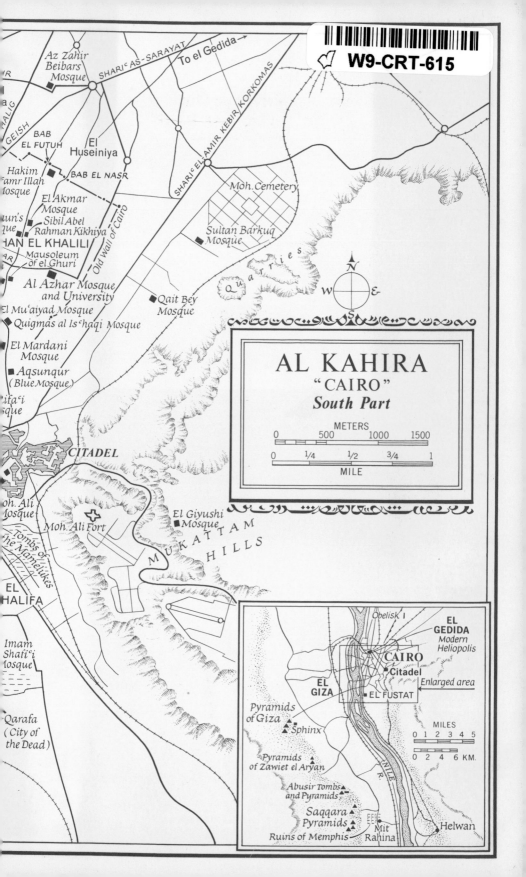

Az Zahir
Beibars
Mosque

SHARI' AS-SARAYAT

To el Gedida →

GEISH

BAB
EL FUTUH

El
Huseiniya

SHARI' EL-AMIR KEBIR KORKOMAS

BAB EL NASR

Hakim
'amr Illah
Mosque

Moh. Cemetery

El Akmar
Mosque

Sibil Abel
Rahman Kikhiya

aun's
que

Sultan Barkuq
Mosque

HAN EL KHALILI

Mausoleum
of el Ghuri

Old Wall of Cairo

Al Azhar Mosque
and University

Qait Bey
Mosque

Quarries

N

W   E

S

El Mu'aiyad Mosque

Quigmas al Is'haqi Mosque

El Mardani
Mosque

Aqsunqur
(Blue Mosque)

ifa'i
sque

AL KAHIRA
"CAIRO"
South Part

METERS

0   500   1000   1500

0   1/4   1/2   3/4   1

MILE

CITADEL

oh. Ali
osque

El Giyushi
Mosque

Moh. Ali Fort

MUKATTAM   HILLS

Tombs of
the Mamelukes

EL
HALIFA

Imam
Shafi'i
Mosque

Obelisk I

EL
GEDIDA
Modern
Heliopolis

CAIRO

Citadel

Enlarged area

Qarafa
(City of
the Dead)

EL
GIZA

EL FUSTAT

Pyramids
of Giza

Sphinx

Pyramids
of Zawiet el Aryan

MILES

0 1 2 3 4 5

0   2   4   6 KM.

Abusir Tombs
and Pyramids

NILE R.

Saqqara
Pyramids

Ruins of Memphis

Mit
Rahina

Helwan

ALDRIDGE, James. Cairo. Little, Brown, 1969. 370p il map bibl
72-79364. 8.50

Well-known novelist Aldridge, in a labor of love, turns his attention
to the history of Cairo. The result is an informative and entertaining
book which presents with clarity the epochs of the city's past. Further,
it is a handsome book, containing vivid photographs and detailed maps
of Cairo's most important quarters. It would make for excellent sup-
plementary reading in a general course in world civilization on both
the high school and junior levels. While the work is not annotated, it
contains a good bibliography to support each chapter or phase of the
city's history. It is also recommended as a "must" for anyone planning
to visit Cairo in the future as it would serve as a useful guidebook.
There is probably no comparable work combining its readability and
logic of presentation.

CHOICE   MAY '70

History, Geography &
Travel

Middle East &
North Africa

DT
'43
A36

James Aldridge was born in Australia of English parents and has traveled extensively. During World War II he was a correspondent for the North American Newspaper Alliance, and his experiences inspired him to write fiction. He is the author of several widely translated novels, including *Signed with Their Honor, The Sea Eagle, Of Many Men, The Diplomat, The Hunter,* and *My Brother Tom.* Mr. Aldridge, who lived in Cairo for many years, married his wife Dina there in 1942. They have two sons and are currently living in London.

Books by James Aldridge

Novels

SIGNED WITH THEIR HONOUR

THE SEA EAGLE

OF MANY MEN

THE DIPLOMAT

THE HUNTER

HEROES OF THE EMPTY VIEW

I WISH HE WOULD NOT DIE

THE LAST EXILE

A CAPTIVE IN THE LAND

THE STATESMAN'S GAME

MY BROTHER TOM

Short Stories

GOLD AND SAND

Nonfiction

LIVING EGYPT

(*with Paul Strand*)

UNDERSEA HUNTING FOR INEXPERIENCED FISHERMAN

CAIRO

CAIRO

Modern apartment buildings along the Nile. In
the background, on the horizon, the silhouette
of the pyramids.

CAIRO

by James Aldridge

LITTLE, BROWN AND COMPANY
BOSTON / TORONTO

Published simultaneously in Canada
by Little, Brown & Company (Canada) Limited

PRINTED IN THE UNITED STATES OF AMERICA

Preface

THIS is not an academic study of Cairo, nor is it an amateur history. It is really a passionate involvement in the place by someone who has long admired the city and its people. In fact it was originally conceived by my publishers and myself as a "biography," and my task was to treat the subject as a living, breathing entity, and tell the full story from primitive gestation to modern metropolis.

I have to admit that I am primarily a novelist, and though there is an extensive and sometimes unique historical documentation in this account, I have tried to extract the drama rather than accumulate the dust. There are far too many bloody moments in the story of Cairo, but on the whole I have underplayed rather than emphasized that aspect of it.

There are no footnotes to the text because they do not fit the approach. But the Bibliography (page 353) will produce the relative sources for anyone who is interested.

The book itself owes a great deal to the sympathetic instigation of Harry Sions of New York, who suggested it and nurtured it. During several years of preparation I received a great deal of help from many other people, but I must comment here on the patience of the staff of the Oriental Printed Books Department of the British Museum. James Etherington, also of the British Museum, gave me invaluable help in finding what I wanted, and Mrs. Mary Rackliffe of Boston saw me through the final stages of the book with invaluable editorial help.

Many people in Cairo helped me very generously with their time and interest, in particular Abd el Rahman Abd el Tawab, Director and

Chief Inspector of Excavations of the Islamic Period, and Shafik Abd el Kadir, Chief Inspector of Islamic and Coptic Monuments. Also Dr. Victor Girgas, Chief Curator of the Coptic Museum of Old Cairo, Mme. Leila Gaad, Mlle. Esmat el Ayyat, Mohammed el Bazzara, Samir Khalil, and above all Mme. Malak Abd el Aziz, who gave me so many vital clues to the intellectual life of modern Cairo. Professor K. A. C. Creswell was kind enough to go over some of his own remarkable volumes on Islamic architecture with me, for which I will always be in his debt.

Contents

Picture Credits

Elliott Erwitt/Magnum: Frontispiece, 273 (top), 350

A. F. Kersting: pages 10, 10–11, 26, 34, 35 (both), 44–45, 54, 89, 111, 112, 121, 122, 132 (bottom), 190–191, 243 (bottom), 268–269, 278–279, 280, 285 (top), 291, 298–299

Egyptian State Tourist Administration, Photo by Sobhi Afifi: page 33

J. Allan Cash: pages 119 (both), 260, 283 (bottom), 301 (bottom), 311 (top)

Popperfoto: pages 125, 132 (top), 143, 154, 192, 200 (both), 201, 243 (top), 307 (bottom)

Stuart Heydinger, Camera Press Ltd: pages 259 (top), 307 (top), 345 (both)

Fox Photos Ltd: page 259 (bottom)

René Burr/Magnum: page 273 (bottom)

PMR Photo by International Photographic Associates, Inc.: page 283 (top)

Henri Cartier-Bresson, Magnum Photos, Inc.: page 285 (bottom)

Günter R. Reitz Pressefoto: page 287 (both)

John Pratt, Keystone Press Agency Ltd: page 301 (top)

Ian Berry/Magnum: page 311 (bottom)

Photograph by Mavis Ronson: page 331

Illustrations

Illustrations

CAIRO

1
Foundations

Piecing together the origins of an Oriental city like Cairo is probably easier for a European than it is for an Egyptian, because there is too much in Cairo's history that is not Egyptian at all. Until 1952 the city was built by almost everyone except Egyptians. The modern half of Cairo is obviously European, but even the old medieval city was built by outsiders, invaders, conquerors; even more by heretics, mercenaries, and one or two madmen. Cairo's most beautiful and enduring monuments to its own religion, Islam, were often built by rulers whom modern Egyptians would hardly consider to be true Moslems; and even now that the city is Egyptian for the first time in its history, the new boxlike architecture makes the huge hotels and the ambitious new suburbs look more like the speculative upheavals of Paris and Rome than anything especially Egyptian.

But though Egyptians did not always conceive their city they have always been its traders, boatmen, masons, carpenters, doctors, servants, artists, historians, and occasionally its aristocrats and almost always its slaves. For over two thousand years the population of Cairo has been fighting someone or other for possession of their city. It has always been a prize, not so much for anything specially its own but for the huge accumulation of trading wealth which it handled. Cairo would probably have remained an insignificant village if it had not been the most important port of Greece and Rome for transshipment of grain from Upper Egypt to the Mediterranean, and later the medieval merchant bank, warehouse and customs shed for the east-west trade routes of the world, which crossed Egypt and which brought

[3]

Cairo its real wealth and made it (some say) and not Baghdad the fabulous city of *The Arabian Nights.*

There have been seven distinct Cairos. In fact there have been nine if you include its role as a royal farm when the pyramids were being built, and also include the ancient city of Heliopolis, which for several thousand years was the world's most advanced university for preclassical science and learning. Both these dead ancestors are now outer suburbs of modern Cairo. The exact position of each of the seven (or nine) different Cairos is quite well known, yet to unearth them now, one after the other, is still a fascinating exercise in detection. The trouble is that almost nobody bothers to look for Cairo any more, neither the historians nor the archaeologists nor even the tourists, because there is too much surface exotica lying around to divert them. In this respect the pyramids are a confounded nuisance.

In any case it's not much use being an archaeologist in search of Cairo; it is better to be a genuine student of melodrama, because the events and the characters which created the seven acts of the city are often so fantastic and so grotesque that their documentation hardly proves anything except the awful continuity of its violence and the indestructibility of its citizens. The natural character of the city has always been far too exotic.

What has probably saved the city's inhabitants from succumbing to the excesses and the brutalities has been their moral resilience and a ridiculous sense of humor. Unfortunately, after they had suffered and indulged and finally undone one oppressor, another monster would always arrive from out of nowhere before the people of the city could take advantage of their moral victory. Cairo was never quite moral enough long enough to anticipate and defeat each ambitious new arrival.

But that's all gone now. Cairo today is very moral, almost puritanical. Maybe this suggests that it is now pretty dull; but not yet, and the complicated overlapping of a new moral resolution on the old corruption has produced some delightful results.

The best place to see Cairo now is from up on the thumb of the Mukattam Hills, which look right down on the metropolis. There is a nightclub there called the Casino de Monte Bella, where you aren't allowed to gamble because gaming is forbidden in Cairo except in one official casino for foreigners, but where from dawn till midnight you can get a very sensuous view of the city. It's only a self-indulgent man who can sit up there from dawn till midnight, but it can be done, and the point of doing it is to see the city lying there under all its Oriental veils. In a day and a night about twenty different curtains of thin dry light are pulled over the city, and every one of them is a subtle trick — the dusty mirages of illusion which decorate the rooftops and lift the city into the sky or sink it firmly into the desert.

The other reason for sitting up on this terrace is that you can take a good look around at the plains and the desert and the river, and when you see Cairo in this full setting the whole city suddenly makes sense. Look south and you can see the long flat river coming out of Africa; look west and you can see the first veins of the rich Delta; look north and the river is heading determinedly for the Mediterranean and for Europe. Up on the Mukattam itself you are in the east, sitting literally on the very edge of Arabia because these hills are the end of the Arabian mountains, part of a limestone range that runs across Asia as far east as China. Cairo itself is built on this little meeting place of Africa, Egypt, Europe, Arabia and Asia.

The city below lies in a valley which was once 820 feet under the sea; the valley rose and sank twice before settling down to its present bed. Torrential rains then cut out the long alluvial basin, and when man began to hunt from these hills the river was so wide that geologists describe it as the "enormous Nile" — it was probably thirty or forty miles across. This enormous river gradually dried up, and the open plains visible all around from this respectable Casino de Monte Bella were heavily forested and teeming with gazelle, wild oxen, baboons, antelopes, elephants, hippopotamuses and the sort of game you can find only in Central Africa now.

It was so rich that the excitable and savage men who killed with flint clubs and stuck spears into hippopotamuses must have been among the most prosperous hunting men of the time, which may be a reason why sophisticated man developed here so early. Archaeologists are still arguing about the origin of agriculture on the Nile, but most of them think that originally a Stone Age hunting people living along the river was invaded from outside by a more vigorous race who already knew a higher culture than that of the Nile hunters. Historians who favor this theory call them the dynastic race because they are the people who supposedly began the great dynastic history of Egypt. The rival theory says that there was simply a steady enrichment of the Nile people because of their unusually favorable conditions, a natural emergence into a higher and higher culture, into dynastic beginnings.

In any case there must have been a moment down there on the plains when all the men hunted and the women did the agricultural work. Farming was always women's work in early societies, so women controlled production and therefore controlled society. Their sexual life was the model for all the fertility magic for which man was merely

[5]

the symbolic fertilizer. Only when warfare for territory developed into a serious necessity did these early Nile women lose their powerful status. Warfare was the natural sideline of the hunter and this allowed man rather than woman to conquer and control the wealth. Even the social emphasis in magic and religion shifted from the divine mother to the divine son.

And somewhere during the latter part of this shift from matriarchy to patriarchy, organized Egypt began. The sad thing is that much of the evidence of it has been buried here under layer upon layer of Nile mud, which has filled up the Delta and swallowed the artifacts. All we have now in solid stone is the rotten-ripe end of the process — the great pyramids; and this is where the drama of Cairo begins.

2

Dynastic Cairo

W HEN I first read in Adolf Erman's famous old *Handbuch* on the Egyptian religion that the largest of the three pyramids was exactly the same size as Lincoln's Inn Fields in London, I was so unbelieving that I hurried down to Lincoln's Inn to take a look for myself.

I had to admit that he was right. It would obviously fit.

Some time later I stood at the foot of the big pyramid (Khufu's) and tried to surround it with all those London lawyers' offices, but the measurement and the view didn't seem to fit in reverse because pyramid amazement is usually a one-way affair — a form of intellectual gaping. When Napoleon looked at the big pyramid he immediately calculated in his head that its two and a half million blocks of stone would build a wall over nine feet high around France. Herodotus remembered among all the inscriptions which once covered some parts of the pyramids the one that mentioned the huge amount spent on onions and garlic for the workers. All serious literature on the pyramids is full of this kind of wonderment because one is always trying to drag them down to earth somehow.

But if you go to the pyramids looking for their ancient connections with Cairo you arrive at something a little different. In November 1966 I stood at the foot of the second pyramid (Khafre's) with Dr. Ahmad el Sanadili, then the Cairo University Egyptologist on the site, and we began speculating on what the Cairo countryside and Cairo itself must have looked like more than five thousand years ago. El Sanadili said that it must have looked about the same as it does now. "Take away the telegraph poles and the cement buildings," Sanadili said, "and everything left — the farmlands and the clumps of palms

[7]

and the canals and the birds and the people — would have looked much the same when Khufu came up here from Memphis to see how his pyramid was getting along."

It didn't require much imagination to sit up there on the dry limestone corner of pyramid No. 2 (Khafre's) and populate the Cairo area as it was five and a half thousand years ago with farmers, boatmen (handling boats 170 feet long), cooks, artisans, masons, nobles, priests, and oxen and dogs and cats. Cairo, the farm, must have contributed considerably to those expensive onions, in fact onions and garlic and radishes were the only items of food supplied to the pyramid builders at government expense.

We do not really know for sure, but it is fair to assume that what is now Cairo was then a royal estate probably endowed by the Pharaoh for the upkeep of his pyramid temples. In fact all the land of Egypt belonged to the Pharaoh, and since food growing for the pyramid builders and the priests and the royal storehouses was obviously the main business of the local farms, it only remains to ask what sort of food these pre-Cairenes grew in their fields. We know from the hieroglyphics that it was the same sort of vegetables you can still see in the big covered market in Cairo. The ancients, like the modern Egyptians, were big vegetable eaters (and also aperient takers) and the main crops were lentils, cucumbers, melons, leeks, dates and radishes. There were also two other basic foods which were probably the first to be cultivated widely in this valley and which remained the common diet of the poor peasant for tens of thousands of years afterwards — the lotus root and the papyrus root. Papyrus, in its scroll form, was once Egypt's main export, and classical antiquity depended on a cheap supply of it to record much of its art, history, business, diplomacy and literature. When paper was invented and then imported into Egypt, Greece and Rome, papyrus disappeared and it is not grown or eaten any more, nor is the lotus. The staple diet of the poor Egyptian now is a bean called "fool."

Everything grows in these fields with incredible ease, and then as now the man who worked them did so from dawn till dark every day of his life for barely enough to survive on. Yet for millennia before and after the pyramids were built this Nile mud was giving two or more rich crops a year to its rich farmers. It still does so, and the peasant is still poor, though not nearly as poor as he used to be.

Apart from the farms of Cairo there was a fair-sized temporary city built near the pyramids, because for twenty-five or thirty years men were cutting and hacking and rubbing the huge blocks and piling them up — sometimes as many as a hundred thousand men in one year. Near the pyramids is a dusty little discothèque called the Stereo Club, and on the same hill with it are the remains of a row of pyramid workers' quarters; sitting on this sand hill one night I couldn't help wondering why the Pharaoh had decided to build his soul fortress on this dry and sandy plateau. Why not farther north in the Delta, or a little to the south where the valley is wider? The answer is quite important to Cairo, even today. Khufu had two kingdoms, the red kingdom in the north and the white kingdom in the south, and as "lord of the two lands" he not only united them in his person, but it was important that he incarcerate his soul for eternity astride the line dividing them; and the line ran across this plateau. Today Cairo straddles the same dividing line between the same two kingdoms, now called Upper and Lower Egypt. As the capital of these quite different halves of Egypt, Cairo is as much the unifying force for the modern nation as Khufu was for his ancient kingdom.

Even so — why up here? Why not nearer the river? This dry little plateau is itself the answer because it *is* dry; it provided an unlimited supply of workable stones, and was also on the west side of the river, which was essential for royal burial because the west belonged to the dead. Almost all the interior blocks for the pyramids were quarried from this sandy plateau, but the stone for their glossy surfaces was quarried at Tura on the other side of the river just south of Cairo, and the stone was floated up to the foot of the plateau during the flood. Some of this surface stone is left on top of Khafre's pyramid. It is a dull yellow now, but once it was brilliant white, and all three pyramids were covered with its whiter-than-white glaze.

Late in 1966 I went out to see Dr. Ali Hassan, who was excavating some tombs behind Khafre's pyramid. He had just dug away a giant heap of rubbish which had been left lying against the back of the pyramid for hundreds of years. Underneath it he had uncovered many of the original Tura facing blocks which were perfectly preserved in color and condition, and this sudden scar of pure white stone leaning against the old yellow limestone of the interior blocks was a revelation of how dazzling the entire surface of these pointed white monsters must have been. The high white cliffs of Tura (now a suburb of Cairo) are today the quarrying ground for the nationalized Egyptian cement work. They dig out thousands of tons of it every year and powder it into one of the best cements in the world. Modern cement-Cairo is really built of this marvelous stuff, and all the streets of Tura and the buses and houses and boats and donkeys are covered with its hanging white dust.

Good stone has always been one of Cairo's attractions for its build-

Looking over the desert
from the top of the Northern Pyramid
of Dahshur to the Blunted Pyramid.

Sphinx and the pyramid
afre at Giza.

ers, but the people who had the subtlest appreciation of it were the sculptors and the architects of Khufu and Khafre. They could not only cut it to the proportional accuracy of optical glass and carve it into perfect colossi, but they used it *in situ* in a very inventive way. It is now believed that the base of Pyramid No. 2 is actually built into the natural basin of solid stone, and the Sphinx, which is probably an idealized portrait of Khafre himself, is really a cleverly worked natural outcropping of very soft rock which was left exposed after the pyramid quarriers had used up all the good hard stone around it. It already looked like a crouching lion; and Dr. Ahmed Fakhry has written in *The Pyramids* that Khafre's architects visualized it as a magnificent Sphinx and transformed the offending eyesore into a sublime monument for their royal master.

If you stand just above the Sphinx and look south towards the distant pyramids of Sakkara you can still see, only a few hundred yards away, the outline of another raw Sphinx which is just as the old quarriers left it. It too is a lump of soft stone and is obviously a natural twin of the finished Sphinx. But this other one was far enough away from the finished monuments for the architects not to bother about. It lies there still, uncarved and unnoticed.

Unfortunately the Sphinx's stone is so soft that it has suffered heavily from erosion, and even more from awful disfigurement by over a hundred generations of visitors. It was not Napoleon who knocked its nose off but a religious sheik who tried to demolish it entirely in 1496. And the *sgraffiatores* began their work on it almost the day it was finished. The most famous of the Sphinx's graffiti is a short poem in classical Greek which was written on one of the Sphinx's toes in Ptolemaic times. In a short verse the writer says he prefers joy and dancing to the "slashed throats of men," and he claims to represent the Sphinx's point of view on world events thus:

. . . *they are perished also,*
Those walls of Thebes which the Muses built;
But the wall that belongs to me has no fear of war,
It knows not either the ravages of war or the sobbing.
It rejoices always in feasts and banquets
And to the choruses of young people united from all parts.
We hear the flutes, not the trumpets of war,
And the blood that waters the earth is of sacrificial bulls,
Not from the slashed throats of men . . .

I had read of this Greek offering in the late Dr. Selim Hassan's book *The Great Sphinx and Its Secrets,* and since Dr. Ali Hassan, whom I

have already mentioned, is his nephew, I persuaded Dr. Ali to leave
his diggings one day and go over the Sphinx from top to bottom with
me, looking for this gem of classical vandalism. But we couldn't find it
anywhere, it had simply disappeared. Where to?

"I don't know," Ali Hassan said in despair after we had looked high
and low for it. "I just don't know."

I still don't know whether we simply missed it (unlikely), or
whether it has really gone forever, which also seems unlikely since it
was one of the few graffiti worth preserving.

Graffiti and tourism have always gone together, and ever since the
pyramids ceased to be a royal enclosure people have wanted to take a
look at them. Serious tourism began here about 700 B.C., and since
then so many people have climbed to the top of the big pyramid and
written their names up there that I once asked the peasant who makes
a profession of climbing to the top and down again in seven minutes
how many names had been scribbled on the peak. "About a million,"
he said with a shrug. The only two names he remembered among the
million were King Edward VII and King Farouk, which may be significant. The most important name-scratcher in modern times was
Belzoni, the nineteenth-century circus strong man, tomb robber and
primitive archaeologist who broke into the Second Pyramid in 1818
and not only chiseled his name on the entrance hole but wrote in big
black letters across the tomb inside: *Scoperta da G. Belzoni 1818*.

Until people like Belzoni made a sensation of them in Europe and
brought the middle classes flocking to see them, visiting the pyramids
was restricted to professional travelers, soldiers, politicians, explorers
and philosophers — men who really came to Cairo for other reasons.
Some of them made a serious study of the pyramids, but fundamentally they were all tourists because they all came simply to stand and
stare. Caesar and Cleopatra must have taken a look at the pyramids
when they were on their way upriver in Cleopatra's luxurious barge.
Herodotus came here with a Heliopolitan priest as guide, and Plato
probably came when he was studying at Heliopolis nearby. So did
Strabo, Diodorus and almost every traveler in Egypt for the next two
thousand years, and the records of most of them are more or less the
same. A few famous visitors to Cairo avoided going near the pyramids, but very few. The only interesting man I know of who refused
to go anywhere near them was Chateaubriand, but even he sent a
servant to climb the big pyramid and scratch his name on the top to
prove that he was not unaware of them.

Today the package-tour tourist to Cairo can see and hear all that is
important about the place in an hour, because the whole technique of

pyramid viewing has been so perfected. The pyramids' value to Cairo now is inestimable, and though international wars and local wars have often interrupted the flow of tourists coming to see them, sooner or later the flood returns. So do the scholars, because archaeologically they are by no means exhausted. The 1967 war interrupted a new adventure in pyramidology. Dr. Louis Alvarez of the University of California was about to "x-ray" the Second Pyramid with an electronic gadget which could determine whether there were any more tombs inside it or not. Alvarez, unlike Belzoni, will never write his name on the tombs he discovers, but the results of this scientific exploration (which have now been resumed) may create as much new interest in the pyramids as Belzoni's butcheries did; in fact in December 1968 Alvarez announced in Stockholm that it had already detected a new, hidden room in the Second Pyramid.

Naturally Cairo gets richer and richer on all this pyramid activity because one cannot separate the pyramids from Cairo any more, or Cairo from the pyramids. Yet of all the hundreds of thousands who have visited the place in the last couple of thousand years only a few have ever taken any notice of the most significant "pyramid" of them all — the fourth. On its own this little tomb means nothing, and you have to hunt to find it, but historically it is the foundation stone of some of the complex historical mess we have inherited from the pyramid builders.

The first and biggest pyramid (Khufu or Cheops) was built at the very height of the economic power which had steadily centered on one king and one god. It represented the accumulation of enormous surplus in the hands of a ruling class which required a considerable organization to perpetuate. The absolute Pharaoh had evolved from this process. He was the one man in Egypt allowed to worship God, and must therefore be protected and maintained by the entire economy. When Khufu died he was buried safely and magnificently in Pyramid No. 1, but in the next sixty years the noble-priest faction, who had always administered and maintained Egypt's economy for the benefit of the Pharaoh, began to revolt against the absolutism which deprived them of the wealth they handled.

They lived in the nearby city of Heliopolis, which was theirs, and what they wanted was the real power, because after all they were running the country. The pyramids built by Khufu's successors were therefore smaller and cheaper as this conflict sharpened, and by the time Menkure had built the third pyramid the conflict between Pharaoh and priests was so fierce that the next Pharaoh, Shepseskaf, had to leave the pyramid area altogether and even abandon the pyramid form for his tomb. By doing this either he was trying to break the power of the priests who controlled the pyramid temples or the priests were forcing him to abandon this colossal expression of kingly waste and power. In any case Shepseskaf built a mastaba, not a pyramid, miles away in the desert at a place now called Mastabat Far'un.

But it is really Shepseskaf's sister, Kentkawes, who represents the end. In her lifetime the God-state cracked, and the priests took power. According to Dr. Ahmed Fakhry, Kentkawes married a Heliopolis priest, and the transference of power to the priests took place. Two of her sons, Weserkaf and Sahure, began the Fifth Dynasty, which was really a feudal kingdom under the priests instead of a God-kingdom under the Pharaoh. The Pharaoh was dragged down to earth as a man. Ra, the abstract sun-god, was now more powerful than the living Pharaoh, and naturally Ra was in the hands of the Heliopolis priests. The Pharaoh himself remained powerful and vital to the society as a semi-God, the son of God, but the absolutism of the long years from pre-history was gone forever. Kentkawes was very important to this historical revolution, and it could be said that this early form of feudalism was really a preview of European history yet to come.

The beautiful queen (plenty of evidence points to her beauty) could probably have been buried with her brother at the new Mastabat Far'un if she wanted to, but she obviously preferred to be buried with her forefathers on the old pyramid plateau. Her grave there is the unnoticed fourth "pyramid." It is a pretty little place just behind the Sphinx, rather like a chapel carved into solid rock, with niches all round and a huge sepulchral opening. The approach to it is a sandy black terrace — the powdered remains of the mud brick quarters of the artisans who built it for her. There has been some dispute about whether the tomb is a pyramid at all. Dr. Selim Hassan, one of Egypt's first important Egyptologists, has said that it is definitely a pyramid; but his successor in the Antiquities Department, Dr. Ahmad Fahmy, says that it is not.

In fact both are right. Outside it is a pyramid, but inside it isn't. Archaeologically it isn't, yet visually it is. Historically it is both, which is really the point. Kentkawes could not quite escape the past, and she mothered the future, and this feminine little pyramid is now worth as much to a historically minded man as all the enticing dimensions of its three big brothers on the hill. But it closes the chapter on the influence the pyramids had on the origins of Cairo, because after Kentkawes was buried in her chapel, and the huge stone door was sealed up forever, the power of the living and the authority of the dead shifted across the river to ancient Heliopolis — now one of the poorest districts of Cairo but in Kentkawes' time already the capital of science and learning in the ancient world — and it became in effect the real capital of Egypt.

3

Heliopolis

TODAY if you ask someone in Cairo to take you out to Heliopolis you will end up in a prosperous Belgian-British–built suburb called Heliopolis which has nothing to do with the city of antiquity. Ancient Heliopolis is utterly forgotten, and to get to the site of it by taxi you must first go to a suburb called Matariya and then say to the driver in Arabic: "To the packing needle!"

Lost in a little patch of classical Egyptian landscape, on the poorer edges of Matariya, is a solitary stone pillar looking naked and neglected, which is all that is left standing of the magnificent temple to Ra. It was once the heart of ancient Heliopolis, and buried under the village of Hosn el Arab just across the fields is the rest of the city.

Heliopolis is the Greek name for the place which the ancient Egyptians called "ei-n-re" (the abode of the sun), which the Hebrews corrupted to "On." It is attached to modern Cairo less by its stones and its ruins than by a special Egyptian tragedy which began here: foreign occupation. When the Persians conquered Egypt in 525 B.C. they had to break the authority this religious and administrative city had over Egyptian life before they could be sure that Egypt was theirs. Cambyses, son of Cyrus, therefore razed Heliopolis to the ground, thus establishing an occupation of Egypt which was to last unabated, with one conqueror handing over to another, until 1952.

Cambyses knew what he was doing, because the connection between Heliopolis and Egyptian life was not only a religious one, it involved the entire social structure of the country, from its origins in earliest man to its most sophisticated condition in decadence. What Cambyses destroyed therefore was not the religion of Heliopolis but

[17]

the *authority* of the religion, which it never quite recovered again. Actually, the Egyptian religion itself outlived the Persian and Greek occupations, and even the Roman; in fact, it survived well into the fifth century A.D., when it was finally absorbed into Coptic Christianity, which anyhow encompassed most of its ancient ideas brought along stubbornly from pre-history, pre-religion and even pre-magic. Plenty of its most ancient rituals are still left in the daily life of any Egyptian peasant. The last time I was walking over this antique rubbish tip of Hosn el Arab with Dr. Ali Hassan and some other Egyptologists, we suddenly found ourselves at the tail end of a village wedding procession of dancing peasants, led by two huge oxen with decorated horns. The whole character of the procession was so ancient and so pagan and so close to the same thing that must have taken place in the city under our feet that we all stopped to watch it, and someone finally said: "Ghosts!"

But the real ghost here was the ancient city itself, which is the spiritual parent of most civilized religions. When Heliopolis sun worship was at its height in 2500 B.C. it had in it not only the outline of the future messianic Hebrew God but an immaculate son of God, a holy trinity and a moral code of commandments (in the pyramid texts) which anticipated a great deal that emerged almost two thousand years later in the Old Testament. And the passage of this Heliopolitan religion from early totemism to the sophistication of an abstract God is really the social history of primitive and dynastic Egypt.

The primitive clans had always used animal and bird totems as their own magical images, and when they finally became refined mythologies there were two cults that overwhelmed all the others: the sun god Ra, and the river god Osiris. Osiris was portrayed as the "mummy with the long phallus . . . father and mother of men, they live on your breath, they eat of the flesh of thy body. The primeval is thy name." The entwined myths of these two main deities became the basis of the Egyptian religion, however many variants were later introduced. But eventually the sun god became the most powerful because this cult was the implement of the powerful priestly nobles of Heliopolis. They controlled the complexities of agricultural production because in their cult of the sun they had knowledge of the stars. Astronomy gave them not only the power to predict the arrival of the Nile flood, which governed Egyptian agriculture, but also the geometry and trigonometry necessary for remeasuring every year, when the flood had gone down, the obliterated boundaries of the resurrected land.

The Heliopolis priest, through his science rather than his religion,

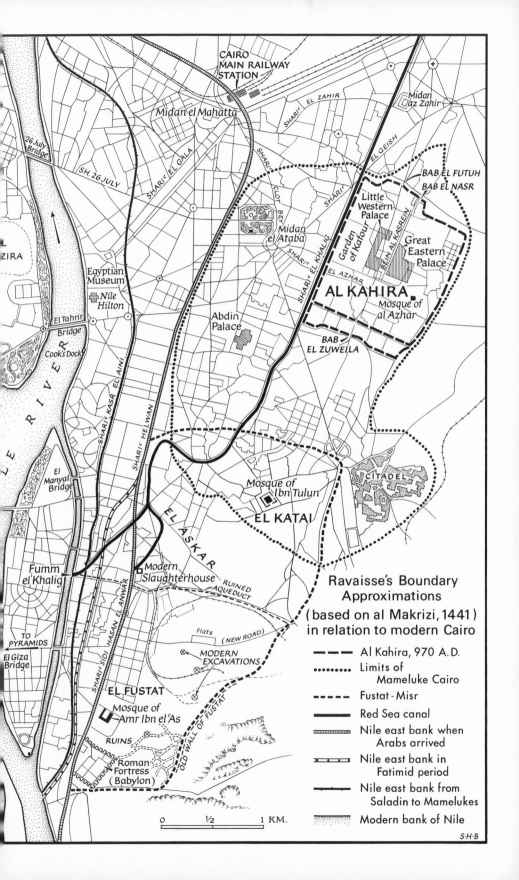

CAIRO
MAIN RAILWAY
STATION

Midan el Mahatta

26 July
Bridge

SH. 26 JULY

SHARIC EL ZAHIR

Midan
az Zahir

SHARIC EL GALA

SHARIC CLOT BEY

SHARIC EL GEISH

BAB EL FUTUH
BAB EL NASR

Little
Western
Palace

Garden
of Kafour

BEIN EL KASREIN

Great
Eastern
Palace

Egyptian
Museum

Nile
Hilton

*Midan
el Ataba*

SHARIC EL KHALIG

EL AZHAR

AL KAHIRA

El Tahrir
Bridge

Cook's Dock

*Abdin
Palace*

Mosque of
al Azhar

SHARIC KASR EL AINI

BAB
EL ZUWEILA

ZIRA

LE RIVER

SHARIC HELWAN

El Manyal
Bridge

*Mosque of
Ibn Tulun*

CITADEL

EL KATAI

EL ASKAR

Fumm
el Khalig

Modern
Slaughterhouse

RUINED
AQUEDUCT

TO
PYRAMIDS

El Giza
Bridge

Flats

(NEW ROAD)

MODERN
EXCAVATIONS

Ravaisse's Boundary
Approximations

(based on al Makrizi, 1441)
in relation to modern Cairo

EL FUSTAT

*Mosque of
Amr Ibn el'As*

SHARIC SIDI HASAN EL ANWAR

OLD WALL OF FUSTAT

RUINS

Roman
Fortress
(Babylon)

	Al Kahira, 970 A.D.
·········	Limits of Mameluke Cairo
- - - -	Fustat-Misr
————	Red Sea canal
▦▦▦▦	Nile east bank when Arabs arrived
⊢⊢⊢	Nile east bank in Fatimid period
———	Nile east bank from Saladin to Mamelukes
░░░░	Modern bank of Nile

0   ½   1 KM.

S·H·B

became the decider, the judge, the measurer, the calculator, the architect, the planner, the engineer and the accountant of Egyptian life. Everybody in Egypt came to depend on him until finally his real authority surpassed the Pharaohs'. And when that happened the religious and scientific city of Heliopolis meant to Egypt what perhaps no other city has meant to any nation since, because never again were morality, science, technology and authority centralized so singularly in one group in one place at one time.

It is hard to picture the old city now, standing where the temple was in the middle of an absolutely naked beanfield, listening to Cairo's modern mechanisms whirring over your shoulder. Yet the attraction of the site is electric when you know that some of the ruins must still be lying there under thirteen feet of Nile mud.

In 1966 the Egyptians began to dig here after a gap of more than fifty years since the English archaeologist Sir W. M. Flinders Petrie had made the last serious excavation (later ones contributed very little). Petrie came here in 1912 and made a few brilliant jabs at the muddy fields, looking for the outline of the city walls and for at least one other obelisk which he thought should be here as a mate to the one still standing. He found the walls and obelisk, and reading the account of his rather hurried excavation is like reading Sherlock Holmes, and Petrie used the same logic as Holmes's. He considered the obvious first and if that failed to produce anything then whatever was left over had to provide the answer.

What surprised me, when I was last there with some of the archaeologists of the Egyptian Antiquities Department, was that they had never read Petrie's account and had never seen his map of the site, which I happened to have with me. They had hopefully dug two pits near the standing obelisk to see what was on either side of it. They were very pleased to discover a broken pillar lying over four yards deep under the watery mud. But Petrie had already described in fascinating detail how he had found the pillar by digging and bailing out a large pond of seepage water. He had covered the pillar up again. He couldn't afford to get it out, or rather, he knew he was not allowed to take it away, so he simply left it there. Some senior archaeologist in the present-day Egyptian Antiquities Department must have known about Petrie's excavations, but the assistants on the site in 1966 did not know.

The city walls which Petrie found are visible all round the obelisk if you know where to look. To the right, the walls have become the ridge of the village of Hosn el Arab. In front, there is a hill with a few trees on it and a cemetery, and this was the corner of one wall. Running across the forward view is an embankment which is another line of the wall. And somewhere to the left, and also behind, is a raised dirt road (the road you come on) and this too is another wall of the old city.

The obelisk still standing is where the open court of the temple used to be. At one time there was probably a holy of holies in the courtyard where a winged phoenix was perched on the pyramidal peak of a stone called a benben, but worship of the sun god was usually carried on in the open air.

Heliopolis was never a big city, so it was easy for the Persians to raze it to the ground. Petrie decided that the Persians destroyed it not only for its religious power but also to prevent the Egyptians' using it as a fortified outpost on their eastern road to Memphis. If this is true then Heliopolis briefly played the same role in the ancient world that Cairo was to have in medieval times — it was a defensive place essential to anyone from the east who wanted to plunge into the rich interior of Egypt and suck it dry. The original Nile–Red Sea canal which ran behind the walls of Heliopolis was also a vital artery which connected the interior of Egypt to the Red Sea, and this too made Heliopolis important for anyone coming from the east. Unfortunately the city was too far away from the river to be treated as a valuable port, so it was simpler to destroy it as a nuisance.

Heliopolis was rebuilt many times. Ramses II and Sesostris I, two of the most extraordinary Pharaohs in Egyptian history, both built at Heliopolis. The obelisk still standing in the beanfield belongs to Sesostris I, who put it up there three thousand years ago to mark the foundation of a new temple. But the four other obelisks which are now in Paris, New York, London and Istanbul were erected by Thutmose III, celebrating a military victory in 1450 B.C. when he had "crossed the great bend of the Euphrates." In 1966 when the obelisk in London was being cleaned, a letter-writer to *The Times* regretted bitterly the degradation of the ancient pillar, which, when it was put on the Thames Embankment in 1878, was bedded down on a hollow stone containing a baby's feeding bottle, a box of cigars and a Bradshaw's railway timetable, symbolic offerings typifying a supposedly humorless Victorian era.

Imagination will rescue these pillars anywhere. In fact it is hard to stand at the base of the obelisk in Heliopolis without living through a couple of centuries; all you need is a little information which two or three good contemporary commentators can supply. Herodotus walked around Heliopolis and the pyramids about 430 B.C. and reported his astonishment with everything. Sir Henry Rawlinson, the English Orientalist who translated him, said that the old Greek was inclined to "indulge in the marvelous at the sacrifice of truth."

Herodotus, who came to Egypt between Persian and Greek conquests, is supposed to have been greatly deceived by his Heliopolitan priest-guides (he was among the first tourists), but he was not deceived by his own eye and his own touch. "The country swarms with medical practitioners," he says, and moreover they were all too specialized. He tells us how the Egyptians baked papyrus, how they anointed themselves with an oil called kiki, how they slept under nets because of gnats on the marshes, and he admires the respect with which young Egyptians treated their elders, standing up when a senior entered a room. The Heliopolitan townsman is visible in all these credulous, marveling descriptions.

Alexander, who saw Egypt in 331 B.C., came in awe of this old civilization, and on the whole Greeks respected it and respected Heliopolis and used it. But the Greeks shifted all the gods and scholars of Egypt to their new capital of Alexandria, which was much nearer home. By shifting the capital to Alexandria the Greeks took Egypt out of Africa and established it firmly in the Mediterranean. One of Alexander's generals, Ptolemy Lagus, established his family as the future Pharaohs, and Heliopolis fell into decay, although it resisted its decline for a very long time.

Herodotus had seen the Greek mind already established in Egypt (even in its time of the Persians), and Diodorus the Sicilian was to see it depart. Nobody knows how much of what Diodorus wrote was firsthand, but he was certainly in Alexandria between 75 B.C. and 60 B.C. when the first Roman mission came to arrange the takeover of what was left of Hellenized Egypt. He even reported one of the Roman emissaries being torn limb from limb by the Egyptians because he had accidentally killed a cat in the street. A few years later Pompey, then Caesar, and then Mark Antony arrived, and none of them was in awe of Egyptian culture the way the Greeks were, so Heliopolis meant nothing to them.

The epitaph for this old city has been written by Strabo, the Greek geographer who visited what was left of it in 25 B.C. "In Heliopolis," he writes, "I also saw large houses in which the priests lived; for it is said that this place in particular was in ancient times a settlement of priests who studied philosophy and astronomy; but both the organization and its pursuits have now disappeared . . . The houses of the priests and schools of Plato and Eudoxus were pointed out to us, for Eudoxus went up to that place with Plato [about 380 B.C.] and they both passed thirteen years with the priests as is stated by some writers." Strabo's claim that Plato was in Heliopolis for thirteen years seems exaggerated; the *Epitome* says three years and Diogenes Laertius says sixteen months. Plato himself never bothers to mention when he was there. How much he learned from the priests we will never accurately know.

What we do know is that Eudoxus, who was not only a student of Plato's but also an astronomer, probably took back with him from Heliopolis to Athens the first accurate measurement the Greeks had of the fractions of the day, and the exact length of the year, which they didn't know. It was probably Eudoxus who invented the sundial after his years in Heliopolis.

It is still very tempting to tramp around the mud walls of Heliopolis and take an inspired guess at where, in that beanfield, Plato lived. I once tried to do it myself but got fascinated instead with a ramshackle old building which looked exactly like an exhausted old man — all skin and bone, all corrugated iron and broken windows. It hissed and coughed and rumbled. It was about a hundred yards from the obelisk, standing alone in the fields. What on earth was that, I asked. I expected some extraordinary answer, but it was nothing more than a very old textile factory still rolling out cloth, which is appropriate here because the shaven-headed Heliopolis priests once made quite a business of linen manufacture.

I never finished my journey back to Plato, because some Egyptologists took me off over the bumpy hills of Hosn el Arab village to see a temple they had just uncovered. A hill of dry mud had been sliced like a cake, and inside the pit were the remains of a small temple built by Ramses II. We had to get down on our hands and knees to see a perfectly tinted frieze which had been taken by Ramses from one of Sesostris' buildings and used wantonly as a foundation stone for his own temple.

It was a pretty little tablet and my Egyptian friends began to discuss the meaning of the cartouches, but by then I was more interested in two naked children sitting above us, pulling the tail of a goat and listening to it bleat unhappily. In desperation it finally flushed the children's bare feet with the only defense it had, and the hilarity of it shook the village. Temples, filth and hilarity are about all that is left of ancient Egypt in this village, which is well inside the boundaries of modern Cairo. Yet it is built over the ruins of one of the most illustrious cities in history. In fact this village of Hosn el Arab tells you all you need to know of Egypt's sad heritage from an antique past. Egyptians have always been long-suffering, but even in their foreign-ridden poverty they've always been in love with every little thing, and they are never — strictly speaking — miserable and they can always laugh. So far they have outlived the destruction of all their own culture and all their own cities, yet their only real bequest has been the garbage and the work.

What is left of Heliopolis in this village is still tied to Cairo by the ties of land, like everything else. Once, the priests used to float down the Red Sea canal to the river and then cross over to the pyramids to see how everything was getting on. They would leave Heliopolis to inspect the royal estates where Cairo now is. There they would judge the peasants or calculate the water allowance or allot the seed. Their authority was an economic and social one, and when that passed there was only the religion and when that passed there was nothing.

When Rome eventually came the legions took everything. In three hundred years the Greeks had failed to overwhelm the southern people of Egypt; Roman legions managed it in fifteen days. They needed a fort somewhere in this area, where the Mukattam Hills come close to the river, but they ignored the pathetic old ruin of Heliopolis and built a new fort on the river a little to the south. They put three legions in it and began in effect the history of modern Cairo, which could only be born when the long gestation of antiquity was over, when antiquity itself was finished forever.

4

Babylon

UP till a few years ago you could still take a tram from the middle of Cairo and ride it almost all the way out to the Roman fortress that founded the city. Nobody in Cairo except the very interested has ever known much about the old fort, and many educated Cairenes have never even heard of it. Christian Egyptians know it far better than Moslems because their most ancient Coptic churches are built into its walls. What all Egyptians now call this curious little corner of their city is simply Masr el Atika, Old Cairo, which is exactly what it is — the oldest part of Cairo, and it was here that Rome lost Egypt to the Arab conquerors, and here too that Egypt's unique form of Christianity somehow survived the persecutions of Rome and Byzantium.

The first fort was built in the sixth century B.C. by the Persians on a rocky ledge above the river, and you can still see where it was, high on the cliffs above Old Cairo. The Romans used the Persian fort for a while, but they soon found that it was far too vulnerable up there on the cliff. All the water for the fort had to be raised by a complicated and exposed system of screws and buckets, and a hundred and fifty men were permanently employed at it, so they abandoned the cliffs and came down to the river's edge. The Roman Emperor Trajan built the present fort, which is no longer attached to the river because in the last six hundred years the Nile has changed its course and left it high and dry.

The Romans obviously chose the river site for its military advantages, but there was already an old Pharaonic settlement thriving in the same place, probably as a Nile port for the grain and tropical goods which arrived from Upper Egypt. This older riverside settle-

One of the towers of the gateway to the Roman fortress of Babylon in Old Cairo. It adjoins the Coptic church of al Mu'allaka.

ment was called Babylon, a name it kept until the Arab invasion, and Cairo was still called Babylon by Europeans for a long time even after that. Why the older settlement was called Babylon has always been in dispute. Almost certainly it is a corruption of the ancient Egyptian *per-hapi-n-On* which means the House of the Nile of On, the Egyptian name for the nearby island of Roda. But Diodorus the Sicilian says that some prisoners whom Sesostris had brought back from Babylon in Mesopotamia revolted when they had to work too hard. In Egypt they were probably quarrying stone at Tura, nearby, and the revolt was so successful that the Pharaoh gave them the present site as a free colony, which thereafter they called after their own city — Babylon.

Rome had complicated needs of Babylon. Trajan dug out the old Pharaonic canal, dating from about 2000 B.C., which linked the Red Sea to the Nile, and he brought it out on the Nile near the fort. Trajan thus opened up a maritime link between the Mediterranean and Arabia, between Rome and India, and Babylon became a big port. In this sense the Amnis Trajanas, as it came to be called, was the first Suez Canal, because ships coming up the Red Sea from Aden, Arabia, India and Africa could turn into the canal at Kulzum (now Suez) and sail across the desert to Babylon on the Nile and then continue the journey downstream to Alexandria, into the Mediterranean and across to Rome.

What used to be so pleasant about riding down to Babylon in Tram No. 1 was that the tramline had been laid over the filled-in bed of the Amnis Trajanas, which was still full of dirty water as late as 1899. Now you can only ride down Shariʿ el Khalig (Canal Street) by bus or taxi, but it isn't quite the same thing because Cairo trams are built like galley ships and they dip and fall and roll and smack as they plow along the streets in permanent storm. Sailing down the Amnis Trajanas by tram was part of the old maritime tradition of the city.

Babylon itself was never the capital of Greek or Roman Egypt. As long as the occupying power of Egypt was a Mediterranean power it was Alexandria which had to be the capital. Alexandria literally tied Egypt to the European skin, to the European sea. All Greek and Roman roads in Egypt led to Alexandria, all authority led there, all art, all politics, all trade, all wheat and money and religion and corruption and pleasure led there. What came nearer to Babylon were the revolts of the Egyptian peasants and artisans, which were partly the reason for the fort's being there, because Rome needed Egyptian wheat, and at one moment in her history she would have starved without it.

The fort is all that is left of Babylon, because none of the dilapidated streets around it in Old Cairo contains a remnant of Babylon township. And today, when you walk into the neat little gateway of the fort that is used as its ground-level entrance, you are really standing on top of the walls, not at the bottom of them. The walls themselves have been buried under thirty feet of debris, sand and mud, on top of which the surrounding buildings and roads of Old Cairo are built. But once you step through the gateway you have come visibly upon something that is no longer Roman at all and not even Arab, and if you have a little imagination here you can easily see how Egypt's hatred for conquerors is impressed in every grain of sand and in every flower in the gardens and in every brick of the old Coptic churches built into the fort.

Coptic Christianity came to Egypt illegally during Roman occupation, but only after Rome had broken the back of the older Egyptian religion, which was always the center of popular resistance. One of Rome's first decrees in Egypt took all property away from the temples and gave it to the state, thus breaking the last vestiges of real power which the pagan Egyptian priests had. Rome also laid down strict laws for Egyptian life, and legions were sent to forts like Babylon to put these laws into effect. The point was, of course, that Rome needed everything Egypt could produce. But Egyptian revolts staggered the Romans, and the ideology that finally brought Egyptian resistance to the very walls of this fortress was not the old native religion but a new Egyptian version of it — the subversive cult of Christianity.

Under pagan Rome the secret cult of Christ was the cult of the impoverished colonial artisan, the revolting slave, the rebellious peasant and the viciously treated minorities, all of whom found in pre-Platonic Christianity a simple creed that might help them support their miseries and unify their resistance. But as a religion it was not exactly new to Egypt. J. G. Milne, in Volume V of *The History of Egypt* (1898), has written: "It is not improbable that the conception of the Trinity, which formed no part of the original Jewish Christianity, may be traced to an Egyptian origin; the whole of the older Egyptian theology was permeated with the idea of triple divinity." Not only the trinity, but the old Egyptian ideas of resurrection, judgment, redemption, hell and heaven, life after death, the cross (the Egyptian ankh), Isis with her child Osiris, Horus attacking a crocodile (dragon) — all these Egyptian concepts go so far back into their Pharaonic past that they cannot even be traced. Christianity was therefore at home in Egypt.

About A.D. 323 a Rome in decay adopted Christianity as its own religion, and suddenly there were two Christianities in Egypt: the

Coptic Christianity of the downtrodden Egyptian and the Melchite (orthodox) Christianity of their oppressive Roman rulers. In this situation a schism between the Christianity of the rulers and the older Christianity of the oppressed was inevitable, since the Egyptians still hated Rome. The superficial character of the split concerned the nature of Christ. The Copts said Christ had "one nature" and one nature only — a divine one "separate but inseparable." Their orthodox rivals, the Melchites, said Christ had two natures — the divine and the human. This was no more than a tiny doctrinal difference but it was excuse enough for the orthodox Roman Church to set about annihilating the Egyptian Copts. Technically, Coptic Christianity was now legal, and even orthodox, but Roman executions of Copts went on more viciously than ever before, only now they were done in the name of Christian dogma.

For three hundred years Roman and Byzantine orthodoxy tried to suppress the Egyptian mind and the Egyptian peasant, and Egyptians went on resisting them bitterly with their own unique Coptic dogma as a national ideology. The old fort was one of the places where the conflict was sharpest, because Babylon was still Rome's principal stronghold in central and southern Egypt. The old canal fell into disuse, but the town itself continued to be a vital port for the transshipment of grain downstream to Rome and Constantinople, and it was always full of the Egyptian traders, artisans, peasants and boatmen who organized resistance to Rome.

The conflict with Rome came to an end only when Arab horsemen, with the little green pennants of their new religion fluttering on their lances, crossed the northern borders of Egypt and made straight for Babylon. The Arab force was a small one, about thirty-five hundred horsemen, whereas Roman soldiers in the Babylon region alone numbered more than twenty thousand. Late A.D. 640 there were battles all around Babylon and Heliopolis, but finally the fort itself was besieged and the Arabs demanded its surrender.

Inside the fort was the Roman viceroy of Egypt, a Melchite orthodox bishop named Cyrus, and for the last ten years Bishop Cyrus had been persecuting the rebellious Copts of Egypt as no one had ever done before. In the name of his Byzantine orthodoxy he had ordered thousands of them to be whipped, burned, drowned and mutilated. In his ten years of power all Coptic churches were closed, the priests dispersed, the religion driven underground, and the ordinary follower of the Coptic ideology cut down wherever he stood up to announce his defiance of Rome. It was Cyrus who was in charge of Babylon's defense.

[29]

The story of the Arab conquest of the fort has always been complicated by a mysterious figure called "the Makaukus," who seemed to be a Coptic traitor inside the walls trying desperately to surrender it to the Arabs. But A. J. Butler, an English scholar who came to Egypt in the 1880s to tutor the khedive's sons, proved brilliantly that the Makaukus was in fact none other than Bishop Cyrus himself, who wanted desperately to save what he could from inevitable defeat by talking his way out of abject surrender.

The Arab commander, Amr Ibn el 'As, offered Cyrus the classic Moslem alternatives: accept Islam or pay tribute or fight to the death. At first Cyrus tried to avoid all three, but there was no way out. One of the envoys whom Amr Ibn el 'As sent to negotiate with Cyrus was a Negro called Ubadah Ibn al Samit, and Cyrus the Christian was so shocked by the sight of a Negro that he said: "Take away that black man. I can have no discussion with him." The other Arabs pointed out that Ubadah (one of the select body called the Companions of the Prophet) was Amr's chosen negotiator, and that black and white were equal among Moslems. Ubadah himself said: "There are a thousand blacks as black as myself among our companions," and expressed his passionate devotion to God, and to the cause of Islam. Cyrus was so shaken that he turned to one of his followers and said: "Do you hear this? I very much fear that God has sent these men to devastate the world."

Bishop Cyrus reluctantly agreed to the Arabs' second alternative, tribute, and Amr Ibn el 'As allowed him to go down to Alexandria and on to Constantinople to get it from Heraclius, the Roman Emperor. Heraclius refused, exiled Cyrus, and told the legions in the fort to fight on, which they did until April 641, when the Arabs stormed the fort behind a romantic hero called Zubair. It was the excitable Zubair who first scaled the difficult walls of Babylon. He reached the top shouting "Allahu akbar," only to find that the part of the wall he had chosen happened to be bricked up at each end, and there was no way to reach the steps leading down to the inside of the fort. While Zubair was fuming helplessly at the top, the Roman commandant calmly walked out and surrendered the fort to Amr, to the disgust of Zubair, who later complained to Amr: "If you had only waited a little I would have been able to get down the wall inside the fort and then it would have all been over anyway."

There was one last tragedy for the Copts in the capture of Babylon. Even when they were about to surrender their fort, the orthodox Melchite Romans dragged out all the Coptic prisoners they had kept in jail for years. They were all scourged and their hands were cut off, and then they were turned loose at the gates. The Coptic historian John of Nikiou describes the groans and tears and cries and misery of these mutilated Copts, who literally walked out of the fort and into the arms of their Moslem liberators. On this sort of evidence there can be little wonder that the Copts had immediately welcomed the Moslem Arabs in Egypt, and Amr and his thirty-five hundred horsemen could never have operated so freely and effectively in Egypt without the help of the Coptic peasants and townspeople.

Babylon was now Moslem and Arab, and in effect so was Egypt. But the fort was never an attractive place for the Arabs, who hated to be shut up inside defensive walls, and what is still curious about Babylon today is its lack of any Moslem influence. It was the non-Moslems of Egypt who eventually reoccupied the fort and used it, and now it is a tight little island of the three main religious minorities of Egypt: Orthodox, Copt and Jewish. They all huddle together in this old compound as if clinging to the lost memories of their faded youth.

It is ironic that the first church you see as you step into the main west gate is an Orthodox church which is built on top of one of the Roman towers. It is ugly inside and out, and it was recently rebuilt in the worst possible taste. Over the southern gateway, and built into the walls of the fort, is the beautiful little fourth-to-sixth-century Coptic church of Mu'allaka, called the Hanging Church because it literally hangs across the bastions. Its ceiling is ribbed and shaped like an upturned boat, an upside-down ark in fact. The third of the minorities, the Jews, have a dark but rather domestic little synagogue called the Ben Ezra. It used to be the Coptic Church of St. Michael, but the Jewish community bought it from the Copts in the twelfth century. There are other Coptic and Orthodox churches and monasteries hugging each other in the narrow alleyways inside the fort, and there is a village of sorts with streets, cemeteries, gardens, a museum and an avenue of eucalyptuses.

When I was last in the old fort, in 1966, I went there specifically to do three things: to find some of the mysterious passageways and cells that A. J. Butler, with schoolboy fascination, found in the tower churches when he was here in the 1880s; to see the main south gate, because the old Roman walls there were clear and visible; and to look once more at the Coptic Museum.

But following in Butler's Victorian footsteps was not easy because so much rebuilding had gone on. Like Butler I had a little difficulty getting into the Orthodox Church of St. George, which was locked. Relations are still not perfect between Copt and Orthodox (although the Copts now call themselves Orthodox), but a whistle down a side street, a man's head at the window of a mud house, a few words in Arabic, and the guardian took me up the main steps and opened the big doors of the modern Greek façade. I wasn't much interested in the new church itself, but I wanted to find the staircase in the Roman tower under the church which Butler had persuaded a priest to open up for him in the 1880s. Butler had described the tower as "a place of mystery and horror, said to be peopled by devils, and is unknown and undiscovered — happily even by the whitewashers."

At first I couldn't find any sign of the entrance, but then I realized I was looking too mysteriously for something that was now too obvious. What Butler had seen in 1882 was a boarded-up hole. What I saw in 1966 was a neat cellar doorway in the middle of the floor of the new church, with steps leading deep down into the tower underneath. Butler had plunged down here into darkness and mystery, stumbling over debris and neglect. He was "glad to escape from the thick black dust and spiders and centipedes and other noisome creatures." What I saw was a clean staircase lit by electric lights, and a clean descent to the very bottom of the tower. The noisome creatures, the centipedes, the dark mystery, the horror and the devils had unfortunately gone away.

Without the mysteries the Church of St. George had little else to offer, so I walked across the sanded interior of the fort to al Mu'allaka, the Hanging Church. I was very lucky there; the resident priest himself was sitting under one of the little windows in black robes, one swollen leg propped up on a cushion. This was the Reverend Father Shenouda Hanna, Chief Priest of the Church, and I arrived in the middle of his conversation with two handsome Egyptian women who were asking him just how credible any of the numerous Christian relics in Cairo really are.

This was a useful subject for me, because Egypt is the only foreign country the Holy Family visited, and Cairo is full of associations which make some claim on Christ and his family. Matariya (near the Heliopolis obelisk) has a sycamore tree called the Virgin's Tree which the Holy Family supposedly rested under in their flight into Egypt, and near it is a well which Christ the Child is reported to have brought from the earth. Fifty years ago Christian souvenir hunting was so bad that the angry owner of the sycamore tied a knife to the tree and put up a notice begging people not to hack at it any more with axes, and to leave some of it for others. Babylon itself is also full of Christian relics. There was once a date stone in al Mu'allaka, which had the Virgin's tooth mark on it. The bones of St. George himself (demoted by the Vatican in 1969) are in the Convent of Mari Girgis, where the old prioress in a dusty black dress took off her shoes and

Coptic church of al Mu'allaka (the Hanging Church), built into the walls of Babylon.

Coptic Church of al Muʻallaka. ABOVE: Doors. OPPO
ABOVE: Interior from the north a
OPPOSITE BELOW: Pu

led me into a chapel which was littered with old newspapers and took a green bundle out of a niche, unwrapped it, and offered me the cedar casket of St. George's bones to be kissed. St. George smelled rather sweet. The crypt of Abu Sagha, a Coptic church, is where the Holy Family "rested" or "slept" or "waited" for days. Even the Ben Ezra Synagogue proudly claims Christian associations. In the little booklet outlining its history, the Communauté Israelite du Caire says: "The Virgin Mary, Joseph and the Child Jesus fled to Egypt and sheltered in this crypt [in the synagogue] for three months. It is positively known that Joseph was a Jew, and that the logical thing for him to do was to go to his own people for a refuge for his family and himself."

Quite right, I decided.

It was therefore something of a small surprise to hear the Reverend Father Shenouda Hanna saying to his Egyptian friends: "Nobody knows where the Holy Family was in Egypt, or what they did. There is no historical support of any of these Christian claims." Father Shenouda Hanna is a cultured man and a strikingly handsome one. He has written a short history of the Copts, and as the ladies and I helped him to his feet he thanked us and then showed the ladies his Hanging Church, which looks so stubbornly Coptic and still stubbornly Egyptian. Everything in this fortress, in fact, looks stubbornly Egyptian and Coptic. Even the Ben Ezra Synagogue just across the courtyard looks Egyptian and Coptic, which is not surprising because these two religions were always minorities together here and got on very well. There have always been Jews in Babylon, and in the last count a few years ago there were still forty-two Jewish families among the 133,000 Mohammedans and 10,000 Copts in the town of Old Cairo itself.

I wasn't too sure what to expect in the synagogue of Babylon these difficult days, but I needn't have worried too much, because a very excitable guardian pushed his little cap back on his head and referred me to Jeremiah in the Old Testament to support the Jewish claim that this synagogue is built on the site of the original synagogue of Jeremiah. The Christians got the site, he said, by a mistake when the Romans were defeated and Amr handed back all seized properties to churches and synagogues. It was the famous Rabbi Abraham Ben Ezra who, in the twelfth century, he said, bought it back from the Copts and rebuilt it. Not only is Jeremiah himself supposed to be buried underneath the synagogue, but Moses had something to do with the rock of its foundation.

The enthusiastic old guardian of Ben Ezra gave me the old Torah to touch "for luck." The original Torah of this synagogue was very famous, one of the oldest in existence, dating back to Ezra the Scribe; this one was a very modern copy of it. All the documents of the synagogue, as well as a huge number of books and Torahs, had been "taken off" to America in the last century by American-Jewish historians for safekeeping, just as so many Coptic furnishings and ikons and books from Babylon's Coptic churches had been "taken off" to Europe by European-Christian historians for safekeeping (which made A. J. Butler furious.) But the original old Torah of Babylon has been cut up and sold and scattered all over the place. Parts of it are in Columbia University, the British Museum and the Bodleian Library at Oxford.

There is one other historical collection in this old fortress which I always dread going into — the Coptic Museum. The whole place opens up so many new avenues for speculation on Egypt's role in the history of religions that it would require a lifetime to follow up any single one of them, so I always leave feeling frustrated and ignorant. The mythologies of ancient Egypt, Greece, Rome and Christianity are so thoroughly entwined with each other in the artifacts of this museum that sometimes the origins of one religion in another seem almost crude.

In the year 300 Egypt was mainly (officially) pagan, but by 330 it was predominantly Christian. These were the thirty vital years when Rome was changing sides. In this Coptic Museum all the little altars for Egyptian shrines and temples up to the first half of the fourth century are pagan, but then suddenly like a biblical clap of thunder a little pagan Aphrodite shell substitutes the beautiful goddess for a deeply cut Christian cross — still in the shell.

Official Christianity had thus arrived in the pagan shrines of Egypt.

Victor Girgas, the museum's chief curator, took considerable pride in showing me a sixth-century niche of Jesus being suckled by Mary, just as Isis had suckled Osiris three thousand years earlier. It was a modest boast of the continuity of his own Coptic ancestry from ancient Egypt into modern Christianity. Even Father Shenouda Hanna was proud of the origin of the Christian cross in the Egyptian ankh rather than in the crucifix.

It was Girgas who took me twenty-four feet down into the excavated bastion of the south gate of the fort, which had been cleaned up about fifty years ago. Down here one finally comes to the thick damp walls of Rome, the only part of the fort which does any kind of justice to Babylon's foundation in a powerful empire.

"There are the stripes," Girgas told me.

The construction of its walls was in the classical Roman five rows of stone, three of brick, which give the surface a striped look. It is possible that the Arabs, who were not builders when they came to Egypt, borrowed this construction technique from this fort and eventually developed it into a beautiful and sophisticated architectural decoration of their own — the striped walls which you can find in hundreds of mosques from Samarkand to Casablanca.

When we had returned to the top of the wall I asked Victor Girgas if there was any real relic of the Arab conquest left in the fort, since this was the place where Moslem Egypt began.

"No," he said. "Nothing monumental anyway. The Arabs preferred to start afresh, so they built their own little city just outside the walls of Babylon. Just over there." He pointed vaguely northward.

He was talking about Fustat — the town of the tent. Fustat became the Arab capital of Egypt, and the more fabulous part of Cairo's history begins almost from the moment that Amr Ibn el 'As decided on the site and began to build his modest but very famous mosque, which is still standing, just outside the walls of Babylon.

5

Fustat

W HEN you take the short walk from Babylon to Amr's mosque just outside the walls of the fort you are really walking from Egypt into Arabia. Babylon is like a little Egyptian village, Amr's mosque is a bare, wide-open space enclosed in mud walls, and once you are standing inside it the dry Arabian deserts seem to be somewhere around you: tents, jingling horsemen, pale dust, and the faraway sound of Bedouin children laughing.

The Arabs ruled Egypt for a little more than two hundred years, and there is no building left in Cairo of the original Arab conquest except this mud mosque. The city that Arabs built around it is now itself a desert of smashed potsherds and undug ruins — hills and valleys of them, a surface of artifacts that you can explore for weeks in an endless search for tangible evidence of a vanished city. That is all that is left of Fustat.

The word Fustat is probably a derivation of the Roman word *fossatum* (camp), though Ibn Haukal, a tenth-century Arab traveler, said it was the name of one of the Arab tribes. The most popular Arab account of the city says that during the siege of Babylon the Arab commander Amr Ibn el 'As had pitched his tent on the spot where his mosque now stands, and just as he ordered it to be struck a dove settled on the top of it and laid an egg there. Amr was delighted. "She has taken refuge under our protection," he said. "Let the tent stand until she has hatched her brood and flown away." The tent was left, and when the Romans were disposed of the first Arab town of Egypt grew up around it.

Implied in the story is the desert Arab's sacred law that anyone, friend or foe, seeking shelter and protection in your tent must be given it. And maybe this characterizes, as well as anything could, the arrival in Egypt of a new kind of morality which Egypt had never known before. The heroic figure of Amr Ibn el 'As himself is also the best model we have of the new kind of man Mohammed had conceived in the very practical and yet highly idealized framework of his prophetic theism.

For the most part the Mohammedan religion is still misunderstood in the west because few people outside academics and opponents have had a chance to consider it historically. Like all religions it has now been sadly corrupted, but originally it was a very simple doctrine. Mohammed himself was born of a minor aristocratic Arabian clan of the Quraysh tribe. His family were desert-living merchants who were then part of the expanding merchant society, which was pagan for the most part, though Christian and Jewish minorities lived in the big Arabian towns. The surrounding powers were the Byzantine Empire and Persia, at war with each other. The Roman Emperor Heraclius was saving Christendom from the Persians, but the whole structure of the Byzantine Empire was so full of decay and contradiction that its days were numbered anyway.

Mohammed was about the same age as Heraclius, and his call to religion came when he was forty. He did not claim to be God nor even to be divine, but simply God's messenger, and with his insistence on one God he was obviously trying to unite his people, who were divided among themselves by dozens of rival pagan cults and petty tribal disputes. Hitti, in his *History of the Arabs,* has said that "Allah was the perfection of state supremacy," and in this powerful state supremacy Mohammed wanted a passionate sort of brotherhood, but no hierarchy, no priesthood, and no god but God. All the known weaknesses of Christianity were also to be avoided. Buying indulgence, for instance, was outlawed, and truthfulness and honor were originally the rock of Islam's foundation. The new code of Islam was, in fact, based on the requirements of desert merchants who had to make long voyages and do business in far-off places, which required great trust. The strict laws about honesty in business and courtesy and shelter for all travelers were the ideal conditions for caravan traders operating far away from home and depending on gentlemen's agreements to safeguard their trade. Mohammed's laws about women are laws for women who had to be left behind, unmolested and untouched by others during the husbands' absence, and artificially armored by isolation against the promiscuity which was rife in pagan Arabia.

The original approach was therefore rather straightforward, and even today a mosque of Islam is still a place of business and accommodation as well as of worship. If a Moslem man or woman arrives in a village or town in Egypt and fails to find a place to sleep he can always go to the mosque and sleep there. In any of Cairo's several hundred mosques it is normal to see two or three men sleeping on the rush mats during the day, or a couple of merchants or a few friends sitting down cross-legged, shoes off, chatting. The place belongs, genuinely, to its rich and poor congregation, and this fact, plus two very significant inner characteristics of the Moslem religion, explains some of its appeal to Egyptians previously oppressed by the dogmas and rituals of excessive perfectionism. One of these characteristics is the belief that man is not born evil, just weak, and if he persists in sinning it is simply because he is stubborn. The other is the Moslem acceptance of the idea that God can change his mind. One might add a third point, which is that Mohammed himself was never considered to be perfect, and even his most adoring biographers are quite willing to include his failings as proof of his fundamental humanity.

This was the kind of religion which Amr Ibn el 'As brought to Egypt nine years after Mohammed's death. Authority in Medina and Mecca had by then been given to an elected caliph, Omar, who forbade Amr Ibn el 'As to use Alexandria as his capital because it was a notorious fleshpot. It also happened to be in the wrong place for direct desert communication with Medina, so Amr decided to build a town outside the walls of Babylon. At first he had the problem of dividing up the area among the many different tribes who made up his army. The Arabs were not allowed to own land, so rather in the manner of claim-staking in the Klondike each tribe was given an area of its own, in and around Babylon and Amr's tent. Each area was called a kittaa, which means, approximately, marking out with a line. But all the kittaas had to be separated from each other because Amr considered that any close groupings of the tribes might destroy their distinctions.

We can only guess now where all these kittaas were. What we do know is that Amr built his house where his tent was or where he had set up his standard, which means it was somewhere in the perimeter of the present mosque. Professor K. A. C. Cresswell, probably the world's leading expert on Islamic architecture, told me in Cairo in 1966 that Amr's house was almost certainly in the corner of the mosque where the tomb of Amr's son Abdullah is now.

All the other Arab chieftains built houses in their own kittaas, some of mud, some mere lean-tos. The ground was theirs only as long as they occupied it, and though there were some disputes the original delineations of these kittaas lasted right up until Fustat was burned down over five hundred years later in 1168.

The original mosque was tiny, only 90 by 57 feet. It was roofless, its walls were mud and palm trees, not even plastered, and it had a minbar (pulpit) but no furnishings, and it was not properly oriented towards Mecca, which all mosques should be. When Omar the caliph heard that the little mosque had a pulpit, from which Amr would discourse, he sent a messenger rebuking Amr for raising himself above his fellows and told him to take it down. What stands there now as Amr's mosque is not exactly the original; Amr's little roofless hut was rebuilt and extended several times in the first fifty years of its existence, and its present shape dates from about 711, when it was rebuilt once more-by the Caliph Abd el Malik and surrounded by the wall that is still its perimeter.

It is impossible to walk into this old walled mosque and not feel highly pleased that it is still there, not because of its primitive architectural interest, but because Amr Ibn el 'As deserves an adequate monument. Amr is one of the few heroic figures in history whom it is still difficult to fault on essentials. He was a marvelous soldier and he treated the Egyptians with consideration. He was firm with his enemies (Cyrus and the Romans) and forgave them several attempts to trick him. He extracted no personal revenge, gave back to Copts and Jews all property which the Melchites had taken from them, would not tax old men, children, women, slaves, madmen or beggars, and even quarreled with Caliph Omar when Omar demanded more taxes than Amr could extract humanely from the people. He was a poet and a philosopher, and when Omar asked him to write a description of Egypt he replied: "Know, O Commander of the Faithful, that Egypt is a dusty city and a green tree. Its length is a month and its breadth ten days . . . Blessed are its early morning voyages and its travels at eventide . . . At one time Egypt is a white pearl; then golden amber, then a green emerald; then an embroidery of many colors . . ."

The one finger that can be pointed at Amr is that he died, aged ninety (buried somewhere at the foot of the Mukattam), so wealthy that his sons refused to take it all. But since Islam made no bones about the right, even the duty, of every Moslem to acquire wealth, Amr's money can hardly be considered a false aspect of his character. The greedy one was the Caliph Omar in Medina because he had wars to fight. But it would be foolish to imagine that Amr and Omar had any other desire in Egypt than to take away as much wealth as they could.

What forged Egypt to Arabia with chains of loot and gold was the old Amnis Trajanas canal. In the first year of the occupation, and with considerable use of forced labor (another finger at Amr), the canal was cleared out. It had been neglected for many years, and the usual Arab story is that a Copt had to point out to Amr where its banks were, and this Copt was released of all taxes as a reward. Within twelve months of Amr's victory the wealth of Egypt was already flowing like blood through the canal to the Red Sea and across to Arabia. Amr even proposed to build a Suez canal, but the Caliph Omar was afraid that Romans would be able to sail through it to the Red Sea, so he forbade it.

It is quite obvious that the Red Sea canal made Fustat a city. If Fustat had lacked such an easy and direct route to Medina it would never have survived. Alexandria had been the place of exit for the wealth that Greece and Rome had taken out of Egypt to Europe; now Fustat became the Arab portal to this treasure-house, and from the day that Amr Ibn el 'As cleared out the old canal Fustat replaced Alexandria as Egypt's capital.

Fustat was built with remarkable speed, and there seems little doubt that most of it was built by the Copts, because the conquering Arabs were certainly not bricklayers and plasterers. The indigenes of Egypt, living along the riverbanks in the township of Babylon — the artisans, weavers, carpenters, bricklayers, dockworkers, boatmen and gardeners — all seem to have adapted themselves quickly to Arab demands. It meant work and, for the local merchants, wealth. What could not be overcome, however, was the Arab sense of the tent, and even today the old parts of medieval Cairo still look like a cluster of Bedouin tents.

Arabs didn't like high or elaborate buildings, so most of the houses of Fustat were low to begin with. When Kharijah, one of Amr's lieutenants, put up a balcony, Caliph Omar (who heard about everything in Medina) sent word that it must be taken down. But eventually most of early Fustat's houses, spreading like a baked-brick octupus around Amr's mosque, were four or five stories, and copying some of the Roman essentials of the township of Babylon, they added gardens and wells and bathhouses; but Arab bathhouses were so diminutive compared with the Roman ones that the Arabs nicknamed them Hammamat el Far — mouse baths.

What seems to have kept this expanding boom going was the arrival of whole tribes of desert Arabs, coming very far west to seek their fortune. Stanley Lane Poole in Volume VI of *The History of Egypt* says that in 732 about five thousand Arabs of the Keys tribe were

Courtyard of the mosque of Ibn Tulun, with the ablution
fountain on the left and the minaret in the background.

settled en masse in northeast Fustat. Every new Arabian governor brought a big army with him from Arabia, as many as twenty thousand men sometimes, and these too had to settle somewhere in Egypt, though not all of them did so in Fustat. In any case intermarriage of Arab men and Coptic Egyptian women began immediately, and on the whole Egypt prospered in the first years of the occupation despite exorbitant taxes and heavy tribute. At one time the treasuries of Fustat were so stuffed with gold and loot that the caliph ordered all surpluses to be sent to the mosques for storage.

When the Arabs began building Fustat they took building materials from every other building they could tear down. Not only Pharaonic monuments suffered (as they were to go on suffering for a thousand years), but churches and monasteries and temples were demolished. Fustat must have been built of a fine collection of bastard doors and windows and porticos. What was most in demand was columns, and almost every column of the two hundred in Amr's mosque seems to be different in height, thickness, style and period. The mixture actually becomes very attractive as you walk in and out of the colonnades because every one is a surprise, particularly when one arch has to be brought low to meet a short column, and the next one has to be kept up high to cope with a tall one. Nothing is regular and some of the columns are upside down, but the total effect is unique and exciting.

Columns have obviously had a magical attraction to Moslems. There is a granite column at the northeast end of Amr's mosque, near Abdullah's tomb, which has a deep and ugly wound in it which is literally stained with blood. The hole has been worn into the column by more than a thousand years of tongue licking. The superstitious believed that they would recover health and overcome a disease if they licked this column until their tongue bled. There are two columns near the main entrance gate about six inches apart, and these are the lie detectors of Amr's mosque. When anybody was in dispute the parties would come to these columns, and whoever could pass between them was declared to be the honest man, but it is obvious that only lean and hungry men could ever win a case in this high court.

Unfortunately most of the columns of Amr's mosque will have to be repositioned because the aisles are all pointing in the wrong direction. All mosques have to be aligned on Mecca, and the aisles must flow in the main direction, but in Amr's mosque they all point the wrong way, because an Ottoman governor, Murad Bey, tried to rebuild the mosque during a fit of piety just before Napoleon invaded Egypt, (although Egyptians still say he was digging up the mosque looking for treasure). On the whole this great monument to early Islam in Egypt has been badly treated by Egypt's Moslem occupiers. At one time it became the haunt of thieves. When Ibn Sa'id came here in the thirteenth century it was full of musicians, beggars and dancing girls. The miracle is that, having survived the eventual burning of Fustat, it could still survive the alternating excesses of neglect and restoration which seem to have done it equal damage.

From these very ramshackle beginnings Fustat eventually became a very rich city, but the full story of how it became rich and what happened to it cannot be told until two other official capitals are dealt with: el Askar and el Katai. Both these royal townships were built on the shoulders of Fustat, but they were officially quite separate and distinct from it. Eventually all three grew into each other under the general name of Fustat-Misr, but both Askar and Katai had extravagant enough lives of their own.

6

Fustat — Askar — Katai

E L ASKAR became the capital because the Omayyad caliphs, who had ruled Islam since Mohammed's death, were overwhelmed by a new dynasty, the Abbasids. The Abbasids claimed descent from Abbas, the Prophet's uncle, and they set themselves up in Baghdad. They not only fathered the biggest split in the Moslem religion, between Shi'ites and Sunnites, but they eventually established a non-Arab supremacy in Islam so that the originally pure Arab rule in Egypt finally came to an end.

The Abbasid general Saleh took Fustat in 750. Like all Moslem rulers he disliked the idea of establishing his authority on the bones of the previous rulers, so he built his headquarters on a little flat stretch of dry land on the northern tip of Fustat. Thereafter this became the official town of the governor and his soldiers and ministers. El Askar means "the soldiers" in Arabic, and though it began life as a military camp, it was not long before this township had its own palaces and mosques. A wavy line of gardens and houses connected it to Fustat, which simply continued its own existence as the rich and powerful commercial city of Egypt.

Egypt by now was a much thicker mixture of Moslem Arab and Egyptian Copt, but neither Moslem nor Copt liked the Abbasids at all, and they both revolted and were both suppressed by the new caliphs. A new factor also appeared in Egyptian life. The Abbasid caliphs began to depend on Turkish war slaves as bodyguards and generals and provincial governors. Abu Salih, the first Turkish-born governor, arrived in Egypt in 779, and though classified as an Arab he was born a Turk, and for Egyptians he was typically a Turk. He laid down strict laws for living, behavior and dress and then enforced them. He particularly hated thieves, and he ordered all the gates and doorways of Fustat to be left open day and night, and if anyone were caught thieving he lopped his head off. Makrizi, Cairo's greatest historian, says that when people went to the baths they left their clothes in the dressing room and shouted out, "Abu Salih, look after my clothes," a reminder to anyone with robbery in mind that Abu Salih would lop his head off.

This kind of dictatorial insistence was only a breath of what was yet to come. Between 788 and 809 the caliph in Baghdad was the famous Harun al Rashid. His court of a thousand and one nights attracted poets and singers and scientists and alchemists and dancers and doctors from all over the eastern world. The lavish taste now called Oriental began to be associated with Islam because of Harun's exotic entertainments. But he was an enlightened and intelligent man, and though his Shi'a faith was considered heretical by the Egyptians, it permitted a great deal more self-indulgence in both physical and mental pleasures, and Harun took full advantage of both. Yet the merchants of Baghdad were really responsible for the rich intellectual flavor of their city. They had created a vast network of trade by sea and by land extending over wide areas of Asia, Africa and Europe. With the trade came the intellectuals, who were essential to it and also the product of it.

The influence on Arab intellectuals then was mainly Hellenic, and there is a certain logic in this. The Arab merchants needed science and philosophy and literature, not only because they had the leisure and the money to enjoy them, but because an enriched culture was good for their kind of business, and they found in Greek classic culture a perfect foundation for their own. Baghdad writers translated many of the Greek classics, and Harun's intellectuals were studying Aristotle and the neo-Platonists, the medical works of Galen (Marcus Aurelius's physician), and the poetic dramas of Persia and India when Europe was stifling helplessly in long years of cultural darkness.

Bertrand Russell, in a flattering comment on early Islam, has said that the Arabs at this time gave us so much of what we have of the Greeks that we can hardly trace all the processes. The Arabs thought Aristotle the scientist more important than Plato the philosopher. Sir William Dampier in his *A History of Science* has analyzed the reasons why science and the Moslem religion were so well mated by showing that the Islamic kind of monotheism fitted perfectly the Epicurean idea that space is atomic, quality an accident, and that if Allah were to cease recreating atoms the universe would disappear. But perhaps another explanation for this upsurge in intellect among the Arabs was Mohammed's insistence on literacy. Mohammed himself had been almost choked to death by an angel who had insisted that he read. Literacy for all was part of Islamic doctrine when the rest of the world didn't really care whether ordinary people could read or not.

Mamun, Harun al Rashid's son, was the first Abbasid caliph to visit Egypt. Mamun arrived in Askar in 832, supposedly to suppress latent Coptic revolts in the Delta, and most historians say that he did suppress them so thoroughly that never again did a Coptic movement for independence emerge in Egypt. But what seems to have been the real reason for the reduction of the Copts in Egypt was their comparatively easy absorption into Islam. Christianity had ceased to provide what most Egyptians wanted — a simple and helpful code they could live with. Christianity's dogmatic priesthood and its ideological insistence on darkness were cutting it off from the rich river of culture which Islam had now released. Though Mamun did fight a bloody little battle against the Copts, it seems clear that most of the poor peasants and many (though not all) of the urban and intellectual Christians of Egypt had already embraced Islam because Islam had more to offer them. The countryside held out a little longer, but as the majority of the population embraced Islam, only faraway places like Upper Egypt remained Coptic, and in fact are still Coptic today.

Curiously enough, Copts remained the principal clerks and administrators of Egypt right up until 1952, and Fustat always had a large and strong minority of Copts who administered the city (and the country), no matter what the Abbasids were doing over in Askar. The most accepted theory explaining Coptic supremacy in administration for so long is that they are simply cleverer administrators than Moslems. This may be true, particularly if one allows that they have inherited the tradition of Pharaonic administration, which was one of the best the world has ever known. But what attracted outside conquerors to the Copts *was* their minority role. As soon as Islam became the majority religion of Egypt, almost no conqueror thereafter depended exclusively on Islamic administrators. Moslem occupiers were not above using Christians to divide and rule the population for them.

El Askar had remained an enclave of the greater city of Fustat, though it remained the *official* capital of Egypt for a hundred and nineteen years — the whole span of the power and glory of the Abbasids. But what had begun in this royal city as a shadow of Abbasid power — the use of Turkish mercenaries and slaves to do the dirty work — now became the substance of Abbasid authority. Turkish slaves began to rule the rulers, and inevitably one of them set himself up in Fustat as the master and not the slave.

At first these slave soldiers were simply a sort of accidental byproduct of the Abbasid system of educating "bought" or "acquired" children in the court to grow up into a loyal bodyguard: a violent civil service without any roots in the society itself who could be trusted to do as they were told, no matter what was happening outside the court. As a rule the Moslem slave was not like a pagan or Christian slave. He was not beaten or made to do brutal work; he was more associated with good soldiering, self-indulgence, a powerful and amoral viciousness, inspired terror, and a sort of back-room political influence. This was to become the slave tradition, later, with the Mamelukes.

Tulun was a Turkish slave from Bokhara who was given to Caliph Mamun in 815 as a present. He became a powerful and influential figure in Mamun's court, and his son Ahmad Ibn Tulun (ibn means son of) was educated in the highest traditions of Islamic law and government. As a young man Ibn Tulun was a brave and loyal servant to his caliph, and when his father died and his stepfather was given Egypt as a sort of private estate by the caliph, Ahmad Ibn Tulun was sent to administer it. He was thirty-three when he arrived at Askar-Fustat, and he couldn't even pay his way from Baghdad to Egypt. He had to borrow ten thousand dinars to set himself up in his new job. But by 870 he was so much the ruler of Egypt that he could build his own capital, because El Askar was too small for his entourage of soldiers, ministers, wives and slaves.

There was a little knoll of high ground between Fustat and the Mukattam Hills called Yeshkur, which was at the time a Christian cemetery. Yeshkur was supposed to be the place where Moses had conversations with God, and where Abraham slew his sacrifice. Moslems considered it a holy place, since Christians and Jews were both respected by Islam as "people of the Book." Ibn Tulun cleared the Christian graves from Yeshkur and built his royal capital around the hill. The new town was divided into special katais (districts) for each section of the population who came to live there. Each katai was named according to the kind of population it had: servants, soldiers, guards, Romans (really Greeks) or Nubians. So the little city itself was called El Katai — the districts. Ibn Tulun built a palace at the foot of the Mukattam Hills, a garden, a racecourse and polo ground, a zoo, a palace for his wives, baths, a hospital, and rich houses for his staff. The little hill of Yeshkur was then literally crowned in 876 by a large, original and inventive mosque, which is still sitting on Yeshkur like a beautiful hat on the head of a dried-up old lady. It is, in fact, one of the most important Moslem monuments in the world.

The three capitals of early Islamic Egypt were thus attached to each other like atoms attached to form a separate substance. Fustat, Askar and Katai were really part and parcel of the same city, and most of what we know of this combined city comes from two four-teenth- and fifteenth-century Arab historians, el Makrizi and Ibn Duqmuq, both of whom loved its exotic character. With Ibn Tulun, Fustat-Askar-Katai began to take on the decorative style that made it a genuinely fabulous place. Ibn Tulun very quickly became more than a governor of Egypt. He created a small kingdom of his own out of a united Egypt and Syria, and with this combination behind him he almost conquered Mecca. The caliphate was weak, and it was obviously silly to send all the Egyptian revenue east. Much of the revenue of Egypt was therefore kept in Egypt for the first time in many hundreds of years. Fustat was still the big trading port between Egypt and the east, however, and Ibn Tulun was intelligent enough to keep his trade with the east active.

The nerve (literally) center of Ibn Tulun's royal city was his Midan el Katai, a huge square which extended more or less from the present citadel right up to the hill of Yeshkur. Being a wonderful horseman and an enthusiastic soldier, Ibn Tulun used the midan for parades and polo, and Makrizi says that everybody in Fustat loved this big square. If you asked anyone you happened to see hurrying along the streets where they were going they usually said: "To the midan." Something was always going on there, even at night.

Since el Katai was surrounded by a network of narrow streets (there were eventually a hundred thousand houses in el Katai) and lush gardens and zoos, the many gates into this square had a special meaning, and each one a special name. You could enter only by the gate of your class or profession, though who classified the population we don't really know. But there was also a Gate of Nobles and a Gate of Lions (surmounted by two carved lions) and a gate called el Darmun because that was the name of the captain of the guards there, who was a big black court official. Ibn Tulun himself entered by a special triple-arched gate of his own, and when he reviewed his troops he would lead them through the center of it while up to thirty thousand men would pass through the side arches. At night he would sit in a little summerhouse he had built high up on the Gate of Lions and look down on his square, which would be filled with people and lights and stalls and gaiety, particularly on feast days. By simply turning around he could see the Mukattam on one side and the Nile on the other.

The whole conception of this midan implies a rich and prosperous population — a population that was not under too much restraint. But unlike Roman entertainments, there were no cruel sports and no personally violent combats in the arenas. Ibn Tulun also built a remarkable muristan (hospital), but this he erected in the old royal capital of el Askar. Makrizi says that the money for this hospital was paid for out of a "treasure" which Ibn Tulun's servant found in Upper Egypt. The servant was riding in the country one day and his horse fell into a hole, and in the hole they found treasure worth a million dinars. In gratitude to God Ibn Tulun built a hospital, which was the first of many we hear about in the history of Cairo. Its social methods could be counted as modern even now. You would leave your own clothes when you entered it and put on hospital garments. All food and medicines were free, and Ibn Tulun inspected the hospital himself every Friday. Moreover, it was especially for the civil population of Fustat, not for his soldiers and guards, who were forbidden to go there.

Ibn Tulun was not quite fifty when he got dysentery from drinking too much buffalo milk. He was soldiering in Anticon and he was carried home to Fustat on a camel litter, a very sick man. His doctors put him on a diet, but he became violent and refused to obey them, and when he realized he was dying he had his doctors flogged to death for failing to cure him. He died anyway in 884.

The mosque that Ibn Tulun built up on the hill of Yeshkur is probably one of the most beautiful and stimulating monuments any historical figure has ever managed to leave behind him. Almost everything about it is intriguing. Makrizi, for instance, tells a rather fantastic story about how the building was conceived. Ibn Tulun, he says, did not want to rob any more Christian churches of their columns because he thought it sacrilegious. But he required a mosque of considerable dimensions, and columns had to be found for it. Hearing of Ibn Tulun's dilemma, a Christian who was in jail for some minor offense offered to build a very large mosque with no columns, and he sent Ibn Tulun an outline showing a vast enclosed courtyard with the mosque itself held up not by marble columns but by squat brick piers supporting pointed arches. Ibn Tulun immediately grasped the inventiveness of the idea and freed the Christian and paid him 110,000 dinars, which was not bad pay considering that the mosque itself cost 120,000.

This is a good story, but Professor K. A. C. Creswell says it is obviously a legend, told to explain the use of brick piers, which Egypt had never seen before. Brick was considered necessary in case the city burned down. Marble disintegrates under flame and brick doesn't. But

Looking from the main liwan into the courtyard of the
mosque of Amr Ibn el 'As.

the use of brick has to be very clever to be both imposing and beautiful, and there is something so powerful and individual in those brick piers, even now, with the famous pointed arches rising over them like a ballerina's swanlike arms, that even a non-expert can see the originality of the unusual design. This mosque was the first to use the pointed arch in a vast architectural complex, and it was another two hundred years before Christianity borrowed it for our own Gothic arch. The cloisters, also, were born in this kind of four-walled, colonnaded mosque. The whole concept, brilliant in almost every brick, probably owed its design not to the jailed Copt but to mosques already standing in Samarra. Professor Creswell told me very firmly that there can be no doubt of this. In his own monumental work on early Islamic architecture Creswell also suggests that the façade of the mosque is based on Amr's mosque, so in style at least it is wholly Egyptian. Christian-inclined historians have always thought that the beautiful foliated designs cut into the stone and gypsum around the top were also Coptic in origin, but Creswell again points out that these were Iraqi, and that probably the whole mosque was built not by Copts but by some of the many Iraqi artisans Ibn Tulun brought with him to Fustat. The minaret almost traces its ancestry to the Tower of Babel. A. J. Butler thought it originated somehow in the famous Pharos of Alexandria, because its design is almost exactly the same, but again Creswell says it originates in Samarra, where Ibn Tulun used to visit his mother when he was young, and where there were corkscrew minarets like this one already standing at the time.

For just over a hundred years after Ibn Tulun's death, and up till the time when another new city, al Kahira, was founded (969), Fustat-Askar-Katai became a more and more elaborate metropolis. The tragedy of knowing what it was like becomes quite acute when you walk up and down the powdered remains of Fustat now, or when you climb the minaret of Ibn Tulun's mosque to look for some remnant of Askar, knowing that not a brick of the fabulous city is left. You cannot, in fact, look across the brown bare floor of the little valleys where the city of el Katai was and not regret that something — some single flower or some lonely tree of the extraordinary garden of Khumaraweh — doesn't still stand.

Khumaraweh was Ibn Tulun's son, and like so many sons inheriting a strong father's wealth he was softer and able to indulge in eccentricities. He turned his father's big midan into a lovely and exotic garden, and planted its vast acreage with tropical trees, roses, jasmine, lilies and shrubs. But Khumaraweh hated the unsightliness of the stalks of trees, so every tree had its trunk and branches coated in sheets of

[55]

gilded copper which were lined with lead water pipes, so that every tree was not only a gilded lily but a pretty fountain running through the shady gardens. Not only were there exotic trees but exotic fruits, such as apricots grafted onto almonds, and a complicated and lovely pigeon house. The birds of Fustat-Katai were famous for their color and their noisy singing. Since he had used up his father's sports ground to build his garden, Khumaraweh built another midan even larger than his father's, but a little distance away. And since he was mad over horse racing, there were races almost all night and day.

Khumaraweh lined the walls of some of the rooms and passages of his palace (where the Hasan mosque now stands) with thin sheets of gold studded with lapis lazuli. In one suite called the House of Gold, which was entirely lined with gold, he set up wooden statues of himself and his wives, each statue dressed in cloth of gold. They were larger than life, and his own statue had golden trousers and his turban was encrusted with jewels. Every night Khumaraweh would sit on one of the terraces or in his golden room or in his garden listening to the poets reciting, or to his favorite slaves singing. He also built a magnificent zoo, and he was passionately fond of lions. There was a special house of lions (dar el assad), and every chamber of it housed a lion and a lioness. Each cage had a special door where the keeper could enter to feed them and clean out the place and sand the floor, and each one had running water. It was really a clean and spacious menagerie, and sometimes Khumaraweh would free all the lions into the courtyard of the zoo, and all Fustat would shake with the roars of the lions fighting and playing with each other all night. Every lion was trained to go back to his quarters when his keeper called him by name.

The most extraordinary of all these lions was one that Khumaraweh kept as his own pet and bodyguard called Zouraik (little blue) because it had blue eyes. Khumaraweh led him around by a collar of gold, and Zouraik slept near Khumaraweh, no matter where he was. Khumaraweh fed him chickens and goats and brushed his coat. But as well as lions Khumaraweh kept ponies, racehorses, camels, leopards, giraffes and elephants in his city. What is charming about Khumaraweh is that he could also be kind to human beings. Instead of turning them out on the street as often happened, he installed the mothers of all his prolific father's children in the harem, and he also looked after any of his own divorced wives who had presented him with children — a not illiberal gesture from a ruler as eccentric as this one.

But perhaps this isn't really the half of it, because Khumaraweh conceived what is probably the ultimate in sybaritic self-indulgence

— something even Texas hasn't thought up yet. Khumaraweh was an insomniac, and his physicians told him that he ought to be rocked gently to sleep every night. To achieve this Khumaraweh dug out a lake thirteen hundred feet square in the garden of his palace. This lake was filled with mercury (as from thermometers) and he slept on the lake every night, rocked to sleep on an air mattress made of inflated skins. The mattress was tied to the edges of the lake with silken cords, and the movement of the mercury made small waves which moved it gently to and fro. In an alcove nearby, his favorite singers (four at a time) sang him sacred and profane songs and chanted his favorite verses from the Koran, and if he couldn't sleep on his lake Khumaraweh would get up and walk around his palace or sit in his gardens or entertain his lady friends.

Makrizi loved this sort of anecdote and he finds it difficult to tear himself away from lengthy descriptions of Khumaraweh's excesses. Fustat-Katai under Khumaraweh lived in a sort of permanent nonviolent Roman holiday, and as Lane Poole says: "So brave, so terrible and so gallant a figure was this superb prince that his subjects dared not speak, much less sneeze, as he passed by." It was also considered bad luck if they did speak or sneeze. But according to Makrizi (Casanova), he was never the same man after his favorite wife Bouran died. It was for Bouran that he had built his House of Gold, and after her death everything in life seems to have lost its charm for him.

Khumaraweh was strangled in his bed in Damascus in 896 by his servants and his concubines. His lion Zouraik and his black bodyguard couldn't save him, and his murderers were crucified. His body was brought home to Fustat and buried near his father's, somewhere at the foot of the Mukattam. Just as he was being put into his tomb the reciters of the Koran "happened to be chanting" the verse which says: "Seize him and hurl him into the fire of hell," which is probably a genuinely popular story and comment on what all this sumptuous self-indulgence meant to the people of Fustat-Katai — zoo, gardens, lions, and his personal bravery notwithstanding.

El Katai itself was destroyed by Khumaraweh's successor. The Tulunids had managed to keep Egypt for themselves as a private kingdom for thirty years, but Khumaraweh's sons were too weak to hold on to it. The Abbasid caliph sent a soldier named Mohammed Ibn Suleiman to take it back, which he did in 905. He and his troops spent four months devastating the city, and Makrizi says that "they invaded the houses, profaned the harems, dishonored the citizens, violated the virgins, chased the women, got up to all sort of infamies, and threw people out of their homes." Then they stripped it of its wealth and opened the prisons. They also decimated the beautiful gardens and cut off the heads of most of the black troops who had been the Tulunid bodyguard. The royal city of el Katai thereafter began to die a slow death, so that a hundred and sixty years later it and el Askar were in such an awful state of ruin that a wall was built around them to hide them from the rest of the city.

7

Fustat-Misr

Though el Askar and el Katai ceased to be entities, Fustat itself went on thriving with the exaggerated excess which seems to have been the character of this old city. But there are very sound reasons why this was so. Egypt was always one of the richest provinces in any Moslem empire, it was always therefore a unique prize for ambitious men to fight for. More often than not a new caliphate would arise in Arabia or Iraq, some general would be sent to capture Egypt for the new dynasty, but inevitably the victorious soldier or the new governor or some violent upstart who hated the idea of sending away all the profits of this rich enterprise would simply take over the place for himself.

Living as we do now in an age of cynical struggle for who gets what in our big business enterprises, it sometimes seems as if Egypt under the various Islamic caliphates had itself become a huge limited company offering such a fantastic return on the investment and such a guaranteed and stable and bottomless market for its products that one foreign tycoon after the other tried to get hold of it, forming new combinations on the existing board to give them control, only to find their power weakened as another combination arose and outmaneuvered them. Or some brutal genius would simply walk in and take the lot. Meanwhile the company itself simply went on turning out its products and amassing the huge wealth which the big company men fought over.

The place where these huge profits on the wealth of Egypt continued to be collected was Fustat. One is inclined to forget when reading about the exotic behavior of its rulers that Fustat was built around a port, and that its real existence depended on its harbors, which brought in wealth from the countryside and sent it on through the old Red Sea canal and beyond. A lot of Fustat's lavish wealth was obviously cash wealth from its port, accumulated by taxing everybody and everything that passed through it. One after the other of Egypt's rulers simply used the city as a huge tax-collecting depot, a treasure-house and a private bank. The tax was usually the royal share, while the merchants made their millions in the buying and selling business. But more often than not the ruler was also the biggest merchant of them all.

The wealth itself continued to be founded on Egypt's excessively rich soil, its three crops a year, its poor peasantry, its clever artisans, clerks, dockers and boatmen. Excepting in times of famine, everything the Egyptian soil produced was dirt cheap. Not only was it produced cheaply but it was transported cheaply because of that ready-made highway, the river, which touched almost all the cultivated land of Egypt. The grain and vegetables and fruit and dates and meat which arrived at the Fustat docks had cost very very little up to that point, but by the time they left Fustat the prices had probably increased by anything up to a thousand percent.

As Fustat got larger and richer and acquired satellite towns like el Katai and el Askar (for that is all they really were), something began to happen to its name. At various times Fustat had been called Misr, because it had always been confused with another city just across the river. The original Misr was really a Pharaonic township on the west bank of the Nile, on the other side from Babylon and Fustat where Giza is now. The name Misr goes so far back into Pharaonic history that we don't know the origins of it. The ancient town was, in fact, a continuation of the antique city of Memphis, and it must always have been a long straggling collection of docks and boatbuilding yards, granaries and markets and houses.

The island of Roda, which is in the middle of the Nile near Babylon, was sometimes considered to be part of this township of Misr, and it was always important to all these towns. Roda has always been con-sidered very beautiful, and today it is still one of the most attractive places in Cairo. It has hardly changed its shape in over two thousand years. The river on the Cairo side of Roda is little more than a ditch, but the river between it and the Giza side is wide and full. The island seems to have had an almost separate life of its own, even though it was considered to be part of Misr and Babylon and Fustat. It was, at different times, a big port, a shipbuilding island, an arsenal, a fortress, the site of royal palaces, a rich garden; and on its southern tip there is one of the oldest buildings in Islamic Egypt — the Nilometer. Because the rise and fall of the river decided the whole cycle of Egyptian life, the moment when the rise and fall began and the extent of either one was something vital to Egyptian agricultural life, and it was in this building on Roda that the height of the Nile was measured. The Nilometer itself is simply a stone pit containing an octagonal column which is measured off and marked. According to Professor Creswell's complicated investigations it was built in 847, and it was in this Nilometer that the very first pointed arch was used; it can still be seen a quarter of the way down the stone side of the pit.

When the Arabs first came to Babylon they used the old Pharaonic name Misr for the actual river port there, and they never really stopped using the name. As time passed, Fustat and Misr became interchangeable names for the port and the city combined, no doubt because all trade with Egypt was directed eventually to the river port of Misr, or it came from Misr. So it seems logical that sooner or later it was all known as Fustat-Misr (which is what Makrizi often calls it) and then simply as Misr. Today Egyptians still call both their country and Cairo simply Misr.

With the restoration of the Baghdad caliphate the old struggle for who was going to have Fustat-Misr and Egypt began again, and there were thirteen governors in Fustat-Misr in twenty-nine years. One caliph sent an army of Africans to conquer Egypt. An Egyptian minister of finance accumulated so much wealth that when he made his pilgrimage to Mecca every year everybody in that city got something out of him, and in Fustat-Misr he lived like a king and was far more powerful than any of the governors because he had somehow got hold of the revenue for himself.

In 935, after years of almost anarchic contests for the wealth and power of the city, a Baghdadi Turk named Mohammed Ibn Toughdj sailed up the Nile and captured Roda Island. He then crossed on the boat bridge to Fustat-Misr and pillaged the city for two days and nights unopposed before settling down to its occupation. He was given the title of al Ikshid by the caliph, and once more the man who was really the governor of Egypt became in fact its absolute ruler and principal beneficiary.

The Ikshid was that peculiar mixture which the various caliphates of Islam have often produced: a self-indulgent ruler who nonetheless encouraged the arts and free debate, a formally religious Moslem who allowed all kinds of heresies to be expressed in the discussions and arguments which took place in the mosques. The Ikshid was one of the few rulers of Egypt who restored the mosque of Amr Ibn el 'As

[61]

and used it. On the last night of the Moslem feast of Ramadan he usually went there in white robes to pray, and it is still a custom in Cairo to go to Amr's mosque to pray on the last day of Ramadan. It is supposed to bring good luck.

But on the whole he did not add anything memorable to Fustat-Misr — he seems to have spent a lot of his time organizing and enjoying the various festivals and parades. In one of the parades through old Fustat four hundred thousand soldiers marched through the streets, followed by eight thousand Mamelukes (slave soldiers) dressed in bright armor. He held open house on feast days, and Ali Ibn Husain al Mas'udi, an Arab traveler and historian who compiled a travelogue called *Meadows of Gold,* attended one of these feasts A.D. 941 when the Ikshid was living on Roda, where his palace was. The Ikshid ordered that the side of the island near Fustat-Misr should be lit by two thousand torches. People by the hundreds of thousands packed the Nile on boats and watched it all from kiosks near the riverside or on the banks. Everybody tried to outdo everybody else with the food on their picnic tables and in dress and jewels and entertainments. Music, singing and dancing went on up and down the riverbanks and all the gates of the different quarters were left open and almost everybody bathed in the Nile, certain that this would protect them from illness and cure it as well.

The intellectual life of the city also got the benefits. The Mohammedan religion has four main orthodox sects — the Maliki, Hanbali, Shafi'i, and Hanafi, each one named after a leading scholar who had the right to interpret Islamic traditions in jurisprudence. The traditions of Islam are a means of understanding the social laws of Islam which still operate in Islamic countries, so the debate between the four rival schools of jurisprudence always had a real meaning for ordinary people. In the Ikshid's time these four schools debated with each other all day and probably all night in the courtyard and under the columns of Amr's mosque. A man would usually begin by stating a proposition. Then a very free discussion would develop and sometimes it got so furious at Amr's mosque that the Ikshid had to close the place up.

This method of public exposure to argument was quite often the way the mosques of Islam were used. They were always academies, and more often than not academies for argument, and sometimes even heretical and unreligious arguments went on in them. In literature and poetry the same method was used. A poet would read his verse to an audience in a square, by a fountain, or in a courtyard, and the audience would listen and then comment, then argue, and if the poet was lucky he could stand up and defend himself. The Ikshid thoroughly enjoyed all these debates and quarrels and he loved the literature and the poetry. Fustat-Misr was therefore a rich home for good writers and thinkers, even the heretical ones.

When the Ikshid died he was succeeded by a black eunuch called Camphor (Kafour). Makrizi says that Kafour was big, fat, jolly and clever. He had once been a page and had risen by sheer force of politics to be governor. He was a great manipulator, but he was articulate and he too loved scholars, poets and singers, and he was usually surrounded by debating grammarians and song-writers. When one of the famous lyricists of the time (Ibn el Asin) explained a rather bad series of local earthquakes as Egypt dancing for joy because it admired Kafour so much, he threw the poet a thousand dinars.

Kafour's table at Fustat-Misr was as fat-laden as Kafour. His daily allowance for himself and his guests was a hundred sheep, a hundred lambs, two hundred and fifty geese, three hundred fowls, a thousand pigeons and a hundred jars of sugary sweets. His palace counted on eating seventeen hundred pounds of meat a day, to be swilled down by fifty skinfuls of liquor, usually quince beer. His public feasts were even more gargantuan; one feast had twenty-one baked dishes each containing twenty-one baked sheep, three hundred fifty pigeons and fowls all piled up in a heap, five hundred incidental dishes each one with seven fowls, cakes, bread, two large constructions of sweetmeats each weighing nearly a ton, and of course gallons of wine, cider and sherbet. Additionally there were continuous singing and dancing, clever clowns and witty beggars, and anybody who pleased Kafour had a handful of gold flung at him.

In Kafour's time a large area of Fustat-Misr accidentally burned down. And while he feasted so grossly and indecently there were often food shortages in the rest of Egypt because the Nile didn't always behave. Kafour's kind of lavish court always suggests a terrible burden on the peasantry who had to provide it, and in effect pay for it. Being a city, Fustat-Misr may have benefited from the lavish indulgences of rulers like the Ikshid and Kafour, but the rest of the country got nothing out of it but brutally hard work. It would also be a mistake to imagine that the Egyptians took it dumbly and humbly. Mas'udi quotes a contemporary writer who says of Egypt: "The people who inhabit it are insubordinate, and only obey when they are made to tremble. They never submit, except when they are disunited, and if they revolt it is a struggle to the death."

Kafour was not overthrown by the Egyptians, but the rebellious Egyptians contributed considerably to the end of the Ikshid dynasty.

When the generals of the new Fatimid caliphate arrived in 969 they did not find it difficult to take Egypt, even though the Egyptians considered them heretics and almost non-Moslems because they belonged to the rival Shi'a sect of Islam.

In 969 the Fatimids founded another new royal city to the north of Fustat-Misr, al Kahira, now the center of modern Cairo. But before dealing in another chapter with al Kahira, which begins another kind of Cairo, one must first dispose of Fustat-Misr, which continued to have an exciting life of its own for another two hundred years.

In fact it is unlikely that any other city in the tenth century except Baghdad could compare with Fustat-Misr, and among the side benefits of its fame are descriptions of it left by one traveler after another. These descriptions reveal a very sophisticated city with the sort of social amenities and city services which we are inclined to imagine as typical of ancient Rome or part of our modern lives, but rarely in the line of Arab history. Sewage and drainage, water supply, public gardens, street lighting, schools, street sweeping and the strict regulations for traders and householders were thoroughly systematized and administered. And they must have worked very well, because Fustat-Misr at its height was a genuine metropolis, with a noisy, intelligent and argumentative population who took a lively part in everything that went on in the city, which they considered very much to be their own.

In appearance the city was a warren of tangled streets, lanes, alleyways and passages. Some of the streets were only about four feet wide, and they turned and twisted and joined others and went through courtyards and gardens and by block after block of tall solid buildings and by open squares and very busy marketplaces. One of the first descriptions of the city comes from Ibn Haukal, an Arabian traveler of the tenth century who said that Fustat-Misr was always crowded, was rich, and though smaller than Baghdad its six- and seven-story houses were brick, its markets prosperous, and it was famous for its gardens, palaces and fairgrounds.

The Persian traveler Nasir Ibn Khusrau came to Misr in 1047, about a hundred years before it was burned to the ground, and in his *Sefer Nameh* he says that Fustat-Misr looked like a mountain when you approached it because of its high buildings, some of them fourteen stories. One seven-story house, he says, had a garden on its roof, and the ox that worked the roof garden's water wheel had to be taken up there when it was a calf. The garden grew sweet and bitter oranges and other fruits and flowers.

A merchant told him that there were plenty of rooms to let in Fustat-Misr, and some of the houses were big enough to hold three hundred people. Many of the narrow streets were covered with canvas against the sun, so they were lit day and night by thousands of lamps. There were then seven mosques, and he described Amr's mosque as being "in the middle of the bazaar of Misr." The pulpit of the mosque then was pure white marble, and it was covered with the full text of the Koran. The mosque's courtyard was a place of reunion, and one rarely saw less than five thousand people there listening to the lectures of the professors or talking and arguing — students, foreigners and public writers who drew up contracts or made accounts for traders.

Ibu Khusrau says that the governor of Cairo at the time, Hakim, had just bought Amr's mosque from his decendants. They had come to him cap in hand claiming they were poor and ruined. "This mosque was built by our ancestor," they said, "and if the sultan will authorize it we want to demolish it to sell its stone and brick." Hakim probably saw through this kind of beggary, but he gave them a hundred thousand dinars for the mosque. He fitted it up with a gigantic silver light which had seven hundred lamps in it, but it was so big that he had to break down a door to get it in. Makrizi confirms this and says that it was done before a huge crowd of spectators. And being Fustat-Misr, no doubt there was plenty of noisy encouragement and barracking from the crowd.

On the north side of the mosque was the Street of Lamps, and Ibn Khusrau says of it: "One knows no equal to it in any other country, and one finds there rare and precious objects from all parts of the world." He mentions in particular jugs of cut rock crystal, and two of the most beautiful and precious objects of early Islamic art still surviving are rock crystal ewers. One of them is in the Treasury of St. Mark's in Venice and the other in the Victoria and Albert Museum in London; both of them are from the tenth century. These ewers are so beautiful and are considered so valuable that no price has ever been put on them. In the same street were sold elephant tusks, giraffe skins for slippers, and African songbirds. Egypt, he goes on rapturously, has an abundance of honey and sugar, and he describes what he saw as he walked through another market on December 18, 1048: "I saw red roses, nenuphars, narcissi, bitter and sweet oranges, lemons, apples, jasmine, melons, destenbouriehs, bananas, olives, myrobalans, fresh dates, grapes, sugar cane, aubergines, courgettes, radishes, celery, cucumbers, fresh onions, garlic, carrots and beetroots . . ."

Fustat-Misr had a faïence factory which produced all kinds of jugs and plates and bowls, some of them so fine that they were diaphanous.

[65]

Large quantities of plates, bowls, cups and other utensils were manufactured and sold in the city, and Ibn Khusrau is particularly enthusiastic about their rich colors. "Some glass," he says, "is so transparent that it resembles an emerald." He was delighted when he met a woman who owned five thousand vases of Damascene copper as brilliant as gold, which she rented out daily for water carrying. All the merchandise in the bazaar was sold at a fixed price, and if a merchant was caught cheating he was put on a camel and paraded around the streets ringing a bell and shouting: "I cheated, and I am being punished." Chemist shops, ironmongers, oils for lamps, olive oil, pistachios — he lists dozens of things he sees and likes. He notes that only the army was allowed to ride horses. Merchants, peasants, artisans and people of the pen had to ride asses, but there were plenty of them, and a large number of them were piebald. "The drapers' shops and the moneychangers and the other merchants were so full of gold and jewels and money and merchandise and brocade," he says, "that one could not find a place to sit down." And he claims that Fustat-Misr was so wealthy and so incredible that nobody in his own country (Persia) would believe him. Christians were safe and wealthy in Misr as well as Moslems, and one Christian told the governor during a bad year that he had enough corn in his granaries to supply the population of Fustat-Misr for six years.

Yet there was another side to this city. Ibn Ridwan, who lived in Fustat-Misr about a hundred years before its destruction and who was court doctor to the Caliph Hakim, said that the city was foul. People there threw dead cats, dogs and other animals into the streets where they lay and rotted. The smell of rotting sea fish on the dockside was abominable. The population would also throw the innards of slaughtered animals into the Nile as well as the mess from their own latrines, and Ibn Ridwan says sarcastically that "they drink this putrition, mixed with water." Smoke from the hundreds of public bathhouses polluted the atmosphere, and the dust caused everybody to cough. It was, he concluded, a very unhealthy place.

It is possible that Ibn Ridwan was carried away by his medical ideas on sanitation, but more probably Misr-Fustat was already beginning to rot. The other new capital, al Kahira, which was a few hundred yards to the north, had been growing more and more important. Events too (dealt with in the next chapter on al Kahira) had changed the character of Egyptian life. What seems most likely is that the same thing happened to Fustat-Misr as happens to many modern cities. As al Kahira became the desirable place to live in, the rich and the middle classes moved into the new area, leaving the old

[66]

city to its docks and warehouses and to its artisans and its poor. The city fathers didn't care so much about the state of the old city since they no longer lived in it, so it was no longer the beautiful place it had been.

Nonetheless, the seeds of Fustat-Misr's imminent destruction were, as always in its extraordinary wealth.

By the middle of the twelfth century Egypt was trading almost as much with the Mediterranean countries as she was with Arabia and the east. Even in the eleventh century she had a brisk trade with Italy, and you could always buy fine, rich Sicilian cloth in the Fustat-Misr markets. Her trade with Venice had not yet developed; in fact, Venice at this time was only beginning to emerge and was just making its first fortune transporting crusaders to the Holy Land. But there was a steady and stable Egyptian trade which went very far west. (One of the most important factors in the expansion of this Arab trade was the use of Arab coinage, and someone could make a fascinating study of the relationship of coinage to the extension of Islamic religion and culture. Merchants were given much scope by having good money, which in itself was a form of credit.)

This trading wealth and coinage wealth and agricultural wealth began to attract a new combination of ambitious men — the crusaders. Christianity from the west and Islam from the east had been fighting each other for over a hundred years to see who was going to get the huge benefits of Mediterranean wealth and trade. Most of the fighting was in the east, where the crusaders had come to rescue the Holy Land for their religion and to get what gold and territory and wealth they could in the process. By 1168 the Moslems had lost Sicily, but Byzantine Christianity had lost Syria. Now the tail end of the second crusade was at the gates of Egypt. Once more the Egyptian population might very well have welcomed the crusaders as allies against their heretical and brutal Shi'a masters, but the brutality and avarice of the crusaders themselves ruined any chance they had of finding a friendly population to help them.

Amaury, the Christian king of Jerusalem, did not come to Egypt simply to protect his flank against Nur ed Din, the sultan of Damascus, which is the usual explanation of his attack on Egypt. Egypt was a ripe plum waiting to be picked. Moslems were themselves fighting each other for Egypt, and after several previous attempts to take advantage of Moslem disunity, Amaury the Christian arrived once more in Egypt, and to show the population of Egypt what his intentions were, on November 3, 1168, he massacred every man, woman and child in the Egyptian city of Bilbeis.

[67]

Nothing could have been more certain to unite the Egyptians against him, and the squabbling factions in Egypt agreed, for a moment, to resist this brutal unbeliever. This also determined the fate of Fustat-Misr, because the Egyptians knew that they would have a hard time defending the old city. They had a much better chance in their newer city of al Kahira, which bordered Fustat-Misr but which was walled and was backed closely by the Mukattam Hills. Shawar, the chief minister in Egypt of the caliph, had one other fear. Even if the Egyptians could hold al Kahira, Amaury and his crusaders might capture Fustat-Misr, just outside its walls, and simply settle down there to lay siege to al Kahira. So Shawar ordered the population of Fustat-Misr to leave their city, and then told his soldiers to burn it to the ground.

The panic was so terrible and the rush to get inside the walls of al Kahira so hurried that Makrizi describes the exodus as an "impetuous human flood." The people had so little time to get out that they had to abandon everything they had — houses, goods, personal belongings, animals and shops. It was like the day of judgment. Families were split up, and if you were too old or ill to walk to al Kahira and had to ride, the price of a camel went as high as thirty dinars — a fortune. Every road and alley connecting Fustat-Misr to al Kahira was blocked with a mass of nervous humanity who were arguing and fighting and trying to squeeze their way into al Kahira. People camped in the mosques of al Kahira, in the public baths, streets, and at crossroads, and they continued to arrive en masse, frightened of suffering the same fate as their brothers in Bilbeis.

Shawar then sent his soldiers with twenty thousand pots of mineral oil and ten thousand torches to set the empty city on fire, and the flames and smoke of the burning streets covered the entire sky. "A frightening spectacle," Makrizi says. The fire lasted fifty-four days, and the ruins were then pillaged by slaves and rivermen and others, all searching for what they could find of the treasures which now lay buried there.

Amaury and his crusaders were rather easily disposed of, and Shawar, the vizier who had ordered Fustat-Misr's destruction, was murdered and replaced in Egypt by Shirkuh, who was Saladin's uncle. But al Kahira was filled with the weeping and angry populace of Fustat-Misr, who demanded of their rulers where to go, where to live. Shirkuh thought it over and then ordered them to go back to the ruins of their houses and rebuild if they could. Little by little Fustat-Misr did begin to reappear, and one of the first places rebuilt was the quar-

ter around Amr's mosque, which had itself survived. But though it
struggled to emerge, the old city could not really revive to its former
condition. About a hundred years after it was burned down it was still
a slum, and an epidemic ruined it. Yet it hung on. It even became
briefly prosperous again in its reduced state, but then another epidemic and a very dry Nile ruined the city once more, and from then
on it literally fell to pieces and people from al Kahira demolished it for
its building materials, until finally it ceased to exist altogether.

Whatever the sin and whatever the epoch, it is impossible not to
regret that there is now nothing left standing whole of Fustat-Misr
except the mosques of Amr Ibn el 'As and Ibn Tulun. All you can see
now of it, when you follow the dusty little road that leads to the excavations near Amr's mosque, is acres upon acres of gray rubble which
roll away like knobbly hills almost as far as you can see. And what is
incredible about these mounds of Fustat-Misr is that when you look
closely at the earth you realize that what you are walking over isn't
earth at all but a whole topography of tiny fragments of pottery, brick
and stone.

Yet there must be a large portion of the city archaeologically intact
under the ruins. More, perhaps, than may be realized. One gets an
inkling of it from the first excavations a few hundred yards from Amr's
mosque. In 1966 I went over the whole area with Dr. Abd el Rahman
Abd el Tawab, director of the Inspectorate of Excavations of the
Islamic Period of the Egyptian Antiquities Department, and it was
like hopping over some turbulent undercurrent on huge stepping-
stones. We started off not far from Amr's mosque, and the first excavations show clearly the high, brick-walled houses on the ever winding,
very narrow streets. On a corner house is a large cistern, and each
house not only had piped water but also its own courtyard. Ibn
Duqmuq describes all these streets one by one: marketplaces, fountains, gardens, schools, asylums, convents, wicket gates, holes-in-the-
wall, hotels, kitchens, baths, canals, ponds, and hundreds of covered
passages. I wanted to imagine myself into this city instead of on top
of it, but Dr. Tawab hurried me on because it was hot and because he
knew what I was trying to do and he was anxious to get much nearer
to the heart of the old city.

"Manure factory," he said, and pointed to a big black hut among
the mounds and valleys of the powdered ruins. "We're going to get rid
of that."

A few scavenging dogs appeared on the wilderness of broken pottery hills near the manure factory and howled like wolves. Covered in

sweat we suddenly came down on a perfect little excavation — the work of Dr. George Scanlon, formerly of the American Research Center in Cairo, who dug this part of the city out in 1964–1965.

Scanlon uncovered here a series of Fatimid houses (A.D. 969–1160) which now lie in a little valley in their skeletal state — a model of the rest of this city which must surely be revealed one day in this kind of tangible outline. What is fascinating here, and Tawab delighted in pointing it out to me, is the evidence of the full sanitation which all these houses had. They not only had water closets and a flush system running into cesspits, but you can trace the kitchen drainage, running water, large water tanks in the lofts, and multiple pipes built into the walls. Later on we counted as many as five pipes running through the walls of one house from roof cisterns into lavatories and roof gardens and first-floor fountains and baths. Every house seems to have had some sort of shower bath, some of them with glazed tile walls which suggest beautiful decorations, and they also had clever arrangements for soap and towel.

Another site, a little further on, had been excavated under Tawab's direction, and here were the tent of the Egyptian archaeologist and the teams of diggers with buckets made out of old motor tubes. What this site revealed was how tight the staircases and passages to the houses were — barely wide enough for one person. The rooms were small but plentiful, and they were built on so many different levels and the houses were so attached to each other that quite clearly the whole city must have been one huge linked house, honeycombed with passages and split-level apartments, rich in terraces and fountains in or on the roofs of the houses, so that it would have been an adventure for anyone trying to find his way through the city. One particular house here had a decorative little octagonal fountain and pond on a terrace, and it must have been fairly typical of many of them.

The shards they were finding on the site when I was there were lamps, translucent fragments of bowls, bottle glass, red pottery, Mameluke faïence (some of this was simply tipped here from early Kahira) and a perfect little amphora. There was one pile of pottery which seemed to be indented with fragments of mercury, or maybe it was stone which was encrusted with it. When I saw it I remembered Khumaraweh's pond of the stuff. For many years after the palace was destroyed people used to go to the site and dig all around it looking for quicksilver, which was always valuable.

From this site we went on in the warm sun to the more recent excavations near the mosque of Abu el Suʻud el Garhi, which is a lonely little djameʼ (public mosque) on the side of a dry hill. The archaeologists here use it as their landmark. This too was an Egyptian excavation. Egyptians have been digging in Fustat for a long time, and their most famous archaeologist here was Ali Bahgat, who searched around Fustat just before the First World War but couldn't get enough funds to continue. His work was quite brilliant and almost every subsequent excavation owes a great deal to him. This new site, at the north end of Fustat, really borders on el Askar.

Here they were digging up a Fatimid house which had been built on (and from) a ruined Fustat house of earlier date. The outside walls were a yard thick, suggesting that the building must have been a tall one, perhaps one of the fourteen-story apartment houses. Once again the character of this warren-like city emerged, and one realizes here that not only was the sun kept out of the dark slit-like streets, but the wind too. The multiplicity of the walls must have kept the city cool in summer but cold in winter. The outline of rooms and terraces and the two different foundations were quite clear, and for a while I watched the workers digging out a deep, perfectly rounded cesspit.

On high ground above the Fatimid house was one of the traditional bell tents of Egyptian archaeology. A young archaeologist of the Antiquities Department had spread sand around it and then marked it off with squares, each one representing ten yards of the dig. What came from any particular ten yards of the excavations was put in its particular square. What they had laid out here was red pottery, Coptic and early Islamic (blue-green) faïence, and finally Mameluke ware glazed in orange and brown, which always made it easily recognizable.

Two particular groups of artifacts here were very exciting for anyone looking for Fustat-Misr. One was a handful of broken goulahs. Goulahs are the simple little water jugs with slender necks which Egyptians have used for millennia to keep their water cool. They are porous, and when they are in a draft or on a shady window ledge the evaporation causes primitive refrigeration. They are very simple in shape, so conventional in fact that the pottery artist can do little with them. There are fragments of uncountable thousands of them scattered all over the Fustat-Misr site.

What was fascinating about these particular fragments was the delicate little filter worked into the inside of the neck and carved with all sorts of beautiful designs. These little neck filters were never really seen unless you looked closely for them, nor were they supposed to be seen. Each filter (and they are all different) was carved by the potter for the sheer love of it. Some were very fine arabesque designs, but one had a Coptic cross. The Islamic Museum in Cairo has a beautiful collection of these little filters, and whenever you see the broken neck of a goulah on the dust heaps of Fustat-Misr you leap on it and hold it up to see if it has one of these filters worked in its neck. What adds to the beauty of a goulah is the gurgling sound the water makes as it comes through the neck, particularly through these filters. This gurgling sound is loved by Arabic poets, more so by the Persians, who often say passionately to their ladylove, "If you will be my love, I will be your gurgling sound . . ."

The second group of artifacts on the sand was more dramatic. In one of the marked squares were two or three pots that looked exactly like modern hand grenades.

"What are those things?" I asked the archaeologist.

"Grenades," he replied offhandedly.

"In Fustat times?" I said.

"Certainly," he replied. "These were the grenades they used to burn down Fustat with." He picked one of them up. "They were filled with mineral oil, a wick was stuffed into the opening at the top, the wick set alight, and then they were hurled into rooms and streets, or simply left lying in piles of abandoned cloth and silk."

Makrizi mentions these things. "Shawar," Makrizi writes, "had sent to Misr twenty thousand pots of naphtha and ten thousand torches." I don't know whether these little grenades counted as pots or torches, but whichever it was this pottery pineapple was the implement of the city's destruction, and with the sort of irony that history is so fond of, the weapons of destruction had survived the thing they had destroyed.

I sat in the bell tent for a while drinking tea and listening to a young archaeologist trying to persuade Tawab to let them dig through a wall of debris which would bring them into contact with another American excavation on the other side of it. But Tawab was very cautious about mixing the two areas like that. All these young Egyptians were very enthusiastic about their job, and they were impatient to get on with it because of the limitless prospect of the site. We joked for a while, and then Tawab took me outside and pointed rather proudly to a new road which cut right across the old borders between Fustat and el Askar and el Katai.

"You can travel on that new road almost on a straight line from here to the pyramids across Roda Island and Giza," he said. "And if you go the other way you can go right around the back of Cairo to Heliopolis."

On the other side of this road, towards el Katai, the present city government had built tall blocks of workers' flats, and their high balconies looked right out over the ruins of Fustat-Misr. Each balcony was hung with patchwork quilts and bedding and clothes, and no doubt the balconies of Fustat-Misr once looked like that. In another project directly across the road from the bell tent were dozens of little individual houses built in colorful blocks, each one painted a different and rather Pharaonic color. This was really an experimental village going up in the middle of a modern city.

Since Fustat-Misr began its life on the old Red Sea canal, and since most of its wealth passed through its port, I wanted to see the place where the canal had joined the Nile. The Nile has long ago retreated about a half mile to the west of where it used to be when Fustat-Misr was thriving, and the spot where river and canal used to meet is now, as far as I can judge, the site of Cairo's slaughterhouse. This is very much an inspired guess, based on Paul Ravaisse's maps and Ibn Duqmuq's record of the city, but if it is correct, this dilapidated street corner of modern Cairo is where boats would have arrived from the Red Sea laden with silks, damasks, gold, pearls, timber and books, and where they were loaded with pottery and fine cloth and glass and metals and dates and fruit, and above all the grain which flowed out of Egypt like a river of Egyptian blood feeding one conqueror after the other.

The real end of Fustat-Misr was not so much its destruction by fire but the eventual shifting of the main port to al Maks and al Kahira, a few hundred yards to the north. Fustat-Misr might have gone on surviving prosperously and independently if its port had remained the exclusive exit and entry for Egypt's trade with the east, but the new Fatimid masters of Egypt wanted to establish their own trading monopoly and their own customs stations and their own center of power and affluence, so their new capital of al Kahira was not so much a continuation of Fustat-Misr but a deliberate replacement of it. How well it succeeded is recorded in those crumbling acres of pottery shards which literally bury the old city and leave the new one brightly and glaringly triumphant.

8

Al Kahira

O<small>N</small> August 5, 969, two hundred years before Fustat-Misr was burned down and two years after the death of Kafour, a former slave named Gawhar marched his large Fatimid army into Fustat-Misr behind a mysterious black dog which had shown them the way across the river. The Fatimid attack on Egypt had been in preparation for two years, and though there was some resistance at Fustat-Misr there was too little of it to count, and thus the private kingdom of Egypt was taken away from the Ishkid-Kafour dynasty and handed over to the caliphs of the Fatimid dynasty. Gawhar was a general in the army of the Fatimid caliph Mu'iz.

Like every other conqueror before him, Gawhar had no intention of founding his authority on the very neck of what was already a powerful city with its own established traditions. Instead, on the same night that he arrived, he camped his large army on a dusty site a little to the north of Fustat-Misr and decided to establish his own capital there. Modern Cairo has grown up around Gawhar's city, which is still in the middle of it. Instead of having to take a tram, bus or taxi out to a site, you can walk into the very heart of Gawhar's city and find there the outline and the record — the streets, walls, monuments and mosques of the city that eventually grew up around the original one.

Makrizi tells a typically Arab story of how Gawhar established al Kahira. Gawhar, he says, marked out the site himself, and poles were erected at the corners and then ropes were strung from pole to pole to indicate the perimeter of the future walls. Hundreds of workmen were then lined up around the perimeter ready to begin digging, but nobody was to dig until a special signal was given. The signal would be the ringing of tiny bells which had been hung on the ropes, and the signal would be given only when some astronomically propitious moment had arrived.

At the moment when everybody was poised and waiting for the astrologers to give a sign, the little bells on the ropes began to ring although nobody had given any signal. A raven sitting on the ropes had rung the bells, but the workmen took it as the expected order to dig, so they immediately pitched into it. Thus the city's foundations were laid before the proper moment had come, and the astrologers were terrified.

"Al Kahira [Mars] is in the ascendant," they cried. They said it was a terrible omen and that the Turks would probably come and capture the city. But it was too late to do anything about it, and as a result of this incident the town was called al Kahira, instead of al Mansuriya, which was its chosen name.

This overladen story which most historians have more or less accepted is really a secondhand legend Mas'udi told the same story years before al Kahira was thought of, but he told it of the foundation of Alexandria. What seems to have happened at al Kahira is that the walls were begun under some sort of astrological omen (the Fatimids would hardly breathe without a sign from the stars) which presumably went wrong. In any case the city was first named al Mansuriya (the victorious) until Mu'iz the caliph himself came to Cairo, and he renamed it al Kahira, which can also be rendered as "the victorious." The choice of the site was certainly dictated by military considerations. It was better placed militarily than Fustat-Misr because it was closer to the Mukattam Hills and on higher ground, and it even had a port nearby in a big bend of the Red Sea canal. It was in fact the customs port of Fustat-Misr, al Maks, which was about where the station square is now.

Unfortunately for orthodox religious patriotism, al Kahira was founded not by an orthodox Moslem but by a Shi'ite. Shi'a is a sect of Islam considered quite heretical by the Egyptians, who are orthodox Sunni. And the difference between the Sunni and the Shi'a is very important in the next two hundred years of Cairo's history. Orthodox Sunni believe in the authority of the sunna (literally a path), which is their name for a collection of traditions and interpretations of the Koranic law. The sunna is considered to be as powerful as the Koran itself. This comparatively rational method of establishing doctrine also applied in determining who should be the leader of the faithful after the death of Mohammed. Since Mohammed himself had said nothing about succession, the Sunni decided that an elected (chosen) caliph was correct doctrine, so that the caliph of Islam thereafter was to be an elected head of all legitimate secular power.

On the other hand the Shiʻa (shiʻa means schism) believed that the word of the Koran was absolute and divine, and that the secular authority of Islam should continue only through Mohammed's family, through the descendants of his daughter's two sons al Hasan and al Husein. Mohammed's daughter's name was Fatima, hence the new Shiʻa dynasty was called Fatimid. The fanatical and mystical Shiʻa were originally a very ambitious Moslem minority and they considered that almost any means was justified to achieve their ends. They were, for instance, quite willing to take on the color of their Sunni rivals in order to bore at their enemy from within, and they did not mind pretending apostasy to gain a point. The Shiʻa also believed in the continuous life and reappearance of a Mahdi, who could not die but would simply reappear at any time in history in one guise or another, such as the Mahdi of the Sudan in the 1880s. The sect of the Assassins were Shiʻa, so today are the dervishes and the Ismailis, which is the Aga Khan's sect.

Muʻiz, the Fatimid caliph who had sent Gawhar to conquer Egypt, established himself in the new royal enclosure of al Kahira in 973, and for two hundred years thereafter the Shiʻa Fatimids were to rule Egypt in bitter opposition to the oxthodox Sunni caliphs of Baghdad. The Fatimids almost always conducted themselves in Egypt with extravagant madness, but perhaps their real trouble was that they were so machiavellian in doctrine and so fiercely concerned with a sort of "revealed" and "inner" religion that they could never convert the practical Egyptians, who still felt the scars of that sort of thing from Byzantine Christianity. And logically enough the Fatimids managed to rule Egypt only by using Christians and Jews, particularly Christians, with whom they formed a powerful alliance. In fact they resembled the Christians in many ways, because they too believed in a coming Messiah divinely protected against error and sin who would save them all.

Al Kahira was not supposed to be a public city, it was a private, fortified, royal enclosure, and Ibn Duqmuq says that Gawhar "built palaces for his master, so that he and his friends and their armies were separate from the general public." The ordinary citizen was never allowed to step foot in al Kahira except when he was needed for something. Even ambassadors had to be met and escorted through the proper gate, and it was two hundred years before the populace of Fustat-Misr eventually overflowed into the city and made it theirs and built mosques and houses and pavilions in it. Yet it had a population, even in Mu'iz's day, of between twenty and thirty thousand people, all court officials or soldiers or servants or slaves.

Even as he began to build the walls of the city Gawhar built a palace for his caliph, and he also laid the foundation of the great mosque of al Azhar, whose courtyard today is on the same site as the original, although the mosque itself has been considerably rebuilt. When enough of the city had been built and when the Caliph Mu'iz arrived to take over his new conquest (975), all Fustat-Misr was decorated to receive him, whereas his brand-new capital of Kahira was bare of any welcome, since they didn't expect him to occupy the new city yet. But Mu'iz didn't even look at Fustat-Misr. He went straight to Kahira, preceded en route by the coffins of his famous Fatimid ancestors, whom he intended to bury in the new capital because he wanted to be absolutely sure that Kahira would remain Fatimid forever.

Gawhar's original plan for this walled city was very simple. It was near enough a square: twelve hundred by sixteen hundred and fifty yards, enclosed by a wide wall which had at least five gates in it or, according to Makrizi, eight. The walls were wide enough for two horsemen to ride abreast on them, necessary because men had to be rushed quickly to any spot where an attacking force could throw up one of their big bridging machines, which could mean twenty or thirty attackers on the walls at a time. If the walls were too narrow the defenders would be outnumbered. The city was cleverly sited, too. One whole side (west) ran defensively along the old Red Sea canal — the same canal which was filled in 1899 and had tramlines laid over it, and it is still one of the most dramatic crossings you can make in Cairo — to walk across the tramlines of Shari' el Khalig (Canal Street) and, in effect, cross from Europeanized Cairo into the original city of Gawhar.

Much of what we know of Gawhar's city comes from Ibn Duqmuq and even more from Makrizi, who wrote in the 1420s, which is a long time after its foundation but he deals enthusiastically with every quarter of it as he did with Fustat-Misr. The only really firsthand account of any substance we have of its early life comes from Nasir Ibn Khusrau, who has already described Fustat-Misr for us, and who was allowed into Kahira seventy-nine years after its foundation. The man who coordinated most of this information and produced a brilliant map of the city based on Makrizi's exact description was the Frenchman Paul Ravaisse, and this is the map any Cairo enthusiast must have in his hand when he crosses the tramlines to look for what is left of Gawhar's walls and gates and alleyways. Ravaisse's map of it is now superseded in some details by Professor K. A. C. Creswell's similar map, but even Creswell's is based almost wholly on Ravaisse. Creswell did some digging of his own and corrected some of the details about the gates, and work is still going on, but Ravaisse's is all one needs to see the outline of how Kahira developed (see map on page 19).

These maps show that spaced around the almost straight walls of Gawhar's city were the main gates, and of these the two principal ones were the Bab el Zuweila on the south side (through which Mu'iz entered the city) and the Bab el Futuh (the Gate of Succor) to the north. A later version of these gates still stands. On the west side the canal ran along the full length of the wall, and on the east side was the shadow of the Mukattam Hills. Inside the square enclosure Ravaisse shows how each group in this populous private city had its own quarters, such as the army quarters (Harat al Askar) or the Greek quarters (Harat al Rum). Most of the city's original administrators and staff were Greeks (Christians) or Negroes. The entire enclosure was obviously built around the two great palaces. These palaces had their own gates and were in fact a fortified enclave within the fortified city. The Great Eastern Palace, and later the Little West Palace, sat firmly in the middle of the city. Between them was a courtyard called the Bein al Kasrein (Between the two Palaces) which still has its name on the original site. A little to the south of the Great Palace was the Azhar mosque. On the west side was the canal and the garden of Kafour, with a pavilion in it called the Luli Pavilion — the pearl pavilion.

This is the setting for all that is to follow about al Kahira.

Caliph Mu'iz (his name means dearly beloved) had invested a fortune of his own to conquer Egypt, so he obviously wanted to get back his investment as quickly as possible, and as always the Red Sea canal was to be the implement of his wealth. The customs port of al Maks, which means customs tax, lay in a bend of the river which came almost up to the walls of Kahira on the west side, near the canal, and this Mu'iz immediately took over and expanded into a proper dockyard, keeping its tax-collecting character but also laying the foundation there for a new port of his own, which immediately took away much of the business that usually went to Fustat-Misr.

Here Mu'iz built six hundred ships, and about seventy-seven years later, when Nasir Ibn Khusrau came to Cairo, seven of these ships were still lying on the riverbank. "I, the author of this narrative," Ibn Khusrau says, "have seen them." They measured 30 arech by 60 arech, or 275 feet long by 110 feet abeam. These huge ships were no doubt a brilliant investment because they could move large quantities of cargo at one time, rather like the modern monstrous oil tankers. Nothing that could make money escaped Mu'iz, and he reorganized the whole tax system into a central collecting body, which did away with the local collectors who used to take a considerable rake-off of their own. In one day he collected over $475,000 (modern equivalent) in taxes from Fustat-Misr alone.

Mu'iz lived for only two years after he had entered his city, so he did little but lay the solid and clever and rich foundation for those of his dynasty who followed him, but an idea of his private wealth is indicated by bequests of his two daughters. When the first one died she left among other signs of great wealth 2,600,000 dinars and the other one left five sacks of emeralds, three thousand pieces of silverware, and thirty thousand exquisite Sicilian embroideries.

The description which Nasir Ibn Khusrau gives of al Kahira seventy-seven years after Mu'iz is really a description of the city that grew up almost overnight as the wealth, which Mu'iz had accumulated, was lavished on its construction. Ibn Khusrau found that no buildings were allowed near the palace. A thousand men guarded the palace, and when you approached the city it too, like Fustat-Misr, looked like a mountain because its buildings were so tall and numerous. But once inside it you couldn't see over the high walls. Twelve thousand servitors looked after the caliph in the palace itself, and Ibn Khusrau says nobody knew how many women were enclosed in those palace walls.

The palace had twelve pavilions and ten gates of its own, and he lists some of the names of the gates: the Gate of Gold, the Gate of Oil, the Gate Where You Smell Meat, the Gate of the Emerald and the Gate of the Slippery Ground. There was a special gate, underground, which opened up into a tunnel where the sultan could ride through to his harem led by female slaves. And this second palace was built of blocks so well fitted that it looked as if it were all one piece.

Ibn Khusrau, writing in 1047, says the city itself had five gates and was not quite enclosed by its fortified walls. The original walls had fallen in, and new ones were not yet built. But every house and palace was a fort in itself. Fifty-two thousand camels were used to take fresh water to the city (including Fustat-Misr) though Makrizi says later that al Kahira was a very dry place. The houses in Kahira were all separated by verges and gardens, and the sultan's palace gardens were the most beautiful he had seen, and as in Fustat-Misr, trees and flowers were planted on the terraces. He also says that most houses were built so well and with such luxury that one could say they were built of precious stones.

Yet al Kahira was a different kind of city from Fustat-Askar-Katai-

Misr. All the previous invaders of Egypt had also been foreigners, and though they had built royal capitals like Askar and Katai they had not since the Romans quite enclosed themselves behind high walls the way the Fatimids did. The royal townships of Askar and Katai had easily been swallowed up by rich Fustat, but this time Kahira was going to outlast the old city, because Mu'iz and his son Aziz laid the foundation for an economic and military policy of occupation which would enable al Kahira to dominate Fustat-Misr, and eventually take its place.

All the Fatimids of Kahira were sybarites, and though they encouraged the arts and some of the sciences (mainly astronomy), they did so mostly for their private enjoyment. Artists and writers came in large numbers to Kahira, but though the gardens of the city were sometimes filled with poets, they were usually birds in a gilded cage. Fatimid buildings were always sublime and got better and better, and the library of al Kahira had no equal in its time, but one searches through the history of Egypt during the tenth and eleventh centuries for the wider benefits of this Fatimid patronage. There is little to show for it outside Kahira.

When Mu'iz died, aged forty-five, his son Aziz ruled after him for twenty-one years and five and a half months, and it was Aziz as much as his father who established the organized Fatimid financial administration of Egypt which kept it functioning so effectively for so long. His brilliant chief minister was a converted Jew called Ibn Killis, who had eight hundred women in his harem. Many of the unusual financial methods introduced were his. But there were other outside influences as well. Aziz's wife was a Christian, and her two brothers were orthodox Melchite priests, patriachs in fact. According to Hitti she was a Russian, but there is no doubt that she and her family had considerable power and influence in al Kahira, and not much of it good. Like all the conquerors Aziz needed minorities and mercenaries, and not only did he use the Christians but he was the first Fatimid caliph to adopt the old Abbasid policy of importing Turkish and Sudanese troops to rule Egypt, and their constant quarreling was a very gloomy prelude to what would happen later with the Mamelukes.

But on the whole Kahira prospered rapidly and richly under him. He built palaces, bridges, mosques and a new canal. He built the little west palace, the Luli Pavilion, and he improved the Great Eastern Palace, not a remnant of which survives. He also began to build the mosque which his son Hakim finished, and which is now one of the most romantic ruins in Cairo. Aziz was so sure of his caliphate in al Kahira that he built a golden cage and prepared an apartment in his palace to house the rival orthodox caliphs of Baghdad when they were eventually captured, which they never were.

One longs to know what really went on inside early Kahira, and though Ibn Khusrau tells us a great deal he was probably too prejudiced to give a full picture, because he was a Shi'a like the Fatimids, and he was very proud of their achievements. What has never quite been explained is how its early population lived their daily lives vis-à-vis Fustat-Misr. Al Kahira was a purely administrative city like Washington, only with a lock and key to it. But it did have trade and business. At first it probably had no merchants or shoemakers or bakers or shops, but as it became organized and as the various quarters were set up for soldiers and slaves and servants and administrators and clerks (there must have been thousands of clerks), the method of distribution in the city was eventually typical of any city, and no doubt some local small merchants were eventually allowed in, and then some artisans and shopkeepers and shoemakers.

There was considerable supply traffic in and out of the walled city from Fustat-Misr and from the new port of al Maks. The Red Sea canal was a main thoroughfare for much of the wheat and vegetables and meat the city ate, but donkeys and camels and men also brought plenty through the main gates, which were open from dawn till dusk. The gates were heavily guarded and no man walked through without explanation and permission. Al Kahira's streets and gardens were not as narrow as Fustat-Misr's; in fact, it was far less of a warren, although the soldiers and slaves probably lived in semi-slums. Eventually the really big merchants of Fustat-Misr came to terms with the Fatimids, although how many were allowed to settle in Kahira as part of the new administration we do not know. Christian merchants were probably more privileged than the local Moslems at first, but outside the city the ruling class of Egypt remained the big landowners, the entrepreneurs, the buyers and sellers, the importers and exporters, the administrative class — who were often Copts — and the Shi'a doctrinaires of the official religion.

The rest of the population never quite submitted, because in two hundred years the Fatimids were unable to convert them to Shi'a ideas, even though the Shi'a were fanatical missionaries. By the time Aziz died and his son Hakim had succeeded him, al Kahira's peculiar isolation and self-centeredness had prepared the city for a divine experience. Hakim, the new caliph, would eventually declare himself God.

Hakim was eleven years old when his father died. He was playing in a sycamore tree in a suburban garden when his black tutor Bargawan arrived with the news. Bargawan stood under the tree and said to Hakim: "Come down, my boy. May God protect you and us all." That could mean only one thing in Islam: the boy was now caliph. He entered al Kahira at night behind his father's dead body, which was carried on a litter out of which the two feet of the corpse protruded. In André Gide's novel *The Counterfeiters,* the principal narrator, Edouard, writes in his diary: "The deeper the soul plunges into religious devotion, the more it loses all sense of reality; all need, all desire, all love for reality." This may explain what happened to Hakim, although the unreality came first in this case.

Bargawan, who was a eunuch, had nicknamed his pupil "little lizard" because he looked and behaved like one. He scared anybody who saw him, and like his father he had big blue eyes. His face was frightening, and as if he needed to hide it he preferred the darkness to daylight and moved only at night, wandering through his city on an ass. He ordered all the shops to stay open all night and close all day, but when people began to adapt themselves to this upside-down routine and began to get gay at night he had them punished. When he was fifteen he had Bargawan murdered by his umbrella bearer, who stabbed Bargawan in the belly with a knife. Two years later Hakim had the umbrella bearer murdered. Hakim had handed over Bargawan's ministerial authority to the great Gawhar's son, al Hassan, whom he also murdered a few years later.

As he began thus to exercise his authority, Hakim began to enjoy his powers of unreality. In 1004 he ordered all dogs in Kahira to be killed. He forbade the sale of beer, wine, grapes, mulokhiya (still a national dish), lupin pellets and fish without scales, and if you disobeyed you had your head cut off. He ordered all sorts of fruits to be burned, all vines cut down, and all honey (which was a particular delicacy for Egyptians) in Fustat-Misr to be tipped into the Nile — five thousand jars of it. He then forbade all women to go out on the streets night or day, and this restraint on them lasted seven years and seven months. He even told the shoemakers not to make women's outdoor shoes, and he ordered the signs that designated which baths were for women to be taken down. He is known to have killed slaves in the street for no reason at all, and he would tear out their entrails with his bare hands. There was a piece of harmless-looking wood floating on the surface of the pool in his beautiful palace gardens, and he would challenge (for six hundred dinars) his friends or his enemies to jump on it. A royal challenge could hardly be refused, and when he jumped in the lake the victim found himself impaled on a long thin spear which was hidden under the little piece of floating wood.

[82]

Of the hundreds of stories about Hakim's brutality, perhaps the worst concerns a victorious general, Fadl, who had more or less saved Hakim and his regime from revolting tribes. Fadl accidentally disturbed Hakim when he was dismembering the body of a very pretty child whom he had bought for a hundred pieces of gold, and whom he had amused for a while before killing. He first cut the child's throat and then took out the liver and the entrails and cut them up in pieces. Having seen the operation Fadl knew his own fate; he went home and made his will and an hour later Hakim's soldiers came and cut off his head.

Hakim's power of life-taking and death-giving was a rather dangerous addition to what would otherwise have been a mere religious conceit — as a Shi'a he considered himself the mystical incarnation of the Mahdi (Messiah). His deification was eventually perfected by a Persian named Daraziy, who announced that Hakim had inherited the soul of Adam and that he was in fact the Creator of the Universe. Daraziy created a sect called the Druze out of this fiendish Messiah, and two hundred thousand Moslems in Lebanon and Syria still adhere to it.

Like all God's prophets Hakim was surrounded by factional dissent, and in the bitter quarrels that were going on around him he foolishly called the Sitt el Mulk, his sister, "unchaste," and it is likely that she plotted his death. Ibn Khallikan doesn't go into the sister's role too deeply, but whether the sister had a hand in it or not the end is typical. Hakim, always intoxicated by his self-exalting mysticism, loved to go off alone at night on his gray ass called al Kamr (the moon) and wander through the Mukattam Hills. He would simply disappear in them for days on end. On February 13, 1021, he went out alone on Kamr and spent a night wandering about the Mukkatam Hills, then next day he was seen in the hills near Helwan, and after that he was never seen again. Some of his officers found his clothes down a well, filled with stab holes, and Ibn Khallikan ends his account of Hakim by saying that some foolish people continue to believe that Hakim will rise again, which in fact the Druzes of Syria and Lebanon still believe.

Historians are inclined to dwell on the long list of his horrors, but Hakim did have a taste for literature and poetry, and the great Arab astronomer al Yunus composed the famous Hakimite astronomical tables for him. Hakim also built a remarkable Hall of Science in the palace grounds for the study of the Shi'a doctrine, science and astronomy, and scholars came here from everywhere in Islam because they could discuss and argue anything they liked. But Hakim was always resisted by the Egyptians of Fustat-Misr. When he had Bargawan the eunuch murdered, feeling against him was so strong that Hakim had to stay hidden in his city for days. When he ordered curses against the Companions of the Prophet to be written all over the mosques in Fustat-Misr in 1004 — an attack on the rival Sunni, who believed in the Companions rather than in Fatimid descent — the population of Fustat-Misr objected so violently that he had to remove the insults and issue another order saying that anyone insulting the Companions should be flogged: a clear victory for the Egyptians. The women of Fustat-Misr always hated his laws forbidding them to appear on the streets and they continually ridiculed him. They set up a very well-made female dummy in the streets of Fustat-Misr where they knew Hakim would see it. He mistook it for a real woman and ordered his guard to cut her to pieces, which they did but found her to be made only of paper. The city laughed for days, but Hakim was so incensed by it that he sent his Sudanese troops to burn Fustat-Misr to the ground. The people resisted with force and there was virtually a civil war which lasted three days before Hakim's troops withdrew. Egyptians murdered almost all the followers of his prophet Daraziy, and Daraziy himself was only saved by Hakim, but he had to be smuggled out of the country. Finally, his game of God provoked a real civil war in Fustat-Misr, and once again Hakim had to send troops to suppress the revolt, which they did with a vicious reign of terror, rape and murder. But his black troops (Sudanese) had bitter military rivals in the royal quarters — the Turkis and the Berbers. All three began to fight each other brutally in the streets of the two cities to see who would hold the real power, and it was probably the anarchy of this situation and its danger to the Fatimids more than any insult to his sister which decided the murder of Hakim.

Only one thing points to a possible hereditary explanation of Hakim. His son Zahir, who inherited the caliphate, also liked to indulge in suffering. He once organized a huge party in his palace and invited 2,660 young girls all dressed in their gayest and most beautiful clothes. On the excuse that there was some delay, and while waiting for the revelry to begin, they were asked to wait in a nearby mosque. When they were all inside the mosque Zahir and his masons bricked up the doors and they were left there to die in agony, and six months later their bodies were still rotting inside the holy place.

The Fatimids went on being foreigners in Egypt, living in their own royal city and even breeding among themselves within its walls as if trying to perpetuate a tiny and savage minority in a vast pit of Egyptian opposition. They went on being wastefully rich, cruel and determinedly private with their possessions, but they were not strictly a decadent society, because economically they were using a sound system of accumulation which made their society more than feudal. They used cash extensively and accumulated it almost as fluid capital, and much of their private wealth was turned into cash, and their luxuries and excesses were to some small degree paid for in cash. Their art was not decadent, in fact it never had time to become decadent; and as an occupying force the personal taste of their caliphs for brutalities was offset by the economic benefits which a thriving trading city gave to all its citizens. They remained traders, and they traded very well.

Fatimid Kahira reached its peak under al Mustansir, who succeeded Zahir. He was a baby when Zahir died, and until he came of age Egypt was ruled by his black Sudanese mother, a former slave, who shared her royal authority with the slaver who had once owned her and had sold her in the first place. Al Mustansir reigned for fifty-eight years, and he was caliph when William conquered England. It would be an interesting academic study to compare in detail the landed feudalism of William with the cash-trading feudal society of Mustansir. William, for instance, was collecting feudal rents in kind from his land and farms when Mustansir was collecting cash rents on twenty thousand boutiques he owned in Kahira and Fustat-Misr, and on twenty thousand houses as well. Like William, however, al Mustansir owned his countryside, and he had three hundred and sixty-nine villages along the Red Sea canal alone (by now called the Canal of the Prince of the Faithful).

One can't help wondering what shape the Mediterranean would have taken if Mustansir had used his cash wealth the way William used his landed wealth — to create a very efficient army of conquest. When William was going from one town to another in Normandy collecting their military contributions for his coming invasion, al Mustansir was displaying his private military wealth in a canal-cutting ceremony in Fustat-Misr which had been a traditional Egyptian festival since the first man dug the first irrigation ditch in Egypt millennia before. He rode through the city at the head of ten thousand cavalry, and every horse was dressed in armor studded with gold and gems. Camels and mules encrusted with plaques of gold followed, and Ibn Khusrau lists the retainers who followed him: twenty thousand Kentani Berbers, fifty thousand Moroccans, twenty thousand Masmoudis, ten thousand eastern Turks and Persians (mostly born in Egypt), thirty thousand slaves (bought with money), fifteen thousand Hadja Bedouins, thirty thousand Oustads (black and white slaves), thirty thousand Negroes every one with a saber, and finally the palace servitors, doctors, functionaries, scribes, etc. But this was not a baronial

national army marching to conquest, it was a private army of occupation, and it was showing off its wealth to overawe the local population. Most if not all of these soldiers and followers lived as retainers in
Kahira, the private city.

One reads through Makrizi's long list of Mustansir's collection of
jewels and baubles in amazement, but in effect one is reading through
the figures of a cash account which could be drawn on at will, and was
in fact used to the last pearl when Egypt began to starve and the
economy began to collapse. Ten pounds of emeralds were a fortune in
ready cash, so were two hundred and fifty thousand fine pearls and
rubies and other jewels. He had priceless crystal vases, enameled gold
plate, a gold mattress, four thousand gold vases for narcissus flowers
and two thousand more for violets, fruit made of amber, a jeweled
turban valued at one hundred and thirty thousand dinars, a gold pea-
cock with ruby eyes, a gazelle covered with pearls, a cock with a crest
of rubies, a palm tree with dates of jewels, a silver barge belonging to
his black mother, quantities of damasks and carpets, a richly embroidered map of the world, jeweled daggers, swords, lances and shields,
and a tent of gold brocade with gilt and silver poles. One tent which
took fifty artists nine years to make was sixty-five feet high and
needed ten camels to transport it, and there was another of pure gold
thread which was called "the killer" because someone was always
killed when it was pitched, it was so heavy.

Everything was thickly beautiful and self-indulgent, but as a collector Mustansir was probably no worse than the great art collectors of
our own era who invest in art for financial reasons as well as for
beauty in the object. But just how delicately this trading economy was
based on Egypt's salable crops, and how much more unstable it was
than the landed and feudal economy of William, is shown by the way
al Mustansir lost his wealth almost overnight when Egypt's crops
failed. A combination of bad harvests and the Nile failing to rise adequately, peasant revolts and quick shortages, and the people of Kahira
and Fustat-Misr began to go hungry.

Al Mustansir depended heavily at this time on his first minister, al
Yazury, who had managed to keep the price of grain low and the
supply coming in. It was Yazury who built the famous Joseph's Granaries at Fustat. He had also forbidden merchants to do what they
were still doing up till 1952 — buying a standing crop at a low price,
in cash, which peasants in terror of calamity or outright robbery were
inclined to accept, to their disadvantage. By these measures the
crisis was held off. But Yazury was murdered in 1058, and after him
the collapse of all internal authority in the royal city began because

the merchants obviously resented his firm control, and the merchants still reigned supreme, no matter who starved or what happened to the caliphate.

It was probably the merchants who encouraged the Turki and Berber soldiers to revolt in Kahira and expel the fifty thousand Sudani black soldiers, who were supported by Mustansir's black mother. The Sudanis set up a sort of bandit kingdom in Upper Egypt and began to raid the villages there, so that most cultivation stopped. The Turks then threw out the Berbers as well, and the Berbers raided the Delta and did there what the Sudanese were doing in the south and even destroyed the irrigation system. The result was quick disaster for the capital because almost no crops were planted in Upper or Lower Egypt, and what was produced couldn't get to the docks of Fustat-Misr or al Kahira. The economy stopped dead.

The Turks, in control of the royal city, began to run riot. They smashed into the palaces of Kahira and tore up the beautiful gardens and looted what they could of Mustansir's fabulous treasures and works of art. Worst of all, they eventually ruined what was then one of the world's most extensive libraries. A hundred thousand books were taken out of it and piled up on a hill and left there, and it was known for years as the Hill of Books. The library itself had been run neatly and the books had been efficiently catalogued. Most of them dealt with religion, science, art and poetry of the age. Some were used for shoe leather, and Lane Poole said in 1902 that some of them were books for which Orientalists still search in vain.

But now that there was anarchy at court and no cultivation in the fields and no grain in the city, a period of starvation and then famine began which continued for seven years. Then the plague hit the city very hard and edible cats and dogs were more valuable than pearls, court officials became bath attendants to earn a few dinars for bread, a fortune in women's jewels went for a cup of flour, and al Mustansir not only sent his family to Baghdad to avoid starvation, he had to sell everything he had to survive. His priceless art collections simply disappeared, and in one fortnight "treasures" worth thirty million dinars were sold. Cannibalism finally reached such proportions that human flesh was sold by butchers, and sometimes people walking through the streets were snatched up by huge sharp hooks lowered by body snatchers from upper windows, where the victims were killed and quartered and sold or cooked.

By now the Turks in Kahira were fighting among themselves, and at this time too a detachment of Mustansir's Turkish soldiers sacked Fustat-Misr and set parts of it on fire. The rebels then occupied Fustat-

Misr, defeated the few remaining loyal soldiers that Mustansir had, and rushed into the royal city and the royal palaces, where they found al Mustansir sitting alone and deserted on a bare mat in a bare palace. Everything had gone: jewels, beauty, riches and joy. But they did not dethrone him; there was no point to doing that, since he was obviously broken and they controlled the city.

One unexpectedly good crop in the year 1073 put heart into Mustansir, and he sent to Acre for a soldier who had won a big reputation in Syria as governor of Damascus and later of Acre. He was an Armenian (but a Moslem) named Badr al Gamali, a former slave, who said he would come only if he could bring his Syrian soldiers with him. Mustansir agreed, and Badr entered al Kahira in December 1074. The Turkish soldiers in the city, not realizing what he was there for, welcomed him. Badr's method of dealing with the Turks was very simple. He told each of his Syrian officers to entertain a Turkish officer for one night only. In the morning every one of his Syrians brought to him the head of the Turk they had entertained.

It was Badr and Mustansir who left us the most substantial remnants we have of al Kahira. The city had been steadily overflowing outside its crumbling walls, even though it was still a royal enclosure, so Badr built a new wall to include some of the new quarters, and some of this brick wall still stands. He also took down all the old gates and rebuilt them, not of sun-dried brick like the old ones but of stone. His three gates stand almost perfectly preserved — the Bab el Nasr, Bab el Futuh, and Bab el Zuweila: the Gate of Victory, Gate of Succor, and Gate of the tribe Zuweila.

Badr, who had been given the title Emir Giyushi by Mustansir, also built a mosque which still stands like a monumental ghost on top of the Mukattam Hills. He built it up there because he wanted to see, even in death, the graves of his seven favorite wives in the valley below. Badr, aged eighty, and his caliph died in the same year, 1094, and the biographer Ibn Khallikan lists some of the treasures Badr left for his family: six million gold dinars, two hundred and fifty bags of silver coins, seventy-five thousand satin robes, thirty camel loads of boxes made of Iraqi gold, a hundred gold nails on each of which hung a jeweled turban, and two large trunks of gold needles for his slaves and wives to use. Seventy-five thousand satin robes seems excessive but in the extraordinarily detailed information about the fortunes these great men left, Arab historians pay a lot of attention to rich clothes because they were serious status symbols and represented, in effect, absolutely wasted wealth.

After al Mustansir and Badr, six more Fatimid caliphs (not one of

Mosque of al Giyushi in the Mukattam Hills, looking toward the Citadel.

them quite normal) would rule in the seventy-five years left to them before the great Salah ed Din (Saladin) occupied the city and brought the Shi'a heresy to an end. There was a long period after Mustansir when Badr's Armenian descendants or other Armenians more or less ruled Egypt as the first ministers of self-indulgent and weak caliphs, which always seems to be the situation when a strong dynasty has finally worn itself out and is about to come to an end. Though often corrupt and vicious, the Armenians ruled well enough, but Egypt was now becoming a rich prize for two rival outsiders who were far more aggressive and powerful and confident than the senile Fatimids.

The Seljuks were Turkomans who had already conquered Persia. They had taken Palestine away from the Fatimids even while Badr was alive, and unlike the Fatimids they were orthodox Sunni Moslems. The first crusaders appeared in Palestine in 1096, and from then on these two powers would be fighting not only for possession of the Holy Land but eventually for Egypt as well. The Christian tendency to slaughter innocent populations did not encourage the local populations to welcome them as deliverers, and when the crusaders "massacred seventy thousand defenseless Moslems in the Holy City" (Lane Poole, Volume VI, *The History of Egypt*), there was no beauty or honor in it for the faith, but a grab for territory and a hunger for spoils.

At first the crusaders paid no attention to Egypt, and the Fatimids could go on surviving safely in their hothouse city; but inevitably the conditions of Egypt made it too ripe to resist. The Fatimids were visibly disintegrating, and life in al Kahira had become a continuing record of ugly murders, assassinations and regicide. In Fustat-Misr the population were almost continuously at war in the streets with the caliph's soldiers. One vizier was so hated that when the crusaders captured him the population of Fustat-Misr bought him back with gold in order to cut off his ears and nose and crucify him on the Bab Zuweila. Of the last two Fatimid caliphs, one died a child and the other, al Adid, was only nine years old when he inherited the city of Kahira. He was twelve when the crusaders finally came to the gates of his city, seventeen in 1168 when Fustat-Misr was deliberately burned down, eighteen when Saladin conquered Egypt, and twenty when he died in 1171.

There seemed to be an exact moment now when the invasion of Egypt became inevitable, because both Seljuk Moslems and Christian crusaders invaded Egypt at the same time. The Shi'a Fatimids in Kahira preferred the crusaders to the Seljuks and they made a deal to buy off the Christian King Amaury for two hundred thousand gold pieces if he would help them get rid of the Seljuks. Amaury agreed, and two crusaders were sent to al Kahira to negotiate the deal. From an account of their visit by William, Archbishop of Tyre, in *A History of Deeds Beyond the Sea,* we have the first and only outside report of what the palaces of Kahira were like. The two crusaders, Geoffrey Fulcher and Hugh of Caesara, were led through the palace corridors where the doors were guarded by Sudanese with naked scimitars, through courtyards with cloisters whose ceilings were inlaid in gold, by beautiful fountains in gardens with mosaic pavements and exotic birds and strange animals, and then into rooms within rooms until suddenly a heavy gold curtain embroidered with pearls was pulled aside dramatically and the young Caliph al Adid was revealed sitting on his golden throne. The caliph then bought and paid for the Christian aid against his fellow Moslems, and he was asked by Sir Hugh to shake hands on the deal. The Fatimid court almost fainted at this familiarity, but the caliph graciously offered his gloved hand. Sir Hugh insisted on the naked flesh, and to the astonishment of every Moslem present the sultan took off his glove and obliged.

In effect this first attempt to conquer Egypt ended in stalemate, and both Amaury and the Seljuk general Shirkuh withdrew. In fact they agreed between themselves to withdraw. It was now that Amaury the Christian came back (1168) and massacred the entire population of Bilbeis to show that he meant business, and as he marched on Kahira, Shawar, who was the effective ruler of Egypt, ordered Fustat-Misr to be burned to the ground. The only point of mentioning these events again is to illustrate how they contributed to the emergence of Kahira, as distinct from their influence on the destruction of Fustat-Misr. Even so, as far as Kahira is concerned, it is still difficult to decide whether burning the old city was a clever or foolish piece of military strategy, and the man who ordered the city's destruction is such a machiavellian type that one is inclined to read it both ways. Five years before, Shawar had been Fatimid governor of Upper Egypt, but he had deserted and gone over to the Seljuks in Damascus and made a deal with Nur ed Din, who promised to set him up in Egypt as first minister. When the Seljuks made their first attempt to conquer Egypt they did succeed in setting Shawar up as the authority in Kahira, but it was he who then asked Amaury the Christian to help him get rid of the Seljuks. Now that Amaury had returned and was about to attack al Kahira, Shawar switched sides again and asked Nur ed Din to help him once more.

Nur ed Din agreed and sent his general Shirkuh and Shirkuh's nephew Saladin to get rid of the crusaders. It was not difficult, because the massacre of Bilbeis had made the crusaders so unpopular in Egypt that they could not operate safely in the countryside. Amaury had to flee, and the Seljuks were the victors.

The anarchy and confusion in Kahira after the burning of Fustat-Misr did not encourage the victorious Seljuks to make any quick decisions, and at first they did not attempt to depose the young Caliph al Adid. Nur ed Din had already appointed Shirkuh as vizier of Egypt, but he did not live long enough to make any serious decisions. It was Saladin, his nephew, who inherited the problem. He was thirty-two when his uncle died and he became vizier instead (March 2, 1169), and though Saladin himself would not stay long in Cairo, his extraordinary influence on the city lasted in subtle ways until the end of the British occupation.

Saladin's first problem was to replace the heretical Shi'a doctrines in the mosques with the orthodox Sunni faith, but he was very nervous about doing so because the destruction of Fustat-Misr had robbed him of any clear picture of popular feeling. It was a year before he finally ordered that Friday prayers should be said for the Abbasid caliph instead of the Shi'a. Nobody was upset, and this more than anything else ended Fatimid rule in Egypt.

The Fatimids were still living in their rich palaces in Kahira and Saladin did not bother them at first, but the young Caliph al Adid obligingly died and then Saladin acted. He occupied the royal palaces inside al Kahira and immediately expelled eighteen thousand members of the Fatimid family from the royal enclosure. Makrizi says that of this number the only males were two hundred and fifty-two members of the caliph's own family, but to be absolutely sure that they could not breed any successors Saladin exiled the sexes separately.

Saladin took none of the wealth of the royal palaces for himself and he did not even live in them. He opened up the gates of Kahira and allowed the destitute population of Fustat-Misr to build in and around the royal city, which finally ended al Kahira's two-hundred-year existence as a royal enclosure. And it is only as of now that one can begin to talk about a city called Cairo, which suggests the combination of all the cities which had so far been built on this old site between the river and the hills. In any case the royal exclusiveness of al Kahira was finished forever, because Saladin's city was about to be born.

Saladin's Cairo would be quite different from al Kahira, and though it is difficult now to separate the older royal capital of al Kahira from Saladin's city, it can be done if you walk through the medieval part of

Cairo blind to everything but Fatimid relics. In fact al Kahira is still the nut inside the skin of Cairo, and you can easily trace its outline on any map of the city. The surviving monuments to the Fatimids are simply tangled up in the streets and alleyways of the old part of the city: the mosque of al Azhar (969), the ruins of the mosque of al Hakim, the three gates of Badr and a fragment of the wall which he also built in 1086/7 (and his mosque on the Mukattam named with his other name — al Giyushi), the mosque of el Fakahani (1120), and the Akmar, whose frontage is the oldest stone mosque façade in al Kahira.

To enter al Kahira now, all you need do is walk through the great stone towers of Bab Zuweila and you are in the old royal city, and if you then follow the main street called Shari' Mu'iz Lidin Illah you can walk right across al Kahira from one side to the other. This is, in fact, the same way the Caliph Mu'iz himself entered his new city, but his original gates were over 150 yards inside the present gates. The present Bab Zuweila is one of the three very solid stone gates built by Badr al Gamali in 1087 when the older walls of Kahira were crumbling down. Cairenes call it Bab al Mitwalli because the spirit of Islam's holiest saint, al Mitwalli, is supposed to live behind the west side of it, where he sometimes flashes a light to let you know he is there. Until a few years ago it was hung with rotting teeth, filthy rags, nails, and all sorts of monstrous tokens of sickness and disease. It was thought that if you had a headache it would go away if you drove a nail into Zuweila, and the huge wooden gates were therefore defaced with thousands of nails. If you had a toothache you need only pull it out and hang it on Zuweila and the pain would disappear, etc. So many people have been hanged, maimed, crucified, nailed and slaughtered in and on and under these gates in nine hundred years that they are, in fact, a very bloody memorial to every moment in the life of the city. Now they have been cleaned up, and the last time I saw them, all that was left of these evil decorations was a couple of chains on one gate and some Arabic slogans hurriedly daubed in white paint across one of the stone towers. "To hell with unbelievers," it said. But on another tower was another slogan which said, "Down with those who prevent progress." Obvious ideological substitutes for severed heads.

Once you walk through the Zuweila you can follow the narrow and straight and yet gently winding street of Mu'iz into al Kahira. It is really a medieval street, and now it is packed to capacity with donkey carts, cars, barrows, bicycles, street sellers, kiosks, and an extraordinary crush of people. But the way it looks cannot be very different from what al Kahira and Fustat-Misr looked like at almost any time in the past. About halfway across the city on the Shari' Mu'iz is the Bein al Kasrein (Between the Two Palaces), which was once the great courtyard between the extravagant palaces of Kahira. Unlike Badr's stone gates the palaces were built of brick, and the four thousand rooms, the exotic gardens, the beautiful pools, the hall of gold, the mosaic cloisters and the exquisite fountains and colorful birds have disappeared utterly; not even the dust of their fanatical Fatimid glory is left. They were already crumbling five years after Saladin's arrival, and he undoubtedly encouraged their demolition so that absolutely no lavish reminder of Fatimid power would remain. The doors, windows, lintels, floors, and whatever was movable were taken away for new buildings, and the rest simply disintegrated into rubble, became a nuisance, and was finally pushed aside.

The only Fatimid building left there is the mosque of Akmar, the oldest stone-façaded mosque in Egypt, which is probably why it survived. It was built in 1125 by al Amir, one of the last Fatimid caliphs, who was a rose lover. He was murdered by ten Assassins as he rode home to Kahira from Roda Island, where he had been enjoying his favorite Arab mistress. The whole standing façade is visible now, but not long ago it was hidden entirely by ramshackle buildings, and it took a long fight by interested people to get the rubbish cleared away from it. It looks lopsided because not all of its face is there. What the experts look at lovingly in this mosque is the fluted, hooded arch over the doorway, and it *is* extraordinary and it *is* beautiful. There is an eruption of little domes inside the mosque which may or may not be original, but it was somewhere in the dusty interior of the sahn (courtyard) that the Vizier Malik Rudwan tried to organize resistance to the Caliph al Hafiz, who cut off his head here and sent it to his wife.

You have to turn around rather quickly when you back away from the Akmar because that maniacal Messiah of the Druzes, al Hakim, is almost pushing at you from behind. Hakim's mosque is now a roofless ruin — the heavenly stone skeleton of a very unpleasant god, and the best place to see it is from the top of Bab el Futuh because you look right down into its aggressive stone cloisters and into the hollow outline of its cleaned-up courtyard. It was built from 990 to 1002 or 3, and its subsequent history is almost entirely tragic, as if its murderous patron still lifts his finger up from hell to anoint it every now and then with wickedness and trouble. The crusaders turned it briefly into a church, which Saladin in disgust demolished. By 1359 it was in a dilapidated condition again and it became a storehouse. In 1458 it seems to have fallen into a state of absolute ruin, and the last date that Creswell could find of its being used for prayers was somewhere around 1452. The French made a fortress of it, then it became a glass-lamp factory and later a rope walk, and it was the first site of the Arab Museum. When I was last there it was an elementary school, which seems to be a decent use for it. Its high-walled enclosure was marked out with a basketball court, and children were laughing in its cloisters.

The Bab el Futuh (Gate of Succor), which overlooks Hakim's mosque, is, like Zuweila, the second version of this gate. It was built in 1092 for the great Badr by one of the three brothers he brought from Urfa in Syria, and these three gates (the third gate, Bab el Nasr, was built by the third brother) were considered extraordinary even by eighteenth-century European travelers who were brought up rather exclusively in the Greek classical tradition. The gates are one of the few examples of military architecture of Islam before the crusaders' influence began, since fort building and defensive fighting were never attractive to the early Moslems.

The Bab el Futuh and the Bab el Nasr are really all of one piece with Hakim's mosque, and the whole complex probably has no equal for the sort of medieval stone solidity which can still go on functioning somehow in the middle of a living city. The French named each of the towers of the gates and of the wall after their victorious generals, and the plaques are still there. Outside the gates there used to be a slip-pery granite apron, a glacis, which made any assault on the gates by cavalry difficult because the horses would slip on it. A sultan's horse did slip on it and threw him, so he had all the glacis ripped up, de-fense requirements notwithstanding.

In effect, you have now walked right through Fatimid Kahira, and when you pass out the Bab el Futuh you have closed the gates of the old city behind you. But there are other monuments of Kahira outside the walls of the city. From the top of the Bab Zuweila you can look straight down on a mosque built by the Emir Talai Ibn Ruzzik in 1160, when he had restored some order to Fatimid Kahira in the last staggering days of its downhill run of anarchy and murder. His mosque was built to house the head of Husein, the great Shi'a martyr, but Husein's head went to another mosque, long since demolished, near the Great Eastern Palace which was once described (Ibn Gu-bayr) as so fabulous that it was beyond understanding. (Husein's head is now in the el Hasanein mosque — Saiyidna'l Husein — near the Azhar.) When Ibn Ruzzik died he called his family together and told them sadly that he regretted only three things in his long life: first, building this mosque, because it was just outside the walls and might be used by an enemy; second, his appointment of Shawar, who burned down Fustat-Misr; and third, his taking troops to fight in Bilbeis (probably against Saladin). But the mosque is not the perfect original. It was taken down stone by stone in this century and rebuilt and restored, and it looks almost domestic now because you can see shoemakers and tailors working in its basement.

The mashhad (mausoleum) of Saiyida Rukaya, which was built in 1133, is another of those little Fatimid jewel boxes that al Kahira was once full of, but it was in terrible condition until it was rescued in 1916 by the Comité de Conservation des Monuments Arabes, which was set up in 1906 to preserve Islamic monuments. The mashhad is not inside Kahira but on the old borders of Fustat and Katai, and it was built for the remains of Rukaya, who was the daughter of Ali, son-in-law of the Prophet. It has another tomb near it for Sayida Atika, and once you are inside the walls of these two mausoleums they seem to become an introverted sort of place, quite feminine and almost cosy and more like a nunnery than a Moslem tomb.

The genuinely extravagant remnant of the Fatimids and of al Kahira is the mosque of al Giyushi (1085), which you can see perched up on the Mukattam Hills from all sorts of odd places around Cairo. It looks so strange, so forgotten, so dramatically alone, that even when you are up there beside it the effect doesn't change at all. It is now a military area, but the governor obligingly bent the barbed wire border to leave the mosque outside. It is a classic Islamic ruin, and in this century it was for years the place where a band of pitiful and disreputable and fanatical dervishes collected, probably because it was so lonely and because it was also a shrine built by a Fatimid and a Shi'a. When Gamal Abdel Nasser was having trouble in the 1960s with the Moslem Brotherhood and there were plots in Cairo involving assassination, the dervishes were shifted out of the mosque because they were reported to be using drugs and hiding arms up there. In some future far-off day this will be a very nice place for picnics, particularly in the moonlight when the mosque turns white and you can sit on the step and look out over the wide valley of the Nile below, where Giyushi's seven favorite wives are buried and where the Nile valley stretches south as far as you can see.

The Shi'a always knew how to create this miraculous atmosphere, and if the Egyptians had been more receptive to it Saladin might not have found his job so easy. But Egypt has never liked religions of inner revelation, and when Saladin set about building a practical city he had the sympathy of the entire population. They were quite exhausted by the poetic madness of the Shi'a and were glad to have an engineer in charge rather than a god.

9

Saladin's Cairo

SALADIN brought an entirely different concept of a city to Cairo because he wanted a unified, thriving, fortified place, protected by strong walls and impregnable defenses, but functioning internally with a great deal of commercial and cultural freedom, and with no private or royal enclaves and no fabulous palaces: a city that belonged to its inhabitants even though he would be its absolute ruler.

Most historians have attributed Saladin's plan for Cairo to purely local or military considerations, but Saladin had what would now be called a world view. Unlike the Fatimids, who were simply trying to hang on to a corrupt empire, and unlike his Syrian-Turkish masters, who were trying to build an empire, Saladin was defending a whole culture as well as its territory, an ideology as well as a religion. He looked on Egypt as a source of revenue for his bitter wars against Christian and European encroachments, and against the dissident Moslem sects who divided Islam. He wanted Cairo to be the organizing center for an orthodox cultural and ideological revival, as well as a collecting house for the vast wealth which he needed for his antiforeign wars. There could be no better proof of his point of view than in his determination to re-educate Egypt in orthodoxy rather than simply crush the rival Shi'a with the sword, which he did only when necessary. His greatest architectural contribution to Cairo, for instance, was the madrasah, a college-mosque where the interpretive ideology of the religion and Islamic law could be taught once more instead of Shi'a dogma. He did think first of the city's defenses, keeping in mind the sort of attacks which had always made the city so vulnerable. But having opened up the royal city, he still had to have a genuine fortress inside it which would be invulnerable to any kind of military attack. He began to build the Citadel in 1176–1177. Historians have decided that Saladin built the Citadel because his Syrian background told him that every city should have a kasr or castle, but Professor Creswell rather ridicules this view and says that purely military considerations persuaded Saladin. One must add that Saladin's historical outlook also dictated his need for a center of absolute authority in the middle of his city.

Saladin's idea of Cairo is still visible on any map of the city. Above all, he wanted to enclose the whole lot, including the ruins of Fustat-Misr, in an all-embracing wall, and he began with Badr's wall to the north and extended it west to the Nile to the port of al Maks, which is now the station square — the Bab el Hadid. On the east, under the Mukattam Hills, he brought Badr's walls south to his own Citadel, which was built two hundred and fifty feet above the city on its own little hill. Both the west wall following the canal and the south walls under the belly of Fustat-Misr were supposedly never quite finished because Saladin left Egypt and was fighting the crusaders and his Shi'a rivals in Syria, but fairly recent excavations have uncovered parts of these "unbuilt" walls.

Saladin, like the great Amr Ibn 'As, is a romantic historical figure whom it is hard to fault in essentials; in fact his most ardent admirers have often been his Christian biographers. They, as much as the Arabs, have made a myth of him, and what always attracted Europeans to Saladin was his almost perfected sense of cultured chivalry. There can be no doubt that the rude, self-interested and often bestial crusader knights learned a great deal about chivalry from the Moslems, even before Saladin, from Saladin and after Saladin. On the whole it is hard to find much chivalry at all among the crusaders. Even the *Encyclopaedia Britannica* accuses the great Richard Coeur de Lion of arrogance and brutality and the senseless massacre of two thousand Saracen prisoners at Acre. Hitti says that the Christians brought no culture with them when they came, but took a great deal away with them when they left; and Lane Poole, a staunch Christian, says in his biography of Saladin that any sort of treaty with soldiers of the cross was worse than useless. Largesse was simply not a Christian characteristic, but it was an essential part of Saladin's faith. Mohammed himself had laid down the religious rules for honorable behavior because caravan trade and business demanded a particular kind of trust in the word of others. This is probably the reason the whole Arab outlook later attracted so many Englishmen at the height of Britain's success as a trading nation, not least romantics like Lawrence of Arabia who found something even more in the feudal Islamic creed — the reincarnation of classical Greek heroism.

This was the new air that Cairo was to breathe, and it went on breathing for a long time before it too disintegrated in its own contradictions. From Saladin's arrival in 1169 until the Ottoman conquest in 1517, when the real medieval role of Cairo came to its end, the house of Saladin was to rule for 82 years, the Turkish Mamelukes for 130 years and the Circassian Mamelukes for 135 years, so that an average of 116 years seems to be about the historical length of survival of any dynasty in medieval Egypt. But beginning with Saladin, orthodox Sunni Cairo emerged healthily from the erratic corruption of the Shi'a dogma, and Saladin not only fortified the city but in eleven years he built five colleges as well as a mosque. None of them exists any more; only a small part of the Citadel is his, and some of the city walls which he built to include much more than the old walls of Kahira.

In the many years I have known Cairo I never deliberately set out to see the bits and pieces of Saladin's walls, but I saw them all anyway, except for a fragment below Fustat which Ali Bahgat found in 1916–1920 and excavated. Part of one gate of the west wall running along the old canal, the Kanatara gate, was dug up only in 1920. Then some more of the west wall was revealed, but it had to be destroyed again when the municipality widened a street along there. Only a little piece of the west wall is now left. On the whole Saladin's city wall is too fragmentary to mean much to anyone but the seriously interested.

In fact the only part of Saladin's Cairo I have ever found adequately impressive is the original perimeter of the Citadel when seen from behind. When you come down on the back of the Citadel from the north you suddenly see how the fortress is built on very high ground. Saladin's original structure, which is intact on this side, makes its medieval character absolutely real and remarkably fresh. The main body of the Citadel was built after Saladin, and almost every conqueror including the British added something to it. But Saladin himself must take the blame for building the original Citadel with stone stripped from the small pyramid of Giza. It is too late to regret the pyramid now, but what one does regret in this city of a thousand similar regrets is that nothing is left of the hospital Saladin built in the Citadel, which we know about only from Ibn Shadad, Saladin's private secretary, and Ibn Gubayr, who visited Cairo in 1183. Ibn Gubayr described the hospital's organization almost in terms of any good modern clinic and as "a palace goodly for its beauty and spaciousness." Saladin staffed it with doctors and druggists; and it had special rooms, beds, bedclothes, servants to look after the sick, free food and medicine, a special ward for sick women, and nearby a separate building with barred windows for the insane, who were treated humanely and looked after by experts, even by "psychiatrists" who tried to find out what had happened to their minds.

But it has all gone. So have all his madrasahs (the special college-mosques), which is a pity because the madrasahs built by Saladin and his successors (some of theirs remain) were very important to Cairo's re-emergence. They not only introduced a new architectural form to Cairo — the cruciform mosque — but they were excellent colleges for administration as well as for religion. They were places of worship and religious instruction, but originally they also taught mathematics, geodesy, physics and medicine.

In 1176–1177 Saladin ordered a madrasah to be built near the grave of the Imam el Shafi'i, the founder of one of the four main schools of the orthodox Sunni sect — the school to which most Egyptians still belong and to which Saladin himself belonged. El Shafi'i had been born in Giza, and he was buried in the cemetery south of Cairo known as the Khalifa. The huge madrasah which was originally built as a monument to el Shafi'i, and which was described by Makrizi, is not there any more, but what *is* still there is the mausoleum over el Shafi'i's cenotaph, built in 1211. There is a fairly new mosque attached to it, built at the end of the last century, and though one gets used to the casual atmosphere of a mosque in Cairo, I was startled when I went into this particular one recently and saw a green neon sign over the pulpit which said: *God bless all in this house.* Because it is such a special place for Egyptians this newish mosque was luxuriously carpeted, and in one corner a boy of sixteen or seventeen was praying so fervently that he was rigid, almost blind with concentration. But the mosque is nothing. The point is the original tomb to el Shafi'i just behind it, which was closed to all non-Moslems until recently. When I went in there the sweeps were beating the carpet, and the tall beautiful mausoleum was filled with dust. With the sun streaming through the windows onto the carved wooden cenotaph, which the restrained Creswell calls "magnificent," and the air literally hanging like gold all around it, the effect was heavenly although I coughed and coughed.

Saladin left Cairo in 1182 to fight the crusaders in Syria, and he never returned. By the time he died in Damascus in 1193 — leaving almost nothing — he had not only established his family in Cairo but he had liberated almost all Palestine from the armies of England, France, Burgundy, Flanders, Sicily, Austria and, in effect, from the world power of the Pope. Often he had the aid of eastern Christians, who were as much the victims of the western crusaders as anybody else in eastern lands. The proud Georgians, for instance, preferred Saladin to the Pope, and so did the Copts of Egypt. In fact, Saladin had not only rescued the east from the west, he had recognized and utilized the forces which were able to rescue the east from itself, and he left in Cairo a transformation which would last it for a very long time to come.

This is the groundwork of the city that now developed. It was an enlarged and busy city of cruel, arbitrary, intelligent, cultured, brutal, artistic rulers, and a city with a populace who lived a very full and risky life of hard work, trade, gaiety, terrible suffering, calamity, patience, and extraordinary passions which always managed somehow to break the confines of the religion and the harsh authority which governed their lives.

Saladin was succeeded by his brother al Adil (Saphadin of Scott's *The Talisman*), and he was also succeeded by a terrible famine with the usual plague that followed famine in the Middle Ages. Nobody has quite explained this particular famine in Egypt, but it might well have been caused by Saladin's imposition of a new kind of landed feudalism in Egypt (see page 103). Cannibalism and economic catastrophe brutalized life in Cairo and partly depopulated it. House rents, always a measure of Cairo's prosperity, fell to almost nothing and Abd al Latif, a contemporary encyclopedist, says that all the wooden decorations of the palaces were burned in Cairo's hungry ovens for heating, cooking or baths. The crusaders came back in 1218, but al Adil's son al Kamil thoroughly defeated them. It was al Kamil who finished the first Citadel, and there can be no doubt that crusader prisoners of war built most of it because Ibn Gubayr saw them in 1183 — incredible numbers of them — digging the deep ditches and cutting marble and shifting huge blocks of stone. They almost certainly continued the work until it was finished in 1207, because crusader prisoners were working in Cairo even later than that. This is probably the only time that Europeans have "slaved" in Cairo; it was always the other way around in the years to come.

Al Kamil is, in many ways, more subtly romantic than his uncle Saladin. It was al Kamil whom Richard Coeur de Lion knighted on Palm Sunday in 1192, in what Hitti calls "the romantic excesses of the time." Al Kamil admired the Copts, and the Copts of Cairo still look on him as their favorite Moslem patron. When St. Francis of Assisi was on his way to Palestine he visited Kamil's court and they discussed religion. But what is rather difficult to decide about al Kamil is the character of his "friendship" with perhaps the greatest crusader of them all, Frederick II. To the Christians it was admirable, to the Arabs it was infamous. All that is left in Cairo of al Kamil's now is the Kamiliya — or rather a rebuilt nineteenth-century version of it — in the Shari' Mu'iz. It was first built as a madrasah, but almost nothing of the original remains; in fact there is almost nothing left in Cairo at all of any of these Ayyubid sultans. There is the tomb-mosque of Kamil's nephew al Salih, which is fairly well preserved in the Bein al Kasrein, but it is a pity that al Salih's private little citadel on the island of Roda doesn't exist any more. When I was last on Roda, hopefully looking for some remnant of its walls, there was only a mess of new pipes and ditches where the Roda citadel had been. A brand-new building that looked like a huge theatre straddled the site — a new water filtration plant being built for Egypt by the Czechs.

Al Salih Ayyub, the nephew, is important to Cairo because he and his Turkish wife Shaggar ad Durr (tree of pearls), who had been one of his slaves, were partly responsible for the Mameluke slave system becoming an integral part of Egyptian history and a new type of society for Cairo. Almost everything about Cairo has several beginnings, not least the city itself and not least the use of slaves as a ruling class. Individual slaves, treated like sons, had already graduated to the sultanate, but this was not yet an established system of succession. It was Saladin who unwittingly created the conditions which made the slave sultan the basis of the ruling class for the next four hundred years. Saladin's army was officered by lordly slaves (Mamelukes), and when he came to Cairo victorious his reward for these brilliant mercenary soldiers was, according to Lane Poole, paid by grants of fiefs, lands, castles, towns, or even whole provinces, held on strict conditions of military service. Egypt had never seen this sort of landed baronial system so forcefully used since Pharaonic times, so that Saladin in fact introduced medieval baronial feudalism to Egypt on the backs of his slave officers. And this peculiar combination of slave soldier and feudal lord was the basis of a class who were able to renew themselves by the extraordinary method of purchase rather than breeding, something which gave the system vigor and purpose.

What also gave them strength was the economic advantage of Egypt's highly developed trading society, without which the Mameluke system would never have worked. On the whole the Mameluke baronial system was useful and stable in Egypt, although its real stability was often completely obscured by its violent form of royal succession. Mameluke power was rarely handed on from father to son, it was more often seized by one group of slave lords who then nominated one of their number to be sultan. But this system of violent ascendancy began only when the Ayyubid sultans became too weak to keep their family succession going. When al Salih Ayyub died, Cairo was full of powerful Mameluke emirs and soldiers, and the authority over these lords would have simply passed to the next Ayyub monarch if there was one. But he was in fact too young, so al Salih's widow, Shaggar ad Durr, decided to rule instead, and she was sufficiently respected by the Mameluke lords to win their support at first.

A queen is an anomaly in a Moslem country, but Shaggar ruled as absolute monarch for eighty days. Then it became too much for the caliphate and the Bahri (river) Mamelukes on Roda, so they elected Ayback, their commander in chief, to marry her and take over the power of the Sultanate. But even though she married Ayback, Shaggar ad Durr went on ruling Egypt absolutely, treating her new husband with thoroughgoing contempt. She even made him divorce his favorite wife, and when later on he wanted to marry another wife she had him murdered in the Citadel as he was taking a bath after a hard day's relaxation on the Hippodrome. But this time the Mameluke emirs were thoroughly outraged, so they locked the queen up in the Citadel, where she hammered all her pearls and her jewel case to dust with a mortar so that no other woman would have them. Then the Mamelukes dragged her out, and she was beaten to death with the wooden shoes of the young slave girls belonging to the wife she had made Ayback divorce. Shaggar's battered body, covered only by her underwear, was then thrown out of the Citadel and left to rot in a ditch below. Dogs began to eat the corpse, but according to Makrizi (Quatremère translation) a "man of the people" took pity and carried her body in a basket to the tomb already built for her.

This mausoleum, which she had built for herself in 1250, is on the southern edge of Cairo, not far from the Citadel and opposite the mausoleum of Saiyida Rukaya. I have passed Shaggar's tomb many times and have walked all round it many times, but for some reason or other I never managed to get inside it. It is built entirely of brick, bonded with palm tree trunks, and what I missed by not seeing its interior is the earliest existing example (according to Creswell) of gold mosaic in Egyptian Moslem architecture. The story of the queen continues to the grave. Nobody would bury her in the place prepared for her because she was too unpopular with the Mamelukes, so all the inscriptions on the tomb itself are confused because someone else was buried there officially in her place.

Shaggar had been able to rule as an Ayyubid only with the help of the Mamelukes, but Egypt had really been ruled by the Mamelukes anyway, and now that these special circumstances had given them a taste for their peculiar kind of power the Mamelukes never really let it go until Mohammed Ali mass-murdered most of those left in 1811 in the streets of Cairo. The Bahri Mamelukes now established the pattern in Cairo for the rest who followed, and like most ruling classes, among themselves they had a vicious dog-eat-dog kind of democracy. Makrizi always says that a particular Mameluke was "elevated" to the rank of sultan by the emirs, but in effect it was a brutal contest of the most powerful among them to rule as long as he was able to, or as long as he could stay alive, and always of course as long as the other Mamelukes accepted him. Inevitably the violent rivalry between these feudal lords meant permanent conflicts of factional interests who fought blo𝘳 lily in the streets of Cairo to put one nominee or another on the throne.

Considered alone, each Mameluke sultan in Cairo seems to be simply a rich and lonely plant, emerging from nowhere, blossoming beautifully for a while and then suddenly having its head lopped off and being replaced by another exotic bloom. But if you give each one of them their true environment — the steadily expanding world trade of the thirteenth, fourteenth, fifteenth and sixteenth centuries — their extraordinary continuity makes sense. Instead of each sultan being an isolated example of violent elevation, incredible wealth and private indulgence, there is a certain historical logic to their wealth and the way they used it. The Bahri Mamelukes were not only successful farmers and traders but were also able to defend themselves against outsiders, which gave Egypt many years of economic security. The Bahri Mamelukes, for instance, kept the Mongols out of Egypt, thus saving Cairo from the fate of Damascus, where Houlagou, grandson of Genghis Khan, had made "the blood run in torrents in the streets" (Makrizi). In Damascus the Christians had become allies of the Mongols, and Houlagou as the Khan Supreme sent a long letter with four ambassadors to Cairo telling Sultan Moustafa Koutouz that he had no way of escape from the Mongol forces and claimed his absolute submission. Koutouz cut one of the ambassadors in half outside the Citadel in the Horse Market, the others were sliced up outside the Bab el Nasr, the Bab Zuweila, and in the Ridaniya quarter. Then all their heads were hung on the Bab Zuweila.

By 1260 the Mongols were being defeated thoroughly by Koutouz, not in Egypt but in Syria, but this meant little to the Mamelukes among themselves. Koutouz's rivals murdered him in Cairo with what is recognizable now as Mameluke panache. The Emir Zahir Beibars (who would be his successor) asked Koutouz for one of the women they had just captured in the wars. Koutouz granted the favor and

Beibars kissed his hand in thanks, which was the signal for assassins to cut the sultan's head off. The Emir Beibars then took control of the Citadel, and as sultan went on fighting the Mongols in Syria and defeated them twice. He once swam the Euphrates at the head of his army when he was fighting Louis of France, and in another battle his Mameluke soldiers killed six thousand Mongols and fourteen hundred Moslems who had sided with the Mongols against him. When Beibars rode back to Cairo after this victory he came in through the Bab el Nasr (Victory Gate) and marched with his troops right through the city to the Bab Zuweila, pelted joyfully all the way by the merchants and people with pieces of gold and silver.

Beibars was born in Kipchak (Mongol Russia), and he had blue eyes. Or rather he had one blue eye, the other was filmed over with a cataract. He was originally bought as a boy in Damascus for eight hundred dinars, cheap because of his bad eye. He had brown hair, a strong voice and a violent temper, and it was really his insatiable energy and vigor that took him upward by murder and plot to the sultanate, which he held for seventeen years, two months and twelve days. His court in Cairo was, naturally, fabulous, formal and rich, and every lordly member of it had some elaborate title like Master of the Horse, Cupbearer, Food-taster, Polo Master, Slipper-holder. All were Mamelukes, and all received princely salaries, and the whole lot had to be in attendance when he was holding court in the Citadel.

Any one of these emirs would have killed Beibars and replaced him if there had been a chance. But Makrizi, at the end of a long biography of him, describes how Beibars loved to be in several places at one time. Nobody ever quite knew where he would turn up, which had its effect on anybody plotting against him. He rebuilt all the essential portions of the public works in Egypt, such as canals, shipyards and fortifications, which were vital to Egypt's efficient functioning as a milch cow. But Cairo prospered when Egypt prospered, and though he was lavish with his gifts of money, goods, lands and titles to his Mameluke partners, on the whole Cairo suffered less squeezing under Beibars than with later Mamelukes, because he was so successful abroad. He extracted hard tribute from any foreign city or lord he conquered. He was religious, forbade hashish and wine in Cairo, and "to purify the city" he closed all the taverns and brothels and expelled the European prostitutes (probably women who had been camp followers of the crusaders). He had a reputation for indulging himself privately in his own excessive pleasures, but if he did they never really showed. The Bab Zuweila was often hung with the heads of those who rebelled or opposed him, but when thirteen hundred Mongols surrendered to him in Syria he received them in Cairo, gave their leaders the title of emir and invited them all to embrace Islam, which they did when they had been painfully but legally circumcised.

Zahir Beibars built a House of Justice at the foot of the Citadel and attended it personally on Sundays and Fridays, and he also held audiences there and received envoys. He made strict laws to cope with the bold behavior of the women of Cairo, but Cairo's women have always been irrepressible and they obviously found their own way around the sultan's prudish restrictions, since in 1264 Beibars had to bring in a law forbidding women to wear turbans or men's clothing. In the same year there was a serious famine in Cairo and Beibars ordered all his lords to take on the responsibility for feeding a certain number of the populace.

Makrizi, reporting the details of Beibars' reign, keeps diverting his account with fascinating details of life in Cairo at this time. He reports, for instance, the discovery in al Maks (Cairo's port) of the body of a dead child which had two heads, two pairs of eyes, four hands and four feet. In 1264, he says, the Cairo canals suddenly started disgorging the bodies of murdered citizens. Men also began to disappear mysteriously and were never heard of again. The mystery was then traced to a young woman of great beauty called Gaziya, who went out in the streets of Cairo every day with an old woman companion. Gaziya was always dressed in the very latest fashion, and when men approached her it was easy to entice them to her home, where several male accomplices robbed and strangled them and threw their bodies into the canal. Gaziya was caught when her aged woman accomplice invited Cairo's most famous coiffeuse to a wedding; when the coiffeuse turned up laden with her well-known jewels she was robbed and murdered. The young slave of the coiffeuse came looking for her, and when Gaziya's old crone said she hadn't seen hide nor hair of the hairdresser, the slave complained to the wali, who burst in on the old woman and "applied torture" to Gaziya and her gang. They admitted everything. One of the accomplices was a brickmaker, who burned many of the victims in his brick oven; in fact when he was caught his cellar was stacked with bodies waiting to be incinerated. The criminals were all crucified, probably on the Bab Zuweila, and though the beautiful young Gaziya was unnailed and taken down after two days, she died almost immediately.

In a pretty little drama of his own invention Beibars accidentally poisoned himself. He wanted to murder a rival prince called Malik Kaher, and prepared a poisoned draft of koumiss for him. But in an almost Hamlet-like situation Malik Kaher cleverly switched glasses and Zahir Beibars took his own poison and died, after thirteen days of agony, "just after the sun had set." He was then a little more than fifty years of age.

There are two serious memorabilia of Beibars left in Cairo. One is a small and rather forlorn corner of a building, which is all that is left of his famous Zahiriya madrasah. The Zahiriya was standing till the 1870s, but the minaret fell in and it was pulled down. The sad little lump of it that is left now doesn't mean much to anyone but an expert. What is impressive, as impressive in its way as Hakim's mosque, is Beibars' other mosque, which he built in 1266–1269. It is still marked on Cairo's tourist maps as Fort Sulkowski — the name Napoleon gave it. It is in fact a walled square to itself in the middle of the modern city, but just outside the old city walls and just off Shari' el Khalig on the way to Abbasiya. Today when you come up to these walls they look from the outside more like a fortress than a mosque. The whole enclosed area is over a hundred yards square, and the walls are 36 feet high and quite intact. But once inside the high walls you find a quiet and very domestic sort of garden, a classic Moslem arcaded sanctuary, with the mosque itself on one side, still functioning.

For some reason or other this mosque was neglected in the fifteenth or sixteenth centuries, and when the French arrived in 1798 they turned it into a fort and put cannon on top of the walls. They eventually named it after Sulkowski, a Pole on Napoleon's staff who was killed in Cairo when the city revolted against the French. When it was no more a fort it became a soap factory, a bakery, a storehouse, and finally the British occupation forces used it as a slaughterhouse. It was cleaned up and made respectable again in 1928, but it is one of those corners in Cairo which seem to be forgotten and unused and ignored. The stone gates look stubborn and beautiful, particularly the northwest gate, which looks like a perfect little building in itself. There is very little left of all the expensive building materials which Beibars brought to it from all over his empire, but the cloistered atmosphere remains, and on a hot day in Cairo its courtyard is one of the best places to sit in because it is cool and the high walls shut out the brassy noise of the modern city.

During the wars against the Mongols Cairo became a leading center of refuge for all Islam. Dimishqi, who wrote in 1300, says that in his day the population of the city was a million because there were so many refugees from other Moslem countries fleeing Mongol brutalities. This meant that Cairo became rich in Islamic intellectuals and philosophers (often the first to flee in a war) as well as artisans and teachers and ordinary frightened people, and for the next two hundred years Cairo benefited enormously from this wonderful accumulation of talent. Almost a hundred and fifty mosques, madrasahs or mausoleums, smoothly domed, were built in the city in that time, almost all of them masterpieces of architecture or decoration. "Domed" Cairo (so called by romantics who love viewing the domes from any high point) is, in fact, the product of this whole epoch, and there are so many of these structures left that it becomes quite impossible from Beibars on to deal with every monument left in Cairo.

When Beibars died, Cairo was still thriving on its trade and exports, and there are records of Egyptian traders at this time running a regular trading business with India and China. But once more the sultanate becomes a prize to be fought for bloodily in the streets of the city, with one faction of emirs fighting another faction to "elevate" their man. The whole city would simply close up when these men were on the loose. More often than not one faction would move into a part of the city and use it as a private fortress, and then ride out into the rest of the city, plundering it and pillaging the houses and the bazaars, kidnapping women and children and firing on the rival faction from the roofs of mosques and houses, hurling spears into the streets below and chopping off heads in the gateways. The bazaars would be closed for weeks while this went on, or until one faction outfought the other. And the punishment for those who were defeated in this feudal shift of power was crucifixion on the Bab Zuweila, or their eyes were gouged out or they were pitched into the river or their arms or hands were cut off to make sure they would never fight again.

What finally emerged in 1279 from all this brutal rivalry was one family who ruled Egypt for one hundred and three years, which is very unusual in the Mameluke history of Cairo. The founder of this dynasty within a non-dynasty was a slave called Qalaun who was known as "the Thousand Man" because al Salih had bought him for a thousand gold dinars. He also came from Kipchak, and Makrizi says he was a handsome man with huge shoulders and a short neck, and though he spoke Turkish and Kabjaki he understood little Arabic. His entire reign seems to have been spent soldiering somewhere else. Like all these Mamelukes he was passionately devoted to his sons, and when one of them, Malik Salih, died of dysentery he was heartbroken, and he ordered as court mourning that no one was to cut his hair or change his clothes until Qalaun said so.

Qalaun built one of the most beautiful complexes of buildings in Cairo in the Shari' Mu'iz. It is in fact a three-part building of mausoleum, madrasah and muristan, built in 1284–1285. The mausoleum and madrasah still stand in their sepulchral medieval beauty, but the hospital (muristan) is not much more than its outside shell. For any student of Moslem architecture this L-shaped complex can be one of the most exciting in Cairo, because much of its style and structure is controversial. When a layman takes a look at the façade, however, and sees the Italian-looking minaret and the long Gothic-like windows and rounded arches, he is impressed enough without bothering about the controversy. But inside the mausoleum, staring up at its delicate interior façades, perfect arches, carved windows, and minute and astonishing and poetic decorations, you can compare it favorably with any decorative Gothic cathedral in the world.

The hospital is now a mere yard with almost nothing left except the channels where the water used to trickle soothingly through the shady gardens. It functioned as a hospital from 1284 until the 1850s. Like all these early, endowed Cairo hospitals it was built to the express requirements of the sick; every kind of specialist worked here, the sick were treated with care and scientific skill and great tenderness, and like almost every muristan in Cairo it included a wing for the care of the insane. The hospital was built in a few months, and Qalaun himself would stand up on the scaffolding with a whip and direct operations, while his emirs were told to stop passersby in the street and make them carry stones. Qalaun settled the income from a million dirhems on this hospital for the benefit of the patients. Inevitably the endowment disintegrated, and the last European to write about it as a hospital was Edward Lane, who saw seventeen cells full of insane men and women chained to the walls in 1847 — a sad end to the original care with which it treated the mad.

When I was last at this muristan I was with Tawab of the Inspectorate, and he noticed a new brick wall had been built behind the old hospital without his knowledge or approval. He was furious, but it was too late to do anything about it. The muristan was untouched, but who knew what might be under the foundation of that new brick wall. What I also found on another visit, almost next door to the Qalaun mosque, and hidden by a little green doorway, was one of the few public baths left in this part of Cairo.

These hammams used to be spread all over Cairo and Fustat-Misr in their hundreds, and to use one now, as primitive as this one, is itself a medieval experience. It hasn't changed much, except that it is worn and old and ugly. I wouldn't have even known of its existence if my friend Shafik Abd el Kader, Chief Inspector of Islamic and Coptic Monuments, hadn't pointed out the doorway to me as a little fragment of the medieval city. The foyer inside was not medieval. It was rather like a large railway washroom with naked taps, gray towels and a wet

Mihrab of the mosque of Qalaun in the Suq el Nahhasin.

Mausoleum of Qalaun, showing two of the ancient columns
which support the dome.

floor. Inside the steam room the smell of several hundred years of male body sweat was suffocating. There was a hot bump of stone in the middle of it, a roof with bottle glass to let in light, and some hot skinny old men pouring out their exhausted sweat. Afterwards I didn't think the smell of it would ever leave me. But it was full of Cairo camaraderie, and obviously you came out clean, even if it didn't smell clean. Shafik knew everybody in it, and for anyone wanting the taste, almost literally, of thirteenth-century Cairo, it is still available in this hammam if you can bear it and if you can find it.

Al Nasir, Qalaun's only son by the Mongol princess Aslun Khatun, was even more the builder than his father was. He is the rotten-ripe example of all these Bahri Mamelukes. He ruled in Cairo as sultan of Egypt for forty-two years except for two intervals, totaling five years, when he was still too young to hang on to what he'd got and his rivals were able to depose him until he was strong enough to emerge for himself, which he did with a vengeance. One of the sultans who ruled in this interim period was Lagim, who took part in the murder of Sultan al Khalil and afterwards hid in the neglected mosque of Ibn Tulun. He swore that if he ever got power and wealth he would restore Ibn Tulun's mosque from its existing state of ruin, and when he actually became sultan in 1296 he not only restored the mosque and cleaned it up but built the little mida'a (basin) still in the courtyard. Originally it was a sort of drinking basin, but later on the Ottomans turned it into a proper place for ablutions with taps, because they liked the hygienic Hanafi idea of the fountain in the mosque. Lagim was murdered in 1299 when he was saying his prayers.

Al Nasir eventually succeeded him again and became another of those incredible rulers who made Cairo a brutal fairy story of such wealth and cruelty and art and beauty that it is always hard for a modern European to understand the complexities of the type. He was lame, had a cataract film over his eye like Beibars, was fanatically strict about morals, and ruled so absolutely and so brutally and so viciously and so deceitfully that he kept all the rival Mamelukes absolutely under his thumb. Ibn Batuta, the traveler from Tangier who passed through Cairo on his way to Mecca in 1326, was very impressed with his nobility and morality, but Ibn Batuta tells several different stories showing how al Nasir murdered his opponents, sometimes using the Ismaili sect as private assassins, and sometimes pursuing his rival as far as Iraq, where the Ismailis killed them with poisoned knives.

What seems to have been the reason for Cairo's prosperity at this time is that Egypt had by now settled down thoroughly to the feudal baronial trading system which Saladin had given it, and on the whole the Mameluke barons were now socially secure, allowing for all the usual contradictions of feudalism. But so far the Mameluke system had helped unify the state, and the outlets for trade were also fairly safe (particularly in the Mediterranean), despite the continuing wars with Mongols and crusaders. Al Nasir was clever enough to make good alliances on his borders, the most important of them with the Golden Horde on the Volga, who were bitter rivals of the eastern Mongols. Al Nasir also kept his peace with Constantinople, so that in effect, in the middle of the trecento, Egypt was far more centralized and much less torn by big rivalries than the rising republic of Florence and the other Italian states.

What is always recorded by historians of al Nasir's reign in Cairo is his treatment of the Copts there. Remembering that the Copts were Christians, though eastern, and that the reputation of the crusaders among all eastern people was of monstrous brutality, the Copts had not suffered much as Christians in Moslem-ruled Cairo. On the whole they were as bitterly opposed to the crusaders as the Moslems were, but as always Copts were used by these still foreign Moslem Mamelukes as an implement of rule, because the Copts were a minority like the Mamelukes themselves. The Copts of Cairo had prospered almost too much under the Fatimids and also under the Mamelukes, but they were about to be made scapegoats.

Qalaun, al Nasir's predecessor, had dismissed all the Coptic clerks from the ministry of war, so there was already a sort of two-faced edge in the way the Mamelukes used the Copts. Suddenly, in Nasir's time, there were demonstrations against the Christians. Cairo was still full of Moslem refugees from the Mongols, and no doubt they were deeply involved. There must have been a large and dissatisfied element among them, if what we know of modern displaced persons is any indication. A church outside Bab el Luk which Nasir had ordered to be left intact was razed to the ground by an angry crowd. This incident ripened into other incidents, and there were thousands of people in the streets of Cairo demonstrating against the Christians. Yet it is possible that these demonstrations might have been a hidden way of protesting against Nasir himself, who had used Christian advisers and whose taxes and laws had become very oppressive. The fact that the Mamelukes had used the Christians naturally made the Christians the scapegoats. As a gesture of protest someone began to light fires all over Cairo, and the city began to burn. No sooner was one fire put out than another started, and it was obvious that a skilled group of arsonists was at work.

Finally a Christian was caught in Beibars' mosque with a pot of oil ready to set it alight, and since most of the other fires had started near mosques the origin of the fires seemed obvious. The Christian and some monks were tortured and they admitted setting fire to the city. The Coptic patriarch denounced the arsonists, but a Melchite convent in the Mukattam was razed and four monks were burned alive. By now the streets were filled with angry people who were caught up in this sudden hatred of Christians. The city bazaars were closed up tight, and the whole demonstration got so out of hand and it so frightened Nasir that he arrested two hundred people — all Moslems.

This seems to indicate that the Moslems themselves were against Nasir, and that he was afraid of them. In any case he seems to have been more determined to suppress Moslem demonstrations than Christian ones, because he hanged the two hundred arrested Moslems by their hands on gallows set up along the city streets and alleyways near the Bab Zuweila, and he left them there till they died. He executed no Christians but humiliated them by making them ride backward on their donkeys, and forced them once more to wear blue turbans and a bell around their necks when they were in the public baths. It seems clear that with these measures Nasir was hoping to divert away from himself, and on to the Christians, whatever trouble had stirred people up in the first place.

There was very little respect in Cairo for Nasir, despite his authority. The violence of the Mamelukes often suggests a docile population in the city, but in fact Cairo was never docile. Frequently the more powerful the Mameluke sultan, the more rebellious (or rather disrespectful) the population. In any case Cairo always managed somehow to enjoy itself and thrive in its own way and to protest with raw rude wit when a sultan did anything that was unpopular. Nasir felt this very forcefully when he arrested a Mameluke emir called Tushtu, whose popular name in Cairo was "Green Chickpeas." Tushtu, with all the charitably religious excess of these guilty men, used to give large sums of money to the harafish, who were the vagabonds of Cairo. According to Ibn Batuta, the harafish were a "large, organized body, hard-faced folk and lewd," and when Nasir imprisoned Tushtu, thousands of them demonstrated outside the Citadel and chanted among other rude things: "Listen, thou all-starred cripple [al Nasir]. Let him go!" Nasir wisely followed their insulting advice and quickly turned Green Chickpeas loose.

Nasir's Cairo is briefly but flatteringly described by Ibn Batuta. In his opening paragraph he says Cairo is the mother of all cities, "peerless in beauty and splendor, the meeting place of comer and goer, the stopping place of feeble and strong." He then goes on to say that it was learned and simple, grave and gay, prudent and foolish, base and noble, of high estate and low estate, but known and famous. He says there were twelve thousand water carriers who transported water on camels to the city, thirty thousand hirers of mules and donkeys, and thirty thousand boats on the Nile which sailed up- and downstream laden with goods of all kinds. He says the people were in love with pleasure and amusement, and he attended a marvelous fête in which Cairo was decorated with silks and rich ornaments for days, all to celebrate Nasir's recovery from a fractured wrist.

What counts in this particular description is the thirty thousand ships; Cairo the port was trading in all direction. At this time Venice was just beginning to establish itself on the mainland of Italy, and some of this trade from Cairo began to fill the Venetian markets. The future alliance of Venice and Egypt had not yet developed — Venice was still fighting with the Genoese for supremacy of the Mediterranean — but many of these thirty thousand ships in Cairo went down the Nile to Alexandria, where the goods went on to the maritime cities of Italy as well as to Constantinople. The importance Nasir attached to this Mediterranean trade is shown by a canal he dug between Alexandria and the Nile (1311) on which a hundred thousand men worked.

As long as the Mameluke emirs were powerful as a class, Egypt was not quite al Nasir's private estate, but it was to some degree his private trading organization, and his wealth lived up to all past reputations of waste and excess. He spent a fortune on his stud horses; twenty thousand beasts were slaughtered when his son married; and when he went on the pilgrimage to Mecca he ate fresh vegetables even in the desert, brought along on his traveling garden carried by forty camels.

In 1303, when he returned to Cairo after utterly defeating the Mongols in Syria, Cairo was en fête to meet him, and pavilions and grandstands lined the route of his entry. The whole city was hung with silken banners, rooms on the route were rented for exorbitant prices, and the streets were laid with silk carpets over which Nasir and his soldiers rode, followed by seven hundred Tartar-Mongol prisoners in chains. Around each Mongol's neck was tied the severed head of another Mongol, and another thousand Tartar heads were carried on the lances of the Mamelukes. After this, the city went mad with licentious enjoyment, so that "disorders" were committed with women, soldiers got drunk, and an earthquake which followed this debauch was considered a punishment from God Himself for such wickedness.

Al Nasir taxed everything salable, even salt and slaves, and though the city seemed to thrive fabulously in his reign, it suffered terribly in the aftermath. When Nasir died in 1341 the whole country was ripped apart by civil wars, famine, and finally the plague — the famous Black Death of Europe, which eventually killed nine hundred thousand people in Cairo alone.

A great deal of al Nasir's Cairo is still standing — about fifteen mosques, tombs and colleges, though not all of them were built by him. In Nasir's lifetime all his emirs competed with each other to build beautiful mosques, tombs or colleges, and forty were built between 1320 and 1360, when the man who built one of the most famous mosques in Cairo was in power — al Nasir's son, Sultan Hasan.

Al Nasir's three great works which show his practical and complex nature are the great aqueduct which used to take water from the Nile to the Citadel, his college and mausoleum next to Qalaun's hospital, and the mosque in the Citadel (1318), which was in ruin for years but was rescued in the last century by an Englishman named Watson, who cleaned it up and pulled down the partitions which had been put up when the mosque was used as a prison. Now it is almost a model of medieval purity when compared with its fat modern neighbor — the Mohammed Ali mosque. Al Nasir's magnificent aqueduct, which still runs along the old borderline between Fustat and Cairo, was originally attributed to Saladin, and its origin has always been controversial. Makrizi says that it was Nasir who built it in 1340–1341, which is indisputable, yet there have always been signs of an earlier aqueduct underneath it which could have been Saladin's. It was the Egyptian archaeologist Ali Bahgat who cleared up the mystery. In 1919 he excavated part of Nasir's aqueduct and discovered that what was underneath it was not an older aqueduct at all but part of an old city wall. It was, in fact, the southern part of Saladin's walls. Up till then everybody had assumed that this part of the city wall had been planned by Saladin but never built. Ali Bahgat proved conclusively that it was undoubtedly Saladin's southern wall, so he had cleared up two mysteries with one excavation. The aqueduct was used right up until 1872, and though it doesn't carry water any more it still snakes dramatically across the underbelly of Cairo, and a road and the Helwan railway cross it, and an old quarry railway still runs along the bottom of it. The sakias, which lifted water from the Nile up into the duct, sit very near where the old Red Sea canal used to join the river, and it is still called the Fumm el Khalig.

The aqueduct is more of an architectural curiosity than something beautiful in itself, but it is so much part of modern Cairo that one hardly notices it any more. The real beauty that Nasir left to Cairo is the madrasah-mausoleum in the Bein al Kasrein, which was built in 1295–1304 on the site of a bathhouse, and the thing about it that immediately impresses the visitor is the extraordinary white marble Gothic entrance doorway, which was taken from one of the crusader churches of Acre and shipped to Cairo by sea, where it had quite a career of its own before it ended up here. When you stand back from this mosque to look at its face, the whole building seems to have been built around this ice-cold Christian doorway. Even the minaret and the tall crenellations on top of the façade are built up dramatically over this extraordinary and quite un-Moslem entrance.

The trouble is that you can't really see the building properly because it is jammed too closely between Qalaun's muristan and Barkuq's madrasah, but even so it is far more rewarding outside than in. The stucco minaret is literally dripping with decaying exotic ornament, perhaps the richest of its sort in Cairo, and I always leave the place with a stiff neck from staring up at it. The last time I was there a curved lip of the rich stucco fell off the minaret and I almost caught it, but it smashed to powder on the path at my feet. The whole complex of Nasir's tomb and college always reminds me of a fruit and nut bowl, because the carved minaret looks like a vine laden with ripe grapes, and in the interior the decorations of the mihrab (prayer niche) of the madrasah are like luscious lumpy walnuts hanging down from some upside-down tree. This was the first of a type of cruciform madrasah built in Cairo for the four schools of Sunni orthodoxy, which could all be taught there at the same time, since each rite used one arm of the cross. Creswell says it is a uniquely Egyptian form and was never influenced by the Syrian Byzantine churches, which is always thought to be the case simply because it resembled them.

This cruciform plan reached its most beautiful form in Egypt when one of Nasir's sons, Hasan, built what is still perhaps the most impressively complete and monumental madrasah in Cairo — the mosque of Sultan Hasan. (Nine of Nasir's sons ruled after him, each one managing to survive only a few years because the Mameluke emirs simply went on murdering the sultans as they tried to establish supremacy and as one faction emerged superior to another. The Bahri Mamelukes were in fact reaching the end of their long run, and Cairo was waiting as it always did for someone else to take over, because the whole of Egypt was once more in revolt against its rulers.)

Sultan Hasan's madrasah-mosque is considered by the experts to be the finest existing monument of Egyptian Arab architecture. Hasan himself was a more-than-usual Mamelutic type, but this huge mosque

Mosque (madrasah) of Sultan Hasan. BELOW: Its courtyard.

can be considered as a monument to its architect and its masons and to the Egyptians, who certainly paid in blood for its beautiful simplicity. It is not in the Bein al Kasrein but up on the hill right opposite the Citadel, and in the nineteenth century, when there were Mameluke wars in the streets of Cairo, one lot of Mamelukes would use the roof of Hasan's mosque as a firing platform against their rivals in the Citadel, and cannon would roar across the street from mosque to Citadel and back again.

The first impression is simply of its size. Its walls from the street are sheer, 113 feet high, built of beautifully cut stone brought from the pyramids. It obviously rises above all the vulgar noise of cars and people below, and its gaping doorway is like a big hole in the side of a stone mountain. Outside, you can't see just how much of a cruciform it is, but once inside and standing in the sahn (courtyard) the shape of the cross is clear. When you are standing in the middle of its open court you seem to be hung up on a high wall of light, which floods everything from the open roof above, and I don't think there is any monument in Egypt, not even the pyramids, where you feel the unworthy softness and fleshiness of your own body as you do standing in this very disciplined stone arcade, which is absolutely puritanical.

Hasan himself lies in a marble tomb in the mosque; he was murdered. The dome of the mosque is not the original one, which collapsed in 1660. One of the minarets had collapsed in 1360 and killed three hundred children who were studying in the school below it. The history of the mosque is full of this sort of extraordinary happening. Though it is always dusty, it always looks very clean because of its simple surfaces. But there are hundreds of chains hanging down inside the main sections of the mosque which are an eyesore. Each chain used to have a glass or bronze light bowl on it, but they have all gone now, many to the Museum of Islamic Art, but many were taken away in the last century by European collectors. The Victoria and Albert Museum in London has four lamps from this mosque which have been "on loan" to them now for sixty years. But the atmosphere of the interior is ruined by these naked and rusty chains, and I once asked Tawab of the Inspectorate why someone didn't at least hang some sort of glass balls on the chains to restore the original effect, and he said: "Money!" When we calculated how much it would cost in Cairo to supply even cheap glass copies of the simplest lamps, it wasn't such a huge sum, but I suppose Cairenes themselves don't notice these dead chains any more.

After Hasan, the last four Bahri Mameluke sultans hardly matter, and the dynasty itself came to an end in 1382 when Barkuq, a Circas-

Minaret of the mosque of Aqsunqur.

Mosque of Emir al Yusufy.

sian Mameluke from the Citadel, was "elevated" to the sultanate and began a new line of Mameluke kings — the last — which ruled for a hundred and thirty-five years until the Ottoman conquest of Egypt in 1517. Hitti says that the rule of these Circassian Mamelukes was "one of the darkest in Syro-Egyptian annals." Only one of them had a Moslem father, and that was Barkuq himself. Because they used the Citadel as their headquarters, they were called Burji (towers) Mamelukes, or slaves of the fort. In general however they are referred to as Circassian Mamelukes, because most of them came from the Caucasus, though not always from the Cherkess race which gives them their name. In 1967 I saw a Soviet-Georgian film made from a famous novel which portrayed the horrible business of child and woman stealing for the Mameluke trade in fourteenth-century Georgia. That was one side of it. But what happened, once these Cherkess victims got to Egypt was horrible in reverse because they usually became monsters, and they were not really good soldiers or clever rulers.

Yet they had inherited in Cairo a thriving "Mameluke" culture from the Bahris, not only in architecture and decoration but in the sciences, particularly medicine. Cairo up till the end of the fourteenth century was a glorious place for medicine and physicians. Even gynecology was highly developed, which is not at all usual in a Moslem country, although it must be said that much of the gynecological literature of this time is so erotic and so full of lewd jokes that it is hard to sort out the real value of it from the nonsense. But there *was* science in it. The horse-mad Bahri Mamelukes had encouraged veterinary sciences, which in itself developed a fascinating sideline in literature about horses. Hitti claims that psychotherapy also originated in Cairo at this time, and he tells a story about Saladin's private doctor, a Jew called Ibn Gami, who once stopped a passing funeral because the dead man's feet were still erect rather than lying flat. Ibn Gami said he was therefore still alive, and he was, and the funeral turned around and went home. Cairo eye specialists were famous, and cataracts were removed regularly and with great skill. Arab medical historians of this epoch have left us very rich accounts of Cairo's medical activities at the time of the Ayyub family and the Bahri Mamelukes.

But perhaps the greatest glory of the whole Mameluke period in Egypt are its two great historians, al Makrizi and Ibn Khaldun. Both lived in the time of the Bahri and the Circassian Mamelukes. Ibn Khaldun was a judge under Barkuq, and his famous *Prolegomena* is as applicable to the human condition today as it was then. It is, in fact, far superior to the works of the great Machiavelli, who came a hundred years later, and modern historians could still read Ibn Khaldun's theory of history with considerable benefit. He even anticipates the Marxist view of the influence that tools and the means of production have had on history. Al Makrizi was less of a philosopher but more specifically the great Arab historian almost without equal, and for all students of Cairo he becomes somebody you live with and like, and his death in 1442 always leaves a genuine feeling of regret as you go on living through the cruel years of Circassian brutalities. Ibn Khaldun died twenty-six years before Makrizi, and considering the savagery of his times it is astonishing to read in his *Prolegomena* a statement that "the excellence of rulership arises out of gentleness," which in context is not a Gandhian outlook but an appeal for an end to Mameluke brutality. Both these great men were really products of the Bahri epoch rather than the Circassian one, but above all they were Cairo intellectuals, living in a city that continued to be vigorous no matter what the Mamelukes did to each other.

But already with Barkuq, the first Circassian, Cairo began to be more like a nest of vipers than the city of a cultured sultanate court. Mameluke life in Cairo became almost literally a matter of dog eat dog, and the Mameluke soldiers of Greek and Turkish and Circassian and Tartar origin cut each other to pieces every day in the streets of the city. Ordinary people kept to their houses, particularly the women, who were never safe from the Circassian taste for rape and murder. Barkuq himself once tortured a rival with fire and the rack to make him reveal where he hid his gold, and when the victim refused Barkuq cut off his head and paraded it on a spear and then hung it on Bab Zuweila. Sometimes the sultan nailed rivals to camel saddles and left them to die in the streets. All his soldiers were freshly bought Mamelukes, acquired sometimes in lots of five thousand, and he would send them out to suppress revolts in the country and give them a free rein. The results were always indescribable.

Yet the beautiful buildings still went up, and because all these Circassian Mamelukes left us such remarkable architectural monuments to themselves you can never look at any one of the forty-two religious "edifices" they left behind in Cairo without asking that familiar question about such beauty being born of such bestiality. Barkuq's own mausoleum was built by his son Farag in 1399. It is in the cemetery called the Tombs of the Caliphs, and as if to emphasize all the contradictions the mausoleum has one of the simplest façades of any Islamic building in Cairo. Only the two minarets look indulgent, and they seem to grow cheekily out of the flat, simple roof like two Florentine candlesticks. Every time I have been to this mausoleum it has been haunted by diseased and hungry street dogs, and I always felt there

Door of the Barkuq mosque in the Tombs of the Caliphs.

was some kind of long-nosed justice in their cringing attendance (Moslems don't like dogs near their mosques). The marble pulpit, which Qait Bey added later on, is very famous because it is so finely carved, but I never liked it as much as the wooden ones in the older mosques. I admit to being prejudiced about Barkuq, although he was no worse than most of the other Circassians. His madrasah in the Shari' Mu'iz also has such a simple façade that it is almost naked, but it has the same kind of beautiful minaret, which is something of a talisman for these Circassians. I suppose I have stared longer and more thoughtfully at this particular madrasah than I have at any other mosque in Cairo, not for its architectural beauty so much as for this underlying contradiction between the cause and the effect, the evil and the fruits thereof.

These beautiful Mameluke monuments go on and on through the Circassian period until one suddenly feels trapped by them. But it is simply not right to see thirteenth- and fourteenth-century Cairo only through these magnificent relics. After a while every Mameluke dome in Cairo seems to become the dome of a Mameluke conscience. They were unashamedly trying to buy their way into paradise, and a good deal of the wealth of the nation was the purchase price they offered. One has to escape these temples somehow in order to get back to what else was happening to the city, because even the topography of Cairo had been changing.

During the twelfth and thirteenth centuries the Nile had been retreating to the west of the city, and in the span of a hundred years its course had receded almost a mile, to about where it is now. This quick recession of the river started in a peculiar way. Whether deliberately or accidentally we will never know, but a huge river ship called the *Elephant* (*Fil*) was sunk at a bend of the river about where the main railway station is now, near what was then the river port of al Maks. Silt began to form over the wreck, and within a few years an island was formed called Elephant Island (Gezirat al Fil), which is more or less the site of Bulaq now. At first this little island used to be covered during the yearly inundation, but eventually it kept its head above water and began to force the river to straighten out its banks westward, so that what is now the European part of Cairo — from Ezbekiya Gardens all the way to the river — only emerged from the water in the thirteenth and fourteenth centuries.

Gezira Island, which was originally named Bulaq Island, emerged about 1300 in this process. This island, and Bulaq itself on the east bank of the river, became the big port, which al Maks had been before Elephant Island deprived it of the river. The river continued retreating westward, leaving huge tracts of low swampy land on which almost all modern European Cairo is built. Many pools and lakes were left in and around Cairo, particularly in the south near Ibn Tulun mosque, and many of them were still there when Napoleon came. The one the Cairenes liked best was called Elephant Lake, and it was more or less where the Hilmiya quarter of Cairo is now (not the suburb), just west of the Citadel.

The land which emerged around Elephant Island was marshy and soft, and Makrizi, who tells us all this, says the Mamelukes used to practice archery there. But in the middle of the fourteenth century al Nasir joined the Red Sea canal to the new bank of the river through this new swampy land, thus draining it. This new exit for the old canal was called Khalig al Nasir, and it remained the exit of the Red Sea canal until this century, although it was later diverted again and called the Ismailiya canal. It met the river where the Egyptian Pharaonic Museum is now, near the Nile Hilton. This final version of Nasir's canal was only filled in at the end of the last century to make what is now Ramses II Street, and anyone with a moment to spare on top of the Nile Hilton can look down on this street and trace the line of the old canal right up to the station square which was once the port of al Maks.

The new port of Bulaq became Cairo's link with the Red Sea traffic; merchants and dockers and soldiers and boatmen built houses along the new riverbanks, and a town of Bulaq began to appear. Bulaq, which is now simply a part of the city, was then a mile from Cairo, which was never quite on the river; and a road ran from the port up to Ezbekiya through open fields where the Mamelukes continued to race their horses and practice their shooting. By about 1300, under the Bahri Mamelukes, the city had become a little like the big city that Saladin had envisaged. The remnants of Fustat were still decaying, and that dusty old city would eventually rot right away like a dead limb. The original Red Sea canal, which still continued on down to Fustat along the old western walls of Cairo, went on being used as long as Fustat was still even half alive. But when Fustat-Misr died this canal was used as a sort of local thoroughfare for boats, and finally it became the city's main sewage drain until it became so revolting that it was filled in about seventy years ago and the tramline laid along it.

As surely as Fustat-Misr had always depended on its Red Sea canal and its river ports for its wealth, so did Cairo depend on Bulaq and Maks for its medieval power and stability. But what Cairo had also become during the time of the Mamelukes was a thriving commercial link between east and west.

Cairo's contact with Europe was through Venice; in fact these two cities became inseparable in the fourteenth and fifteenth centuries because they organized a world monopoly on east-west trade, and historians have even described Venice then as a half Oriental city. After the fourth crusade, when the Venetians stripped Constantinople and ruled the Levant and controlled even the Black Sea, the merchants of Venice briefly had had a direct link of their own with the east through their own Levantine ports. But when they lost these ports in 1291 to the Egyptians, the Venetians scandalized the Christian world by making a commercial treaty with the Mamelukes which gave them trading rights of a new kind. Venetian merchants and agents now appeared in large numbers in cities like Cairo, and by 1400 Venice was the recognized European mart for exchange of goods from east to west.

Almost everything from the east reaching Venice and the west now had to pass through Cairo first, and the customs dues paid on this trade were the real bonanza for Cairo's merchants and Mamelukes and sultans. The sultan got a great deal of it, and though there was plenty left for the merchants and agents, the farther down the social scale the more the benefits thinned out, until right at the bottom the peasants got none of it. In any case the two great trading cities of Cairo and Venice would live or die together with this trading pact. They even had similar social characteristics at one moment — the Venetian signori were the twins in violence and rapacity of Cairo's Mamelukes.

It was Ibn Said in 1246 who saw and described how goods arriving in Cairo from the Red Sea were bonded at Fus͗at and then distributed to the markets or sent on. D. A. Cameron in his book *Egypt in the Nineteenth Century* (he was British consul in Port Said at the end of the last century) shows how the Mamelukes levied customs dues on every bale of Oriental produce which arrived from the Persian Gulf and the Red Sea for transfer to the harbors of Alexandria and Alexandretta for retransshipment to Venice. Cameron gives us a typical example of a consignment of raw silks, nutmegs, peppers, indigo and cloves. The cargo was worth $22,000 on landing in Egypt at a Red Sea port where first customs dues were almost $9,000. The goods were then sold at $44,000, and by the time they reached Bulaq in Cairo the price was $66,000. But another $10,000 had to be paid before they could finally be cleared for transshipment to Venice. "Thus, whether in customs or in tolls, or in presents to the local governors and escorts, a quarter of the £35,000 paid by the Venetian would go to the Mameluke sultan and aristocracy merely for the privilege of transit. Arrived at Venice, the produce might fetch any price from £50,000 to £100,000."

The excessive wealth and exotic business that all this trading tribute brought to Cairo convinced Stanley Lane Poole that it was Cairo and not Baghdad that was really the fabulous city of *The Arabian Nights*. He concludes his wonderful little book on medieval Cairo with a lengthy demonstration of this theory, drawing heavily on Makrizi, Ibn Khaldun, al Syuti, Ibn Iyas, al Ayni and other Arab historians to prove his point. He says that *The Arabian Nights* tells the story of the "life of the people" of Cairo, whereas the great Arab historians give only the lives of the great. That seems a little unfair to Makrizi, but Lane Poole goes on to illustrate how the tales are really the adventures of Cairo's ordinary merchants and shopkeepers and sailors. Cairo merchants would even put to sea themselves in search of good trade, although as a rule they simple kept shop and tried to cope with the unpredictable behavior of evil djins which at times could almost be identified with the fickle behavior of the Mameluke lords. Even Sinbad the Sailor could be found on the riverside quays of Bulaq or Fustat.

Anybody walking through the medieval part of Cairo today can still find plenty of evidence to support Lane Poole's theory that this was the city of *The Arabian Nights*. (It is far more believable here than anything modern Baghdad can offer.) The alleyways, bazaars, caravanserais, markets, and even some of the traders are little changed in essentials. Street by street and building by building and quarter by quarter it is often wretchedly but romantically intact. The bazaar of the Khan el Khalili has been functioning since 1400, when it was founded by Garkas al Khalili as a public service and a good investment in rents, and tourists never get tired of it because it is the best preserved of all the great bazaars. To provide the sort of shelter these merchants needed there were many different kinds of markets and merchant residences and places of business in Cairo, each quite distinct, although they are often confused these days. A kasariya for instance was the largest kind of market, and a suq was an ordinary everyday market. A wekala was a sort of caravanserai — an inn around an open court where the merchant could hire one of the simple little rooms and reside there and keep his goods there as well. A khan was explicitly for trade, and its courtyard could be filled with goods and the rooms around it lived in. A foondouk was more of a hotel for all people — traders and customers alike.

Many of the khans and suqs still function, but the wekalas don't operate any more, although several have been preserved as museum pieces. There is an attractive little wekala in the Shari' Mu'iz which has been preserved. It is opposite the madrasah of al Ghury and it was built just before the Turks arrived in the sixteenth century. It is still one of the most attractive places of medieval Cairo, and you can now get some idea in this cleaned-up old caravanserai of what the entire city was like when it was kept neat and dusted and swept and was comparatively free of filth. It is a very simple courtyard with cell-like rooms on all four sides, four stories high, with a fountain in the middle. It was only restored about twenty years ago, and now folk artists live in the little cells and show their work there as well. At one end of it there is a sort of school for handicrafts. In this courtyard you know exactly what Lane Poole is talking about when he shifts *The Arabian Nights* to Cairo.

In Makrizi's time (early fifteenth century) there were eleven such hostelries in Cairo as well as twenty-three kasariyas, fifty suqs, and quite incidentally eleven racecourses. Makrizi describes all the khans and suqs in marvelous detail, and then as now you could buy anything in them — soaps and oils and silks and sesame, jams, fruits, nuts, cloth and indigo and spices. Makrizi mentions one suq which had big and small chests piled up so densely that only a little space was left free in the center. In each of the piled-up chests was gold and silver — "enough to amaze one." The security of these markets and wekalas must have been absolute, otherwise all this open trade and business for cash would never have worked. There were no banks, so merchants had to carry all their gold with them, and it wasn't just their loose cash but their entire accumulation of capital, which was often considerable. But because it was a rich city full of poverty, theft was common enough, although the punishment for stealing was brutal and quick. You either lost your head or your hand, and the city executioner was always busy limb-cutting just outside the Bab Zuweila, which was his headquarters.

What was inextricably attached to all this merchant wealth and its pleasurable excesses was the great decorative art of Islamic culture, not only in the mosques and madrasahs but in the rich furnishings of merchants' and Mamelukes' houses. Even the simple man had something beautiful. "Almost no home in Cairo was without many pieces of inlaid brass," Makrizi says, but he adds sadly that the art was already disappearing in his day. Venice, in fact, inherited it, as it did so many other aspects of Islamic art. Brass work and its inlay is still done superbly in Cairo, but artistically it is moribund and it is little more now than part of the tourist industry.

I never had much of a taste for brass inlay, but what I have always found unique in Cairo is the medieval art of carved stucco. Examples of this fragile art are spread all over the city like rich butter. Egyptian craftsmen first began to carve plaster when wood became expensive, and at first they even used wood-carving tools. I used to think stucco was carved when hard and dry and crisp, like wood. How else could it get its clean lines and perfect design? But I was surprised one day when I came on a new school in the Mosque of Hasan where about a dozen apprentices were learning this old art, and they were working on damp gypsum plaster. I realized then how these bevels and curves and delicate arabesques were cut into the firm white slabs: the plaster *had* to be wet. In Ayyubid and even in Mameluke Cairo there must have been hundreds of workshops for this art, probably one in every mosque or madrasah being built.

The sort of trade and wealth which all this beauty was built on could hardly last forever. What hastened the downfall of the Mameluke system and bankrupted the city was the inability of the Circassian Mamelukes to adapt themselves to changing world conditions. Maybe it was impossible for anyone to anticipate the one event which would change the history of the city, but if the Circassians had at least invested a little more of their wealth in the security of their state, or in a cheaper and more reasonable system of taxes on transit goods, the history of Egypt and even of Europe itself might have been different. But these Circassians were born dissipaters, and the workable relationship between land, trade and state which the Bahri Mamelukes had left them was steadily disintegrated by their greed. They turned Egypt into a free-for-all in which a dozen different groups plotted and fought for any spoils they could get. They not only corrupted the tax system and milked the traders beyond reason, but they played havoc with land tenure and even undermined the unity of the state itself, so that when the moment of crisis came they were utterly incapable of facing up to it.

The last days of medieval Cairo are therefore the last days of the Circassian Mamelukes, who nonetheless still went on building the city even as they ruined it. Almost every one of the great monuments they built is still standing. There are an awful lot of them, but two in particular say all that need be said of their rich and sophisticated and decadent and beautiful taste in heavenly structures. Just inside the Bab Zuweila is the mosque of Sultan Mu'aiyad, which Gaston Wiet calls one of the most luxurious mosques in Cairo. Wiet is enthusiastic about the mihrab and the joggled voussoirs and the colonnettes and the polychrome marble and the inlaid pulpit, but for the layman it is the garden-courtyard and the colonnade and the huge bronze gate

Koran lessons around the pillars in the mosque of al Mu'aiyad.

Dome of the tomb-mosque of Qait Bey
in the Eastern Cemetery.

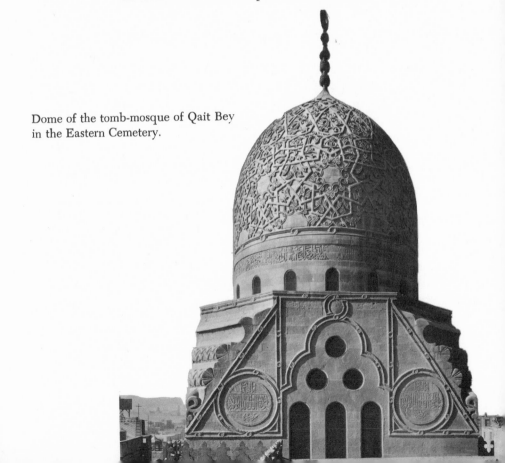

which make this a different sort of mosque. Colonnades are always appropriate in a hot country, but the arcade of this mosque looks almost northern and quite un-Egyptian. The mosque was built by Sultan Mu'aiyad on the site of the prison where he was once locked up by Farag (Barkuq's son), and he swore, as these Mamelukes always swore, that he would build a mosque on the site if he ever got to power. He finally did come to power, but the mosque was only completed in 1422, a year after his death. He was a pious and oppressive man, but he was also a musician and a poet, and his mosque cost a fortune. His reign was cursed by plague and by his own weird currency reforms, so that when he died everybody was so brutally engaged in chosing his successor that nobody attended his funeral, and he was buried without even a towel to wrap his body in.

Forty-nine years and twelve sultans later the very perfection of these Circassian Mamelukes, Qait Bey, was elevated to the throne on the shoulder of a cultured old Greek called al Zahir Timburghi who had been elected sultan as a stopgap. As a boy slave Qait Bey had been bought and paid for by one sultan and he had pushed his way up violently through the reign of nine others to become sultan himself. He reigned for twenty-eight years, sometimes flogging the president of the council with his own hand. He taxed all land to a fifth of its produce, and he put out the eyes and tore out the tongue of the great chemist Ali Ibn al Marshushi because he could not change lead into gold. There are many wonderful monuments left by this man — wekalas and mosques and even a palace (Yeshbek), and his college near Ibn Tulun's mosque is so sophisticated that it is almost perfectly featureless.

It is his tomb-mosque (1472), in that suburb of mausoleums called the Tombs of the Caliphs, which is probably the most sophisticated and beautiful building of medieval Cairo. It was finished at the same time as York Cathedral, Britain's own ripe example of its European equivalent in Gothic. It is so deliberately impressive that the spontaneity and surprise which are always an important part of Islamic architecture are almost totally lost. I always go to it overwhelmed even before I get there, so it usually disappoints me a little.

The striped façade shows how the stripe has come back home with a vengeance. It also has a decorative little balcony-veranda which was once a kuttab (elementary school), and though its floor is dusty and unswept these days, you can lean over the balcony and look at the Cairo sky and wonder where all those Koranic suras went that were once chanted here. The minaret is so restrained that there is not a daring line in it. The dome is the same, and it is so stalactited inside that you can never quite work out how it is done. Carved stone, the richest arabesques, marble mosaics, stained-glass windows, stucco, and also the two footprints of Mohammed himself, which he somehow implanted into stone as hard as iron. But they are smooth and pleasant to touch and they were brought from Mecca by Qait Bey himself.

I was once talking to Professor Creswell about this mosque and I asked him if there was any other mosque among Cairo's hundreds where stone had been so beautifully and elaborately used, and he said: "Of course. The mosque of Qigmas al Ishaqi in the Darb al Ahmar." Al Ishaqi's mosque, which was built nine years after Qait-bai's, is not far from the Bab Zuweila, and though Professor Creswell told me how subtle and beautiful the interior of it is, I have always walked outside the mosque but never gone inside it, because the end for me is Qait Bey's — which is hardly an objective way to look at it, but Cairo is inclined to do that to you.

The event which now put Cairo to sleep for almost four hundred years was the discovery in 1488 of the sea route around the Cape of Good Hope from Europe to India. Western European powers desperately needed a new trade route to the east which was free of the physical influence and the heavy tolls that Venice and Cairo took on all goods they transshipped between them. Just two years after Vasco da Gama had rounded the Cape (1497–99), Portuguese traders were already operating in Calicut, picking up goods from India and delivering them to Lisbon at a fraction of the price that they cost through Cairo. And Spain was already in America picking up gold from the streets. The result for Cairo and Venice too was obvious. By 1502 Cairo's trade was so seriously affected that the Mamelukes tried to get help from the Mohammedan ruler of India against Portuguese ships, which were sailing up and down the Red Sea without serious opposition. No help came. The Portuguese were marvelous sailors, but so were the Venetians and the Egyptians. The issue would obviously be settled at sea, and the Venetians brought to Alexandria timber which was shipped through Cairo to Suez, where a fleet was built. The Egyptians sailed these ships to India and met the Portuguese fleet off the coast of Bombay and defeated it thoroughly. But a year later, in 1509, the situation was reversed when the Mameluke fleet was totally routed off Diu.

The man who presided over this final dissolution of independent Mameluke Egypt and medieval Cairo was al Ashraf Kansuh al Ghury. Al Ghury was sixty when he was "elected" in 1501. He had inherited a mess. He not only had the Portuguese at his back door, but on the other side of him the Ottoman Turks, who had already captured Constantinople from the Christians in 1453. The Turks were emerging not only as the vigorous new conquerors of the east but as the new unifying force which organized the Moslem world to defend itself against European ambitions. In May 1516 al Ghury left Cairo at the head of his army to face the Turks. Already defeated at sea by the Portuguese, he was fighting a purely defensive war with the Turks — Turkey was preparing openly to conquer Egypt. The Turks and the Mameluke forces met just north of Aleppo on Sunday, August 24, 1516, and the Circassians (up to fourteen thousand real Mamelukes and a huge army as well) were badly defeated. Treachery and artillery, which the Mamelukes despised, beat them, and Sultan al Ghury himself was killed on the battlefield.

Once again, as the Turks approached Egypt, the Egyptians had prepared the way. Exhausted by famine and brutality and exorbitant taxes (al Ghury had collected ten months' taxes in one swoop), the Egyptians more or less welcomed the Turks as deliverers from the long burden of Circassian savagery. On January 22, 1517, the Turkish Sultan Selim entered Cairo, and the last Mameluke sultan, Touman Bey, who had ruled for a few months after al Ghury's death in battle, was hanged on the Bab Zuweila. Far from trying to preserve Egypt as a strong and independent state, the Ottoman Turks set about reducing it to nothing, and a new era began for Cairo — the longest and heaviest in its history.

Al Ghury, the last real ruler of an independent Mameluke Egypt, gave Cairo two good monuments, and it is typical of Cairo's ability to produce something appropriate that his college-mosque and his mausoleum are built not far from the crossroads of what are now Shari' Gawhar and Shari' Mu'iz. Thus the first two names of al Kahira's history and the last of its independent rulers are all perpetuated in one place. The college-mosque was built in 1503, four years after Vasco da Gama had appeared off Calicut with his ships. Al Ghury opened it himself, and Cairo was en fête for the occasion. Gaston Wiet says that the decoration of this mosque turns its back on the wild exuberance of Mu'aiyad's mosque, but it has its own kind of exuberance. It has one of the most attractive minarets in Cairo — amusing, lighthearted and lovely, crowned daringly by five little sugar-loaf domes high up over the surrounding buildings. Baedeker called these diminutive cupolas "inappropriate," but for once this admirer must thoroughly disagree with him.

The horseshoe arches inside this cruciform mosque above each of the liwans are also among the best in Cairo because they are so simple. Today the mosque is always richly carpeted and well lit because it is still a place of instruction for all four schools, and the transept has a little square opening in the high dome above which is really a very sophisticated hole. It simply implies the existence of a courtyard below rather than announce it with the usual gaping exit to the sky. Just across the Shari' Mu'iz from the mosque is al Ghury's mausoleum, which he never inhabited because his body was never found on the battlefield at Aleppo. The mausoleum was neglected for years, but was restored in the last century after the dome had fallen in. For a while it was used as the library of Ahmad Pasha Zaki, an Egyptian nationalist, and it is still a library. Or rather, since Nasser it has become a Cultural Center for youths who want to study on their own, and I never saw a young man or woman bounding up the steps of al Ghury's mausoleum without wondering if they realized how significant the place was. Or if they even knew that one kind of Cairo — the rich, aggressive, self-willed medieval Cairo — had ended here, and the new kind of heavily occupied city they were heir to had taken its place.

10

Ottoman Cairo

THE Mamelukes did not die with medieval Cairo but lived on as the powerful feudal lords of a provincial Cairo under the Ottoman sultans. One could rewrite and reinterpret a great deal of Cairo's history under the Mamelukes simply in terms of their feudal trading role and its effect on the economy of Egypt, and not all of it would be bad by any means. Up till Ottoman times the Mameluke role in Egypt had been only a little different from the role of feudal barons in any other country, and not really much worse, except that they were all foreigners. And though rule by outsiders was always to be the curse of Egypt, it still wasn't the worst aspect of Mameluke power. The slave origin of these lords and sultans was probably the biggest evil of the Mameluke system as well as its most vigorous characteristic, because it meant that they had no national identity with any people or any place. They were attached only to themselves, and for Cairo the brutal individualism of their wild behavior was always antisocial in exact proportion to their lack of any identity or ties with the city they lived in. D. A. Cameron made this point very clear when he wrote in 1898 that the Mamelukes were no more than an aristocratic guild of soldiers, and "the real slaves were the Egyptian peasantry and working classes."

The second period of Mameluke rule in Egypt, under the Turks, is quite different from the Bahri-Circassian period because the Turks abolished the Mameluke sultanate without abolishing the Mamelukes themselves. Egypt was now ruled by a pasha who was really the governor of Egypt, and he was appointed by the sultan in Istanbul, to whom he was responsible. Egypt was divided into twenty-four districts, each one ruled by a Mameluke emir, only now he was called a bey. As always the real basis of their power was their feudal posses-sion of the land, and these Mameluke beys surrounded themselves once more with slaves who upheld their purely baronial authority and even collected taxes for them. In fact all the emirs were partly autono-mous in their own regions, although the Turks took tribute from all of them. At first this division of authority, and the deliberate imposition of a sort of provincialism on Cairo, did not affect the city much, but gradually its rulers became burghers rather than monsters, and their tastes became solid and bourgeois rather than erratic and monumen-tal.

Sultan Selim, the Ottoman conqueror of Egypt, made no bones about encouraging rivalry between these feudal emirs so that he could keep them divided and ruled. The Mamelukes simply went on fighting among themselves as before, only now the "elevated" leader did not become the sultan, he was simply the Sheikh al Balad (chief of the country). Even so, he often became far more powerful than the Turk-ish pasha, so that sometimes the faction-fighting in Cairo still decided who was to get the largest portion of the spoils. But this only hap-pened when Istanbul was preoccupied elsewhere, which was quite often. After all, the Turks were the new saviors of the east so they were always busy putting down irritating revolts in their empire, or pressing their defenses deep into the border lands where east met west. They were even aggressive enough to reach the Danube, and for a while they plundered every Venetian ship they could find in the Mediterranean, even as far west as Gibraltar.

Turkey's westward policy and her destruction of Venice reduced Cairo more and more to the level of a provincial city, though still rich and important because it was Egyptian wheat that now fed the citi-zens of Istanbul. Cairo was once more a port for grain and fruit and African goods heading for Islam, not for Europe. And the Turks, like all foreigners in Egypt, took all and returned little.

With this Turkish policy of divide and rule, Cairo's day-to-day diet of events once more became butchery in the streets, plundering rival-ries and frequent assassinations. The Ottoman Turks installed their own kind of Mamelukes in the Citadel — the Janissaries and the Azabs, and these new Ottoman factions complicated the old rivalries. Sometimes the opposing Mamelukes and Janissaries and Azabs forti-fied the mosques and fired cannon at each other across the city. The pasha-governor was supposed to rule the city with his own men, but very soon he could hardly control his Janissaries because the battle for local spoils was too important for colonial loyalties to be bothered with. The Turks did collect tribute for the Porte (Istanbul), but the

Mamelukes collected much of the wealth even before the tribute was levied, and Hitti says that in all this scramble everybody exploited the peasant: "If one got to him first, the other would come and wring him dry anyway."

A great deal of what we know of Cairo's history for the next two hundred years of Turkish occupation is written by another masterful Egyptian — Abdel Rahman Ibn Gabarti, who wrote not only much of what we know of seventeenth- and eighteenth-century life in the city but what is even more valuable and fascinating later on — his own day-to-day diary of the Napoleonic occupation of the city. On almost every page of Gabarti's *Biographical and Historical Marvels* one finds casual sentences like this: "On the 4th day of the month the pasha strangled his deputy . . ." Or ". . . on the 12th day of Ramadan in 1780 a violent storm hit the city of Cairo bringing a dust storm which covered the sky. It was Friday and everybody thought it was the end of the world." Cairo has a long history of thinking that the end of the world has come. One Thursday in 1735 the populace of Cairo even left the city in a panic and went out into the fields and said goodbye to each other because they thought the resurrection (whose, is not clear) was going to take place next day. Friday came and then, astonishingly, Saturday, so they all trooped back to the city not a whit abashed, but laughing and joking about their own stupidity.

Gabarti tells us of all the epidemics, important births, the price of bread, the state of the treasury and lives of the great men, and he gives us the discussions of some of the wonderful scholars of the time. One famine which he records in the year 1695 caused the starving populace of Cairo to demonstrate against the pasha outside the Citadel. The pasha refused to pay any attention to them, and even got on his horse and chased them off. But the crowd broke into the shops and carried off cereals and other food, and eventually the rebellion got so bad that the pasha himself was replaced by another one sent from the Porte. In 1698 a man named al Oleimi set himself up as a saint in a café behind the fountain of al Mou'men, and people flocked to see him. He gave them "permission" to dance, and for men and women to mix freely and scandalously night and day, which they did quite happily until the soldiers came and took the saint away and cut off his head in the Citadel.

The impression of seventeenth-century Cairo you get from Gabarti is of a frustrated but mercurial and quick-tempered populace, always on edge because even the disputes of the pashas and the Mamelukes and Janissaries infected popular feeling, which was always ready to rise up heatedly on any issue which affected their lives. The city was in fact divided for many years into two main factions — the Fikarites and the Kassemites — which seem to have played an inexplicable but leading role in many of the internal conflicts of Cairo. It was originally a division deliberately created by the conqueror Selim out of a jousting match between the Mamelukes of Egypt (Kassemites) and the Turkish Janissaries (Fikarites). Somehow, too, Selim found a split in the artisans of the city, who were divided into Sadites and Haramites and with considerable skill he managed to combine the two splits into one so that half the artisans found themselves supporting the Mameluke Kassemites, and the other half the Ottoman Fikarites. Thus this identity of rivalries often found the artisans caught up in disputes between Mamelukes and Janissaries which really had nothing to do with them.

The situation which these divisions created sometimes affected the whole city with a sort of Montagu-Capulet conflict, and loyalties of workmen were demanded in silly and bloody battles which cost them dear and returned them absolutely nothing. Nobody has ever looked into this situation very deeply, but Gabarti says that the bitter hatred and rivalries of the two groups "passed from masters to slaves, from fathers to sons, and were the cause of many crimes, massacres, pillages, rapes and arson." No wonder therefore that some of the intellectuals of the time felt only despair for man himself. Cairo's life continued to be rich, but no intellectual saw any hope or happiness in Ottoman rule. So normal was the sense of betrayal and deposition among their rulers that the poet, Sheikh Hasan al Hadji, who died in 1718, wrote (my own rather free adaptation):

> *My brother, be intelligent and be on guard*
> *against all men.*
> *Do not cradle false illusions,*
> *For aren't there people of sincere façade*
> *Who, like foxes, betray your insides. . . .*
> *Be above all on guard against your parents,*
> *For they are the sadness of the world, and*
> *they die like scorpions.*

This is rather an unusual sentiment for an Arab poet, who is often cynical and dry but rarely quite so bitter. Gabarti mentioned a poet of Mecca called Sayid al Nabtit, who died in 1713, and who wrote:

> *The frequentation of men is an epidemic,*
> *And his isolation is the result of solid opinion.*

[140]

Thus, any confidence in men is a weakness,
And this has been said in the Holy Book.

On the whole, however, the scholars fought back, and though Cairo had the reputation of slowly dying intellectually under the Turks, this was not so. Cairo's vigorous give-and-take in the wordy battles in the street and marketplace and even in the mosques kept almost everyone passionately committed. Disrespect for bad rulers always managed to foster a sharp popular mockery in the city, and Gabarti reported that one pasha had to listen to the street urchins outside the Citadel chanting: "Pasha, Pasha, with the eye of a flea." But the city was always quite willing to scarify itself as well. In 1705, which was a desperate year because the river was low, everybody suddenly rushed off to the Mukattam Hills to pray for deliverance, and Sheikh Hasan al Hadji was so disgusted by this panic that he composed a poem in its honor:

Cairenes are ignorant,
Their ignorance is beyond understanding,
Their duplicity is one-eyed,
And their ability to lie is absolutely perfect.

But once again everybody enjoyed the joke and returned in a good humor, and Cairo went on living breathlessly as before. But from Gabarti one also gets the feeling that Cairo was now becoming the rather domesticated and bourgeois city that its provincialism made inevitable, despite the oppression and the violence and the repeated famines. By now the sheikhs and emirs no longer built themselves superb mausoleums; they were more inclined to build themselves rich villas on the banks of the river, or preferably on one of Cairo's half dozen little lakes like Elephant Lake or Ezbekiya Lake, which were really no more than big pools left in the hollow ground around the city when the river subsided every year.

For instance, Mohammed Chanan al Maleki, a rich sheikh of the Azhar, built himself a palace on the borders of the Nile at Bulaq. After the famine of 1695, when Ali Pasha — the one mocked by the street urchins — was sacked from the governorship, he went to live in the beautiful house of Ahmed, on the banks of Elephant Lake. Again and again Gabarti mentions these rich and prosperous houses, and there are a few of them still left in Cairo. The most familiar one is in the Khishkadam quarter, about halfway between the Bab Zuweila and al Ghury's mosque. It was built by Gamal al Din al Zahab, who in 1637 was president of Cairo's merchants, and what one finds now in this dusty museum of a house is the sort of Moslem hot-weather domesticity which all these sixteenth- and seventeenth-century houses in Cairo had. It has thick walls and intriguing passages and tiny rooms, and the salamlik (living room) and the qa'a (a sort of entrance hall) were really rooms to receive in, not live in. It is a house for hand-slapping welcomes, and for fat cheerful merchants to sit around on the divans gossiping with their slippered feet up, while the fountain made gurgling noises in the middle of the mosaic floor.

The real art of the musharabiya or finely carved wooden screen, is better seen in these old Ottoman houses than in any museum, even if they are often artistically inferior, and you can also see what the musharabiyas were really intended for. They were simply lace barriers which could hide the women sitting in cramped little galleries above the salamlik, yet allow the women to see the men below and hear everything said, even while they chatted among themselves and ate sweetmeats and giggled. The Gayer-Anderson museum near Ibn Tulun's mosque is of the same period as the houses Gabarti mentions. It is two houses in one: the older one is 1531 and the other is 1641. One was built by a smith and the other by a butcher. (Butchers in Cairo have always been able to build big houses.)

In Ottoman times most of Cairo's merchants were Moslems, but many were Copts and Jews, and some of them were very rich. The Copts were still used by the Ottomans as clerks and civil servants, and during the governorship of Mohammed Amin Pasha (he died in 1752) the prosperous Copts of Cairo were allowed to prepare a rich pilgrimage to Jerusalem. The caravan included many women and children and it was heavy with riches. They camped just outside Cairo before setting out, but the very man who had given them permission to go was persuaded by fanatics to allow Moslem zealots, led by students from the Azhar, to sack and pillage the Copts, and they attacked and stripped the caravan and then went on to loot the neighboring houses as well.

This was fairly typical of the unpredictability of Turkish authority in Cairo, but not all the pashas and emirs were so bad. Gabarti describes in full the rather intelligent rule of at least one enlightened Turk — Osman Bey Zulficar. After Osman there was another enlightened khatkoda (minister or deputy) called Ridwan al Gelfi, who was chief of the corps of Azabs, the Turkish mercenaries, and when he became chief of Cairo itself he built a number of beautiful houses, one in particular by the Ezbekiya Lake which was decorated with gold and had many colored mosaics on the walls. In his kiosk by the canal at Ezbekiya "he led a life of pleasure and debauchery," Gabarti says,

[142]

Harem windows.

"and he never dissimulated his taste for drink, nor the cult that he professed for beauty. Women and boys of a certain class could give, during his power, free course to their excesses and their vicious leanings . . . Cairo then resembled a country of gazelles, or a paradise peopled with houris and mignons, and the inhabitants drank with avidity from the cup of delight."

But even the delights were on a much reduced scale. This Turkish paradise was not to be compared with the mad dreams of al Hakim or the hearty indulgence of Kafour, the Camphor. The glory of Cairo under someone like Ridwan was really an echo rather than a drama. Yet he left a good impression, because he loved poets and they loved him and they would laugh and argue together in his garden. The poet Kassem composed a long poem in honor of Ridwan, and the following two verses, taken at random from it, (and freely transposed) give some idea of what that garden on the lake at Ezbekiya was like.

> The eye of the narcissus, having wept the tears
>   of a rose,
> Made the camomile smile with a pretty mouth,
> And the rose then carrying its purple robe
> And blooming in its opulent cup
> Saturated the air with its own excitations.

> Honor to wine and the vine,
> It is my remedy against my boredom.
> When my wine is poured by the hands of a young
>   god
> I seem to see the sun embraced by the moon,
> And both wrapped up like that in a sky of happiness.

Ridwan's only remaining monument in the city rests rather heavily on it. There is a gate of the Citadel called the Bab el Azab which Ridwan built on the ruins of an older gate, and it was behind this gate that Mohammed Ali massacred the last of the Mamelukes in 1811. The moon wrapped up with the sun seems to be a better way to remember Ridwan, even though he was an Azab, a profligate and a wine lover. He was shot one day by assassins as he was being shaved, but he managed to escape on his horse and flee to the countryside, where he died of his wounds without benefit of his women or his wine or his poets.

By the middle of the eighteenth century we began to have the first serious European accounts of the city, although even before that an almost unknown traveler named Ludovico di Varthema visited Cairo in 1502 and was disappointed because it was not as large as he thought it would be. "Its size in circumference is about equal to Rome," he says, although it had a bigger population. Some years ago I looked through the First Letter Book of the East India Company (1600–1619) hoping to find there some indication of what had happened to the forgotten old trade route from east to west through Cairo, and hoping also to unearth some early European description of the city. But the letters simply show that in the early seventeenth century Britain was allowed to trade freely in Cairo, and the company mainly used the old route through Egypt for written communication from India to London, because it was still the quickest way from east to west. There was no picture of Cairo, no romantic description of the company's agents groping their way dauntlessly through the intrigues and assassinations of this great Oriental city.

In 1741–1743 an Englishman called Richard Pococke visited Cairo and described the city as consisting of three towns a mile apart: old Cairo, Cairo proper and Bulaq. Old Cairo, which was all that was left of Fustat, was then about two miles around, but it seems to have been mainly granaries along the river. The granaries at Fustat were already famous and were called Joseph's Granaries. They were brick courts filled with grain and surrounded by high fences. Pococke says that the aqueduct to the Citadel was functioning, Amr's mosque was in a ruinous condition, and there were still some remains of the old palaces on Roda Island. Pococke rode around the city on an ass, and he describes the old walls and the lakes which were covered with boats in the summer. The city gates were guarded by Janissaries, and "no idle people can go about the streets at night." He saw a Jewish funeral, used a public bath, and gives us a firsthand description of European merchants living in the city. Apparently they lived very agreeably and they spent the mornings at business and the afternoons riding out into the fields and gardens north of Cairo. "Of the Europeans, there are settled here only the French, English and some Italians from Venice and Leghorn." When the English died they had to be buried in the Greek Orthodox cemetery because there was no English chaplain. The big trade these Europeans did was in broadcloths, tin, lead, coffee, senna, flaxes and drugs. They imported raw silks from Asis, and he comments on the manufacture of sugar in Cairo.

One important aspect of Cairo's financial life at this time is that the Turks still did not use credit, which meant that the caravans of goods would still arrive in the city and the traders would take up residence until everything was sold and then go away again. (This meant that a fairly large part of the crowded city's population was not permanent.) Since Europe's great expansion of business and trade in the eighteenth century was already based on credit and exchange, which permitted the serious accumulation of capital, this archaic system of cash and carry kept Cairo firmly grounded in its old medieval habits, which eventually made it so vulnerable to European methods that a hundred years later the sudden discovery of the European credit system would bankrupt the entire country.

About twenty years after Pococke, the German traveler Carsten Niebuhr visited Cairo. His journey began in 1761 and his description of Cairo is substantially the same as Pococke's. But in Niebuhr's account there is a hint of what was about to come. The Cairo he describes has re-established its trading contacts with Europe, but after such a long period of Turkish provincialism it seemed to be poised and waiting now for some big event to come along and shake it back into life again. Niebuhr was, in fact, Europe's first intelligence man in Egypt, and he told Europe just what conditions were really like in the city.

But he did not judge the city by European standards the way later travelers did, and the result is an informed Orientalist's account of a city which, in the very nature of its strange customs and rather sublime unawareness of what was happening in the turmoil of Europe, must have seemed like an attractive prize to farsighted politicians in the west. Many of them (mostly French) already realized that sooner or later some western power would have to establish a foot in Egypt, and unwittingly perhaps, Niebuhr manages to make Cairo a very ripe prospect for them.

Nonetheless, one of the first things he noticed was the Egyptian distaste for foreigners. Only Moslems were allowed to ride on horseback; Christians and Jews had to ride asses. Moreover, they had to get off obsequiously when even the most "inconsiderable" Mameluke lord passed by. The Mameluke lords on horseback were always accompanied by a special servant (sais) who ran ahead with a big stick and beat everybody out of the way and set upon anybody who did not leap off his donkey quickly enough. Europeans suffered from this as much as Egyptians. French merchants were beaten like any other Christians, and many suffered other indignities because the Mamelukes were absolutely contemptuous of all foreigners, particularly Europeans. Napoleon eventually used this "shocking" treatment of the French merchants, which he may have read about in Niebuhr, as one of the reasons for invading Egypt. But until Napoleon's arrival the French had to suffer nobly and go on trying to hold their pride to-

[146]

gether in the streets as best they could, even when street urchins followed them through the city calling them monkeys—because the
French insisted, no matter what, on dressing in the latest French fashion. Only the British seem to have devised a devilish way around all
this undignified kowtowing and mocking. "The British consul appeared on horseback dressed like a Mohammedan lord," Niebuhr says.
That way he doffed his backside to nobody.

What seems to have made the biggest impression on Niebuhr was
the system of quick and summary justice in Cairo's courts, and the
efficient police system which, he said, kept Cairo freer of crime than
any European capital. He also admired the commercial organization
of the big okalas (warehouses) on the riverbanks, and the elegant
houses which even had piped water. He found that one of the old
muristans was still functioning, that Fustat had decayed almost to
nothing, that Babylon was still lived in, that Giza was where all the
rich Cairenes lived, and that the old canal still running through the
city to Fustat was pleasant enough when water was in it, but it simply
became "an exceedingly filthy" street when the river dried up and left
it empty.

It was Niebuhr who introduced European readers to Egypt's Oriental dancers who performed naked to the waist, "with their yellow
hands, spotted face, absurd ornaments and hair larded with stinking
pomatum . . . their movement graceful though indecent . . ." They
were mostly a Turkish taste, quite a normal one. What horrified the
Cairo Turks was the European habit of promiscuous dancing of the
two sexes. A Turk who had been to Italy and seen the carnivals there
told Niebuhr that the Christians simply became mad at certain sea-
sons of the year.

What was particularly exotic to eighteenth-century Europeans was
any form of Oriental dress, and Niebuhr describes many of Cairo's
costumes in intricate detail. The Turks wore a shirt with wide sleeves,
linen drawers, then slippers, large red breeches, a vest, a dagger, a
broad girdle, and often a burnous. The Christians wore more or less
the same, but they were not allowed to wear bright shoes, and in those
days everybody shaved their heads, leaving a little tuft on top, and
rank was determined by the kind of headdress you wore over the tuft.
Niebuhr says he could not report on the women's dress because he
never saw any. They went out totally enveloped in a sort of tent, but
he did know that all the women of the east wore drawers, even where
the men did not wear breeches. Yet the body among Moslem women
wasn't the problem it was to Europeans. "There have been many in-
stances of women," he says, "who, upon being stripped naked, eagerly

[147]

cover their faces without showing any concern about their other charms." But in comparing Egyptian and European customs he was worried that whereas in Europe the men "were daily adopting more entirely the amusements of the women, in the east they were more austere except in the harem." He did not know what passed in those solitary retreats, but "it is very possible that the amusements are extremely childish."

It is trade that brings Niebuhr to the crux of this tempting city. He knew what to look for and found it. Lint and linen went to Marseilles, cotton to Italy, sugar to Europe in general, although it was dearer than West Indian sugar. It was forbidden to export rice, but "the Americans are even said to have brought rice hither for some time, from Carolina. And if this be so there can be no better proof of the astonishing decline of agriculture in Egypt." Egypt was then importing cloth from France and, — strange as it may seem — spices, which had been sent all the way round the Cape from the east to Europe and then sent back to Egypt. Coffee came from the Americas illegally, and caravans from Arabia and Ethiopia brought in ivory, ostrich feathers and tamarinds and gold dust, which the Arab traders bartered in the city for cloth, seed pearls, coral, guns and ready-made clothes.

Though Britain was rapidly expanding her world trade at this time, she did not seem to be much interested in trade with Egypt. What British agents were really in Cairo for was to keep their eyes on the richer jewel of Empire — India. Egypt was the natural barrier between Europe and India, so Britain's main interest in Cairo at the end of the eighteenth century remained strategic rather than commercial, whereas France had already developed a considerable trade with Egypt. France's social interest in Egypt was also far more involved than Britain's. Catholic missionaries were already established in Cairo: Jesuits, Cordeliers and Fathers of the Propagation of the Christian Faith, and though they were mainly concerned (as all subsequent missionaries were) with proselytizing their fellow Christian Copts (they had no hope of making any impression on the Moslems), nonetheless they represented a serious French presence in Egypt, as important in their way as the merchants and the diplomats.

Finally, the most significant passage for any European statesman reading Niebuhr's description in 1792 when it was published was his picture of the Citadel, which was really the center of Turkish authority in Egypt. The Citadel was divided into three parts: the palace of the Ottoman pasha, the Janissaries' quarters and the Azabs' quarters. But Niebuhr says that the palace of the pasha was falling into ruins. Nobody in fact cared what state the pasha lived in, and he says that "the Turkish Pashas are in general ill-lodged." If Napoleon read that sentence it must have told him a great deal about the weak condition of Ottoman rule in Cairo.

It is more likely that Napoleon read the work of a compatriot named Count Constantin François de Volney, who cashed in a small inheritance to pay for a long trip to Syria and Egypt in 1783–1785. Volney's Cairo is utterly different from Niebuhr's, and allowing for the difference in outlook between them, plus whatever had happened to the city in the twenty years since Niebuhr's visit, it is sometimes hard to believe that Volney isn't, like the French merchants in Cairo, being rather determinedly French about the city and simply seeing it as he wanted to see it. But Volney was a far more enlightened man than Niebuhr, and what he brought with him to Egypt was a very lively agnosticism and a revolutionary suspicion of anything as feudal and wasteful as Turkish colonialism, so there is often far more logic in his description than in Niebuhr's.

"At Cairo itself," Volney says, "the stranger on his arrival is struck with the universal appearance of wretchedness and misery. The crowds, which throng the streets, present to his sight nothing but filthy rags, and disgusting nudities . . . Everything he sees or hears reminds him he is in the country of slavery and tyranny. Nothing is talked of but internecine dissensions, the public misery, pecuniary extortions, bastinadoes and murders. There is no security for life or property. Justice herself puts to death without formality. The officer of the night in his rounds, and the officer of the day in his circuit, judge, condemn and execute in the twinkling of an eye, without appeal . . . the head of the unhappy victim falls into the leathern bag in which it is received for fear of spoiling the place."

Volney hates the ugly dogs which roam the streets and the swooping kites. He is shocked by the appearance of the children, who are misshapen and wretched, with pale and puffed faces, swollen bellies, meager extremities and yellow skins, and he realizes that most of them will soon die. But he liked the Cairo bathhouses. "The masseurs," he says, "are boys who knead the flesh, crack all the joints, scrape the scurf, eradicate the superfluous hairs, rub the body gently and are said to be subservient to the pleasures of the bather."

It is clearly a sad and miserable place to Volney, and there is a hint in his description that someone might come and rescue the Egyptians from their misery. "Were Egypt possessed by a nation friendly to the fine arts," he says, "discoveries might be made there which would make us better acquainted with antiquity." Who, to a Frenchman, was the nation "friendly to the fine arts"? He suggests, for instance, that this friendly nation might be allowed to open up the Second Pyramid, and adds that the total demolition of it could be happily managed for about two thousand pounds. But it was Volney (an excellent scholar) who insisted that the pyramids were not temples or observation posts, but tombs.

The young soldier Napoleon seems to be reading all this over the author's shoulder as Volney goes on for page after page about the weak and wretched state of the city. How much, therefore, of Niebuhr's more dispassionate view can one really accept? An English traveler, W. G. Browne, who spent eleven months in Egypt between 1792 and 1798, on the very eve of Napoleon's arrival, says that Niebuhr's serious concern was Arabia, not Egypt; in fact Egypt was incidental to him. And Browne then proceeds to confirm, in cautious English fashion, much that Volney has written. He says that even the Europeans only survive in the city as virtual prisoners, so who can blame them for amusing themselves? To an eye accustomed to Europe's wide streets and uniformity, Cairo appears disgusting.

He too (like Volney) estimates the pasha's role as being a mere cipher for the mercenaries. He also sees the dogs, the beggars, the filthy canal ("a dunghill"), the cheap and very lovely marble bathhouses, the warehouses, and the women who walk around with only eyes and fingers showing. And he says that women are considered beautiful only if they are fair and fat. But he also describes rich houses on Elephant Lake, and good reservoirs and many coffeehouses, brothels and bazaars which are "copiously supplied." He calculated the population of the city in these last days of Ottoman rule as three hundred thousand. In Niebuhr's time the Turks had farmed out the city's customshouse to Cairo Jews, who ran it profitably and well, but in Browne's time the Jews had lost the customshouse to the Syrians. The Jewish population had also decreased, but there were plenty of Greeks, Syrians, Armenians and Moroccans in the city, though strangely enough few Turkish inhabitants. (There never were many real Turks in Cairo.) There was a big business in slaves, spices, shawls and wheat. Rice was now exported. Browne gives us a full description of the Mamelukes, who wore red pants, red slippers, and a peculiar green cap, and they always carried a pair of pistols, a saber and a dagger. They also wore chain mail under their vests. A slave purchased by a Mameluke still automatically became a Mameluke, but Mameluke wives seldom had children because they practiced abortion.

But Browne's better description of the city suggests a little more beauty than Volney saw. Bulaq, the port, was a large irregular town, but full of beautiful gardens rich in vegetables. Masr al Atika (Babylon) was "pleasantly situated and well inhabited," but Fustat was simply a long street running parallel with the river. Gezira Island was covered with gardens, Imbaba across the river had cows, Giza had a palace and a foundry for cannon, and gunboats — all of them about to go up in smoke when Napoleon marched on the city — were anchored at the quayside.

Browne had described the city which Napoleon was about to see for himself, but even more, he predicted what would happen to the Mamelukes if and when it came to a fight. He said that as individuals the Mamelukes were the finest soldiers in the east, but in a regular battle conducted by maneuvers they would be quite inferior to disciplined European troops. This was, in fact, the military difference that Napoleon brought with him. Knights in mail armor, charging bravely into the thick of the fight, meant nothing to Napoleon's well-deployed and unified veterans of the German and Italian campaigns, who had learned to expose themselves only of necessity.

What Browne ultimately describes is a city on the verge of social disintegration. Niebuhr had found it a solid city, Volney a sad one, and Browne shows why it was so wretched. In 1798 a laborer in Egypt was paid one-seventh of a piaster a day, about 50 piasters a year, which was worse than slavery when you consider that Murad Bey, the leading Mameluke took fifteen hundred piasters a day every day out of the mint for his out-of-pocket expenses; 2,100,000 acres of land were taxed by the pasha and the Mamelukes six piasters a day every day — a fortune; and the money came out of the peasants' bread, not out of the Mamelukes' pockets.

The situation in Egypt itself got so bad that Coptic villages in Upper Egypt openly rebelled and refused to pay taxes, and there is no indication that anybody dared try to collect from them. What must have encouraged Napoleon, too, as these reports reached him in France, was the generally accepted view that the people of Cairo had stubbornly preserved their own identity despite centuries of Turkish domination. The Turkish language had made no impression on the ordinary population, nor had Turkish manners. The ruling families took on many Turkish habits, and even kept them to the last, but mentally the city remained thoroughly Egyptian; and far from dying off, the intellectual life of the city, though limited to literature, history, poetry and religious philosophy, was always alive and, more often than not, fierce.

This was the expectant city which Napoleon's disciplined soldiers would find waiting for them without really wanting them. But before

Citizen Napoleon brings all the benefits of the French Revolution to Cairo it is worthwhile to take a look at what is left in Cairo now of that long Ottoman twilight which so dimmed the horizon of this sunlit old city.

In their time the Turks built no "great" buildings in Cairo, but Cairo is full of their very attractive mosques. But what is lacking in all of them is Cairo's usual violence of inspiration. The craftsmanship is impeccable, but the invention dull. Yet the Turks did change the character of the Cairo mosque, because they preferred the public mosque (masjid) to the college mosque (madrasah) and they liked the Byzantine style of Istanbul rather than the traditional Arab shapes.

Simply by comparing one of the first Turkish mosques in Cairo, the Malika Safiya (1610), with one of the last, the Mohammed Ali mosque (1856), you can see how this Istanbul-Byzantium line arrived and survived and decayed, during two hundred years, from a light and pleasant enclosure to the massive indulgence which sits on the Citadel like a fat purring cat in a satin-lined basket. The small mosque of Malika Safiya is just off what is now called Shari'al Qal'a (Citadel Street, which used to be Shari' Mohammed Ali). When you look at its roof of domes, little domes and a big one, and at its cylindrical minaret with a cone on top, you can see in it the true Istanbul parentage of so many other Turkish mosques in Cairo. Malika Safiya herself was not a Turk. She was a Venetian of the Baffo family. Her father was once governor of Corfu, and Safiya was captured (rather like Constanza in Mozart's *Il Seraglio*) by Corsairs when she was about fourteen and sent to the royal harem, where she became a proud Moslem queen and eventually built this mosque for her son, Sultan Mohammed. It is a feminine little mosque, and the whole area of the arcade inside is crowned by delicate cupolas which might well have been thought up by a beautiful and desirable woman.

There are so many more of these Turkish mosques in the city that I have often walked around the streets with a Byzantium sort of mind trying to detect them among the other mosques I didn't know. On the whole it was possible to pick every one of them, and no great detection work was needed, yet the discovery was always surprising, because most Turkish mosques are, in fact, as intrinsically beautiful as the rest. They were reduced in their dimensions and limited in their artistic invention only by a lack of money, not a lack of skill.

What most experts on Turkish art in Cairo like to call a little Turkish gem is not a mosque at all but a sibil, a fountain, which is at the Y junction near Barkuq's madrasah and Nasir's tomb, in the Shari' Mu'iz. It was built in 1774 as a school and a fountain by Abdel Rahman Kikhya, a Janissary turned Azab. The kikhya (deputy) was a clean, charitable, corrupt governor who built a palace at Bulaq and another at Abdin, and added to the Azhar and intelligently rebuilt a number of Cairo's monuments. He was a strange little man because he had a very white skin and an almost white beard, and Gabarti says he was extremely neat and even coquettish, and his lovely fountain *is* the best example of Turkish art in Cairo. It has a façade which is almost too Turkish, but it is so well done that it seems to look better and better every time you see it. I knew it had originally been built as a school, but I was nonetheless surprised when I walked into it one day recently to find that it was still a school, which means that someone among the city fathers is keeping the good tradition of the school-fountain alive here. All the boys and girls from this crowded corner of the city sitting in the classroom were dressed in neat *tabliers*, and they were learning their alif-ba's from a modern textbook illustrated with cars and trucks rather than camels and date palms. The shy young woman teaching them had a cataract in her right eye, and she obligingly stopped her lessons while I looked around at the faïence walls and peered through the windows at the street below, and when I went outside again I could just hear the pupils reciting their lessons above the noisy street sellers and the men hammering copper or tin in the bazaars and the children playing along the street in the dust and dirt of this famous old crossroads.

There was a brief moment before Napoleon arrived when it seemed as if Egypt was about to emerge from this Turkish cocoon under its own steam and re-establish itself once more as an independent Mameluke power. In 1796–1797 the people of Egypt were in revolt against the Turks, demanding that something be done to relieve their misery and cut them free from the dead weight of Ottoman taxes and unbearable economic bondage. There was in fact a sort of historical race between the local Mamelukes and the faraway French to see who would be able to take advantage of this local discontent.

The local men had first go, and one of the Egyptian Mamelukes, Ali Bey, occupied Cairo, thoroughly humiliated the Turkish garrison in the city, and sent the Turkish pasha back to the Porte. Ali Bey then attacked Syria and Arabia and was so successful that he was even acknowledged caliph of Mecca, so that Egypt was suddenly a sort of independent state within the Ottoman Empire. Inevitably Ali Bey was betrayed and murdered, and he was succeeded by Murad Bey, who shared his authority with another Mameluke, Ibrahim, and together they were ruling Egypt when Napoleon appeared off the coast of Alexandria. This time, however, the Mamelukes were historically

The Valid Fountain.

quite unsuited to save Egypt from the Turks and the French alike. They were far too corrupt, ignorant, primitive and selfish.

At first Murad refused to believe it when he heard that Napoleon was off the coast of Egypt. When it finally penetrated his intelligence he sent for the most respected foreigner in Cairo, Rosetti the Tuscan consul, and told him that as far as he, Murad, was concerned the French soldiers were all donkey boys. He asked Rosetti as a European to give them a handful of silver each when they arrived and to send them packing, because he had no desire to kill them. Rosetti tried to explain just who Napoleon was, but Murad knew nothing of history or Europe. When Napoleon began to advance on Cairo, Murad confidently sent ten thousand Mamelukes and thirty thousand irregulars (mainly Egyptians, Albanians, Negroes and Bedouins) to face Napoleon's forty thousand French veterans.

At Imbaba, now a suburb of Cairo and just across the river from Gezira, the Mamelukes and the French under General Louis Desaix fought it out. It was Saturday, July 21, 1798, the feast of St. Victor. "As soon as the Egyptians saw the French army they hurled themselves at it with fury," Gabarti reports, and he does say "Egyptians," not "Mamelukes." "The battle was bloody on both sides," Gabarti adds. But the French maneuvered all over the place and the Mameluke officers didn't, so that the Egyptians were caught in a terrible crossfire. It was a hot windy day and the citizens of Cairo watched the dust and smoke of the battle rising over their city, and they heard the drums, the rifle shots, the cannon; and at the end of it all the Mamelukes were defeated and fled, and nothing they did that day was either brave or intelligent or worthy. Murad Bey himself rushed home to his palace at Giza, collected what he could of his fortune in fifteen minutes, told his soldiers to burn all the military stores and gunpowder and gunboats along the river at Giza, and then fled.

The people of Cairo saw the Giza side of their city in flames and thought the French had done it, so the rich began to pack up and get out as fast as they could, and many of the poor followed them. But they really had nowhere to go, and many of them were attacked by Bedouins as they waited like refugees just outside the city. Pillaging and murder began in the streets even before the French got into the city. In this confusion some of the sheikhs of Cairo gathered at the Azhar and sent a letter to Napoleon, and while they were thus negotiating the surrender of the city to the French, the angry populace, who felt deserted and betrayed, broke into the palaces of Ibrahim and Murad and set them on fire.

On Wednesday, Napoleon rode into the city and took possession, and Gabarti, beginning his diary of this eventful year, says that for Cairo and Egypt it was to become a period of "great battles, terrible events, disastrous facts, calamities, unhappinesses, sufferings, persecutions, upsets in the order of things, terror, revolutions, disorders, devastations — in a word the beginning of a series of great misfortunes."

11

Napoleon's Cairo

N APOLEON did bring a wide selection of these disorders to Cairo, but he also brought Europe with him, and when he left the city three years later it would never be quite the same Oriental town again. The English would come a hundred years after him and occupy Egypt for seventy years, but even during British occupation modern Cairo would go on emerging as a French-looking city, not an English one, with French bourgeois taste rather than English middle-class manners. Looking dispassionately at what is left of this French frontage of modern Cairo, it seems as if the English, when they came, weren't worried about the outward appearance of the city, provided that the real influence on the economy, administration and politics of the country remained theirs, which it did. But the French legacy is written all over the European part of Cairo.

The British-French rivalry for empire had brought Napoleon to Cairo in the first place. As Nelson but nobody else seemed to understand, Napoleon was eventually on his way to India, and to get there he had to cross this barrier of Egypt. Volney had already mentioned the possibility of cutting a "Suez" canal through the isthmus which separated the Red Sea from the Mediterranean, thus opening up direct communications with the east. This was obviously in the French mind from the beginning. The European trade war and the European empire war had been escalating for years, and now it had reached the point where the east had become the highest stake in it. Long ago Leibnitz had suggested to Louis XIV that he invade Egypt, and Bourrienne had told Napoleon that the conquest of Egypt would make up for the loss of the French West Indian colonies to the British.

The point anyway was that the route across Egypt was still the fastest and potentially the best trade route to the east, provided that Egypt and the trade itself were in European hands and not at the mercy of some hungry Oriental despot laying fantastic customs dues on everything that passed through Egypt.

Yet it wasn't quite so simple. Talleyrand is supposed to have thought up the invasion of Egypt as a means of "ostracizing" Napoleon to a faraway place, and by the time Napoleon realized it the expedition was too far advanced to be canceled. But machiavellian plot or genuine drive to the east, the French looked upon this invasion of Egypt as a sort of left wing for the eventual invasion of England.

Napoleon needed three hundred ships to get him and his forty thousand soldiers to Egypt. He was taking with him not only the cream of his staff officers — Murat, Kléber, Bessières, Desaix, Davout, Savary, and Berthier, but also a hundred savants led by Monge and Denon who would produce for Napoleon, even after he was dead, what is still the greatest European work on Egypt — the *Description*. Napoleon's three hundred ships set out from Toulon and other Mediterranean ports, and the British admiralty thought they were going to sail westward to pass through the Straits of Gibraltar to attack England through Ireland.

Nelson was sent to intercept them with a fairly small squadron, to prevent their reaching the English Channel. But Nelson was convinced that they were heading east not west, and he cleverly anticipated them and chased the French squadron as far as the Egyptian port of Abukir (near Alexandria), where he wrecked their fighting fleet, having just missed (by the idiocy of his seniors) a possible earlier engagement in which he might have met up with Napoleon's own ship *L'Orient*, with what possible results we can only guess.

Though the French landed their soldiers in Egypt, Nelson's victory over the French fleet at Abukir meant that Napoleon never again had safe communications with France. He was in fact defeated in Egypt even before he conquered it, because he could never get any reinforcements from home. His landing was successful enough and he had no difficulty in capturing Alexandria, but as he marched south through the Delta he met the first signs of popular resistance, and Vivant Denon describes how peasants and townsmen rather than soldiers fought the French.

When Napoleon had defeated the Mameluke armies at Imbaba, but before he entered Cairo, he sent for the sheikhs of the city and told them that he intended to set up a grand diwan of ten of their number to rule the country and institute the laws, and this ultimately was the way he did rule. He rode into Cairo on Wednesday, July 25, 1798, and took over a brand-new palace which Mohammed Bey al Elfi had built at great expense but had not yet occupied. It stood in its own gardens in the place which eventually became the site of Shepheard's Hotel, and that too is a little bit of Cairo melodrama, because European occupation began on that particular spot and really ended there when Shepheard's was burned down in 1952.

Only a few French soldiers entered the city with Napoleon. Most stayed over the river with their units, probably as a precaution. In any case the ordinary Egyptians of Cairo were not yet involved in the fight. Until now the Mamelukes had been responsible for the defense of Egypt and they had failed miserably. The Egyptians themselves had not yet realized that the responsibility was now theirs, because at first they were a little stunned by their new masters. The French also seemed to realize that there was a hiatus, and they too were cautious, as if they didn't know yet how to go about occupying the city.

For the first few days, therefore, French soldiers were able to walk the streets of Cairo unarmed, and they gave nobody any trouble. They joked with the people and paid exorbitant prices for everything they bought, which encouraged the population to come out of hiding. Soon the merchants were selling the French soldiers bread, sugar, soap, tobacco, and the shops began to open up and the city to come to life again. Almost overnight the French merchants of Cairo opened up a French restaurant for the army—the first restaurant Cairo had ever seen, and the idea of people sitting at a table and eating with knives and forks and then paying a fixed price for what they got amazed and delighted Egyptians. French-style cafés for the French soldiers also appeared, and like this the French stepped very lightly into Cairo, and it was a clever beginning for them.

But in the meantime Napoleon was quickly and efficiently establishing himself militarily in the city. He not only occupied all the strategic positions and buildings which he considered absolutely desirable for his defense of the city, but he quietly set up artillery all around the outside of the town, and from this fairly secure military position he tried to establish closer contact with the diwan of sheikhs he had persuaded to cooperate with him after the defeat at Imbaba. Some of these sheikhs were of the Mameluke families, but they were, strictly speaking, religious or political leaders who were a sort of professional class. In fact one of Napoleon's principal ideological weapons in Cairo was these sheikhs, who were impressed by European culture.

What Napoleon also did in the first few weeks was to set up his Institut d'Egypte, so that his hundred savants would begin their great work throwing light on Egypt past and present. Initially, Napoleon was more interested in the present than the past, and the first recorded discussions in this Institut reveal something of the French problems in the city and what they had found there. Citizen Napoleon was part of the mathematics section in the science division and he attended the first meeting to propose the following question: "Can the ovens that bake the bread of the army be improved? How?"

In another session, Monsieur le Baron Lavicy, who was surgeon of the guard, contributed a dissertation on the problem of the health of his soldiers. He said that since their arrival in Egypt the French soldiers were suffering from three principal diseases: ophthalmia, tetanus, and atrophy of the testicles. Bad luck on the French, but Lavicy's description of his sick soldiers is a rather sad comment on the arrival of French enlightenment, because he concludes it by noting that the army had just established a syphilis hospital for their troops. There is no comment from Citizen Napoleon on this state of affairs because he concentrated on his own interests, and one of the first things he asked the Institut to do, besides improving the ovens, was to prepare him a good and accurate map of the city. So the geodesists began by simply drawing a line from Cairo to the river and measuring it: 1042 meters 36 centimeters; and from this they built up the first accurate map of the city, which was published eventually in the *Description.*

What the savants at the Institut also did for Napoleon was to go around Cairo finding out, firsthand now, just what the mentality and the condition of the city were. They investigated trade, industry, work and language, and one of the first of these reports was by Citizen Louis Frank on the slave market. The slaves in Cairo then were all African, and most of them were kidnapped adults or children who had been seized in payment for debts. They were "stored" in local warehouses like any other goods for sale. "When a European sees this market for the first time," Citizen Frank says, "with the Negroes for the most part naked — boys and girls of all ages and mothers with children at the breasts — it is almost impossible to resist the painful sentiment it occasions." But if you return, he says, when they are about to be sold, which meant they would have a home, their gaiety and insouciance was much less pitiful, and the women always tried to please their prospective buyer by covering themselves with oil and plaiting their hair.

Napoleon obviously got all this material on his desk at the Ezbekiya Palace, and using it almost as military intelligence helped him get the best grip he could on the city. He seems to have realized that he was always vulnerable to popular rebellion, so he began to open up those streets which he considered militarily dangerous to him, and he ordered all streetlamps to be lit outside the houses. But he also began to insist now on some visible and real signs of submission from the populace, so he issued an order that everybody in Cairo should wear a cockade as a sign of "submission and friendship." This was obviously the sort of pressure which was becoming inevitable as the population began to show the first signs of serious unrest. So many people ignored the order in fact that Napoleon had to withdraw it. He then called together all the sheikhs of his diwan in his Ezbekiya headquarters and presented each of them with a cockade, but when he pinned one on the breast of Sheikh al Shackhoui the sheikh tore it off in a fury and stamped out.

Almost everything Napoleon did in the city was now resented by the population. He tried to level the graves of a cemetery at Ezbekiya to have clear ground around his headquarters, but the people were so hostile that he gave up the idea. He taxed all buildings, and again the people resisted the scheme angrily and volubly. Step by step his decrees were resisted, and eventually the citizens of Cairo became so incensed simply with the French presence that they demonstrated outside the Azhar. Napoleon sent General Dupuy to make a show of force and to disperse the demonstrators. But the Egyptian populace bushwhacked the general and killed him and many of his soldiers. They then occupied the remaining street gates of Cairo and raised barricades all over the city, and thus, in 1798, began Cairo's first revolt against French occupation.

The French met the revolt by setting up cannon in the Citadel and bombing the Azhar and its surroundings, doing a great deal of damage to the mosque and the surrounding houses. "It was the most terrible damage the inhabitants had ever seen," Gabarti says. Some of the rebels were deterred by the cannon, which were a totally new experience for the city, but in the Huseiniya quarter they refused to be frightened, and they stopped fighting only when they had run out of ammunition. In the night the French sent in a force under cover of darkness and demolished the barricades in the streets, and the cavalry smashed their way into the Azhur and (according to Gabarti) tied their horses to the kibla, urinated on the walls, stamped on the Koran, drank wine in the courtyard, and undressed anybody they could catch. And Gabarti adds: "God alone knows how many people died on this day."

But from now on the citizens of Cairo would never stop for a moment their harassment of the French, and it is clear now that what they did they did alone, without any help from outsiders or Mamelukes or soldiers. Napoleon was shaken by this violent resistance, and he insisted, under threat of more reprisals, that the sheikhs tell him who the ringleaders of the revolt were. The sheikhs refused to inform at first, but eventually they betrayed some of the "leaders." One of those named was the chief of the Corporation of the Blind, and he and four others were immediately arrested and shot. The French then demolished parts of Giza, old Cairo (Babylon) and Shubra, and they built fortifications all around the city, including many little forts which still survive in the troughs of the Mukattam Hills. They also razed mosques and small palaces and houses in the city, in fact mosques in Cairo were now treated by the French as dangerous little fortresses for the population.

As a hopeful demonstration of French power, and maybe as a sort of divertissement as well, a hot-air balloon was sent up from Ezbekiya. But the cupola collapsed and the balloon came down with a crash, and the French "blushed with shame." Next day the French poisoned all the dogs in the city because they always barked a warning when French soldiers approached. Napoleon also began to add to the Citadel, and it was at this time that the French took over the ruined mosque of Hakim and turned it into a fortress. Napoleon also planned to open up new wide boulevards from the Citadel to various parts of the town. He had in mind especially a wide straight street from the Citadel to his headquarters in Ezbekiya. But even the Frenchman Paul Ravaisse says that happily this was never done, not by Napoleon anyway, although the Khedive Ismail would do it thirty or forty years later and call it Shari' Mohammed Ali. But Napoleon did cut a wide road from the Bab el Luk to the Bab al Adaoui, slicing through houses and older streets and using French workers and paid (!) Egyptians and "simple, perfect tools" (Gabarti) and not primitive panniers but handcarts. He also cleared the ground around his headquarters at Ezbekiya, despite the protests, leveling houses and trees to keep the space open, and he turned Zahir Beibars' mosque into a fortress and put cannon on the roof.

Napoleon had once again secured the city, but by the end of 1798 his role in Cairo seemed to have become entirely repressive, punitive and military, and as far as the ordinary people were concerned this was definitely so.

Yet despite this brutality there can be no doubt that the French occupation was beneficial to Cairo, not for its military presence but for the enlightenment it brought with it. Napoleon really had two headquarters in Cairo, one military and one intellectual, and at first he managed to combine these very well, but as the military situation outside Egypt began to press on him he seems to have suffered from a sort of growing lack of interest in the intellectual future of the city. In France he had prepared the expedition to Egypt with very long-range eyes, as if he intended to stay there forever. He had planned to establish, from the moment of his arrival, a sound French cultural basis for the future. The difficulty and expense of importing a hundred savants with all their equipment as part of the military arrival could hardly be considered merely a means of satisfying French scientific curiosity about Egypt. But from the moment the British defeated his fleet at Abukir, Napoleon knew that his chances of staying in Egypt were slim, and one always gets the feeling, reading Napoleon on Egypt, that his mind was already somewhere else; that he was attending to the affairs of Cairo all right, and even involving himself intellectually with his savants who were preparing to spread enlightenment and science among the Egyptians, but in effect he was really thinking militarily of Syria and Turkey, or some future battle which would rescue him from this strategic trap he had got himself into.

There seemed from the very beginning therefore to be two distinct French policies in Cairo: the military and the intellectual. And they steadily grew farther apart as the occupation had to defend itself more and more against attack in the streets and subversion in the administration. Meanwhile, the nonviolent scholars made a deeper and deeper impression on Cairo's intelligentsia in the richly endowed academies of the Institut de l'Egypte.

This valuable Institut had been set up in two houses in the Nasriya quarter of Cairo. It was divided into four sections — industry, health, science and mathematics, art and literature — and there were thirty-six French scholars in the four divisions. The industry, health and science sections, with laboratories and workshops and libraries, were established in the brand-new house of a Circassian Mameluke named Hasan al Kachef, who had fled the city with Murad and the rest of the Mameluke lords. The artists and painters were in another house nearby which had belonged to a Turkish deputy named Ibrahim al Sinnari.

The Kachef house opened every morning at ten and stayed open all day. "Simple soldiers themselves go to read in this library," Gabarti says. If a Moslem wanted to visit the establishment they didn't forbid him but on the contrary encouraged him warmly, particularly if he were interested in the sciences. The French would also show their Moslem visitors chemical experiments and give them electric shocks and very fine books in Arabic. The French had even brought with them a sort of mural which pictured Mohammed himself ascending to heaven, and although it was forbidden in the Moslem religion to portray Mohammed in any form, Gabarti is not shocked, and he describes the portrait as accurate according to known description. Just across the street in the Sinnari house the painters were usually engaged on scenes of Cairo (which we now have in the *Description*), and a well-known French portraitist named Arago painted many of the principal sheikhs who came to visit the Institut. Sometimes the artists were also busy painting animals or insects or fish the French scientists had discovered in Egypt.

Knowing today how significant this Institut has been to Cairo's new link with Europe, and the long history of benefit and evil that followed the cultural contacts it began, it is always worthwhile for anyone going to Cairo to take a look at this corner of the Sayida Zeinab quarter to see what is left of this old headquarters of French enlightenment. Kachef's house, which was the main part of the Institut, has gone; it was pulled down and rebuilt as the Government Saniya School for Girls. The Sinnari house, which the painters used, is still standing, and after 1952 it was handed over to Cairo's artists. They use it now as a sort of collective headquarters, and they also exhibit there. When I was last there the attractively restored courtyard of the house had an exhibition of sculpture by Anwar Abdel Mowela, one of modern Egypt's best young sculptors, who died in 1966; and the upstairs rooms were also exhibiting modern paintings and products of Egyptian folk art revival. Almost all the modern paintings exhibited now in the Sinnari house could trace their ancestry to the French, so Napoleon is still around somewhere.

But for all the long-range success of this intellectual activity, Napoleon's destiny in Egypt had become such a brutal one that the Institut didn't really help him. Every day he had to execute more and more citizens of Cairo as the population openly opposed him. During one day alone ninety people were shot in the Citadel, and two women and five Jews were arrested and thrown into the Nile to drown. Gabarti also complained that certain Copts, Syrians and Jews who were in service to the French were becoming insupportable because they now rode horses and carried arms and insulted Moslems. Napoleon seems to have encouraged this newfound "arrogance" of his friends, because as always he needed the minorities to help him rule. But nothing they did or Napoleon himself did seemed to help, and it is hard to say at what point he finally abandoned all hope of staying in Egypt. By the end of summer 1798 he was looking nervously north because he believed that Turkey and Britain, in alliance, were preparing to attack him from Syria. He decided he would have to strike first, so he began to prepare an attack on Syria. On September 22, 1798, he rode out of Cairo to make a reconnaissance as far as Suez. According to Gabarti he went without benefit of a kitchen, but he took along three chicken sandwiches wrapped in paper for lunch, and French soldiers marched with their bread stuck on the tips of their lances. One thing that seems to suggest that Napoleon still hoped to keep some hold on this great crossroads between Europe and the east is that he told Citizen Peyre to make geometric measurements of the level of the ancient canal which once ran from Suez to the Mediterranean. His chief of staff, General Berthier, considered the proposed canal "one of the greatest and most useful works in the world."

But Napoleon returned to Cairo almost immediately, and in February 1799 he and his army set out to take Syria from the Turks and the handful of British forces who were there helping them. Napoleon's departure from Cairo says a lot for what had happened to his army after less than a year there. The baggage train was an incredible sight, according to Gabarti; it included beds and mattresses and white and black slaves whom the French had acquired from the Mameluke houses, and women of the city who had become camp followers and who now wore French clothes, and all sorts of wasteful and quite unmilitary equipment which Napoleon seemed to simply ignore as if his heart weren't really in it anyway.

The French failed to take Syria. They were defeated at Acre mainly by British sailors. Napoleon hurried back to Cairo with his tail between his legs, and with only seven thousand men left of the twelve thousand he had taken with him. The defeated column entered Cairo through the Bab el Nasr — drums, carts, women, children and pale soldiers, and Cairo knew he had been beaten. Everybody was delighted, and almost at the same time that he returned to Cairo the Turks landed at Abukir. Suddenly Cairo began to expect something big to happen. Utterly on the defensive now, Napoleon rushed north to face the Turks, and because this time there were no British bluejackets to help them, Napoleon easily defeated the Ottoman armies, and he returned to Cairo with thousands of Turkish prisoners.

But by now it was only a matter of time before some better-prepared Anglo-Turkish attack would crush him, and rather than face inevitable humiliation in Egypt and knowing there were richer pickings at home he fled to France, where he became First Consul after the overthrow of the Directory by the coup of 18 Brumaire (November 9–10) in 1799. He left Kléber in charge of Cairo, hoping at least for a long delaying action. But Sir Sidney Smith, who had defeated Napoleon at Acre, now appeared on the Egyptian borders alongside the Turks, and Kléber, knowing he could not win a battle, signed a convention agreeing to evacuate the country (1800).

It was now, the nonviolent Gabarti says, that the "low inhabitants" of Cairo began to prove themselves blind, because they showed their hatred of the French to their faces, insulting and ridiculing them. The French began to evacuate the city, and Murad and the other Mamelukes, who had been hanging around like jackals since their defeat at Imbaba in 1798, appeared on the outskirts ready to reoccupy the city the moment the French left it. The Turks too were not far from Cairo, waiting. For weeks the Turks, the Mamelukes and French all eyed each other nervously around the city. In the meantime the ordinary Egyptians began murdering French soldiers in the streets again. Only the people actually fought the French now.

The real problem for Kléber was that he couldn't leave Egypt so easily. The French had no ships, and the British had quickly repudiated the convention for the French evacuation because they believed that the French were stalling. The Turks and the Mamelukes began massing again near ancient Heliopolis as if preparing for an attack on the city, and Kléber felt trapped. He was caught between a hostile city at his back and enemies all around him, so he marched out of Cairo and hit the Turks quickly and savagely at Heliopolis. The Turkish command and troops fled after the first attack. The Cairenes heard the gunfire and armed themselves with clubs because they had no firearms. Then the fleeing Turks and Mamelukes actually arrived on the outskirts of the city, and the citizens knew as they fought the French that they were in as much danger from the Turks. So far no soldier in Egypt, not the great Mamelukes nor the Turks, had really fought the French, only the Egyptians had. In particular the citizens of Cairo had fought disciplined French soldiers with a great deal of spirit and determination.

Though they had been defeated in battle, the Turks and Mamelukes knew that the French were unable to go on launching strong attacks, so they took up positions on the edges of Cairo. In semioccupation of some parts of the city, the Turks needed a scapegoat to divert attention from their own failure and cowardice, so the Turkish commander ordered all Christians to be massacred. The Turks knew that there was popular ill feeling against those Christians (by no means a majority) who had identified themselves with the French. But Moslems too were arrested and murdered or manhandled by the same gangs who were killing the Christians, so it was much more than a religious issue that inspired this brutality.

The Turks even managed to occupy Ezbekiya, but the French bombarded them from the Citadel, which they still held. The whole city was now in a state of civil war, and in effect what was happening was a new popular uprising against the French. The people asked the Turks and the Mamelukes to help them fight the French, but both refused and went on tightening their own grip on the city. But by now the people more or less controlled the streets, despite the confusion and the Turks, and the French regiments under Kléber began to bombard the city from all the forts around the city perimeter.

Besieged and battered, the city began to go hungry, and at one point the sheikhs were so worried about the city's being reduced to ruins by the French bombardment that they tried to negotiate with Kléber, but when they came back to the city the people insulted them and knocked their turbans off. The French then tried another tactic. They began to set fire to the city, including Bulaq. But still Cairo resisted. Inevitably, however, French troops came back into the city, breaking through the barricades at Bab al Hadid. Once again the waiting and expectant Turks and Mamelukes were the first to collapse; they agreed to evacuate Cairo, and the French even gave them money and camels to speed them on their way. The population wanted to kill Osman Bey and Nassouh, the leaders, for giving in so easily, but they barricaded themselves in a mosque. As the Turks and Mamelukes finally left Cairo the angry population insulted them.

Deprived of any serious military help by the Turks and Mamelukes, the unarmed population were overwhelmed and once more the French controlled the city, and thus the second revolt was defeated. The revolt had lasted thirty-seven days, and almost every quarter in Cairo had suffered, particularly Ezbekiya and the rich houses around the little Lake al Rotli near Ezbekiya. The French had reoccupied the middle of the city in force, although they no longer wanted it and desired only to get out of Cairo and go home. But there was still no way of getting out unless the British let them go, and there was no sign of that. By now the French soldiers and the people of Cairo lived in such an atmosphere of mutual hatred that only something dramatic could bring all this to a head, and on June 17, 1800, General Kléber was stabbed to death on the terrace of the palace headquarters at Ezbekiya. When the news spread through the streets the population expected half Cairo to be annihilated as a reprisal, and the city literally held its breath. But the French were afraid to unleash any excessive revenge, and they gladly seized on the admission of the assassin, an Azharite (a student of religion) named Suleiman Alepin, that he was more or less alone in the plot — an almost impossible condition for any political assassin. But Alepin and two "accomplices" were all tried very formally and then legally sentenced to death. If the French had spared the city from any wild act of revenge, they did not spare the assassins. Alepin, the confessed assassin, first had to watch his two companions have their heads cut off. Then the French burned off Alepin's right hand and he was then impaled and left to die slowly; the official British historian, Sir Robert Wilson, says he took three days to do so. All three executions were enacted as a sort of savage divertissement as Kléber's funeral slowly marched by.

But the French had no logic or coherence left in their behavior in Cairo. They were trapped tigers who still had plenty of fight left in them, but little else. General Jacques Menou succeeded Kléber, and never was an occupier of a city left in such a dangerous and critical situation. Some time before this Menou had become a Moslem and married a Moslem wife (their son, Said Soliman Mourad Jacques Menou, was the first "citizen" recorded by the French in their census of Cairo), but Moslems never really believe in Europeans who become Moslems, so Menou remained just another Frenchman. In any case he was simply waiting for the end, and all he could do to soften the last few months of French occupation was to organize entertainments in the public gardens, which were rather vitiated by the fact that the people had to pay to get into them — another French innovation in Cairo which intrigued the Cairenes but hardly pleased them.

On March 8, 1801, British soldiers under Sir Ralph Abercromby landed at Abukir. The Turks also arrived at al Arish on the eastern frontier of Egypt, and the French knew that it was all up this time. Menou was a bad general and he was easily routed when he attacked the British near Alexandria. Militarily speaking, he should have waited for the British to attack him. Two of Britain's most famous and most orthodox and most poeticized heroes were casualties in this battle — Sir Ralph Abercromby, who was killed, and Sir John Moore, who was wounded but lived to die another day at Coruña. Sir John Hutchinson, who succeeded Abercromby as commander, isolated Menou in Alexandria by opening the sea dikes and flooding the surrounding country, thus cutting Menou off from Cairo.

With the Mameluke landowners of Egypt as their main and most admired allies, and with a Turkish army which still liked to cut off the heads of its enemies and of their own dead colleagues to claim war bounty on them, the British invested Cairo. "Deserted by Napoleon," D. A. Cameron has written, "deprived of Kléber, disheartened by the incompetence of Menou, General Belliard [French commander in Cairo] cogently argued that only some eight thousand out of a garrison of thirteen thousand remained fit for duty, that the natives were in revolt and that the plague was raging." But the British did not want to risk an attack which would involve them in street fighting, so they lined up along a canal across the river between Giza and the pyramids and waited there for the French to come to their senses and give in.

A few years ago, after a somewhat adventurous search, I found the old positions which Generals Craddock, Doyle and Sir John Moore took up near the village of Zaneen. The countryside there looks as if nothing at all has changed it in the intervening years since 1801, except that the canal the British used as a frontal defense has silted up for lack of use. Otherwise you could walk along the old dirt road and watch the dust rising and quite easily imagine those young soldiers (many of the British troops were mere boys, and many were foreigners too) sunning themselves in these fields, waiting to attack the city or set siege to it or simply march in.

Inside Cairo, General Belliard begged the Egyptians "to remain faithful to the French . . . otherwise their houses would be burned, their goods pillaged, children orphaned and women violated" (Gabarti). The French swore that Napoleon had successfully invaded England, and arranged a fireworks display at Ezbekiya to prove it, but the real fireworks were shots exchanged across the river at Bulaq between the British and the French.

On the Cairo side of the river, and once again on the edge of the city, the Turks hoped to occupy it before the British. The first official entry into the city was by twenty-five Turks, who came to a café in Huseiniya quarter, met no French resistance, and ate some biscuits and boiled beans and then returned to their camp. But the Turkish commanders were more cautious than their soldiers, and they waited.

The people were now starving because the entire city was completely surrounded by British, Turks and Mamelukes and nothing could get in or out. Sir John Hutchinson offered to revive the old convention for the evacuation of the French originally negotiated with Kléber, and the French readily agreed. An armistice was arranged, and Cairo was officially handed over to the British, Turks and Mamelukes. A Colonel Stuart entered the city first and tried to get into the Citadel, but it was abandoned and nobody had the keys to the gates, so he couldn't get in. But a French officer, who had been left behind somehow, finally opened the gates and Stuart took his dragoons in. The British then offered to protect the lost and lonely French officer, but he refused and walked off into the city, where the people stoned him to death. Then the Turks suddenly arrived at the Citadel and were furious to find the British already there.

Officially Cairo was Turkish again, not British, so the Ottoman flag was raised over the city even though the British held the Citadel. What the British found in Cairo is described by Sir Robert Wilson in his official *History of the British Expedition to Egypt,* published in 1802. He says the French had expected much of Cairo, but the British expected nothing, and even that was pitching their hopes high. He said Bulaq was in ruins and had been since the 1799 insurrection (probably the 1800 revolt). Cairo itself was shattered. Kléber's house in the Place Béquier (Ezbekiya) was still standing, and the French had even left the stains of Kléber's blood on the terrace floor. (The palace was eventually destroyed during the Mohammed Ali revolt a few years later.) Wilson says the Citadel was a miserable, paltry castle and the people of Cairo were excessively dirty, "mostly afflicted in their eyes; and swarms of beggars, distorted or unnaturally formed and wretched, crowded the streets." He describes one man who had an exposed belly "hanging down from his navel to his ankle; a blue skin contained his bowels, but which seemed so thin as to be liable every moment to burst." There is a picture of this unhappy monster in the *Description.*

Among Hutchinson's soldiers in the city were 448 men from the East India Company's artillery, a significant attendance at this victory. What was even more important was that General Hutchinson remained in Cairo to "reinstate the Mamelukes," whom the British officers admired far beyond reason for their dress, swordsmanship and horsemanship. But there were, of course, practical reasons for this admiration. With the French gone, and all ideas of a canal across the Suez isthmus with them, Britain wanted back the old status quo — the sort of feudal barrier the Turks and Mamelukes had been before. But when Sir Robert Wilson had looked around Cairo a little, he saw that "Egypt must be considered as the natural emporium for the riches of three-quarters of the world, and in her own soil could rival America in any of her productions." The status quo ante in Egypt might therefore be the safeguard for imperial India, but this soldier knew what Britain had captured, and even regretted that Egypt was not immediately constituted as an Indian colony to be properly occupied by the British and not the Turks. But the security of India came first, so the "tottering Ottoman Empire" (Wilson) and the Mamelukes were restored, to once again hold this old barrier of Egypt in the safety of darkness and ignorance.

The thirteen articles of the treaty of capitulation allowed the French fifty days to get out of Egypt. The French opened up the tomb of Kléber and took his body with them, and for some reason or other they also took the remains of his assassin Alepin. But Menou left his

Moslem wife and Moslem son behind him, and wrote into the peace agreement a request that the sheikhs of the diwan in Cairo take care of them. (One wonders now what became of them, and of their descendants.) As the French left the city the Turks began looting. The Turkish vizier's troops ravaged everything they could get their hands on, and Turks and Albanians and Janissaries and Mamelukes began their usual quarreling again. As the French soldiers left, the British officers also arrived — to visit the bazaars.

Most of the English army followed the French out of the city and marched behind them all the way to Alexandria to see them out of the country. In a remarkable little journal of letters, a British officer on Hutchinson's staff calling himself "Carlos Bey" (probably Major Charles Holloway) wrote in his *Non-Military Journal* . . . of the extraordinary scenes at the embarkation of the French at Rosetta, where he watched the enlightened spectacle of the departing French soldiers and officers selling their women to the English for a dollar each.

One way or another the women of Cairo had made a big impression on the French, and the French on them. Some of the experience was liberating for the Moslem women, but not all of it, because the French usually treated them as chattel slaves and concubines, much the way the Turks did.

Volney had once described the women of Cairo as phantoms, but Gabarti poured hatred and humiliation on those non-phantom Moslem women of the city who went to live with the French and dressed like the French and abandoned the veil, particularly in the last desperate days when the French were inclined to enjoy themselves at debauching parties on the river. Vivant Denon and "Carlos Bey" found the Syrian and Christian women in Cairo excessively beautiful, but "Carlos Bey" says that the Arab women (he means the peasants) are "poor, stupid, ignorant animals . . . who hardly know how to speak." (How little he knew them.) But after a critical analysis of Arabs in general, this young English aristocrat says that you can't conceive how the Turks "knock about the poor Arabs," and he adds: "I have proved that nothing can be more hospitable than the Arab; he gives you a share of all he has." And when the Turks in Cairo began to butcher Christians, Jews and Copts (he doesn't even count the Arabs), he says unhappily: "What blessed allies we have."

The British were to remain in Cairo only long enough to restore the Turks. English soldiers were glad to leave the city, even though they had inherited all the French army's women. The plague killed 173 British soldiers in 1801, and Sir Robert Wilson reports casually the death of an unsung medical hero named Dr. White who, in the interests of some experimental cure, inoculated himself with plague and died. Among the considerable quantity of loot that changed hands in the treaty of capitulation with the French, Sir Robert Wilson lists seventeen pieces of ancient sculpture. No. 8 of this lot is "a stone of black granite with three inscriptions, hieroglyphics, Coptic and Greek, found near Rosetta." The British Museum's short history of the famous Rosetta stone says that the French tried to claim it as General Menou's private property. There was in fact some very acrimonious discussion about it before the British finally got it out of Menou's house in Alexandria.

Among the Turks that were left in charge of the city was a young officer named Mohammed Ali. Colonel Stuart, who had been leading the British troops fighting with the Turks on the east bank of the river, had noted that Mohammed Ali distinguished himself in a cavalry charge against the French. He was immediately promoted by Husein, the Turkish capudan (admiral) who was in charge of the Turkish forces. Mohammed Ali was an Albanian who had distinguished himself before — as a gendarme and tax collector in his own native district near Philippi. He was born in the same year as Wellington and Napoleon, and he was thirty-three when he came to Cairo as a Turkish officer. In 1806, five years after the British had left Egypt to the Turks, and after a bloody contest with powerful Turks, Mamelukes and Janissaries, he made himself pasha of Egypt with the help of his Albanian troops, and he was reluctantly acknowledged by the Porte as the head of a more or less autonomous state within the Ottoman Empire. Mohammed Ali would rule Egypt for forty-three years, and for forty-one of them the whole of Egypt would be his private estate and Cairo would become, in effect, his private city.

12

Mohammed Ali's Cairo

THE Cairo that the Turks came back to was not the one they had left, because the French had undone forever the pure Orientalism of Cairo. The comparative freedom of European behavior, and the organization of this behavior, had made a deep impression on the ordinary people of Cairo, but what Mohammed Ali did as the ruler of Egypt was to channel all the benefits of this new horizon into his private welfare.

On his way to the top Mohammed Ali had changed sides several times, sometimes supporting the Mamelukes against the Turks and sometimes the Turks against the Mamelukes, but he knew that if he wanted to rule Egypt he would have to contend with the Mamelukes, who were still the feudal owners of the land. The land had remained the real source of power and wealth in Egypt. Napoleon had changed much, but he hadn't changed that.

Mohammed Ali began to attack the Mamelukes in 1804 and 1805. They knew what was in his mind, and in 1805 in one of their attempts to defend themselves the Mamelukes forced their way into the city to fight Mohammed Ali, but his Albanians killed or captured most of them. This was his first serious blow at the Mamelukes, and as a special lesson to the rest of them Mohammed Ali tortured and murdered the captives, and their heads were skinned by the butchers and stuffed with straw, while the surviving Mamelukes were forced to watch what was in store for them. (*Time*, July 22, 1966, reported South Korean soldiers killing and skinning and hanging up the heads of captured Viet Cong.) Mohammed Ali sent eighty-two of these stuffed heads to the Porte to prove his loyalty there.

In the course of this particular clash the Turks and Albanians had pillaged Cairo, and it got so bad that the populace rose in revolt against the Turkish governor. Despite his involvement with his Albanians, Mohammed Ali was the only apparent enemy of both Turks and Mamelukes, so he was "elected" pasha almost by public assent, and from here on Mohammed Ali, though still nominally the governor of Egypt, began to look upon the country as his own.

Perhaps someone in London had read Sir Robert Wilson's description of Egypt as an Oriental Eldorado, or perhaps it was the new and dangerous alliance of the French and the Turks against the Russians; in any case, the British attacked Egypt in 1807, intending to throw the Turks out and restore the authority of the Mamelukes, whom they still admired. Mohammed Ali's clever leadership and his five thousand Albanians, who were far better soldiers than the Turks, cut the British to pieces, and now it was the turn of the British to be sold into slavery and to have their heads cut off and for British prisoners to be led starving and miserable into Cairo and paraded at Ezbekiya, where four hundred and fifty British heads on poles were lined up along an avenue of victory. To the everlasting credit (in English eyes) of the city, the populace of Cairo took pity on the captured British and gave them food and helped their sick and put them on donkeys. Four hundred and sixty-six British soldiers and twenty-four officers were thrown into the Citadel dungeons. Many of them were later ransomed from Mohammed Ali by General Frazer in command of the British invasion, but some remained behind, and one Scottish soldier named Keith became a Moslem and fought as a Moslem and after considerable courage in battle became the governor of the Holy City of Medina.

Having defeated the British, Mohammed Ali was now in an almost impregnable position. The Turks were no problem, since he was technically their representative and they had to go on confirming his authority, however independent he was. The Mamelukes' cause had also been badly weakened by the British defeat, and Mohammed Ali was able to seize their lands in the Delta. By 1808 he was strong enough to confiscate all land in Egypt, even the lands held under the wakf (literally mortmain), which is an Egyptian organization of religious endowment vital to the social heritage of the country. Mohammed Ali destroyed all title deeds but his own, which was rather like burning the Domesday Book, and he even did away with the middleman and used the peasant as a beast in the field. The system of omdehs (local government representatives) and mudirs, (provincial governors) which Mohammed Ali set up remained in use until the revolution in 1952, and vestiges of it are still in operation. It was such a retreat into almost prefeudal conditions that, D. A. Cameron says, "Not a clod of earth, not an ear of corn, not a piaster of profit from sale of grain belonged to anyone but himself."

But he still didn't quite have the land as long as enough Mamelukes were alive to go on resisting and claiming their ancient baronial rights. On the excuse of a big celebration for his son Tusun, and implying that he wanted to come to terms with them, he invited five hundred leading Mameluke lords to attend a ceremony in Cairo. They accepted and arrived in the city in their most beautiful and ceremonial clothes, wearing costly armor and riding richly caparisoned horses. Many legends have grown up about what happened that day, but Gabarti, who was in Cairo at the time, gives a detailed description.

On March 1, 1811, the Mamelukes led by Shahin Bey marched in the military procession of Mohammed Ali's celebrations as one of the rearguard contingent. As they rode out of the Citadel down the narrow little hill to the gate of Azab, which opened out into Roumaliya Square, the huge doors of the gate were suddenly slammed shut in front of them, so that they were trapped in a narrow defile with high walls on either side and a detachment of Albanian soldiers (the rearguard of the procession) behind them. The moment the gates closed the Turks outside were ordered to get up on the high walls and kill the Mamelukes trapped below, who were so packed in that they couldn't escape the merciless fusillade which poured down on them from above and behind.

The panic of five hundred caparisoned horses and men in that small space can only be imagined when you see just how tight a space it is. Horsemanship meant nothing now, and the Mamelukes got off and stripped themselves of their heavy clothes, and naked to the waist tried to use the sword. But there was no one near enough to use it on, and the firing was relentless. Some of the Mamelukes managed to crawl up the walls, but they were shot down before they could escape. The famous story in Thomson's *The Castle of Indolence* of Amin Bey, who supposedly leaped his horse from the gate into the square below, which is still told by guides to the Citadel, is the sort of story the Mamelukes inspired in Britain at that time, but in fact Amin Bey was never in the Citadel. He was late and couldn't get in, and when he heard the firing he sensibly galloped out of the city and hardly stopped until he reached Syria.

Shahin Bey, the Mameluke chief, was wounded in the first fusillade, and then a soldier cut off his head and rushed off to Mohammed Ali with it to claim a bounty. Some of the Mamelukes tried to find shelter in the harem palace nearby crying "Fi 'ard el harim" (Protection of the women), but the harem kept their doors closed tight. Not one of the Mamelukes trapped in the Citadel escaped, and the Albanians went on shooting and beheading into the night. Outside, when this bloody massacre was going on (the defile was a horrible mess of blood and limbs and rich clothes and screaming, wounded horses), the population fled from the district and the merchants shut up shop. Gabarti says that as soon as the remaining soldiers knew what was happening they "jumped like grasshoppers" on the houses of the Mamelukes and began to scour the city and pillage and murder and give "free reign to their appetites." The Mameluke women were victims with the men; loot was the prize, and a woman who had bangles on her arm had it cut off when she wouldn't hand them over.

While the massacre in the Citadel had been going on, Mohammed Ali himself was nervously awaiting the outcome, and as long as the firing lasted he was in a state of terror. But when the firing stopped and the heads of the victims began to appear at his feet, he calmed down a little. Félix Mengin, in his *Histoire de l'Egypte sous le gouvernement de Mohammed-Aly* (1823) says that Mohammed Ali, waiting for the news, was finally relieved when his Italian doctor, Mendrici, rushed in and announced gaily: "It's all over. It is a fête for your highness." Mohammed Ali couldn't say anything except to ask for a glass of water.

Mohammed Ali immediately went after the lesser Mamelukes who had remained in the countryside, and thousands of followers and retainers were slaughtered and heads began to grow on the Bab Zuweila like pox. Five hundred had been killed in the Citadel, and thirty-five hundred more were murdered in the streets of Cairo. But that first five hundred counted most, and when they were dead the Mameluke power was dead and the long and incredible rule of these Georgian slaves in Egypt was over forever. There were forty thousand Mamelukes in Egypt when Napoleon came, about twenty thousand when the British left in 1803, and the five thousand murdered all over Egypt in 1811 accounted for the bulk of those remaining in 1811. In their prime they were good medieval soldiers; in their decline they were not even good soldiers in the streets of Cairo against the unarmed population; and at the end there was nothing to show that they were good soldiers anywhere else. In the nineteenth century they were better soldiers than the Turks but not as good as Mohammed Ali's Albanians, which proves nothing. And they certainly left very much more beauty in Cairo than the Turks did, which might prove something, if only that they served and enjoyed the expansive times they lived in.

Mohammed Ali Pasha, in absolute power after their annihilation, behaved like a Mameluke sultan himself. He immediately began to expand his new kingdom, and his favorite son Tusun and his not-so-favorite son Ibrahim became his best generals. The pasha, at the invitation of the Porte, went to war immediately with the Wahhabis of Arabia and subdued them enough to get personal control of the Red Sea coast, which he then controlled on both sides. He occupied the Sudan and also began to modernize Egypt, as the new property owner improving his private domain. He imported foreign experts, built armories, factories, shipyards, laid down a system of canalization, and sent some Egyptians abroad (mainly to France) to study.

But Cairo in the hands of this ambitious man hardly changed its visible character, because the modernization which Mohammed Ali brought to Egypt was private rather than social. His schemes were clever and extensive, but he tried to keep the city as a feudal-merchant marketplace under his absolute thumb. There was almost no relationship at all between his industrial schemes and the population he didn't care about. So he couldn't suddenly lift the city out of the past and put it into the future, because he wasn't really there himself. Many of the intellectual benefits that accrued under Mohammed Ali were really the leftovers of French revolutionary thought brought along with Napoleon.

The sort of city Cairo was when Mohammed Ali got hold of it is well illustrated in the fifty-six plates on Cairo in the *Etat Moderne* volume of the French *Description,* and anyone who knows modern Cairo would probably find many of these views of the city quite extraordinary. There were, for instance, about eleven lakes in Cairo in 1798, and a large number of boats and boatmen operated in the middle of the city. The Birket al Fil (Elephant Lake) is pictured in the *Description* as a large Venetian-looking waterway (including a troubadour) surrounded by rich and solid houses. Ezbekiya Lake, on Napoleon's map, was about half as big again as Ezbekiya Gardens now, and three engravings show it to be very busy with boat traffic, and surrounded by hundreds of little houses which had been built in the middle of the seventeenth century. Most of the western side of Ezbekiya was taken up by Napoleon's house and headquarters, and I found in Félix Mengin's *Histoire* a picture of the palace which Mohammed Ali had built on the same site, which was still a lake in 1823. Almost all these lakes were wet for only four months of the year; during four more months they were gardens, and in the remaining four months they were dusty squares. They also became stinking pestholes because they were used as refuse dumps.

Ezbekiya, which had been named after Ezbek, a Mameluke lord who once built a mosque in the area, had become the radial point of the city ever since Napoleon had set himself up in Elfi Bey's house there. When Napoleon arrived in Cairo there was already a sort of special European quarter established between Ezbekiya and Kahira, where local Europeans lived and did business. It was then called the Frank quarter from the word afrangi, which means foreign. Later, Europeans called this the Rosetti quarter after the famous Italian, Rosetti, who was the doyen of the European merchant-consuls in Cairo when the French arrived. The French admired Rosetti, and General Hutchinson stayed with him while seeing the French out of the city. Sir Robert Wilson, the official historian of the British expedition, praised Rosetti's "superior qualities" and even claimed that it was from Rosetti that Volney and others got most of their information about Egypt. The more popular name (now the only one for the Frank quarter or Rosetti quarter) was the Muski, because it was flanked by a road leading to the Muski Bridge over the canal. The bridge had been built by Iz ed Din Musk, a relation of Saladin's. Some of the other details of the city from the *Description* show Roda as an island of lovely gardens, Shubra as a pretty little village, and Kasr el Aini already as a hospital. In 1798 Gezira Island was only about two-thirds its present size.

This was really the city the French left behind them. What did Mohammed Ali do with it? Unfortunately, one almost has to leave the character of Mohammed Ali out of Cairo's topography. It was rather his grandsons and great-grandsons down to Farouk who changed the appearance of the city. What was more noticeable about Mohammed Ali's reign in Cairo, and was really his most direct influence on the city, was the new form of foreign influence which he imported into Egypt. He had a mania for foreigners, and as Cameron says, "the pasha and the foreigners were drawn together by a mutual necessity: they both wanted money."

Under Mohammed Ali the Europeans began to be the privileged class of Cairo. He created absolute trading and manufacturing monopolies which he shared with European consuls, who had to agree to his exorbitant terms but who reaped the benefits anyway. As a result of these deals "a wail of agony rose from every peasant in the land" (Cameron).

Foreigners now came to Cairo looking for something subtly different. They were mostly Europeans sniffing the African air, and many of them had an uncanny nose for what was going to happen and for what might be useful to some future situation in their favor. They came to Cairo to dig up profitable lumps of antiquity, or to "investigate" the slave trade, or they were on their way to discover darkest Africa, or women came to be European women in the land of the harem; and eventually the traveler began to turn into the tourist, though not before an exotic path had been opened up for them by the tomb robbers, the antiquarians, the professional Orientalists, and the romantic tasters of ancient ruins.

About the first — and certainly the prince — of the tomb-robber-archaeologists was Giovanni Belzoni, and his influence on this particular aspect of Cairo's future was considerable. Belzoni was the son of a Paduan barber and he became a professional strong man in a traveling fair. In Egypt he seems to have turned overnight into a fanatic of ancient ruins. He arrived in Cairo in 1815, and his own description of how he simply crushed his way through mummies and utterly destroyed uncountable sarcophagi in search of their papyri makes frightening reading today. But Belzoni was one of a curious trio who did a great deal to popularize Egypt and Cairo among Europeans, and they were all in Cairo at about the same time. John Lewis Burckhardt, the Anglo-Swiss traveler, was a scholar and explorer who discovered some of the Pharaonic sites that Belzoni later exploited. Herbert Salt, the British consul in Cairo, was Belzoni's patron and partner in business, and he made a fortune from the antiquities which he shipped to Europe in large quantities. Burckhardt discovered, and Belzoni and Salt robbed. It was these last two who sent to England the huge head of young Memnon, the trunk of Ramses, and the straight left Pharaonic arm which now menaces all who visit the British Museum's Egyptian section.

Considered as a serious archaeologist, which he also was, Belzoni was not the first tomb searcher to come to Cairo, and there were others who came after him with something else in mind besides sensation and profit. The French had already been inside the big pyramid (Khufu), and illustrations in volume 5 of the *Description* show the French architect le Père inside one of its narrow passages. The most successful British excavator was probably Colonel Richard Howard-Vyse, who came in 1836–1837 and used gunpowder to get into the pyramids and bored holes in the Sphinx to find out if it was hollow. But unlike Belzoni, he had no vandalism in his method, despite its violence. In 1826 Edward William Lane, another serious scholar, arrived in Cairo hoping to recover from tuberculosis, and he stayed there the rest of his life, producing the first good Arabic-English dictionary as well as some extraordinary illustrations of the pyramids which he drew with his camera lucida. They were never equaled in accuracy and scope and detail until the camera itself came along. Auguste Mariette, the archaeologist whom Egyptians themselves still respect above all others, came to Cairo in 1850, and anyone walking around that unbelievable storehouse of Egyptian antiquity, the Egyptian (Pharaonic) Museum in Cairo, can thank Mariette for it, since it was he who founded the museum and collected much of what is in it.

In the long run the serious scholars outlasted the vandals, and by 1827 the French had set up an Egyptian section in the Louvre. Jean-François Champollion was put in charge of it, and two years later the first chair of Egyptology in Europe was established for him at the Collège de France. Seventeen years later Berlin had a similar chair which Lepsius, the German Egyptologist, was given. In 1828 Champollion, who had made his name deciphering the Rosetta stone hieroglyphics with the daring theory that hieroglyphic script was in fact phonetic, came to Cairo as head of a French expedition.

Because of all this fascination with the Pharaonic past, Egyptian antiquities were a steadily increasing attraction in Europe during the first half of the nineteenth century, and inevitably a lot of this rubbed off on Cairo. Orientalism also helped, and whereas the earlier travelers had been more or less professionals, now scores of gifted amateurs began to write up their journeys to the city as mildly exotic adventures, and volume by volume one can use these travelogues to build up a picture of Cairo in the 1820s, 1830s and 1840s and see its steady transformation in European eyes from a place of Oriental mystery into a city that was well within the reach of anybody rich enough to get there. And it was, of course, Mohammed Ali's Cairo which they wrote about.

At first these amateur travelers to Cairo were mostly English, but the Americans were not far behind them. The best description we have of Cairo's streets and traffic in the early nineteenth century comes from Captain Moyle Sherer, one of the first of these amateur travelers, who was in Cairo in 1822. He sees in the narrow, crowded streets "a stream of turbaned men, long files of camels, the quick rumbling asses of scribes and merchants, here and there a solitary horseman, or a small group perhaps, a wealthy man on a mule, a poor man with the small-sized overloaded ass, a party of armed Albanians, a file of women going to the baths enveloped in their black mantles and closely veiled, slaves before clearing their path with a cry and a blow, and they raised very loftily, upon saddles high above their animals, with one servant leading and one at each stirrup — nor shape, nor face, nor foot discernible; nothing save the dark flashing of the eye."

The Americans began to arrive in the 1830s, and for most of them Cairo was a rather delicious tailpiece to their respectable little pilgrimage to the Holy Land. The most interesting of these early Americans was John L. Stephens, a fairly innocent traveler who came down to Cairo from Petra and Palestine. Stephens was taken to see Mohammed Ali by the American consul in Cairo (an Englishman named George R. Gliddon) and Stephens almost sounds like Mark Twain as he describes what they said to each other. "His [Mohammed Ali's] dragoman Nubar Bey (an Armenian) was there and presented me," Stephens wrote. "The pasha took his pipe (hubble-bubble) from his mouth, motioned me to take a seat at his right hand on the divan, and with a courteous manner said I was welcome to Egypt. I told him he would soon have to welcome half the world there; he asked me why: and, without meaning to flatter the old Turk, I answered that everybody had a great curiosity to visit that interesting country. . . . Knowing his passion for new things, I went on and told him that he ought to continue his good works, and introduce on the Nile a steamboat from Alexandria to Cairo. He took the pipe from his mouth again, and in the tone of 'Let there be light and there was light' said he had ordered a couple. I knew he was fibbing." In fact the old Turk was not fibbing to Stephens at all; in the next ten years fifteen thousand people would travel by steamboat up the Nile to Cairo from Alexandria.

On the way home from visiting the pasha, consul Gliddon suggested that they call on the governor of Cairo, and as they mounted the steps of the Palais de Justice they saw a prostrate Arab lying face down on the ground and being beaten into unconsciousness by two men with cowskin whips. They went on to the slave market, and being an American Stephens was more familiar with slaves than Europeans were, and less shocked; he saw "an Abyssinian who had mind as well as beauty in her face; she was dressed in silk, and wore ornaments of gold and shells, and called as I passed, and peeped from behind a curtain, smiling and coquetting, and wept and pouted when I went away."

On the whole, Americans always had a slightly different view of Cairo than European travelers, and they still have. They were usually more practical-minded and far more realistic about the filth and misery. In this respect James Ewing Cooley is an archetype for many an American who followed him. Cooley had also been in Petra and the Holy Land, but what he saw above all in Cairo in 1839–1840 was the stupid customs, the high hotel prices, and something worse: "The natural consequence of these long ages of despotism and slavery are," he wrote, "that the people themselves, accustomed to be plundered by the government and its officers, and unused to its care and protection, have lost all moral courage, and are stranger to every principle of honesty." When he visited the pyramids long files of half-clad Arabs armed with clubs suddenly appeared running down the slope toward him at top speed, most of them lacking an eye, many minus a finger, some with their front teeth knocked out, and all carrying leather bottles of water for the visitors to drink from, candles to light their way through the pyramids, and clubs to fight off other "guides" with.

The most important "American" in Cairo at this time was the consul George Gliddon, and though some Americans admired him enormously, some, like Cooley, hated him. Gliddon was the only foreign consul in Cairo who condemned the wholesale extraction of antique artifacts from Egypt, and he wrote *An Appeal to the Antiquaries of Europe* in 1841 begging Europeans to be more discriminating, though not suggesting that they desist altogether. He was contemptuous of Napoleon's hundred savants and their *Description,* and he launched a long and bitter diatribe against Mohammed Ali and the French, in contrast to what he considered to be the gentlemanly behavior of the English in Egypt. He said that every other consul in Cairo took part in the monopolies that Mohammed Ali had set up, and that they were all involved in the big racket of exporting antiquities. (Later Dr. John Bowring, an Englishman, would say that Gliddon was in it too.) The only other consul Gliddon admired was the Russian; he said that the Russians were most efficient and their men were gentlemen. The Russians were ahead of everybody else in setting up language institutes for their young diplomats to learn the languages of the east, and only Gliddon himself and the Russian consul could speak colloquial Arabic. In 1837 he sent an urgent report to President Van Buren on the role of the consuls in Cairo, and what he seems to have been worried about was that the United States was being left out of this grab at Egypt's trade which all the other consuls were involved in. He also mentioned that the P & O (Peninsular & Oriental) Steamship Navigation Company was going to bring vast numbers of tourists to Egypt as part of these "vast and all-comprising plans" to capture the Egyptian market.

Burckhardt, Lane, Stephens, Cooley and Gliddon wrote the sort of books that gave British and Americans an intense desire to get to Cairo, not only to see the antiquities of Egypt but to dabble a little in the exotic life and customs of the city itself, and inevitably it attracted the women travelers as well as the men. Simply being a woman in Cairo was enough in itself, but when they described in detail what they saw in the streets, houses and palaces, they seemed to be adding another dimension to the attractions of this Oriental city for the far-away Victorian readers who were sitting in their drawing rooms seeing it all through the eyes of these intrepid females. What they also did was to add the domestic, gossipy touches which seemed to be expected of them. In 1839 the Honorable Mrs. G. L. Dawson Damer wrote a very down-to-earth description of her stay in Cairo which included a visit to Mohammed Ali's palace at Shubra. She describes the vulgarly furnished apartments and adds, "The taste, alas! of an English upholsterer." She also went to a theatre on Roda Island, half amateur and half artist, which was performing Italian vaudeville to an audience which was mostly "Levantine women" and "pretty Jewesses." She found a Dr. Abbot in Cairo trying to establish a library, and she went to an English service in a Protestant chapel arranged by German missionaries.

A year after her an American woman, Mrs. Sarah Haight from New York, arrived in Cairo after traveling to Moscow, Turkey and Alexandria. Mrs. Haight felt that the natives of Egypt ought to be given a little more taste of the cane, and she longs for the French bayonet or the British cannon to teach the barbarian Mohammed Ali a lesson. But she stays in Mrs. Hill's boardinghouse, where a hair mattress on her bed is a luxury she hasn't known since Moscow, and her room has 475 little panes of glass in it. Mrs. Haight's visit to Cairo was at the time Volney's long-established book *Les Ruines* was sending European romantics into a sick ecstasy for the pleasures of ancient piles. They inspired, Volney said, "a thousand delicious sentiments, a thousand admirable recollections." Already a British officer had committed suicide by flinging himself off a pyramid, after leaving his watch and wallet in his hotel and telling his friends that this would be a glorious way to die. Mrs. Haight and her husband indulged themselves romantically in another way. They spent the night in one of the pyramid chambers of the dead which, she says, had been turned "into a pretty good restaurant" by a local Frenchman. She spent a satisfyingly ecstatic night, but was glad when morning came.

What readers also expected of these women, and what they always got, were the juicy tidbits of Oriental harem life. All women travelers had to visit at least one harem. Mrs. Dawson Damer found the one she went to quite respectable: the ladies were rearing silkworms, and one wife was copying a picture by Ackerman, and a white Circassian beauty actually discussed religion with Mrs. Damer. Mrs. Sarah Haight missed her visit. She had to leave Cairo urgently because of an "explosion" of the plague. Mrs. Sophie Poole, the sister of Edward Lane, who lived with him in Cairo, described several harems. In one the women were "painfully anxious" about the conflict between Russia and Turkey then raging. "I find," she says, "the feeling very strong in favor of England in the harems."

So far it was all tantalizingly discreet, almost unbelievable, and it took a Frenchman to open up the subject properly. Gerard de Nerval was a writer with a wonderful facility for devilish innocence, and he went to Cairo, he claims, to look for a wife. His search finally brought him to a harem, though *par force* it was empty. He was shown into a little room with almost no furniture in it, and he notes that "the one thing which these harems, even the most principal of them, seem to lack is a bed."

He asked the sheikh attending him: "Where do the women and their slaves sleep?"

"On the couches," the sheikh replied.

"But they have no covers," de Nerval pointed out.

"They sleep fully dressed," the sheikh said. "In the winter there are woolen or silken covers."

"I can understand that the husband doesn't like the idea of spending the night in a room filled with fully dressed women," de Nerval told him. "But what happens if he takes two or three of these women in with him . . ."

"Two or three!" the sheikh shouted indignantly. "What sort of dog would behave like that? Good God! Is there a woman in the world, even an infidel, who would agree to share her husband's bed with another woman? Is that how they behave in Europe?"

But there was another view of the seraglio which was probably the real one, and it came from Harriet Martineau, who was a sort of Simone de Beauvoir of the 1840s. She saw two harems and found them utterly disgusting. "I declare," she said, "that if we are to look for a hell upon earth, it is where polygamy exists." In one harem she found that "all the while romping, kissing and screaming went on among the ladies," and she thought the women silly, ignorant, jealous, miserable, and reduced almost to childish savagery. What particularly upset her were the harem children. "The children born in large harems are extremely few," she says, "and they are usually idolized and sometimes murdered." If the child was a boy, "he remains among the women till ten years old, seeing things when the eunuchs come in to romp, and hearing things among the chatter of the ignorant women, which brutalizes him for life before the age of rationality comes."

Victorian readers thus had their fair fill of the respectable, sinful and evil harems of Cairo, but the most sensational view of Cairo's women was not in a harem at all, but in a public bath which Mrs.

Sophie Poole visited. Wrapped in a towel, she decorously enters the steam room. "On entering this chamber," she reports, "a scene presented itself which beggars description. My companion had prepared me for seeing many persons undressed, but imagine my astonishment on finding at least thirty women of all ages, and many young girls and children, perfectly unclothed. You will scarcely think it possible that no one but ourselves had a vestige of clothing. Persons of all colors, from the black and glossy shade of the Negro to the fairest possible hue of complexion were formed in groups, conversing as though fully dressed, with perfect nonchalance, while others were strolling about, or sitting round the fountain. I cannot describe the bath as altogether a beautiful scene; in truth in some respects it is disgusting." And she concludes: "The eyes and ears of an Englishwoman must be closed in the public bath in Egypt before she can fairly enjoy the satisfaction it affords."

By the 1840s and 1850s, and with the aid of this sort of literature, Europe and America had a pretty good idea of what Cairo looked like, even if it was all fairly superficial. But Mohammed Ali was very glad to have this European interest because he knew not only that he would have to contend with European ambitions in Egypt but that there was a gold mine in it if he could somehow attach Egypt to the rapidly expanding industrial and trading wealth of Europe. Two particular events made this connection possible. In 1822 Mohammed Ali introduced cotton into Egypt, and in 1845 Lieutenant Thomas Waghorn delivered the mail from Bombay to London in thirty days, a record time, using the overland route which passed through Egypt.

Egypt already had a native (baladi) cotton on its own, and Pehr Forskal, the Swedish naturalist, mentions it in his book on the flora of Egypt in 1775. But what was desperately needed by the cotton mills of Europe was a superior quality of cotton which could stand ginning and milling and emerge strong enough and with a staple fine enough to be woven into high-quality cloth. In 1818–1819 a Frenchman named Jumel, who had been in America and knew something about cotton, tried to persuade Mohammed Ali that an Ethiopian cotton called Maho, after a Turkish bey who grew it in his garden, could revolutionize the whole agricultural output of Egypt. Mohammed Ali wasn't convinced, so Jumel and a merchant took a plot of land near the Heliopolis obelisk and planted the Maho cotton. By 1820 they had shipped three bales of it to Trieste, which convinced Mohammed Ali enough to put Jumel in charge of his own cotton plantations.

In 1822 some Americans arrived in Cairo to show Mohammed Ali a "Whitney Saw-gin" cotton gin, but he didn't buy it. He bought a roller gin instead, but it failed too because in fact the fellah's hands and feet were cheaper. The introduction of cotton hardly went smoothly, but nonetheless it began to shape up in the pasha's mind as the gold mine he was looking for. All cotton in Egypt belonged to the pasha, and he began to extend his crop all over the Delta. The fellahin were forced to plant it, and in his pamphlet on cotton in Egypt (1841) George Gliddon says that "much opposition was encountered by the government when first the fellahin were compelled to cultivate Jumel's cotton." Fellahin who resisted were beaten or bastinadoed or press-ganged into the army. "Cotton," Gliddon says, "was the article most attractive to European capitalists," and as the area of the crop began to increase in Egypt, Mohammed Ali began to sell the whole crop each year at a fixed price. "Capital flowed into Egypt," Gliddon says, and Mohammed Ali's credit "was really extraordinary."

What this gradual concentration on a single crop eventually did to Egypt's economy can hardly be measured even today. It not only created a new European interest in possessing Egypt, it began the process of turning Egypt into a single-crop colonial country, tied as a source of raw material to the apron strings of manufacturing Europe. It also brought capital to Egypt from Europe, but as Gliddon points out the money was always concentrated in the hands of the few individual merchants who handled the cotton and who eventually began to deal directly with the big European bankers. But it was Mohammed Ali himself who sat on the top of this pyramid of cash from Europe.

Cotton also brought the credit system to Cairo, but the wrong way. Credit became Europe's enticement to Mohammed Ali and his successors to go on borrowing and borrowing at the exorbitant rates of interest that eventually gave Britain and France the excuse to foreclose on the entire Egyptian economy and control all Egyptian life, as if that were the fair price to pay for the pasha's debts. Mohammed Ali had tried to industrialize his country, but he had failed because he considered it *his* country and nobody else's. It was Mohammed Ali, for instance, who built the first barrages across the Nile near Cairo in 1847, because a dam was vital to irrigation and cotton growing. But by then he was in such debt to Europe that in 1841 Gliddon, the American consul, went to England to persuade the British government to interfere in Egypt, using the depressed condition of the people as a moral reason and the rapacity of Mohammed Ali as justification. Nobody in London listened to Gliddon because he talked like an American. He wanted the peasants of Egypt to have the right to plant what they wanted. But that was not the idea that was developing in the minds of

[186]

British manufacturers and politicians. The British government had already sent Dr. (later Sir) John Bowring to report on the state of Egypt's finances, and his Blue Book (1840) gave the British government enough material to realize that it was only a matter of waiting for the plum to ripen a little more before it was finally ready to be plucked.

The other event which was to affect Egyptian life and eventually give Cairo its biggest face-lift was the inauguration in 1845 of the direct route from India across Egypt to England. The young English naval officer Thomas Waghorn had tried for years to get his East India Company mails transported by this direct route across Egypt (there is an excellent description of how it was eventually done and the itinerary of it in *Voyage en Egypte et en Grèce* by Adolphe Joanne, 1850), and when he finally succeeded, it simply predicted and made inevitable the next stage — the Suez Canal. In 1847 Mohammed Ali gave his ready permission for a mixed group, which included Robert Stephenson, to investigate the possibility of digging a canal from the Red Sea to the Mediterranean. French engineers advising Napoleon had decided that there was a difference in level between the two seas, but the commission of 1847 disproved this. It wasn't until Mohammed Ali was dead and buried that de Lesseps actually began to cut the canal (1859). Nonetheless, the foundation of the canal began in Mohammed Ali's lifetime, and when it was finally opened in 1869 Egypt was thereafter tied by these two big instruments of European expansion — cotton and canal — to a future which would bring it misery and degeneration, but which would finally force it to fight for some sort of genuine independence.

In this period of hiatus Cairo itself changed very little at first, except that people like Waghorn, de Lesseps, Bowring, and the increasing number of European experts and travelers began to give the city a European character in its social and political life, even though its outward appearance didn't change much. In fact for years the topography of the city did not adequately reflect any of this underlying upheaval. We have a brief but purely descriptive picture of Cairo in 1847, two years before Mohammed Ali died, by Edward Lane in *Cairo Fifty Years Ago.* He says western innovations haven't reached the city, except that the houses of the rich Turkish bourgeoisie now have glass windows (Mohammed Ali forbade musharabiyas in new buildings); and European-style glass-fronted shops, as distinct from Arab booths, have appeared in the Muski. "Franks" have begun to wear European clothes, and there are European workers in the local arsenal. The road from Ezbekiya to Bulaq which Napoleon had built still ran through beanfields and marshes flooded during the annual inundation.

In 1847 the streets were still mostly narrow, five to ten feet wide, but the introduction of carriages by the rich Turks meant that the new streets had to be built wider and straighter. There used to be little stone benches (mastabas) outside all the shops of Cairo, but Mohammed Ali had them all removed to accommodate the carriages. By 1847 European goods were beginning to appear more and more in the markets and bazaars. Lane mentions "shawls of Kashmir, England and France, muslin shawls of British manufacture for turbans . . . and European linens."

Turkish merchants sold ready-made clothes and Turkish silks and sabers and prayer carpets in the Khan el Khalili, and there were public auctions of goods, usually Turkish, on Mondays and Fridays in the Khan. There used to be a wekala al Gellaba, a slave market, a little to the south of Khan el Khalili, but in 1847 it had just been removed to the area around Qait Bey's mosque, because the slaves were said to be too crowded and unclean and were supposed to be the cause of the spread of infectious diseases. (Cairo had a very bad plague again in 1835.) Slaves were beginning to be a little better off, though dressed only in loincloths. There were still Circassian white slaves (incipient Mamelukes or decadent ones?) in the city. There was a big Jewish quarter in the old walled city, and Jews shared with Moslems the important canal-cutting ceremony every year. Edward Lane says that the external appearance of the houses in the Jewish quarter "was mean, but some are sumptuous within." The Greeks had two quarters: Harat al Rum (they still used the word Roman for the Greeks) and the Inner quarter. The Copts had two quarters, one northeast of Ezbekiya and the other Harat al Nassara (the quarter of the Christians). By 1849 the lake of Ezbekiya had been more or less filled in, although a canal ran around it, and some European-style houses had been built near it. All the travelers I have quoted here talk of the European hotels around Ezbekiya. Harriet Martineau mentions that both the Hotel d'Orient and Shepheard's Hotel were quite full during her stay in Cairo in 1846, and she comments on the agreeable "society" which could be found there. This must be the first society notice of Shepheard's we have. The same travelers also mention the European social life in the hotels they are staying in as a special aspect of Cairo's seasonal European society life, which was to remain active until almost the end of foreign occupation.

But apart from this European presence, the mark, the scar, the memory, the beauty or the monument that Mohammed Ali left Cairo

[188]

is his Byzantine mosque up on the Citadel, which has become the most recognizable landmark of tourist Cairo. Almost every expert in Islamic art looks upon this mosque with cautious distaste. It has big fat domes and thin spherical minarets which seem far too slender and insecure for the voluptuous cupolas below them. The mosque was begun in 1824 and finished in 1857, and Mohammed Ali brought a Greek architect from Constantinople who modeled his designs on the Nuri Osmaniya mosque in Constantinople. For anyone with Constantinople in mind the mosque looks quite normal, but for Cairo it has always been something of a foreigner. I once asked Shafik Abd el Kadir of the Antiquities Department what was the latest opinion about the mosque, since Mohammed Ali is thoroughly disliked in modern Egypt, and he said: "It doesn't really fit. But it has its own beauty, and we can enjoy it now."

The mosque is still luxuriously kept. Inside, it is carpeted and well lit, but if you stand in the middle of it and imagine that this was once the way some of the other great monuments were furnished, the Mohammed Ali mosque loses a little of its flavor, because the imagination is never really stirred by any breathtaking intrinsic beauty. The façades of yellow alabaster, which the much respected Baedeker of 1929 calls poor-quality stuff, were described by Charles Didier as of "incomparable beauty," although Didier really disliked the mosque. The twisted grain of this translucent stone and its lovely tints are very soft on the eyes when you are up on that brown bare hill. Baedeker also called the Chinese-looking hanafiya (ablution basin) in the courtyard "debased Turkish," which is still fair comment. Every tourist visiting the mosque has the tower in the courtyard pointed out to him. It supports a clock which Louis Philippe of France presented to his good friend Mohammed Ali, but no modern Egyptian points it out these days without commenting that this is about all the Egyptians got out of the French in exchange for the Suez Canal.

What one can also get from the walls of this mosque is a famous view of the whole city below, which is like the close-up of a familiar face after the longer view of it from the Mukattam. Those with a special taste for city roofs can see from the mosque a few of the unique Cairo ventilators from up here. These ventilators have been part of the Cairo skyline for centuries, and they will always be part of it as long as the north wind blows.

The mosque of Mohammed Ali is really a last gesture of fading Ottomanism. Its Byzantinism had nothing to do with Europe, and even less to do with Arab or Egyptian tradition. It is, in fact, an excellent portrait of Mohammed Ali himself, and it dates the time when

Looking toward the Citadel, with the mosque of Mohammed Ali — the "Byzantine" mosque of Cairo — on the left.

Interior of the mosque of Mohammed Ali —
what a well-attended mosque should look like.

Ottomanism ends and Europe begins to take over, because the money and the credit which cotton and the canal brought to Egypt also brought the speculators with their cosmopolitan tastes, and in the next thirty years, until the British occupied Egypt in 1882, they would change the city's appearance beyond recognition.

13

Europeanized Cairo

"WE, who call ourselves Christians," D. A. Cameron wrote in 1898, "cannot but feel ashamed when we learn how during that thirty years (1849–1882) Christian adventurers victimized the Moslems of Egypt, not shooting them down, it is true, but nevertheless cruelly wronging them by the abuse of privileges and capitulations, by the mysterious processes of European law to which the Orientals were quite unaccustomed."

What Cameron is talking about is what he called "foreign swindling and roguery," mainly by the greatest banking houses of Europe, aided and abetted by their governments, who finally got hold of the economy of Egypt by a process of unscrupulous and dishonest mortgages. The insatiable rates of interest on their loans to Egypt were so excessive that the sums deducted at source before the ruling pasha got a penny of his loaned money were sometimes up to 25 percent through one legal trick or another, and the loans themselves were so arranged with these deductions that repayment became quite impossible. In fact the only way to collect these debts was by foreclosure, by taking over the entire country. Some of the most famous merchant banking houses of Europe today raised fortunes on this theft of Egypt. But the initial blame lies with the ruling pashas, who were spendthrift madmen, to whom Egypt and its economy and its people were no more than an easy collateral against whatever cash they could get.

When Mohammed Ali died insane in 1849 he was already succeeded by his grandson Abbas (1848–1854), then by one of his own sons, Said (1854–1863), another grandson, Ismail (1863–1879), and his great-grandson Tawfik (1879), and then by the British, who came in 1882. During these four ineffectual reigns Egypt was simply swept off her feet by the European whirlwind, since the free-for-all to get hold of this succulent prize brought merchants, bankers, tourists, soldiers, engineers, explorers, priests and mountebanks to Cairo in its golden wake.

To some extent Mohammed Ali had kept back this flood, or kept a fairly tight control on what Europeans did in Egypt. But none of his descendants was strong enough to stand up to even the most rascally European. And underlying this European presence, which simply spread over Egypt like a disease, was the continuing British and French rivalry in Egypt. The French brought inventive ideas, the French language, French culture, and French social and diplomatic influence. The British came with railways, politics and money, and they won without much difficulty. In the thirty-three years between Mohammed Ali and the British occupation the French wanted desperately to build and finally succeeded in building the Suez Canal. Britain still did not want the canal, still thought of Egypt as a vital barrier between Europe and India, and for her part was far more interested in cheap cotton and the financial basis of land ownership and crop buying. But once the French had built the canal Britain had to have it, or have Egypt, and eventually she got both.

Though the French and British were the instigators and beneficiaries of a great deal of this Europeanization of Egypt and particularly of Cairo, they were by no means the only ones. Almost every European country was well represented in this gold rush city, and almost every class of European as well. By 1872 there were three hundred thousand people living in Cairo, and eighty-five thousand of them were non-Egyptians. Twenty-five thousand of these were complete foreigners — Europeans who had settled there — and another two or three thousand were permanently "passing through."

The Europeanizing of Cairo was therefore more of an influence rather than an act. It isn't as if the French and English said, "Let there now be a European city." They almost did that, but not quite. It began with the Europeans bringing their own standards and their own ideas on almost everything: what they lived in and how they lived and what sort of bathrooms they used and the kind of brothels they liked. These imported tastes influenced the local pashas and merchants and princes, and by the 1850s and 1860s many Egyptians had also been abroad, and they too brought back their own ideas on what sort of trousers they should wear and what the stores, streets, entertainments and houses should look like. Foreign architects and engineers imported to do this new work came with Italian, French, Austrian and

[195]

English ideas, and the combination of rich pashas and imported capital and foreign experts really began the process of changing Cairo. It started with a few houses and palaces and eventually became a deliberate policy, even an exaggerated one. Long before the British came you could draw a north and south line through Cairo, down the edge of the Ezbekiya Gardens, and you could say that almost everything to the east was the old medieval Arab city and everything to the west (except Bulaq) was the new European one — a division which still exists.

There were real reasons for this east-west division of Cairo. The city could not go east very well because the Mukattam Hills were in the way, and there was little point building on the hillsides because there was no water up there. The city had to go west. The Nile had been steadily shifting westward from the city anyway, leaving behind low brackish land which had to be drained and filled in before it could be used — an expensive prospect. But imported capital and imported techniques made it possible, and European Cairo began to build on the old bed of the retreating Nile.

What one traces, therefore, in this new Cairo is a complex matrix of novel circumstances, new techniques and new transport, new money, new social habits, and a new sort of traveler. Locally the result was a new kind of businessman, a new kind of foreigner, a new kind of courtier, soldier, khedive, a new style of shopkeeper, a new kind of middle class and a new kind of money, and of course a new kind of corruption and exploitation. The only part of society which did not benefit from this change was the lower level of it, which, as Cameron points out, suffered more, not less, from this new kind of foreign invasion.

Perhaps the first and in some ways the most important vehicle of this European arrival in Cairo was the railway line which Robert Stephenson built in 1852 between Alexandria and Cairo against bitter French opposition — the French wanted everything in Egypt concentrated on building the Suez Canal. A telegraph line was added a few years later, and thus Britain had set up an excellent land and communication link with her Indian colony, through Egypt but without breaking the Egyptian barrier. (British troops were sent to India during the Mutiny by this new route.) The real result of this railway was the arrival in Cairo of hundreds and thousands of Europeans who would simply remain or spend a "season" in the city, or simply come and go, to and from India. Naturally most of these new train travelers were British, and when Charles Didier, the French writer, came to Cairo in 1855 he was disgusted by the English and their shopkeeping instincts in Cairo. In the English hotels, he said, "*la voix glapissante des femmes"* — the yapping voices of the women — *"formait le soprano de ce concert mercantile."*

An important part of this English mercantile concert which the railway had also brought with it were the new tourists — the clergymen and teachers and middle-class girls looking for husbands. And with them, like a guardian guiding angel, came Thomas J. Cook. Cook himself paid his first visit to Cairo in 1860, and within a month of his return to England he had organized a tour to Egypt for thirty-two ladies and gentlemen, for which he hired two steamers on the Nile. Commercial tourism had begun, and Thomas J. Cook and Sons was to play a useful role in the future of Cairo for the British, and not only with their lady and gentleman tourists.

What coincided, too, with railway travel and tourism to Cairo was the Civil War in the United States, 1861–1865. The European demand for another source of cotton besides America raised the price of Egypt's new crop to dizzy heights, and Egyptian exports of it rose from 16 million dollars in 1862 to 56 million in 1864. Cotton thus began its fateful role for Egypt. The last link which tied Egypt irrevocably to Europe was the Suez Canal, which de Lesseps had built with Egyptian labor and in the end with Egyptian money. It took ten years to build, and when it was opened in 1869 it was undoubtedly the product of Egypt's "blood, sweat and tear-wrung millions" (Byron).

By this time Egypt was ruled by Ismail, Mohammed Ali's grandson, and it was in Ismail's time that the accumulated store of European affluence did its best and its worst for Cairo. Ismail had been educated in France and had traveled extensively in Europe, and he wanted Cairo to rival the modern quarters of Paris. It was Ismail who deliberately divided Cairo into east and west in an ambitious scheme to build a Paris on the Nile. Ezbekiya was again to be the centerpiece of this new scheme, and though Ismail did rebuild the Ezbekiya area and opened up two new boulevards into the old city — Clot Bey, and the Boulevard Mohammed Ali which cuts straight through to the Citadel — his real plan was to establish a new quarter to the west quite separate from the old city.

Ismail's new quarter was laid out to a French plan with straight streets and roundabouts, and the organized pattern of modern Cairo is the result. The complaint by the European old guard in Cairo, who were attached to Ottoman Cairo and medieval Cairo, was that Cairo was being Haussmannized, which in fact it was, because Baron Haussmann had just devised the original radial plan for the new centers of Paris. The khedive gave a site in this new Ismailiya quarter free

[197]

to anyone who would build on it within eighteen months a house or building worth at least thirty thousand francs, and the rich instantly obliged. At first the buildings were mainly residential as the big European merchants and the pashas built villas along the straight new streets, but the banks and consulates also built their new headquarters there, moving across the borderline of Ezbekiya from the old Rosetti quarter to develop this new commercial and business city which was not going to be Arab, but European.

Ismail's personal contribution to the European look was the wooden Opera House which he built on Ezbekiya, symbolically facing the western side of the city. Ismail wanted his theatre for the inaugural celebrations of the opening of the Suez Canal, and it was put up in five months in 1868 by gangs of forced labor. Verdi was commissioned to write an opera (*Aida*) for it, but *Aida* wasn't finished in time, so it was *Rigoletto* which opened the Opera House and the canal, November 1, 1869. Hurriedly built as it obviously is, Ismail's white Opera House is still the loveliest landmark left of his Parisian Cairo, although it is almost useless now for opera or ballet because it has almost no wings and little dressing room space, and the orchestra and its conductor have to walk down the main aisle of the theatre to reach the orchestra pit.

There are only one or two of the villas of the 1860s left in the European center of Cairo now, but the contrast between the old city and the new was so great that even walking through the same streets in Cairo today you can look at the later-nineteenth-century European façades and still feel the enormous difference which these wide planned streets made to Cairo. In 1870 Ismail brought gas to the city, and electricity eventually replaced it in 1898, so that Cairo was one of the earliest cities in the world to use electricity. Running water came later, but from the outset Ismail put down well-paved carriage roads to Abbasiya, Matariya, Masr al Atika, the pyramids, and to Shubra, where his palace was.

The acacia-and-sycamore-lined avenue to Shubra was at this time the most important street in Cairo, because the rich had followed the khedive and built big houses along the road, and it was along this thoroughfare that the rich came out to show off their wealth and their finery. New hotels went up in the new European quarter, and though Shepheard's remained the heart and soul of visiting English society in Cairo, a new hotel had been built opposite Ezbekiya Gardens by an English company and for a while it was called the New Hotel. It was taken over almost immediately by the khedive to house his guests for the canal opening, but later on it was sold to a French company, and eventually it was renamed the Continental-Savoy and became in fact the rival and then the ally of Shepheard's as the giddy center of the city's seasonal social life.

Greek and German brasseries and French cafés also appeared like spring flowers in all the new streets, and many of them had orchestras or bands. On free ground overlooking the Ezbekiya Gardens the Duke of Sutherland built the new Khedive Club, a copy it was said of the best London clubs of the day. It was under local royal patronage and its chairman was the British consul, then the highest British diplomatic official in Egypt. Within a few more years what used to be beanfields and rather desolate country around the railway station was built up with bijou villas and small "country" houses, and from the railway terminus into the city the new streets were built up very quickly with smaller European houses and busy second-class shops. By 1877 you no longer had to ride a donkey into town from the railway station — omnibuses ran from the station to Shepheard's, or you could take a carriage.

For almost ten years new Cairo was one huge building site; by European standards most of these big houses were very palatial, and even the rather middle-class quarters were lavishly built. Ismail himself had four palaces in Cairo, and one of them (Kasr al Nouzha) was reserved for the entertainment of visiting dignitaries. Every time a British viceroy of India or a duke or even a wealthy aristocrat or a French or an Austrian prince passed through he was given a lavish welcome in this palace. Ismail also had another palace to house many of his royal guests who came especially to Cairo to open the canal with him. It was just across the river on Gezira Island, and it was here that the Empress Eugénie of the French, the Crown Prince of Prussia, Henry of the Netherlands, Prince Louis of Hesse and their large entourages were put up for the Suez Canal celebrations.

This palace was later sold by Egypt's European bailiffs to a foreign company which immediately used most of the land for speculative building. Then a rich pasha bought the palace itself, which was finally turned into a hotel after the 1952 revolution. It is now called the Omar Khayyam, and its Suez-Ismail atmosphere is still intact. Today it is a favorite place for big bourgeois weddings because of the romantic double staircase which winds itself gracefully from top to bottom, and fully flowered Egyptian brides love to walk down this marble pathway to the grandiose foyer below.

The year of the canal opening, 1869, was an astonishing one for Cairo. Life for the rich and the foreign became one long festival of balls, banquets, theatres, operas, races. Ismail even built a special

Shepheard's Hotel

Shepheard's Hotel (OPPOSITE ABOVE), once the heart and soul of visiting English society. OPPOSITE BELOW: Members of the British smart set on the veranda. ABOVE: The New Hotel, later the Continental-Savoy — sister to Shepheard's.

racecourse in the city, and anybody who knows modern Cairo will be surprised to hear that it occupied the block of the city which begins at the Rond Point of Mustafa Kamel and runs along on the righthand side going down Shari' Kasr el Nil. What the populace had to enjoy in this new city were the packed streets, the gay lights, the hundreds of kiosks and booths, street performers, and the traditional Moslem festival decorations. A temporary bridge was built over the Nile to Giza, and in February of that year the Prince of Wales (Edward VII) and his princess paid an official visit to Cairo; the round of balls and banquets was only a small part of the *Arabian Nights* entertainments they were given. Six steamers and dahabiyas on the Nile were put at the disposal of the prince and princess, and nothing was spared to impress them with the sybaritism and size of Oriental hospitality.

Finally, after Ismail himself had made a quick tour of Europe, the canal opening celebrations began. As well as the royalty and aristocracy of Europe, a whole army of *hommes de lettres* and newspapermen had arrived, and a still larger crowd (said to exceed three thousand) of comparative nobodies had managed to procure invitations. All were housed and fed in Cairo and transported in royal luxury by the khedive. The whole entourage of princes and hangers-on and serious newspapermen and *hommes de lettres* were moved from Cairo to Port Said in November, when a Moslem alim and a Catholic priest from France (who later married de Lesseps to a local half-European beauty) blessed the canal, which was officially opened to extraordinary scenes of banqueting in the desert (three thousand guests) and festivities on the water on November 17, 1869. The canal company was French, but the first ship through it to pay dues was British.

So much of the momentum of Ismail's planning had been directed towards this great climax of the canal that Cairo had a very difficult time returning to normal after 1869. In any case Europeans continued to pour into the city, speculators went on looking for gold in the streets, and Ismail's ambitious attempts to create a copy of Paris went on unabated. In 1872 a new iron bridge was built over the Nile from Kasr el Nil to Gezira Island by a French firm for £108,000. It used to open up twice every twenty-four hours for river traffic to pass through. The river on the other side of the island between Gezira and Giza was deliberately blocked so that Gezira and Giza became one, but this put so much water strain on Bulaq when the river rose that the barrier was hurriedly dug out again. A British firm then built a swing bridge on the Giza side of the island. It never worked, but it didn't matter because the Kasr el Nil bridge had opened up Gezira Island as part of the city, and eventually it became one of the city's wealthiest quarters. Cairo also became the base for British expansion into Africa — at Egypt's expense. In 1869 Samuel Baker spent four months in Cairo preparing his expedition to the White Nile, ostensibly to put down the slave trade. He left Cairo with a detachment of black troops and English trade goods and British ships, all of which cost Egypt half a million pounds, and J. C. MacCoan points out that though a lot of new territory was acquired the slave trade remained exactly as it was.

So much money had been spent in Egypt during ten years that it seemed to come from some bottomless pit, but everything that Ismail had done for Cairo was really bought and paid for by high taxation of everything and everybody, and by lavish loans which Europe lovingly heaped on him. Ismail had borrowed his first £5,700,000 in 1864, of which he only got £4,900,000 after deductions. But this was a minor loss compared with later loans, and reading the story of these loans in MacCoan's *Egypt Under Ismail* is like reading the inside story of a huge confidence trick. For instance, the Rothschilds loaned Ismail through the state £8,500,000 against a collateral of 435,000 acres of the richest land in the world. The net sum he got after "deductions" was £4,360,000, and MacCoan says that even this was largely eaten into to pay off "judgment" debts. During eleven years the banking houses of Fruhling-Goschen, Anglo-Egyptian, Imperial Ottoman, Oppenheims and Bischoffsheims loaned Ismail £68 million, but only £48 million reached him after deductions at source. In 1875 Ismail was forced to sell his shares in the Suez Canal to the British for four million pounds, payable on draft to Rothschilds — a sum which in a very short time would itself be the annual turnover of the canal in shipping tolls.

Ismail struggled on lavishly, desperately trying to survive this European generosity and the mounting revolt which his hard and oppressive policies towards the peasants made inevitable. As always before, it was becoming a race between local upheaval and a foreign invader. Ismail knew he could never escape the financial grip which Europe had on him; in fact, his only hope of survival was to have some kind of help that would be quite clean of local corruption. The trouble was that he could trust nobody in Egypt or in Europe, because everyone wanted his cut. If, for instance, he could have depended on his army he would at least have had some sort of support against the European embrace and against rising popular hatred. If he'd been a Mameluke sultan he would simply have purchased a new supply of Mamelukes to replace his corrupt Turkish and Albanian officers. But the Mameluke system was dead, so he looked around for other outsiders and he found them in the United States of America.

There was a lot of sense in this idea because American officers in the Sixties knew more about modern war than any soldier in Europe. The Civil War, the first modern war, was just over, and the Southern states were full of officers and gentleman who were penniless and futureless but not yet finished with soldiering. In 1869 Ismail employed an American officer, Captain Thadeus P. Mott of the late Union army to engage American officers for the Egyptian army. Within the year Mott brought to Cairo an Indian fighter named General W. Loring, two more generals, nine colonels, two majors, and a doctor and a professor of geology. All but four of the soldiers had served in the Confederate army, so they were mostly Southerners — Southern colonels.

How effective these soldiers were for Ismail's purpose, and what role they eventually played, is measured by their behavior in the two most important events they took part in: the Anglo-Egyptian expeditions into Africa, and the long-expected internal revolt which came in 1881. But while they lived and served in Cairo they were easily the most exciting of the foreign imports, and they added a sort of d'Artagnan–Wild West dash to the city which it had never had before. They were almost always in trouble, mainly because they refused to bend the knee to anyone, but also because they insisted on being treated as gentlemen, and as gentlemen they were determined to enjoy themselves at all times and at all costs.

One night, for instance, a Major Morgan was at the Théâtre Français with General Loring and another American officer, Colonel Chaillé-Long, and they were drinking at the buvette during the intermission. The prefect of Cairo's police, Ali Bey, who was wearing a very fancy uniform, came into the buvette and ordered Major Morgan, who was after all a junior officer in service to the khedive, to get him a glass of water. Morgan was incredulous. He carefully filled his glass with water and threw it in Ali Bey's face, and then slapped the bey hard to make sure the insult was understood. Ali Bey hurried up the steps to the royal box, furious, and reported the matter to Ismail, who more or less said, "Serves you right," and added, "I did not bring Americans here to wait on you . . . Go and ask his pardon," which Ali Bey did.

Morgan, who was only twenty-five, had been a midshipman at Annapolis and he was a remarkable horseman. On one occasion he was out riding in the usual society parade on the Shubra road when a ladies' coupé with the khedivial crown on the door passed him, followed by two mounted eunuchs with drawn swords. The rule was that men, at least gentlemen, should look away when a lady's carriage passed, but Morgan rode close enough to take a look inside and saw a pretty girl who suddenly gave him some roses and a kerchief, which so surprised Morgan that he let them fall. Everybody in the street was now aware that someone of the royal harem had just flirted with an American officer. Morgan did not hesitate, however. He snatched the flowers off the ground without getting out of his saddle and then took off on his horse, which happened to be the thoroughbred being trained to carry the Empress Eugénie when she came from Paris for the canal celebrations. Morgan was instantly chased by the two guards, with scimitars in the air, and they wanted his head.

At the point where the Shubra road crosses the railway line there used to be a double railway gate (now there is a bridge), and these gates happened to be closed as Morgan arrived at the gallop. He dug his spurs in and cleared the first gate. In the true style of the Wild West, a train also happened to be coming along. So Morgan dug his spurs into his horse again, and though the run was short he cleared the other gate, putting the train between himself and his pursuers. He got away, but he had to hide in the Russian Embassy for days, where he burned the kerchief and the roses and enjoyed himself with his Russian friends until it had all blown over.

Another American officer named Major Cameron, who was a religious maniac, tried to poison a fellow American officer — Colonel Chaillé-Long — so a third American challenged him to a duel. Cameron made such a noise practicing with his pistol all night in his rooms that he was arrested, and on some excuse was quickly deported. All Americans dressed like Turkish officers, beards and all, but their imperturbable boyishness always gives them away in their stern and soldierly portraits. They seem to have spent a lot of time and money giving champagne suppers for the Italian and French actresses who came to the Théâtre Français and the Italian Opera.

For the kind of serious work the Americans did one must read Chaillé-Long's book *My Life in Four Continents*. Colonel Chaillé-Long was sent by Ismail as chief of staff to General Gordon when Gordon was being sent up the Nile to become governor of the Egyptian Equatorial Provinces. Ismail knew that Gordon was really looking after British interests, and this was also the time when Stanley was preparing his expedition to rescue Livingstone. Ismail told Chaillé-Long that in fact the Stanley expedition was being prepared to plant the British flag in Uganda. He told Chaillé-Long to anticipate the

[205]

London expedition and to slip away from Gordon when he could and get into Uganda and make a treaty for Egypt with the king there. At Gondokoro, when Gordon wasn't looking, he jumped off the paddle steamer just as it shot out into the Nile current, and waving goodbye to the astonished Gordon he did as he was told. Chaillé-Long also went on to discover the Keoga lake system in Central Africa. When the colonel came back to Cairo, all skin and bone and looking like a dirty Egyptian beggar, they would not let him into the grand New (Continental-Savoy) Hotel, but he eventually got in somehow and went up to General Alex Reynolds, another American who happened to be standing around, and begged a piaster from him. Reynolds was about to pay the beggar the usual European price with his cane when Chaillé-Long said in English to him: "What a reception . . ."

There is little doubt that Ismail trusted his Americans in Cairo more than he trusted anybody else on his military staff, but there were not enough of them, nor were they involved enough with his cause, nor were they brutal enough to form a caste able to come to grips with the corrupt court they served. Ismail thought enough of their services to give General W. T. Sherman, in gratitude for his part in lending the Americans to Egypt, a bag of diamonds worth sixty thousand dollars. Sherman came to Cairo in 1872, and a special act of Congress had to be passed to let him take his diamonds home untaxed.

But none of this helped Ismail. In 1876 self-appointed Europeans, sitting in judgment on his financial situation, told him that he owed them £91 million. By 1879, according to MacCoan, his debtors claimed that he owed them about £100 million. Ismail's apologists say that he never got this amount, and almost nobody believes that he did; at least £25 million of it was spent on the Suez Canal, on building new irrigation canals, railways, bridges, telegraphs, lighthouses, harbors, docks, and sugar factories, and on Haussmannizing Cairo. Ismail did spend large amounts on these projects, but no one knows exactly how much. In 1879 Britain and France did what they had been waiting to do for a long time. After their experts had added up the debts they simply stepped in and took over Egypt's finances with two comptrollers general, one British and one French. What right they had to do this nobody has ever quite resolved. On June 19, 1879, they took another extraordinary step. The British and French consuls general called at Abdin Palace and told Ismail to abdicate, which he did because there was nothing else he was capable of doing. He wasn't facing an invading army, he was facing something far more complicated and dangerous — the very face of the great powers of Europe who themselves wanted Egypt. He couldn't even call on popular support, since the people were so burdened by the misery of his taxes and corvées that they hated him and they were glad that he was going. He simply collapsed, and he left the country for Europe and died in exile in 1895.

Tawfik, his son, inherited what was left of Egypt, and these last few years of Egypt's "independence" were even harder on the population. Since the 1860s every Egyptian had been "at the mercy of some seventeen petty consular tribunals" (MacCoan) because no foreigner in Egypt could be tried by or even sued in an Egyptian court. He could only be brought before his own consulate, and in matters of business and in cases of assault the abuses that this system encouraged, and the ruthless stealing of the land and the goods of Egyptians, provoked Lord Milner to denounce these consular courts as "a severe plague." Some of them even claimed outright jurisdiction over Egyptians and delivered judgments against them. And the judgments were enforced often by diplomatic pressure. This system of foreign protection came to be known as "capitulation." It became one of the most important implements of British rule, and it played an important part in the growth of this new European domination of Cairo. It was eventually codified into a collective foreign court, the Tribunaux Mixtes, which went on protecting all foreigners from Egyptian law until the system was finally abolished at the Montreux Conference in 1937.

In 1866 a Frenchwoman, Olympe Audouard, published a book, *Les Mystères de l'Égypte Dévoilés*, which caused something of a sensation because she denounced Ismail as a brute and a savage who only wanted to suck the blood out of the people. Vehemently and factually she showed that Ismail seized whatever estates he wanted, wrecked whole villages with his corvées, and even behaved brutally to his wives. In 1868 Lady Duff Gordon wrote in *Macmillan's Magazine* from Cairo: "I cannot describe to you the misery here now . . . Every day some new tax. Now every beast, camel, cow, sheep, donkey, horse is made to pay. The fellahin can no longer eat bread: they are living on barley-meal mixed with water." Not only were they taxed for their goods, but peasants were taxed for being born, for marrying, for dying, for entering a town, for buying salt, for a dead animal as well as a live one; whereas all foreigners in Egypt were exempt from all taxes. It was not surprising to anyone who knew Egypt that the Egyptians could finally take no more and rose in revolt.

The Arabi revolt took its name from its popular leader Ahmad Arabi, who liked to call himself Ahmad the Egyptian. He was the son of a peasant, and he had managed to get a few years of schooling at the Azhar. He then switched to the army and was made a colonel

[207]

almost immediately because Tawfik was trying to appease the Egyptians in his army. But Arabi became the spokesman for the bitterness and the nationalism of three separate groups of Egyptians: the downtrodden peasant, the young Egyptian officers in the army who resented their Turkish and Circassian superiors, and the nationalist intellectuals of Cairo and the other cities.

The revolt began in 1881 with a mutiny in the army. The rest of Egypt joined the revolt immediately, and in February 1881 Arabi with four thousand men and eighteen guns marched into the square outside Abdin Palace in Cairo and called for the khedive to come out. Tawfik was not in, and when he eventually arrived at Abdin he found the square surrounded by soldiers, with cannon pointing at the palace windows. His own "loyal" regiments had joined the revolt, so Tawfik had to creep into his palace the back way and Mr. (later Sir) Auckland Colvin, the British comptroller of the Egyptian receipts, urged him to make a personal appeal to his troops. With Colvin on one side and General Charles P. Stone (the West Pointer who was then commander in chief of the Egyptian army) on the other, Tawfik walked down the staircase towards the group of colonels in the square, and on this level at least the Americans were fulfilling loyally their contract to the khedive. Two of the three rebellious colonels (Arabi and Abdullah Bey) were on horseback, and according to Thomas Archer in *The War in Egypt and the Sudan* (1885) the khedive said to them: "Get off your horses."

Wilfred Scawen Blunt in *Secret History of the English Occupation of Egypt* says that Colvin told the khedive to shoot Arabi down as he talked, but Archer says that Colvin advised the khedive to order Arabi and Abdullah to give up their swords. Tawfik was not quite equal to that, so he simply told them to sheathe their swords, which they did.

The khedive asked what they wanted. Arabi replied that they came in the name of the people to ask for liberty and for the three points formulated in the letter sent that morning to the Ministry of War: an assembly of notables, a constitution, and the establishment of a system in which all Egyptians were equal before the law.

"Have you forgotten that I am the khedive and your master?" Tawfik asked them.

Arabi answered by a verse from the Koran: "The ruler is he who is just; he who is not so is no longer ruler."

The khedive asked, probably on Colvin's advice, for time to think it over and returned to the palace. Later Arabi was sent for, and he either apologized to the khedive or thanked him, but in any case the Egyptians have never quite forgiven Arabi for doing either. But he was still the leader of the military revolt; Tawfik had to compromise, and Arabi was made minister for war. The nationalists tried to push through social and economic reforms, but they were blocked by the British and French advisers. When in February 1882 the nationalists forced through an organic decree establishing the basis for a chamber of deputies — clearly the beginning of a government which would be Egyptian for the Egyptians — the British and the French saw what was happening and sent a combined fleet to Alexandria to suppress the nationalists, demanding Arabi's arrest and exile.

Egyptians made no bones about their hostility to British and French intervention. They were supported by a "fatwa" from the Azhar, which said that no more obedience was due to the khedive, and a sort of national committee was set up to take over the country. In fact the Egyptian revolution was on the very eve of liberating the country from Turks and Europeans. But once more an outsider would step in and frustrate Egypt's struggle for genuine independence.

On July 11, 1882, the British fleet bombarded Alexandria. The harbor was full of ships, including Russian and American warships, and all the Europeans who could get out to the American and Russian men-of-war did so. The scenes in the water that day were described as "incredible." Colonel Chaillé-Long, who was in Alexandria at the time, played a considerable part in saving some of the city, although the British bombardment was, according to almost every report of it, a savage piece of military politics. The British said they expected the city to be attacked by Arabi with thirty thousand men, and Major Edwin N. McClellan, who was in charge of the marines on the United States warships, has said that the marines were determined "to stick to the British and take their chances."

Arabi had lined himself up along the Suez Canal, intending to block it so that the British couldn't get at him from the rear, but de Lesseps persuaded him not to, giving Arabi his word that no British ships would be allowed to use the canal. De Lesseps then broke his word, and the British sailed up the canal to Arabi's exposed rear. The British landed at Ismailiya, and Arabi met them at Tel el Kebir nearby. Much has been written about this battle, and the general opinion of European writers is that the Egyptians fought badly at Tel el Kebir and were easily routed. But Sir Archibald Alison, commander of the Highland Brigade at Tel el Kebir, said in a speech in Glasgow in October 1884: "I must do justice to the Egyptian soldiers [at Tel el Kebir]. I never saw men fight more steadily. Retiring up a line of works which we had taken in flank, they rallied at every re-entering angle, at every battery, at every redoubt, and renewed the fight. Four or five times we had to close upon them with the bayonet, and I saw men fighting hard when their officers were flying."

The Egyptians were ill equipped and badly led, and Arabi personally did nothing that day which Egyptians can remember with pride. On September 14 British cavalry reached Abbasiya in Cairo, and the next day Lord Wolseley, with the Brigade of Guards under the Duke of Connaught, entered Cairo. Arabi, obviously frightened for his life, drove out to Abbasiya and handed over his sword to the British, and that was the second act of obeisance that Arabi is not forgiven for, even now. The Egyptian army — if it could still be called that — in Cairo surrendered to the British without fighting. The garrison in the Citadel surrendered to Major Watson, an intelligence officer who had 130 men with him. Watson entered the fortress alone and asked for the commandant. The commandant was asleep. "Then wake him up," Watson ordered, "and tell him to surrender." The commandant appeared and Cairo was then officially handed over to the British by this sleepy Turkish officer, who gave Watson the keys of the castle and said he was delighted to do so.

14

Cromer's Cairo

B̲ʀɪᴛɪsʜ rule by occupation brought no sudden physical change to
Cairo because the British had been ruling Egypt indirectly for some
years anyway. Tawfik went on being khedive, the administration remained foreign, the consular courts went on dealing out justice, and
British troops now occupied the Citadel, Abbasiya and the barracks at
Kasr el Nil on the riverside. The most important influence the British
would have on the city was the increasing division of it.

Like the Ottomans before them the British needed foreigners to
help them rule Cairo, because they did not want commercial Cairo to
be Egyptian-owned. They wanted no accumulation of financial capital
in Egyptian hands; in fact they wanted Egypt and Egyptians to remain fundamentally feudal, particularly on the land where the cotton
and the cheap labor came from. On the other hand it was vital for the
sort of commercial investment they were making in Egypt that Cairo
at least should be thoroughly organized in a modern way by depend-
able non-Egyptians. Britain therefore encouraged into Cairo not only
her own administrators but commercially inclined foreigners from all
over Europe who flocked into the city and took over the Europeanized
part of it, creating a sharper and more brutal division of the city than
ever before. But this was to be a steady process rather than a sudden
one.

The initial period just after the occupation was used by the British
to consolidate their absolute rule in Cairo, and the man who was responsible for it was Lord Cromer — then Sir Evelyn Baring. Cromer
took over Egypt as British Agent in 1883, and he ruled Egypt for the
next twenty-four years. But even before the occupation he had been

the British Commissioner of the Public Debt in Cairo, and it was his manipulation of the Egyptian debt and the politics he played in the court that helped bring about British occupation. Englishmen still consider Cromer to be one of the greatest diplomatists produced in the nineteenth century. Modern Egyptians consider him to be one of the most cunning scoundrels who ever ruled them. But whatever else he was, Cromer was a brilliant financier in the tradition of his old and powerful banking family. He always knew exactly what Britain's real economic interest in Egypt was, and he did everything possible to protect it. He was a stubborn, dictatorial, Victorian Englishman who treated Egyptian peasants as "not unkindly" children, and Egyptians in general as intellectually inferior Orientals who, if they ever gained anything from contact with Europe, picked up the worst (revolutionary) ideas rather than the best ones.

It was Cromer more than any other man — not excepting Gordon and Kitchener — who kept the French, Belgians and Italians away from the Nile and established the condominium with Egypt over the Sudan in 1899, after its recapture by Kitchener. The point of "protecting" the Nile, and also of Cromer's subsequent schemes for building new barrages across the river in Egypt, was simply cotton. But the other role that Cromer gave the English in Egypt was rather larger than cotton. In his own book *Modern Egypt* (1908) he wrote: "The Englishman came to Egypt with a mission to perform . . . He looks towards India, and he says to himself, with all the confidence of an imperial race — I can perform this task; I have done it before."

The English imperial task as Cromer saw it was perfectly clear, but what Cromer and his successors had to contend with in Cairo was an increasing awareness among the rich Egyptians that for every penny they got out of the cotton they grew, the European merchants and eventually the English got a lot more. The national bourgeoisie also wanted more say in Egyptian political affairs, and together with the Moslem hierarchy they formed the most articulate opposition to the British. This combination produced almost all the leading politicians in Egypt in the next fifty years, and many of them would rise to power from nothing on the very promise that they would get rid of the British. But with rather sickening regularity they would inevitably compromise or backslide or simply collapse before the determined physical opposition the British met them with, including prison. Only a handful of Egyptian politicians between 1900 and 1952 can be considered now as uncorrupted men.

Cairo under Cromer was therefore an intensely political and socially weighted city, but according to Sir Ronald Storrs (*Orientations,* 1937) the golden epoch of Cromer's Cairo began to end in 1904. Up till then the kind of social and regal authority the British exercised in Cairo was at its peak, and Storrs says that if 1904 began the decline then 1914 was the fall. Storrs himself was to bridge the decline and fall of Cromer's Cairo as an Oriental Secretary at the Agency, and his study in *Orientations* of the manners and customs of the young British diplomats in Cairo and of the Turkish-Egyptian court between the decline and fall of the Cromer era are written so nostalgically and intellectually that one begins to see why Cairo attracted so many of these young English intellectual diplomats and soldiers like Storrs, Phillip Graves, D. G. Hogarth, T. E. Lawrence and dozens of others. Their life was perfect, even if the rarefied regal atmosphere that Cromer had enjoyed was changing to a more vulgar and attenuated involvement.

Cairo for them was all comings and goings, good company, intellectual exercise, public-schoolboy classicism; and if you spoke Arabic, which many of these young men now did, Cairo life was full of exquisite "Oriental" titillations. Men like Storrs did their day's work from eight to one, then they would hop on a bicycle and ride to the Turf Club, and after lunch play tennis or golf all afternoon until dark, then back to the Turf Club or to their houses or to somebody else's for dinner. The night was spent at the French or Italian theatre (the English had none of their own) or at one of the endless soirées which went on around the fringes of the court. Yet there was also a certain modesty, then, to the requirements. Even Kitchener, who was commander in chief of the Egyptian army, would ride a donkey to his office. All donkeys in Cairo then had number plates, and Storrs swears that they loved to have cigarette smoke blown up their noses.

Cromer himself left Cairo in 1907, and Storrs says that Cromer made his farewell drive to Cairo railway station along streets lined with soldiers with loaded guns and in a "silence chillier than ice." But it was not only on the streets that Cromer's imperial mentality made itself felt. When he left he bequeathed to his compatriots in Cairo the sort of outlook and behavior which was never to leave them as long as they were there in occupation. British society in Cairo had become so narrow under Cromer and so excessively introvert that his successor, Sir Eldon Gorst, was almost ostracized by the local English when he tried to invite Egyptians to the British Agency. Even the idea of it was so scandalous to the English in Egypt that Sir Eldon had to ask the Foreign Office if he could sue an Englishwoman who had written in an English paper that he was so vulgar that he had gone to Cairo station on a motorbike wearing a cloth cap to meet a British royal prince.

It was this sort of super-English presence which began to change the outward appearance of Cairo simply by being there. The English not only took over the court and the politics and the banks, but they introduced the sort of modern city amenities that English colonial society found essential for its comfort and its commerce. By 1900 there were four tramways in Cairo: from the Citadel to the railway station, from the Citadel to Bulaq, from the railway station to Abbasiya, and from Ezbekiya down to old Cairo, Masr al Atika. A fifth was being built from Giza out to the pyramids. The suburban train to Helwan and Tura had been built, and its Cairo terminal was at the old Bab el Luk. Victorias and dogcarts also packed the streets. There was an English nursing home, and also the Victoria Hospital, which is still standing in the Shariʿ Abdel Khalid Sawat Pasha. An English society weekly called *The Sphinx* was founded in 1893, and it continued publishing until after the 1952 revolution. (The European Cairo newspaper then was still a French one — *Le Journal d'Égypte*.)

There were three English department stores and an English estate agent. In the new shopping districts of the Ismailia quarter you could find "English" booksellers, cigar importers, religious libraries, sanitary engineers, confectioners (not the famous Groppi's yet), drapers, dressmakers, florists, glovers, gunsmiths, hairdressers, hatters, livery stables, milliners, outfitters, photographers, saddlers, solicitors, tourist agencies and tailors. Among the tailors was the famous Collacot, who dressed several generations of English gentlemen and officers up till the burning of Cairo in 1952.

By 1900, apart from polo and the mixed sporting clubs (where the main sport was not always outdoors), there were tennis courts, golf links and shooting clubs. A steam laundry had been built, some of the hotels had European chambermaids, and after 1898 almost all the main streets and shops of the Ismailiya quarter were lit by electricity. In the 1890s the old palace grounds of the Kasr el Doubara along the Nile was cut up into streets and plots, and the first new building in this new quarter was the British Consulate General, which was known in turn as the Agency, the Residency, and is today the British Embassy. Most of the ministries also moved to this area, which is known now as Garden City. In 1896 an Anglo-French-German commission had drained the swampy parts of European Cairo, and what was left of the old lakes in this area finally disappeared.

By 1914 Cairo was fairly well Anglicized, but the dedicated Englishman that Cromer had pictured so fancifully as typical before 1900 was simply no more. Englishmen, in service to the empire or not, came out to Cairo now to be served and to enjoy themselves, and almost all came to lord it over anybody considered inferior. One lot of English would look down on other English, but all the English would look down on all the foreigners. All foreigners would look down on all Egyptians, and rich Egyptians looked down on middle-class Egyptians. And everybody of all races and classes looked down on the fellahin, who in fact dug and watered and nurtured the wealth the whole structure was built on.

One can find a sort of distillation of this atmosphere in the once popular books of Douglas Sladen, who was an excellent and amusing observer of Cairo, but whose comments on Egyptian-English-foreign relationships in the city are a little embarrassing to read now. He claims, for instance, that one of his books, *Egypt and the English* (1908), "unmasks the Egyptian and shows him to be a shifty, imperfectly educated Oriental." This was about the time that the word "wog" became popular (though Eric Partridge says the word comes from "golliwog" and not from "worthy Oriental gentleman"). Sladen also says that the Khedivial Club, once the best club in Cairo, was now "essentially a club of foreigners and gyppos." The two clubs patronized by "the best English people" were the Turf Club and the Khedivial Sporting Club (Gezira), where there were no gyppos.

This sort of behavior merely reflected the expanding British middle-class presence in Egypt, and the importation of the English class structure in toto. But what finally changed the physique of Cairo between 1900 and 1914 was not English snobbery but the big cotton boom of 1903. This was in fact a legacy of Cromer's early policy in getting Egyptian soil almost totally under cotton, so that it was there when it was needed. This boom brought an extraordinary gulp of cash wealth to the feudal landowners. They still could not invest the wealth in anything like industry or trade, but they could spend it on themselves which they did with a vengeance. Among other indulgences they built themselves in Cairo some of the most luxurious villas in the world, and though many of them still stand today, every year now these beautiful old houses in rich and exotic gardens fall into disuse or are pulled down to make way for modern apartment blocks. But one can still walk around Gezira or Garden City and marvel at the wealth that went into these small palaces.

Coinciding with this 1903 cotton boom, a European-style land speculation arrived in Cairo. By 1908 thirty-one land companies, not one of them really Egyptian, were operating in the city. It was not only the Ismailiya-Tawfikiya area that was torn up and rebuilt but Gezira, Roda Island, and the Pyramid road and Garden City. The beautiful grounds of the Gezira Palace Hotel (the former khedivial palace which is now the Omar Khayyam Hotel) were the first to be exploited, and by 1910 the area around this hotel had been built up with huge and costly houses, foreign and Egyptian. Roda Island, which had remained a sort of vegetable garden for Cairo with Ibrahim's large decorative gardens on the north end, was now turned over to the speculators, who built French-style villas down the middle of it. Today, what saves Roda from the usual modern ugliness is the dilapidated charm of these houses, which now seem very attractive and nostalgic — isolated like little Frenchified islands in the middle of a later and more repulsive development.

Both Shubra and Kubba suddenly became garden suburbs, or part of them did, built in the French or Italian style. Most of the architects of this boom were French or Italian, and most of the masons were Italian, according to Lord Cromer. The rich Egyptian villas were built with Egyptian cash, but most of the European companies now invested in apartment blocks, office blocks or stores, and most of this sort of building went on in the center of the European city. Foreign-owned banks, hotels (including the new and luxurious Swiss hotel, the Semiramis) and department stores began to grow like lilies in the field, and many of the comparatively new private houses in the Ismailiya quarter were simply pulled down and rebuilt in the modern four- or five-story apartment blocks, many of which still stand like black romantic ghosts among the gray and yellow realities of modern cement construction. But the big cotton boom suffered a temporary bust in 1907, and Cairo was left full of holes where buildings had been demolished and rebuilding had suddenly stopped.

What signified the permanency and domination of the Europeans in Cairo more than anything at this stage was their religion and their schools. British missionaries have often claimed that they brought education to Egypt, but in 1876, before the British occupation, there were already 4,817 Arabic schools in Egypt and 110,803 pupils, a higher percentage than there were in Czarist Russia at that time. There were 8,875 pupils in Cairo schools alone. There were also twelve separate Coptic schools in Cairo, a large Jewish school which taught Hebrew, Arabic, French and Italian, and two Greek schools, a Syrian Maronite school, a free Armenian school, and a remarkable institution called the Free, Gratuitous and Universal School, which had Tawfik's patronage and which taught only professional and scientific subjects — no religion of any kind. It had 262 Egyptian pupils;

the rest of the 486 pupils were European, including fifteen English boys. And unlike the European schools that followed it, Arabic was a basic subject, though not the main one.

On the whole, none of the Mohammed Ali family had any interest in Arab culture or even the language, which they did not speak, and one khedive after another encouraged foreign schools, even Christian schools, in preference to local ones. The oldest mission school in Cairo belonged to the Sisters of Saint Vincent de Paul and the Lazarist Fathers; Mohammed Ali had encouraged them to set up their school by giving them a big piece of land in 1844. The Christian Brothers followed, then Franciscans and Sisters of the Good Shepherd. Proselytizing in these Catholic schools was secondary to giving a good secular education.

It was Said (1854–1863) who brought the American Protestant missions to Cairo in 1855 and gave them a building. By the 1870s they had a boys' college, two girls' schools and a mixed school — an innovation in Egypt and a good one. The American Board maintained the schools, but they got a generous subsidy from Said and later from Ismail. Ismail also gave them a plot of land on the northwest corner of Ezbekiya and donated seven thousand pounds to their building fund. They built a church and a school there, which are still marked on Cairo's maps but which are now a rather sad little corner of Ezbekiya. The British "educators" came last, in 1862, and the first school they established in Cairo was not really a mission school but was more or less a private venture run by a Miss Whately, who was the daughter of an Anglican Bishop of Dublin. Miss Whately's school had many poor Arab pupils and it taught Arabic.

That was the situation in education when the British occupied Cairo, but after 1881 the conditions changed rather subtly. Most of the mission schools became middle-class European schools with no poor Egyptian pupils, and eventually the large English population dominated their own schools. Major A. W. Sansom, one of the most honest observers of Cairo's political life later on (he was the security officer of the British Embassy in 1952) describes in *I Spied Spies* (1965) his own English education in one of these schools between the wars as: "that ghastly prep school in Cairo, run by those female horrors from Cheltenham who regarded the French as wogs and Egyptians as a bare cut above camels."

Egyptian schools were steadily and deliberately neglected in favor of all these foreign schools, and rich Egyptians either sent their children to them or packed them off to Europe if they wanted any higher education. The people who had to put up with inferior Egyptian schools were the poor townsmen and the ignorant villagers. Egypt's greatest writer, Taha Husain, who is almost unknown in the west but who is undoubtedly one of the most important literary figures of this century, wrote in two autobiographical volumes just what it was like to sit at the feet of the ignorant teachers in these forgotten and impoverished Arabic schools, trying to acquire from them some inkling of knowledge beyond the ninety-nine names of God and the meaning of every single word of the Koran. As a child, Taha Husain had been accidentally blinded by his ignorant peasant mother, but he not only got an Arabic education in Egypt — he graduated eventually at the Sorbonne, became for a while minister of education in Egypt and is today Egypt's most venerated intellectual. What he writes of Cairo at the end of the last century and into this one shows just what a large gap there was between the privileged rich in the European schools and the underprivileged Egyptians sitting around the pillars of the Azhar listening to nothingness. This is not simply an Egyptian view of the situation. Sir Valentine Chirol in his book *The Egyptian Problem* (1920) says that education under British occupation was "unquestionably the worst of our failures."

By 1906 this British encouragement of foreigners had reached a point where it was possible to build them a whole new suburb. A Belgian company, the Cairo Electric Railways and Heliopolis Oasis Company, began to develop a stretch of the desert north of Cairo, just beyond Mataria and not far from the site of old Heliopolis. The man in charge of this new Heliopolis was an Englishman, Sir Reginald Oakes, although its Belgian inspiration was the Baron Empain, who built himself an exhilarating palace on the very edge of the new city in the style of one of the palaces of Angkor in Cambodia, although it always reminded me more of the Kandaha Mahadewa Temple. The little city was laid out, in fact, as an entity which was originally intended, according to the 1914 *Baedeker,* to house, among others, the British officers and officials who ruled Egypt. But it was overtaken by circumstances and prosperous Europeans long before it was finished, and it became the suburb of Cairo where the upper middle classes lived, and where rich Egyptians also built their private villas on the desert perimeter.

Architecturally the style was a consistent but peculiarly European Mooresque, and almost every apartment block had wide balconies and a rather opulent façade of yellowish desert-colored stone. Streets of shops were built along arcaded footpaths; gardens ran down the middle of wide avenues; a racecourse, sporting club, hotel and swimming pool, clubs and mosques and churches were added, mostly with

[218]

a nice European taste for comfort. The point was, of course, not only to collect the rents from this vast new city but to collect the cash on the metro railway which was built to bring all these officials — and later the clerks, shopkeepers, dentists, doctors, teachers, chemists, lawyers, and European shopgirls and typists — into the city.

In Cairo itself, in European Cairo, the sidewalks had long ago been invaded by the poor population from across the Ezbekiya hoping to do some sort of street business with the foreigners. Just before the First World War you could buy, outside the Continental-Savoy Hotel, anything from a boa constrictor to a fully grown leopard in a cage, as well as a *New York Tribune* or a *Daily Mail* which were not too old. Outside the Continental there also used to be a performing baboon (you still see them in Cairo) who did somersaults while riding a donkey. His act was decorously modified by a pair of red flannel trousers which an outraged American woman missionary had given him to cover his raw red nakedness. All the area around Clot Bey and the northeast corner of Ezbekiya, which only thirty years before had been fashionable, was now half brothel and half cheap cafés specially catering to Tommy Atkins. The streets here were always a twittering miasma of electric lights, and every café had a tinkling piano or a pianola in it. The prostitutes operated in the alleyways off the quarter, in the fish market and under the arches.

Parts of Bulaq were also evil; in fact prostitution was widespread all over the city — most of it European. Shari' Rod el Farag had once been the leading Levantine brothel quarter, and even before that native women used to stand naked in the Bab el Luk area begging custom, which for a while gave prostitutes in Cairo the name of Bab el Luki. Just before 1914 the Haret al Roui, near the Ezbekiya, was the principal and perhaps the worst quarter for prostitution, and the taste then was for fat women who used to sit out on the sidewalks with their legs bare. Many were Italian, some were even white Circassians, and at night the British military police used to patrol these honky-tonk districts mounted on pure white Arab thoroughbreds. There was also another kind of brothel — for Egyptians and Turkish middle classes — in the Shari' Wagh el Birkett (also near the Ezbekiya), and here the prostitutes used to lean over the balconies on the first floor dressed in virginal negligees. The best belly dancing in Cairo in the early 1900s was in the fish market at a café called El Dorado.

The British in Cairo could thus enjoy themselves on all levels. The rich Europeans and Egyptians entertained lavishly, the middle classes lived like well-kept domestic gods, and the soldiers got drunk in the cafés and enjoyed the brothels. It was soft, pleasant, succulent, boring; yet always rather edgy because of the Egyptians, who could not be quite forgotten. As early as 1883 Britain had promised to get out of Egypt the moment Egyptians were capable of ruling themselves. But Egyptians were always convinced that this was an interminable subterfuge for permanent British occupation. The man in particular who emerged after the Arabi revolt as the true defender of the Egyptians, and who remained incorruptible in this belief, was a French-educated lawyer named Mustafa Kamel.

Mustafa Kamel wanted an untrammeled Egypt free of all foreigners, including the Turkish court, but he knew it would never come from the politicians playing political chess with the British in Cairo. Mustafa Kamel put his own faith in a populace whose national consciousness was aroused to resist. He was one of the few Egyptian politicians who considered this appeal to the populace the only real policy for Egypt, and it was his policy to open popular schools for children and even night courses for adults all over Egypt to teach Arabic and Arab culture. In Cairo, Mustafa Kamel founded the Hizb al Watani, the Nationalist party, in 1905, and its platform was no negotiations with the British until they had left Egypt. Mustafa Kamel was a little before his time, and his party did not survive subsequent events.

If Mustafa Kamel was untouchable for the British, the man they respected was Saad Zaghlul, whom Cromer considered an honest young man with a brilliant future. Saad was honest, and he did have a brilliant political future trying to get rid of the British. But the growth of Egyptian political life in Cairo, whether it was hostile or friendly, was always choked to death by patronage. The great Saad Zaghlul himself was under the patronage of Princess Nazli, a niece of Ismail's, and he was also her lawyer. Princess Nazli was something of a politician in her own right, although she was far too patrician to do anything but encourage the others. She was a royal bohemian who spoke four languages, even some Arabic, and was brave enough to invite men to her salon. The reception room of her house was papered with illustrated weeklies, and while you waited there her Abyssinian slave would pedal out "Home, Sweet Home" on the pianola. She was cultured and European but also a good Moslem who treated Kitchener, whom she had known as a young captain, as a sort of overgrown boyfriend. She was very pro-British, while Saad Zaghlul, who had fought well at Tel el Kebir, was anti-British. Saad got a little too deep into this fashionable milieu when he married the daughter of a former prime minister, Mustafa Pasha, who was a close friend of Cromer's.

But somehow he survived all the Turco-British blandishments of court politics and remained a dedicated Egyptian. It was the articulate policy and the popular following of Saad Zaghlul and others which forced Lord Kitchener (who followed Sir Eldon Gorst as resident minister and who spoke some Arabic) to set up a legislative assembly in Cairo. Thus the parliamentary life of Egypt, in imitation of the British, began.

The relationship of British resident minister to prime minister to court to parliament and to politicians established the pattern Egyptian politics would have until the British left Cairo. The comings and goings of one group to another, man to man, office to office, parliament to palace, palace to Residency, Residency to politicians gave the city the atmosphere of an Italian operetta being sung to the angry chorus of a national upheaval. Almost all foreigners in Cairo except the clever ones laughed at this spectacle of Egypt trying to learn how to rule itself in the European parliamentary manner.

But what terrified every British resident minister, from Lord Cromer to Sir Miles Lampson (the last), was the possibility that Egypt might somehow discover that it did not have to rule itself in imitation of a European parliament, and that there might be another way. The political events that came out of the First World War did suggest to the Egyptians that there might be another way, and it erupted eventually on the streets of Cairo.

15

Revolutionary Cairo

W HEN Storrs said that 1914 was the fall of the old society in Cairo
he really meant that the First World War broke the enchantment of
absolute British rule. The First World War undermined almost every
aspect of British authority in Egypt, yet, the war itself barely came to
the Europeans in the city except pleasurably. "From the London
newspapers it is clear that Cairo is imagined to be in a state of tense
and bellicose anxiety," Storrs wrote in 1914, "but . . . yesterday there
was a race meeting numerously attended, the tennis courts are overcrowded; you cannot get a table at the Club, bazaars are open and
doing a certain amount of business." But he goes on to say that Egyptian students, politicians and journalists who spread rumors against
the British did so in fear of arrest and deportation to Malta.

Within a very short time the war brought eruptions of British, Australian, New Zealand and colonial troops to Cairo, which once again
influenced the city's manners and customs more than it did the city's
real appearance. Since Egypt in 1914 was still under the fiction of
being an independent part of the Ottoman Empire, Turkey's entry
into the war on the side of the Germans, and the rather timorous
Turkish attack on the Suez Canal, complicated the problem of British
authority in Egypt. Britain had based her authority in Cairo not on
Turkish rule but on rule by Turks. But now the Turks were enemies.
Moreover Britain, through that extraordinary paymaster T. E. Lawrence, was also encouraging the Arabs of Arabia to revolt against the
Turks, in fact to fight a war of national liberation. This lesson was not
to be lost on the Egyptians later on — self-determination became the
one policy all Egyptians could agree on, and while European Cairo

gradually became a sort of madhouse of self-indulgence for the British army, Egyptian Cairo became a place of whispers and politics and preparation. While newly arrived British soldiers enjoyed the sort of pleasures in Cairo they had never tasted in their lives before, Egyptians began to suffer from steeply rising prices, and in the countryside poverty and malnutrition were so bad that in 1918 more people died than were born.

But soldiers did bring a measure of prosperity to Cairo, and Storrs, reporting the arrival of the Australians in Cairo in 1914, says that they spent between three and four thousand pounds a day in the city. This association of soldier with Cairo, of Tommy and Digger with Cairene, would become something that neither side would ever quite forget. Storrs thought the arrival of troops improved the appearance of Cairo. He reports that the Australians began turning over donkey buses which wouldn't wait for them and firing pistol shots into cafés they liked. The Egyptians, Storrs said, feared but admired the Australians. On the other hand the Honorable Aubrey Herbert in *Mons, Anzac and Kut* (1919) says that there was little love lost between Australians and Egyptians. He admired the Australians himself, but he adds that "The native Egyptian was, it must be admitted, constantly very roughly treated, for the average Australian, while he was at first apt to resent superiority in others, felt little doubt about his own claim to it."

The truth is that Cairo and foreign soldiers have always been oil and water. Soldiers enjoyed Cairo to the point where they would always look back on it nostalgically, but they always felt they were being "gypped," and more often than not they were. But Cairo became a problem for the British because it was too attractive to officers and soldiers who should have been thinking war when in fact they were thinking pleasure. Even people like T. E. Lawrence would wrap themselves up in Cairo when they got back to it, and Storrs describes Lawrence ("my little genius") as an eager and unfatiguing bazaar walker and mosque hunter.

This continual mutual corruption of British and Egyptian during the war is very hard to measure properly now. How many British soldiers learned any sympathy or dislike for the Egyptians during the war? How many Egyptians, watching the behavior en masse of British soldiers, learned to hate them or admire them? The Egyptians, as almost everyone who has lived in Cairo and written about them says, have always been reluctant to hate anybody, even those who have treated them hatefully.

Nonetheless the Egyptian contact with British soldiers in Cairo was a contact with reality, which increased rather than diminished Egyptian determination to get rid of them. Saad Zaghlul said: "I have no quarrel with them personally . . . but I want to see an independent Egypt." And on the whole most Egyptians felt this way. Most British soldiers got on well with the individual Egyptian, but British soldiers in Cairo saw only the mischievous, tricky, nightshirted Egyptian who packed the streets and bazaars and lived in medieval squalor and seemed to enjoy it. He couldn't see the man who lived under this miserable, filthy, starving skin in a world absolutely his own, into which no foreigner penetrated unless he understood what Egyptians really wanted of themselves as well as of others. And so few foreigners bothered to find out, and those who tried to were so easily blinded by their own intellectual superiority that almost every Englishman except those in the secret police of Cairo underestimated Egyptian feelings at the end of the war, when there was a revolution in Egypt and Cairo became a city of barricades and strikes.

What led up to this situation was the wartime British declaration that Egypt was now a British protectorate. Britain was, in fact, ruling directly by diktats. Martial law was introduced in 1916, and military courts judged civilian offenders and punished them. In fact Britain treated Egypt more like an enemy country than a friendly one, and in 1917 Britain began to force and even allow the kidnapping of peasants to serve in their labor battalions in Palestine. "It was the corvée unashamedly reintroduced," Colonel P. G. Elgood says in *The Transit of Egypt* (1928). "Fellahin were seized on the highway and in the fields and sent under escort to the army." Donkeys, camels and other belongings were taken with them, and food was commandeered. It had been Kitchener's boast that he had done away with the corvée after millennia of recourse to it by Pharaohs and occupiers. Emil Ludwig says in his book *The Nile in Egypt* (1937) that during the 1914–1918 war the British sent one hundred thousand "free Egyptians" to Syria, eight thousand to Mesopotamia and ten thousand to France.

It was President Wilson's Fourteen Points which gave Egypt hope of independence at the end of the war, and when Saad Zaghlul knocked at the door of the British Residency one day and demanded Egypt's right to self-determination under the Fourteen Points, he was allowed to talk and then allowed to leave, but he was arrested a month later and deported to Malta. All Egypt immediately revolted. Every city and town was seized by Egyptians, and overnight Cairo became a revolutionary city.

Trams and trains stopped, all life stopped, nobody went to work, and the workers themselves organized strikes and joined with students in big demonstrations which took over the city. On March 18, 1919, eight English soldiers were killed on their way to Cairo. According to Sir Thomas Russell, who later became commandant of Cairo police, the city lay behind barricades. Trenches were dug so that mounted police and troops couldn't operate. The police were told to isolate the Azhar, which was a sort of headquarters of the revolt, but Russell says the Egyptian soldiers couldn't be relied on, and he persuaded the British authorities not to try it. Women in particular played a new and considerable part in the revolution, throwing off the veil, haranguing the strikers, forming picket lines, building barricades and following in large crowds the funerals of Egyptians killed in the street fighting.

The situation was so tense that Britain was reluctant to expose her own troops in Cairo. At one dangerous moment, when Russell and his policemen were desperately and delicately holding the balance of British authority, Australian soldiers arrived on the streets with hockey sticks, dying to get into the fight, and Russell only saved the situation and their lives by talking them out of it and promising them some "useful street fighting" later on. But he couldn't stop it for long, because by now the Egyptians, he says, were shouting "Long live the Revolution," and parading in the streets carrying chisels, adzes, tree props and iron gratings. Demonstrations went on and on and shots were exchanged, but Russell says that much of the real trouble was started by "low-class Europeans losing their heads and firing at the demonstrations from their houses." When Egyptians in Cairo attacked lorry loads of troops with sticks and stones, the troops opened fire and killed thirteen and wounded thirty. And for "murdering" British officers, thirty people including intellectuals and political figures were executed on April 9. But British troops themselves were fed up with the war and there is every evidence that they could not be trusted either. The British government sent General E. H. H. Allenby as special high commissioner to replace the Resident, and Allenby was intelligent enough to read the signs.

He immediately ordered the release of Zaghlul from Malta. Perhaps more than any other political or military act this one saved Egypt for Britain for years to come, although Allenby was attacked bitterly in England for compromising too much. Saad Zaghlul's original delegation to the Residency had now become the basis of a new party called the Wafd (delegation), which wanted to negotiate the British out of Egypt, as distinct from the Nationalists, who still demanded instant and absolute British withdrawal. The 1919 revolution was rather quickly taken in hand by the Wafd, who continued with strikes and demonstrations to dominate Cairo, but they gave Allenby time enough to organize his own forces. Most of the Wafdists hated violence and didn't want it. Allenby was a soldier who wasn't afraid to use it, and having undermined Wafdist opposition by releasing Zaghlul, he declared martial law in Egypt and crushed the strikes one by one.

Though free to leave Malta, Zaghlul was not yet allowed back in Egypt. He went to Paris, where he knocked on the doors of the peace conference with his Wafd, still hoping to get Egyptian independence under Wilson's Fourteen Points. But on April 20, 1919, the United States itself recognized the British "protection" of Egypt, and thus knocked the bottom out of any hope the Egyptians had (and most of their revolution was based on it) of persuading the big powers that Egypt had a right to rule herself.

Worse, the end of the war brought cotton back to the world market, and once more food crops were replaced by cotton, and fortunes were made on cotton by rich foreigners and the feudal landlords who were Britain's steadfast allies. But according to Sir George Young in *Egypt* (1927), "More than a million urban and landless proletariat were starving." That meant Cairo. The Egyptians boycotted a special mission under Lord Milner which the British then sent out to "work out the details of a constitution" for Egypt. The women in Cairo played a considerable part in this boycott. They would kidnap tramcars and drive them through the streets shouting out "Down with Milner" and waving slogans under the nose of any European who tried to get on the tram, and Sir Valentine Chirol says that the schoolgirls of Cairo became so passionately anti-Milner that they were more violent than the boys, and teachers could hardly hold them. The boycott was so effective that the Milner mission failed.

Once more Britain got the message, and Zaghlul was allowed to return to Cairo after presenting the British in London with the Wafd's demands for independence.

British-Egyptian politics simply continued to worsen, although Britain allowed Egypt her "sovereignty" in 1922, and Fuad, who was then khedive, became king. But during the next eighteen months seventeen British officials were assassinated and twenty were attacked in broad daylight. In 1924 Sir Lee Stack, British commander in chief of the Egyptian army, was shot by seven men as he rode in a car through the streets of Cairo. Much of this Egyptian violence was simply a reflection of vigorous popular reaction, and Britain retreated slowly and skillfully before it, seeming to give way a great deal but in effect giving up very little. By 1936 an Anglo-Egyptian treaty was signed which gave Egypt a little independence, but more in name than in fact. In 1937 Egypt was finally freed of the Tribunaux Mixtes, the foreign courts, but still the Egyptians were not satisfied, because Britain was still in occupation, still controlled most of Egyptian economic life, still ran the canal. The land, the cotton, the canal and the old strategic link with India were still the reasons for Britain's reluctance to give up her grip on Egypt, and the continuing violence and denunciation and threats of revolution made Cairo an exciting city for those who lived in it, but not a particularly threatening or dangerous one.

The apparent status quo, which Britain had managed to keep going somehow for almost twenty years, meant that the balance in Cairo between Europeans and Egyptians also remained about the same. In other words, it still favored the Europeans. The British, in fact, needed the Europeans more as their own direct control became less. It was now, however, that the middle-class Europeans signed their own expulsion warrant, although it would not come into effect for another twenty years. Up till 1937 it was obviously advantageous to be foreign or even stateless in Cairo because that way you were safe (under the capitulations) from Egyptian law and free of Egyptian taxes. Greeks, Italians, Cypriots, Maltese, Syrians, Rumanians, French, Austrians, Germans, Armenians and European stateless Jews all lived in Cairo as permanent foreign residents, and by now their children were being born in Cairo and knew no other city. But the silly arrogance, stupidity and ignorance of this prosperous European community became almost unbearable to Egyptians, and it even took on an air of tragedy. Jews fleeing Hitler were permitted into Egypt freely and were allowed to work and establish businesses in Egypt. But being European, and mostly middle-class Jews, they did not bring their Semitism with them (which would have been brother to brother in Egypt) but their Europeanism, which made them contemptuous of poor Arab and poor Egyptian Jew alike.

Though there were always some poor Europeans (mostly Armenians) in Cairo, almost every European had at least one servant, and many of the middle classes had more. Medically they had more than an ample supply of doctors, hospitals, and the latest 'rugs, and they certainly ate far better and much more cheaply than anybody in Europe. But according to a survey the Egyptian Association for Social Studies made in 1938 (quoted by Charles Issawi), poor Egyptian families (and about 90 percent were poor), lived five to six persons in one room, got seven and a half weeks' work per year, earned an average annual income of nine Egyptian pounds, spent fifty-two piasters (ten shillings) on food a month, and lived permanently in debt.

Egyptians had the highest death rate in the world, two children in every four died before reaching the age of five, 65 percent had malaria, there were more blind per head than anywhere else in the world, and the people lived on a diet which had little or no fish, eggs, milk, meat, butter or even wheat. Seventy to eighty percent of the fellahin had bilharzia or ancylostomiasis. Bilharzia is a waterborne disease which was partly spread by the irrigation waters that grew the cotton.

During her occupation, Britain never drilled an artesian well to bring pure water to a village, never established a medical service for Egyptians in city or country, never made any serious attempt to school, house, bring health to or improve the conditions of the majority of the population. The British were not brutal occupiers, but the real list of Egyptian condemnations against British rule (and almost every serious British economist and sociologist dealing with Egypt agrees) admits this absolute failure to improve the conditions of the ordinary citizens of Cairo and the countryside.

It is hard to blame the individual Englishman or European born in Cairo for this situation, even though he contributed to it. The Europeans themselves were byproducts of this old tragedy of foreign occupation, and if they lived well, ate well and slept well they were only fulfilling, they felt, what was expected of them. As individuals, the Europeans of Cairo were by no means unattractive, and physically the various mixed marriages among these many-faced races produced a very beautiful middle-class girl — some of the most attractive to be seen anywhere. Looking back on it, the situation of these Europeans was obviously self-indulgent, but they did play a big part in the continually expanding commercial life of the city. Between the wars, when their life was at its best, you could see them arriving every morning to run the ordinary life of the city: beautifully groomed typists, secretaries, students, shopgirls, teachers. They came in the trams and buses from the garden suburbs of Mataria, or Kubba or Heliopolis or Maadi. Decorum was high among these European girls, and a good bourgeois marriage was about the only hope they had for the future. The subdivisions of these middle-class Europeans were often determined by their passports, but religion was probably more important than nationality. On the whole Catholic was married to Catholic, Protestant to Protestant, Jew to Jew, but since they all emerged as Europeans from, say, the English Mission College or the Lycee Français, any graduating class in these numerous European schools could include Greeks, Italians, French, Armenians, Syrians, Spanish, Central European Jews, Copts, Moslems, English, Germans, Swedes, and maybe a Hungarian or a stateless European or a White Russian.

[228]

This mixture of European youth was really a non-Egyptian collective whose members did not speak the proper language of the country, but who felt nonetheless that Cairo was theirs.

The memory Cairo has given the majority of these people is of the sort of carefree and happy youth that all youth ought to have. Not only were the cafés and bars and cinemas and swimming pools and sporting clubs and theatres gaily and specially theirs, but in this soft climate, warm and sunny most of the year, the Cairo countryside itself became a fascinating playground, and so did the desert. In the summer when they had finished work at one they would sleep naked in cool sheets behind shuttered windows, in the buzzing heat. At five they would emerge into a warm bright evening to dance or swim or drink sodas and eat cakes in wonderful patisseries, and they would pack the restaurants, cinemas, the desert, the pyramids, the gardens, hotels.

Cairo was a huge village for them. Everybody knew everybody else's business, not only by birth, marriage, and death but in the scandalous intrigues which this wicked old city could breed simply by autosuggestion. European women went unveiled and enjoyed all the freedoms that European women enjoyed in Europe. Most Egyptian upper- and middle-class women had abandoned the veil after the 1919 revolution, although as long as Fuad was king the royal harem wore the veil in public, or watched the opera from behind the polished metal screen in the royal harem box. Yet as European as the manners were, the curious intimacy of the strict family life, the entwined middle-class morality of Moslem, Copt, Catholic and Jew which agreed on essentials about sex, marriage and good behavior, created an almost erotic, fenced-in atmosphere of stricture and abandon, of moral dogma and moral evasion, and of that curiously intense delight in the subtlest and in some ways the most sensual byplay of sex which no girl in Europe would have even understood. But on the whole this youthful happiness brought little or no culture with it, no indigenization, no sense of belonging to city or country, no real future, and no hope of a life that was any further away than tomorrow. If they were all doomed, none of them knew it, because they were incapable of even imagining that Egypt could do without them.

Rich and middle-class Egyptians also shared these foreign privileges, and if there was a meeting point between Egyptian and foreigner in Cairo between the wars it was a class rather than racial one. The prosperous young Egyptians still wanted a foreign education in Cairo or abroad because Egyptian higher education was struggling to emerge and was still below the standard that any modern society de-

[229]

manded. The American University in Cairo absorbed most of the young Europeans and some of the Egyptians, but most middle-class and poorer Egyptians who wanted an education went to the Fuad I University across the river at Giza. The 1922 independence had been responsible for the real establishment of this state university, but it had a prehistory in people like Taha Husain and Mustafa Kamel. Low tuition fees and improved secondary education gradually filled the Egyptian colleges and universities, and what they really reflected was the widening demand by Egyptians of all classes for a basically Egyptian education, even if it was slightly inferior to European schooling. Sons and daughters of small landowners, government officials, Egyptian merchants, lawyers, doctors, teachers and officers were now getting a higher education in Arabic in Cairo. But for what?

Egypt was still grimly and interminably feudal. Britain, the court and the feudal landowner still controlled the economy. Anatole M. Galatoli in his book *Egypt in Mid-Passage* (1950) has pointed out that before World War II Britain persuaded the Egyptian government to impose heavy duties on locally manufactured goods, even up to 8 percent on locally made cottons. Yet somehow industries did begin to emerge in ways that did not compete with British trade — sugar refining, vegetable oil processing, alcohol, cement, hides. But in 1939 almost 50 percent of Egyptian industry employed nobody but the owner of the factory, 35 percent employed only one to nine workers, and only 19 percent employed more than ten. Seven-eighths of the amount invested in industry was owned by one-half of one percent of the population. So there was nothing much in Cairo to absorb all these young Egyptians being educated to rule and administer and engineer and teach and soldier for a modern country. The modern country did not exist, so they lived from day to day in politics. Politics was their only occupation, their only hope, and Cairo was never free of student demonstrations and outbursts of street violence.

For some of them it was always a problem of what to put their faith in, whom to trust, whom to hate, and whom to kill if necessary. They were the up-and-coming generation, and something would have to be done for them, otherwise another 1919 seemed inevitable in Cairo. Quite often the very issue which impassioned them was the same one which nullified them, because they were frequently infuriated by idiocies and inflamed by charlatans. Some became Fascists, some were good bourgeois liberals, some were religious fanatics, some were Communists; and though they were all nationalists they fought among themselves as furiously as they fought the British.

There was therefore no clear way to national liberation; the basis of

Egyptian party-political life was still too corrupted to get itself out of the gutters. Divide and rule still worked very well among them, not only in favor of the British but for the old politicians and the king and the landowners. Yet there was another factor, an old one, which was becoming increasingly important even among the youth. Feudal accumulation and wastage of wealth was beginning to debilitate even the landowning class which had so far benefited most from it. They longed now to get their money into something else besides crops and trade and the occasional block of flats they put up in Cairo. Egyptian capitalism was trying very hard to get off the ground in 1939, and in some ways it had even become identified with national liberation itself.

What postponed this "natural" economic emergence, and the attempts to unify the poor peasantry, city workers, young and unemployed professional classes, disgruntled officers and frustrated feudalists behind it, was the Second World War, which again changed the character of Egypt. The war brought sudden prosperity to Egypt, particularly to Cairo, but it also sharpened every aspect of Egyptian thinking and Egyptian politics, and once again the issue of Egypt's future would come to a head on the streets of Cairo.

16

The End of Occupation

REMEMBERING what Storrs had written about Cairo at the outset of
World War I, it is worth reading what that other excellent observer
Alan Moorehead wrote about Cairo at war in 1939 in his *African Trilogy* (1944): "The Turf Club swarmed with officers newly arrived
from England, and a dozen open-air cinemas were showing every
night in the hot, brightly lit city . . . We had French wines, grapes,
melons, steaks, cigarettes, beer, whisky, and abundance of all things
that belonged to rich, idle peace. Officers were taking modern flats in
Gezira's big buildings looking out over the golf course and the Nile.
Polo continued with the same extraordinary frenzy in the roasting
afternoon heat. No one worked from one till five-thirty or six, and
even then work trickled through the comfortable offices borne along
in a tide of gossip and Turkish coffee and pungent cigarettes . . .
Madame Badia's girls writhed in the belly dance at her cabaret near
the Pont des Anglais."

History was laughing at itself, and once more Clot Bey's brothels
filled to overflowing with British Tommies. Once again Shepheard's
and the Continental were jammed with staff officers with suede boots,
fly whisks and swagger sticks. Once again the nightshirted street
Egyptian began to invent a thousand new ways of getting a few piasters out of the pockets of these red-faced soldiers. But as it was before,
so it was again — the street Arab got the pickings, and the European
and Levantine speculators and black marketeers and the rich Egyptians and the British as well made the fortunes. But Cairo blossomed.
British soldiers seeing sun and desert and clean air for the first time in
their lives looked hungrily at the beautiful European girls who

swished their pretty legs in the streets and on the trams and in the cafés. Many of these soldiers had come from appalling conditions in the black and grimy back streets of British cities not yet recovered from the depression. Many of them had never seen before what they now enjoyed every day in Cairo, and Cairo's Europeans were generous with friendship and help. But it was not long before the relationship between the British soldiers and officers and the European girls in Cairo became an intricate and complicated entanglement which very few escaped, and many good British marriages foundered in those soft Cairo evenings when love rushed through the city on the wings of an exotic escape.

Cairo filled steadily with soldiers other than Englishmen, Scotchmen, Welshmen and Irishmen. This time the Egyptian authorities asked that the Australians should be sent somewhere else, so they were sent to Palestine instead, but the Free French arrived and so eventually did Greeks, Czechs, Poles, Danes, Slavs, New Zealanders, Cypriots, Maltese, Palestinians, South Africans, Rhodesians, Americans and Indians. The British had two headquarters in Cairo: British Troops in Egypt (BTE), which was set up in the Semiramis Hotel on the Nile, and General Headquarters Middle East, which was given a large block of commandeered flats surrounded by barbed wire in Garden City. BTE was really part of the old British forces still occupying Egypt, mainly in the canal zone, but GHQ(ME) was the headquarters of the army that was facing the Italians and would pursue them into Libya. Of all the generals who fought in Egypt during the war, only Wavell (the first) and Montgomery (the last) always knew what was going on in the desert. Nonetheless Wavell's staff officers were among the worst in their attachment to Cairo.

The sight of these thousands of officers playing their games in Cairo and living like petty princes in the clubs and around the swimming pools disturbed the British soldier in the second war far more than it had in the first one. But in fact the situation never really changed at all until Montgomery took the Eighth Army clean out of Egypt to chase Rommel across North Africa. There were, of course, brilliant and dedicated officers and generals in the desert as well as incompetent idiots, but for most of the war Cairo was occupied by an old-boy network who kept their firm grip on it to the very end.

All the local Europeans enjoyed the British presence because they benefited from it, excepting perhaps the Italians, who were interned whether they were for or against Mussolini. Egypt was technically not at war with the Axis until 1945, but she broke off diplomatic relations with Germany and Italy at the outbreak of the war. The

Italians were therefore interned by the Egyptians, not by the British, because they were on Egyptian soil. But the Egyptians were not anti-Italian, so the internment regime was mild and the British didn't object to it. A fair number of local Italians were Fascists, but they made no serious attempt to help Mussolini. On the whole the Italians were probably the most popular foreigners in Cairo.

The real enemy agents in Cairo during the war were German, and the British secret police were very efficient in catching them. In *I Spied Spies* Major A. W. Sansom, who was in charge of one section of the British counterespionage security police in Cairo during the war, tells story after story of how clever the British were, almost always using — and developing as their best agents — prostitutes and petty criminals and people they deliberately got involved. Sansom's account of Cairo in the war is one of the seamiest and dirtiest ever told, but it is also one of the most honest and informed, and it reveals a great deal about British methods in keeping Cairo safe for the British presence.

Some of Sansom's officers were distinguished men, and he mentions a raid he made in Cairo with Christopher Soames, later Minister of Agriculture in the Conservative government, and later still British ambassador to France, and Churchill's son-in-law. Sansom says that Soames "distinguished himself" while under his command when they were making a political raid on a café in Cairo. The brother of Hussein Sirry Pasha, a former Egyptian prime minister, "came into the café for a quiet cup of coffee," Sansom says, and "Soames felled him with a single crack" of his swagger stick. Sansom divided his security interest in Cairo about half and half between rebellious Egyptians and German spies. Sometimes they both mixed, because many young Egyptians had no more sympathy for Britain than they had for Germany, and would willingly play one off against the other. It was Sansom, with the aid of a Jewish cabaret dancer, who unearthed a coven of German spies who came to Cairo loaded with English money and a radio transmitter and set themselves up in fabulous luxury in a houseboat on the Nile. But Cairo got the better of them. They were so delighted to be in this succulent old city with a fortune in their pockets and girls in their beds that they didn't bother too much with their espionage, and it was comparatively easy for Sansom to catch them in a dramatic raid, though not before he had gone through all the weird and shady business of plots in low cafés and tip-offs and the usual double-faced deceptions.

What was most significant about this raid however was that it led to the capture of a young Egyptian officer named Anwar el Sadaat. The captured German spies would not talk, so Winston Churchill, who happened to be in Cairo, personally questioned them and offered them their lives if they would reveal all their contacts in Egypt. The Germans betrayed one of the Egyptians they knew — Sadaat. He was arrested, cashiered from the Egyptian army, and imprisoned. But what the British police did not know then was that Sadaat was one of a group of young officers who had just formed the Revolutionary Committee which would eventually seize power in Egypt.

In fact the British knew little or nothing at all about this committee of young officers right throughout its existence, and they were never able to really penetrate it. The committee was set up to get rid of the British, and though it would change its plans many times before it finally took power ten years later, it did not have much chance of success until it had a better social basis than mere machiavellian plots against a machiavellian occupier. And ironically, it was Britain herself who helped create this new economic and social basis for her own expulsion.

Economically the British began to need some industrial and technical help from Egypt during the war because they couldn't possibly supply even their own needs from faraway, hard-pressed Britain. Overnight great repair workshops for the army were set up in Cairo, and the British employed and trained thousands of Egyptians as fitters, mechanics, electricians, drivers, engineers. Later, when the Americans set up a vast repair depot near Cairo, they too trained Egyptians to grind lenses and repair instruments and reconstruct complicated lumps of sophisticated equipment. Not only military equipment was repaired by Egyptians, but their own trams and trains and machinery and cars and buses had to be kept functioning with what they could manage for themselves. It was nothing in those days to see a dozen boys working with primitive equipment in the back streets of Cairo duplicating in cast or on the lathe almost any part of a motor car engine.

Consumer industry also had to develop, if only to help supply the British forces. Just before the war fewer men were employed in industry (1937) than ten years earlier. The big excise duties had succeeded in wrecking local manufacture. But now Egypt began to weave its own cloth, not only cotton but silk and wool. Food processing became very important for the army, and sugar refining increased, cottonseed presses produced more and more oil, hide tanning went up to spectacular levels of production, and even Arabic films became one of Egypt's major industries. But the most important advances were in mining, petroleum refining, cement, and in the new chemical and metallurgical industries.

[235]

As local industry and technology expanded, labor became far more sophisticated than it had ever been before. There were unions in Egypt where the workers were supposed to be able to organize themselves, but they were really company unions or government unions which "cooperated," so they were hardly useful to the growing labor force in the city. Yet Cairo was never quite free of strikes. In 1942 there was a series of them caused by the big increase in the cost of living while wages were low and hours were long. The police suppressed them very brutally and imprisoned hundreds of workers, but at least the genuine unions won their right to be legal. In more and more of this mass behavior the Egyptian worker was gradually changing. The British, by employing so many, were helping in fact to create a new working class in Cairo. Britain employed two hundred thousand Egyptians during the war, and of these eighty thousand became skilled or semi-skilled workers.

Nor was it only the working classes that were being added to by British war demands; Egyptian cash and capital were also accumulating. During the war British forces spent about ten million pounds in Egypt every year, and in England Egypt was accumulating huge sterling balances from her cotton payments, which came to four hundred million pounds at the end of the war. This big accumulation of cash in Egypt and capital abroad had to have an outlet which feudalism simply could not give it, and more and more Egyptians of all classes wanted Egypt to get on with this new industrial prospect which Britain had reluctantly encouraged. There was therefore a big capitalist crack appearing down the middle of Egypt's feudal face which was obviously going to widen. But first things still came first, and it was still the war that was deciding what kind of government and life and economy Egypt would have, and what sort of city Cairo would be.

In July 1942 Rommel pushed the British back almost to Alexandria, and he was stopped at Alamein only because his troops were exhausted and his supply lines overextended. British trucks and soldiers and equipment poured into the Delta, and the British army retreated as far as Cairo in a disorderly panic which became known in Egypt among the British themselves as "the flap."

Not only did Cairo fill with soldiers in retreat from the desert, but resident soldiers from the various headquarters were quickly packed off to training camps, while others prepared for a total retreat from the city. The flap infected the entire population of Cairo, though the Europeans were far more upset by it than the Egyptians. British officers finally abandoned the Gezira Sporting Club to get into the queue which stretched around several city blocks and led to the military branch of Barclay's Bank, where their money was. This time it really looked like the end. British headquarters and the British Residency were literally under a cloud of smoke for days as they burned all their vital papers preparing to get out. Refugees began pouring out of the city, and Cairo railway station was a daily madhouse of soldiers and civilians and Englishwomen hurrying in overcrowded trains to Palestine or to Luxor, or heading for the Sudan. And tragically, many of the European Jews who had fled Hitler in Europe now tried to flee once more before Rommel.

Auchinleck, who was then commander in chief, finally had to move his headquarters out of Cairo, but most British soldiers laughed bitterly at this belated gesture, and in fact it meant nothing militarily. There was about a week in July when nobody knew how things would turn out, but as Alamein held and Rommel failed to move forward, Cairo returned almost to normal. But it would never again be quite the place it was before this scare. In any case Auchinleck was about to be replaced by General Alexander, and Montgomery was about to take over the Eighth Army in the desert.

Between August 1942 when Montgomery took over the Eighth Army and October-November 1942 when he won the decisive battle at Alamein, Cairo was almost a serious military city. But after Alamein, when the war left Egypt and disappeared like a setting European sun over the western horizons, the city lost almost all the fantasy and glamour which those balmy years of occupation had brought it. Now it settled down to its unfinished contest between the feudal-foreign regime and the young moderns, and the first requirement was still national liberation.

The complicated and very dirty politics that led to the 1952 revolution seem almost unimportant now. In fact Cairo politics in the 1940s seem more and more like mere stage directions for the essential drama that was being fought out unseen between the will of the old and the hot passion of the new. It seemed inevitable, for instance, that the king, representing the wasteful disposal of all the feudal cash which could not be reinvested in the economy, should become more and more self-indulgent and corrupt. Farouk's rules for pleasure could very well be described in much the same terms as the old caliphate courts, but that would really be flattery. Farouk was simply a vulgarian, a sexual vegetable which grew and grew. His companions were mostly lumpen lackeys, particularly men like Pouli, who was his evil factotum for almost everything he wanted in sex or politics. Pouli was an Italian who was originally the palace electrician until Farouk made him one of the most powerful backroom men in Egypt. But it is hard to decide now whether Farouk was the corrupter or whether he himself was corrupted. It hardly matters now, because, like the mad caliph Hakim, Farouk's extraordinary power to do as he wished turned what would have been merely the repulsive appetite of an abnormal prince into a sexual omnipotence which threatened lives and claimed real victims. It was said, for instance, that anybody in Cairo with a beautiful wife was a fool if he let her out in public, because if the king saw her and wanted her there was no way of resisting him, short of being maimed or ruined.

The same sort of moral corruption and indulgence also contaminated the old political parties like the Wafd, who wanted a little more power, a little more reform, a little trouble, but had no desire to lead a revolution or to rip everything up by the roots and start again. In that at least the Wafd agreed with the king and the British, and when one or all three fell out, it was never on what should be done but on how trouble could best be avoided. Even Gamal Abdel Nasser and his young officers' movement wanted only to re-establish a government of respectable politicians who would free them of the British and of corruption and begin the reinvestment of Egyptian wealth in the building of a modern state. It was only subsequent events which suggested to them that there was no other way than to get rid of the entire structure of parliamentary politics which, they decided, had become far too corrupt to serve any further useful purpose.

The revolution of July 1952 succeeded for several reasons. Economically there was almost no alternative, and socially Egypt was finally ready. The Wafd no longer spoke for the farmer, artisan, intellectual or worker, it spoke for its own corrupt privileges. Yet there was no disciplined and organized political party in the country which could rival the Wafd, so that when the young officers suddenly appeared at the gates of the Abdin Palace, all Egypt was already with them without really knowing who they were. Actually a popular revolution preceded their military coup, but it was without leadership or discipline until the young officers' movement took it over as their own.

Almost all the planning for the 1952 revolution was done in Cairo, either at the Officers Club or at the house of Gamal Abdel Nasser or in the cafés and streets of the city. But strictly speaking it all began in 1946. In that year a Communist students' committee, working with trade union leaders, called a strike for February 21, and thousands of students and workers marched together through the streets of Cairo and attacked the Kasr el Nil barracks where the British were still in occupation. The British opened fire and killed thirty and wounded fifty. The whole city was instantly in chaos, and Major Sansom, who was still the British security officer, wrote in his book: "They marched in their thousands into Midan Ismailiya and defied British cordons that had been thrown round the Embassy and the Kasr el Nil barracks. Virtually unarmed, they hurled themselves against the iron railings, from behind which our machine-gunners mowed them down." And he adds: "If the Communist intellectuals had been able to agree among themselves, if they had had more real contact with the workers, and above all if a few efficient organizers had taken charge, they would surely have been swept to power, and no doubt would still be the rulers of Egypt."

Though it failed to develop into a full-scale revolution, this was the demonstration that forced the British to withdraw from Cairo and Alexandria. A Labour government had been elected in Britain, and one of Prime Minister Attlee's first acts was to remove British troops from Cairo. On July 4, 1946, the Citadel of Cairo was handed over to the Egyptians; on March 28, 1947, Kasr el Nil barracks were also handed over; and as the British marched out of Cairo, a historic event, they settled down firmly on the Suez Canal, which of course meant continued occupation of Egypt.

But this was only the beginning of the Egyptian pressure. For the next five years demonstrations and strikes and riots against the continued presence of the British in Egypt never abated, and most of this furious activity took place on the streets of Cairo. On May 6, 1947, Cairo was in a state of revolt, and Cairo's luxury cinema, the Metro, was blown up, killing four Egyptians and wounding thirty-eight. In the riots that shook the city at this time an American tourist was killed, and in March 1948 Cairo's police went on strike. In May 1948 Britain gave up her mandate in Palestine, and in the ensuing war between Jews and Arabs the rotten, untrained condition of the Egyptian army became a national scandal. Not only had they no heavy arms, almost no transport, not enough food, but most of their ammunition wouldn't go off. Somewhere in Cairo men were making fortunes from this faulty secondhand armament, and as Major Sansom has shown, not only was Farouk involved but many of the leading ministers in the government.

Every day now seemed to be a day which would surely bring a violent end to all this corruption and evil. In Cairo assassination followed assassination. In December 1948 General Selim Zaki was assassinated while directing operations against students at the Fuad I university who were demonstrating against the government.

Within a few weeks Nokrashy Pasha, the prime minister, was also murdered as he stepped out of a lift in the Ministry of Interior. In retaliation for these killings, the palace told the political police to murder Hassan al Banna. He was the head of the Moslem Brotherhood, the terrorist organization which had probably planned the murder of both Selim Zaki and Nokrashy. Hassan al Banna was shot in the back and bled to death in Kasr el Aini hospital. Then the police officer who murdered him was himself murdered on the Suez road one night, also shot in the back by the orders of the men who had employed him in the first place. In August 1951 fifteen people were wounded when police fired on a demonstration in front of the British Embassy.

The violence seemed to be continuous and endless, but by now the Egyptians were almost at the end of a long, long road. In 1951 there were forty-nine strikes and four peasant uprisings in the country, including one on the king's estate. They were all bloodily suppressed. In October 1951, Nahas Pasha, the Wafdist prime minister, finally abrogated the Anglo-Egyptian Treaty. All the Egyptians working for the British in the Suez Canal zone went on strike, and a sort of guerrilla warfare broke out against the British which culminated on January 25, 1952, in a battle between eight hundred Egyptian auxiliary police at Tel el Kebir and the British army, who attacked them with tanks and heavy artillery. The eight hundred police, armed mainly with rifles, were barricaded in their quarters in the desert, and they asked their government in Cairo what they were to do. They were told to resist, which is what they did. Seventy were killed, and the government which had urged them to fight on did nothing to send them help. This time the population of Cairo could no longer be restrained. On Saturday — now known as Black Saturday — January 26, 1952, European Cairo was set on fire.

There are many conflicting accounts of what happened that day, and no one has yet decided who really did most of the burning. At various times the Communists, the king, the Moslem Brotherhood, Serag el Din (the Wafdist minister of the interior), the secret police, and the British were all blamed, and Major Sansom accuses a right-wing section of the Free Officers (the Revolutionary Committee). Nasser once blamed the Communists, but later changed his mind and said he didn't know. The accumulation of evidence now suggests that it was started in a popular demonstration of anger which was quickly exploited by a small group of right-wing experts in terrorism, who then set a large part of the European city on fire. The one group that satisfies the description, almost the only one, is the Moslem Brotherhood, and most people in Cairo now accept the theory of its responsibility.

The day seems to have begun as a demonstration outside the cabinet office in support of the auxiliary police besieged at Ismailiya. Students at Fuad University and the Azhar demanded arms to help the police resist the British, and as huge crowds accumulated around parliament, students and police and army officers and soldiers were, for the first time in Egyptian history, all on the same side. The demonstration was really an uprising, and as much as anything it was the beginning of the revolution which the officers simply crystallized a few months later under their own leadership.

At first the crowd was absolutely united, and they marched on Abdin Palace but did not stay there. Instead they headed north towards the Place de l'Opéra. There was already a series of separate demonstrations going on in the big square, organized by left-wing organizations and the Moslem Brotherhood. In the Place de l'Opéra there was one of the many cabarets which had specialized in the *danse du ventre* and had always been a favorite with British officers — the Casino de l'Opéra of Madame Badia. The trouble started when the crowd found an Egyptian police officer sitting at one of Badia's tables with one of the dancers. It was 11:30 in the morning, and someone shouted that he ought to be ashamed — amusing himself while his brothers were dying in Ismailiya. He made some cynical remark and so did the girl, and after a sharp argument a section of the crowd suddenly burst into Badia's, smashed up a few tables and chairs, and set it on fire. Badia's was full of dry, combustible materials, and in ten minutes the whole place was ablaze. The fire brigade arrived, but someone cut their hoses and thousands of people watched this old headquarters of foreign indulgence go up in Egyptian smoke. The police did not interfere at first, though later they did force the crowd away from the fire.

It was now that the real confusion began, because what had started as a spontaneous display of anger at Badia's was continued efficiently by that mysterious small and highly organized unit of pyromaniacs. About twenty men ran or rode down Shari' Fuad el Awal and threw bottles of petrol into the Rivoli Cinema. This was not spontaneous, it was deliberate. These same men were seen all over the place that day wherever the fires were being lit. The Metro Cinema was next, and almost opposite it the famous Turf Club, and though the secretary had urged his members to leave hours before, about twenty-five stayed and ten of them were burned alive or killed. Now foreign shops and cabarets and restaurants were dealt with, one after the other. Almost every street in the center of European Cairo was in flames at one part of it or the other. Cicurel's big modern department store was set on fire and flames poured out of the windows and roof. The famous Groppi, the Chrysler agency, European art galleries, Barclay's Bank, airline offices, dozens of small European boutiques, and motor cars were all set on fire. And finally the very jewel in this old British crown in Cairo — Shepheard's Hotel. It was early afternoon, siesta time, when a dozen men rushed up the front steps and across the terrace and piled up wooden chairs and wicker furniture into a heap and poured petrol onto it and threw in a match. The old hotel was dry and brittle, and its creaking corridors were perfect stuff for a good fire, and it all went up so quickly that in a few hours not only Shepheard's but the street on either side of it looked like the stark ruins of a bombed city — a Warsaw or a Rotterdam.

While Cairo burned, dozens of demonstrations were going on at the same time. The British Embassy was well protected by a high wall and iron railings, but there was hand-to-hand fighting all around it as some of the police tried to keep the demonstrators out of it. Some did get into the compound and were seized by British guards, but finally the police cleared up the area, and the embassy was unscarred. There were two distinct forces at work in Cairo that day. They overlapped briefly, but on the whole one, the majority, was interested in political activity and violent protest but not in fire, and the other, the minority, was more interested in burning down all the old landmarks of eighty years of British and foreign occupation.

On the second floor of Abdin Palace the king watched his capital burn. He had been giving a banquet that day and he doesn't seem to have interrupted it. Anwar el Sadaat says that the prime minister, Nahas Pasha, was visiting his manicurist, and the minister of the interior was shifting some expensive furniture he had just bought, while building after building in Cairo was being set on fire. Perhaps Neroism was deep in the soul of feudal Egypt, and when the day ended four hundred buildings had been destroyed, and the estimated cost of the damage was twenty-three million pounds. An unknown number of people were killed, probably about a hundred, mostly Egyptian.

When the king did finally react he dismissed Nahas as prime minister and brought in Ali Maher, who lasted thirty-two days. Government then began to replace government in helpless succession as the king and the politicians tried to rule a country they no longer had any hope of ruling. Finally the king, realizing now that British influence was coming to an end, turned to the United States ambassador, Jefferson Caffery, and asked for help. But it was not forthcoming. While the palace wriggled about like a fat worm, the Free Officers decided on the date of their own coup — March 1952. But one of the officers, Rashed Mehanna, deserted the committee, and because they thought he might betray them, the young officers changed the date. On July 16

Great entrance hall of Abdin Palace. Up this staircase went every diplomat and politician, British and Egyptian, in every crisis; and here, in 1952, King Farouk watched the city burn.

Midan el Tahrir (where the British Kasr el Nil barracks used to be), with the Arab League Building and the Hilton Hotel in the background.

the executive committee of the Free Officers met secretly in Cairo under the presidency of Gamal Abdel Nasser, who was then an instructor at the military Staff College, and decided on immediate action because the king was getting ready to crush them or disperse them. On July 20 all the revolutionary officers were therefore told by the committee to go to the assembly points and be ready for the coup, which had been worked out as a military operation. The plan was simple: the young officers would take their units and seize the military and civil administrations and depose the king. If this failed there was a second plan (which Nasser vigorously opposed and which was later abandoned) to assassinate all the leading figures of the regime.

The coup was postponed one more day because Nasser wanted to ask General Mohammed Naguib for his support. Naguib was sympathetic to the young officers, but he knew nothing of the planned revolution and had taken no part in its preparation. Nasser went to Naguib's house, but Naguib was entertaining two guests and nothing could be said to him. So the officers' committee decided to go ahead without him. The one factor which never seemed to be in question in all this was that the soldiers of the regiments who would carry out the revolt would unhesitatingly do so, although they were not told what they were doing until the last moment. The day finally agreed on was July 22, and even on that day Nasser and the committee had to put the revolution forward by an hour to forestall the king, who was about to arrest the lot of them.

The first step was to take over military headquarters. The general staff was actually meeting at GHQ to decide how to deal with the young officers. Nasser, who had been correcting cadets' examination papers all day in his office at the Staff College, was told about the generals' meeting and said it made everything simple. "We can start an hour earlier and take them all together." Nasser then set out in his little Austin car to warn all the other officers, and one by one these young revolutionaries were told that the time would be tonight, at midnight. The rendezvous was at eleven o'clock at the house of Abdel Hakim Amer, Nasser's closest friend.

The coup itself went off like the clockwork that all military operations are based on but rarely achieve. There was simply no opposition. There was even time for one of the young officers who nearly missed the revolution to catch up with it: Anwar el Sadaat found nobody at his rendezvous because he had been at the cinema with his children and had not been told that it was all to happen an hour earlier. He rushed off to GHQ anyway, but the soldier at the gates would not let him through, although the place had already been taken over. He was standing at the gate arguing with the guard when he saw Abdel Hakim Amer in the distance. He shouted at the top of his voice and Amer heard him and let him in.

There were brief moments when it did look difficult. When the officers began to invest Abbasiya an armored column suddenly appeared out of the darkness with its lights off. The young officers thought it was hostile and prepared for action, but it turned out to be one of their own revolutionaries named Youssef Sadek who had moved his armored column early and had already taken prisoners. The various regiments then occupied GHQ, the rest of Abbasiya barracks, Manshiet el Bakri, Kubba, Heliopolis, and the Nile bridges, and they met no real opposition. Just before they marched into GHQ a detachment of troops had been sent out by the general staff to surround the Free Officers, but their commander, Captain Mohammed Shadid, shouted as he approached that he was placing himself and his soldiers under the authority of the revolutionary committee. Nasser sent them back to GHQ under the command of Abdel Hakim Amer, who marched into the headquarters and took the place with only one defending officer firing — three shots which hurt nobody.

By 2 A.M. the entire city was in the hands of the Free Officers. But they were very worried about British intervention, so they sent an armored brigade down the Suez road to prevent any British attack from the canal. The British knew absolutely nothing about the coup, and it must have been one of the few times in Egypt when they didn't have an inkling that something was going to happen. Nobody in Cairo knew. Cairo woke up on July 23 and heard on the radio, at seven o'clock, that a revolution had taken place. When the population went outside on the streets they saw tanks and soldiers occupying key places. General Mohammed Naguib didn't know until five o'clock, when he was made nominal leader of the revolt, which he had taken no part in. But though Naguib assumed command, and almost got control of the revolt, in effect it was Gamal Abdel Nasser who had engineered it and who remained in effective control of it. And it was Nasser who eventually removed Naguib as president when it looked as if the general wanted to bring back the old-guard politicians and the old methods of government.

The problem now was what to do politically. King Farouk was in his palace at Ras el Tin in Alexandria. He was told of the coup by telephone, and now he tried to bluff his way out of the mess by offering lavish compromises, even suggesting that the Free Officers form a government under the existing constitution. But they were not that naïve, so they refused. In the meantime Farouk was also playing the usual game of backroom manipulation. He eventually made contact with the British Middle East Headquarters on the canal and asked for help. By July 25 the threat of British intervention in support of the king was so real that Nasser decided to depose Farouk without further delay.

Not everybody among the officers or the population wanted Farouk to be politely dethroned and allowed to walk out of Egypt a free man. Some of the officers wanted him tried, condemned and shot. The officers who had been sent to Alexandria by the committee to negotiate with the king couldn't decide what should be done, so one of them, Gamal Salem, flew back to Cairo at 2:30 A.M. to consult the committee, which met and debated among themselves for several hours and then sent the officer back to Alexandria at 7 A.M. with their decision. The majority, including Nasser, had voted for immediate exile.

In one last attempt to save his life, since he assumed he was going to be shot, Farouk sent the famous Pouli secretly to Jefferson Caffery, begging him to send an American battleship to help him get out of Egypt. Caffery, according to Anwar el Sadaat, persuaded Farouk that this would be behavior unworthy of a king. The American military attaché had been present at the interview, and some of the Free Officers met him coming away from the palace. He demanded an explanation of what was happening and said that Washington demanded a guarantee of the safety of Farouk's person. But there was only one way now that Farouk could save his person, which was to accept the document of abdication the officers sent him. He signed it with a shaking hand, illegibly, even making a spelling mistake in the Arabic version of his own name, because Farouk still could not write the language of the country his family had ruled for more than a hundred years.

Farouk was allowed to leave with two hundred pieces of baggage on his royal yacht the *Mahroussa,* and by six o'clock on July 26, 1952, he sailed out of Alexandria harbor to bring to an ugly end this Turco-Albanian dynasty which Egyptians still consider to be one of the most hateful they have ever suffered.

The British tried only once to reassert their old political authority. The embassy in Cairo ordered the revolutionary committee to impose a curfew on Cairo in order to protect foreign nationals, to set up a regency council and to uphold the monarchy. The Egyptians laughed at this affront and ignored the commands, and in effect this was the last order the British would give an Egyptian government, directly or indirectly. From now on, for the first time since the Persian conquest of 525 B.C., Egypt was to be ruled entirely by Egyptians.

17

Egyptian Cairo: Survival, 1952–1956

W HAT you see now when you step out of a hot, crackling jet on Cairo's airport and drive through the streets in the airline bus is a thoroughly modern city with the usual skyscrapers, thick-necked traffic, nervous taxis, neon lights, buses, trams, metros, department stores, boutiques, cafés, street sellers, and everything in fact that Cairo always had except maybe the beggars and the foreign troops.

Since the 1952 revolution Cairo has been through four distinct periods, and each of them has reflected the changes that have taken place in the Egyptian revolution itself. The first period, 1952–1956, was mainly one of survival and primitive reform; the second, 1956–1962, the emergence of a sort of national consciousness; the third, 1962–1967, of intensified socialism; and the fourth, 1967 and after, has been a period almost of destiny itself. Cairo has lived through these four episodes of the Egyptian revolution holding its breath — a situation which the city is used to. But what has made it an altogether unique situation is that Egyptians have been deciding what Egyptians will do and where Egypt will go.

This is a very new experience for these people, and by no means an easy one. The ordinary Egyptians have been oppressed for so long that they are still trying to get up off their knees, something which they have been sharing lately in an upside-down sort of way with the Jewish people. Perhaps the Jews and the Egyptians have been persecuted and oppressed more continuously than anybody else on earth, though if anything the oppression of the Egyptians is the longer. But their emergence from it has been later, since they have not experienced en masse the enlightenment which millions of European Jews enjoyed before their savage persecution by Hitler.

What has been happening in Cairo during the last fifteen years therefore must always be judged by the sort of fears and humiliations and hopes and suspicions which are always deep in the consciousness of anybody who has suffered for such a long time.

In the first period of the revolution, between 1952 and 1956, the young "Free Officers" hardly knew what they were doing. They had no planned projects for the future. Their point of view was not socialist, if anything it was capitalist, and the majority of the Revolutionary Council of young officers were right-wing rather than left-wing. Their only serious plan was to "liberate" the country from the past, and while they were learning how to do it they made life very puzzling for the people of Cairo because nobody knew exactly what was happening. For the most part nobody had ever heard of these young officers. Nasser was utterly unknown, so were Abdel Hakim Amer and Anwar al Saadat and Ali Sabry and Zakaria Mohieddin. The only man most people did know of was General Mohammed Naguib, whom the young officers had elected at the last moment to be president of Egypt as a sort of respectable figurehead for their coup. Most people in Cairo came to believe that Naguib was one of the principals of the revolution, and he was treated as a hero of it. So the city was stunned when Naguib was deposed for taking his paternal role a little too seriously. The man who had really led the revolution and was the most important man of it, the man who began to feel that there was no safety in going back to the old parliamentary ways, was Gamal Abdel Nasser. Though the populace did not know of him, all the young men who now ruled Egypt knew that he was the man that mattered. But even after the revolution Nasser had no appeal to the Egyptian people because he made no attempt to approach them.

At first the young officers considered themselves to be simply the force that would open up the way in Egypt so that others would follow and take over. Because nobody among the barrowloads of politicians seemed willing to follow the "incorruptible and patriotic" path the soldiers had so naïvely prepared for them, Nasser decided after about six months of watching all the old political tricks being played that the soldiers would have to do it all themselves. And what they had to do seemed quite clear to them. Above all they wanted to get rid of the British troops who still occupied the Suez Canal, and they needed to devise some means of rescuing the population of Egypt, which was increasing faster than the food supply.

After a series of clever and conciliatory moves by both sides, British and Egyptian government representatives sat down in Cairo in July 1954 and signed an agreement which would finally get British troops out of Egypt and demilitarize British bases on the canal, although Britain and France would still own and operate the canal itself and get the bulk of the royalties. That was the first problem dealt with. The next difficulty was to get arms from somewhere to revitalize the Egyptian army. Almost immediately after the revolution Nasser sent his emissaries to Washington looking for military equipment. The English and the French and the United States between them had equipped six Israeli divisions with modern weapons, while Egypt had three ragged divisions equipped with prewar and faulty surplus World War II weapons, which was all she could get. According to the French observers Jean and Simonne Lacouture, in their book *Egypt in Transition* (1958), Washington made it quite clear that Egypt would get arms from the United States only if she "bound herself to the Pentagon staff," which Nasser refused to do. Reluctantly, since he was firmly against communism, and after a heavy Israeli attack on Gaza, Nasser made a deal in September 1955 to buy Czech arms without any strings attached at all. He had thus solved Egypt's second problem.

To solve the third and largest problem — feeding the expanding population — Nasser and his economic experts, who were mostly trained in the United States and Britain, planned two complementary solutions, and the first of these was to break up the old feudal estates and give land to the peasants. Under the agrarian reform law of 1952 no one was allowed to own more than two hundred acres of land. No family together could own more than three hundred acres. This was one of the first important decrees issued by the Revolutionary Council, but it would not of itself solve the agricultural problem of Egypt. Egypt needed more land if she were not to starve, and the only way to get it was to build another dam across the Nile above Aswan, which would not only provide rich sources of power for Egypt's new industries, but would irrigate enough new land to allow Egypt to hold her existing standards, if not to raise them a little. The building of this new dam was clearly a matter of life or death for Egypt, and every Egyptian knew it and so did every statesman, friend or enemy, who had any dealings with Egypt.

To get the money to build the Aswan High Dam the Egyptians asked the International Bank for a loan, and on January 1956 Egypt was offered two hundred million dollars at 3.5 percent, payable in twenty years. But there were strings to it. In effect the bank claimed the right to control the Egyptian budget until the loan was repaid, a condition which Nasser, who had just rid Egypt of that kind of influence, flatly refused. He then tried the Russians, who said at first that they would lend him money for the industrialization of Egypt but not for the high dam. In the meantime, too, the French and British governments, and according to the Lacoutures and the *Encyclopaedia Britannica* (1968 ed., "Egypt") the Israeli lobby in Washington, were putting pressure on Washington to cancel United States support of the loan. Nasser, realizing what was happening and knowing that there was no other way of getting the money, decided to accept the terms of the loan. But the State Department announced on July 18, 1956, that it was withdrawing its support of the loan because of the instability of the Egyptian economy. This was such a deliberate blow to Egyptian hopes that every politician in London, Paris and Washington assumed that its effect would be to bring Nasser down. But on July 26, in a speech in Alexandria, Nasser announced to the huge crowd gathered in Mohammed Ali Square that Egypt was going to nationalize the Suez Canal in order to pay for the high dam at Aswan.

What was important about this speech of Nasser's is that he not only did what every Egyptian wanted done, but he told the Egyptians about it in Balladi, the popular language of the people, which is quite different from the educated Arabic which Nasser would normally use. "The shy and awkward Nasser had suddenly discovered how to talk to the Egyptian people," the Lacoutures say, and the response was wild enthusiasm from every section of the population, from extreme right to extreme left. But three months later, on October 29, 1956, Israel invaded the Sinai, and the next day Britain and France, in what is now accepted as a carefully prepared collusive alliance, also attacked Egypt, and the political effect on Cairo was profound. But in this first period of the revolution, in these first four years of independence, Cairo had already changed a great deal, though not so much in texture as simply in the color of its skin. The young officers had based so much of their revolutionary outlook on the dispatch of all foreigners from Egypt that they wanted not only the British out of the way but also the mixed Europeans of Cairo who had been the lever of British policy in Egypt for almost a hundred years. The real pressure on these local Europeans had started long before the 1952 revolution. Various prerevolution Egyptian governments had passed ambitious laws stating that Arabic must be used in all business houses and a certain percentage of Egyptians employed in every business, and later on a tougher law was passed which said that all businesses had to have an Egyptian director or an Egyptian partner.

At first, Europeans always found an easy way around these laws, but after the Second World War they had to be taken much more seriously as Egyptians demanded a bigger say in running the economy of their own country. Between 1945 and the revolution of 1952 the stiffer enforcement of these laws began to make Cairo a little more Egyptian, but foreigners still did not feel that they had to leave, nor even that they were losing their grip on the city, although the clever ones could see what was going to happen to them sooner or later.

The event that made many foreigners realize that their day was done was the burning of Cairo in January 1952. This, more even than the revolution, suddenly made every European in the city realize that the era of foreign predominance was coming to a close, and many of them began slowly to prepare to leave. Most foreigners of French or Italian or Greek or British nationality who had good businesses in the city had always kept a part of their money abroad anyway, and so did many European Jews, but when the foreign shops were burned and the Egyptians were looking hungrily at the potential spoils of foreign business houses, the serious departure of Europeans began. Foreigners (including European Jews) were not told to leave, but they were encouraged to do so. Just after the revolution they were allowed to take with them everything they owned and up to five thousand Egyptian pounds in money, which was fairly generous under the circumstances, since Egypt was already getting short of foreign currency and needed all she could get.

But there was no real exodus. Cairo's foreign minorities still managed to behave with old-fashioned arrogance, even after the revolution, although now their powers of authority were confined more and more to the hangers-on, to the large body of impoverished wretches who depended on foreigners for their existence — servants, drivers, laundrymen, nursemaids. After 1952 if a foreigner was insolent to a middle-class Egyptian he was liable among other things to get his face slapped. But the sporting clubs of Cairo were still full of the city's foreigners, and the restaurants and cafés and cinemas were still oriented more towards Europeans than towards Egyptians.

The people who began to take the foreigners' privileged place in Cairo after 1952 were the young officers. Nasser himself was always a disinterested and incorruptible man, and that was perhaps the singular characteristic which made him important to Egypt. Most, but by no means all, of his close companions were like him. But many of the older higher officers suddenly became very prosperous men, being in the best possible position to legally acquire the lucrative shops and agencies and factories which Europeans were finding it difficult to hang on to. For a while the officer class became the social elite, which was a far cry from the days before the revolution, when the Egyptian army was looked upon as the weak arm of the ruling class. Almost everybody had looked askance at it then, excepting the young men in it who believed that the army would liberate the country. So the officer now became a powerful figure in Cairo, worth flattering and bribing and marrying, and after the revolution too many young officers became ready substitutes for the rich and powerful sons and the feudal politicians whom they were trying to eradicate. The kind of officer-businessman who emerged in this situation would remain a serious factor in Egyptian life until 1967, when many of them were arrested and discredited after Egypt's defeat in the June war.

Naturally the young officers began to appear in the exclusive sporting clubs, in particular Gezira — that old temple of British snobbery. There you could hear the barking young voices of Egyptian officers, who wore peaked caps now instead of the Turkish fez, and who brought with them the sort of horseplay which was peculiar to their class and their culture and their age and which jarred on the nerves of anyone who preferred the British kind of horseplay. Almost imperceptibly, too, army officers and their families began to appear in Cairo's modern blocks of flats, which they could not have afforded before. But though the army took advantage of its new status and enjoyed its new privileges, Cairo did not look like a militarist city, and it hardly felt itself to be ruled by soldiers. It never had that kind of atmosphere about it.

Capitalism was still the working basis of the Egyptian economy. Nasser himself seemed perfectly willing to be capitalist. The only thing that really interested him was not the ideology but what would work, no matter what it was called, and between 1952 and 1956 the best alternative to feudalism seemed to be a form of controlled capitalism rather than socialism. Egyptians were still being encouraged to go on investing their money in profitable enterprises, and high dividends were still desirable. Until 1956, therefore, Cairo was still a capitalist city. There were still plenty of foreign cars and foreign goods from Europe, clothes still looked as if they had just arrived from London and Paris and Rome, and the usual cosmopolitan flavor in the city's sybarite tastes in food and drink and entertainment were not greatly disturbed.

Cairo had also benefited in bricks and mortar from the agrarian reform law of 1952. The big landowners realized that their accumulated cash was going to rot away in the banks if they couldn't invest it in the land, so they were eager to build rentable office blocks and apartment houses in Cairo. This would give them a return of up to 25 percent on their investment because building costs were low and rents were then fairly high for Cairo. Some quarters of Cairo boomed in these first four years.

But this laissez-faire approach just after the revolution, which often seemed to be more like a shift in power than a real revolution, was in difficulties from the outset, because Nasser soon learned from his experts trained at Harvard and the London School of Economics that some sort of overall capitalist planning was necessary, not only for big schemes like the Aswan High Dam, but to get urgently required increases in production of fuels, fertilizers, chemicals, transport, arms, cement, et cetera. Money itself had to be planned, and so did investment and imports and exports. And if an industrialized Egypt was hoping to absorb the great part of Egypt's nonworking population, then some form of state guidance, state control and state investment seemed inevitable. Nasser began to learn, as he tried one scheme after another, that he was not going to revitalize his very poor country without in fact organizing it all ahead. And Cairo became the center and the headquarters of dozens of new organizations which were set up to reorganize Egypt's economy.

What had to be established first was the material basis for Egypt's industrialization. Light industry was already well established, but serious industrialization needed heavy industry, so in 1954 a contract was given to Demag, a West German firm, to build Egypt a new steel mill at Helwan to exploit the 168 million tons of iron ore buried under the deserts near Aswan. The whole scheme was to be financed by mixed private and government capital and The Helwan ovens would provide all Egypt's new future, but in some ways it was also an end, because this sort of "mixed" investment was about as far as the young officers were willing to go with their interference in the financial structure of the economy.

In time, the presence of this steel mill on the outskirts of Cairo would create a new kind of working class in the city, as well as a new concentration of technologists, chemists and engineers who would have to come from the universities and technical institutes. But that was in the future. Up to 1956 there was still not much apparent change in the life of the populace of Cairo. All that can be said now of those first four years is that something was being born, only nobody quite knew what it was. As the capital of this undefined and often contradictory system, the city seemed to live in a state of permanent expectancy, as if it would all become clear tomorrow, as if some new event would bring everything to life in a recognizable perspective.

This was the situation in Egypt when, on October 29, 1956, the Israeli army marched into the Sinai, to be followed next day by the British and French attack on the airfields and towns of Egypt. The first period of the revolution was over, and the second period was about to begin.

18

National Consciousness,
1956-1962

CAIRO awoke on the morning of the Israeli attack without feeling
any great threat to the city or even to the country, because nobody
believed that Israel was invading Egypt. The unsettling mixture of
army arrogance and Gamal Abdel Nasser's claims for Arab strength
had persuaded Egyptians that Israel was no threat. The real problem
for Egyptians had remained "Western imperialism," which they denounced far more rigorously than they did Israel.

Egypt's attitude to the state of Israel in 1956 was a fairly simple
one. The Egyptians took the position that there had been no large
indigenous Jewish population in Palestine — about 5 percent — for
two thousand years, and that it was only in modern times that European Jews had come to Palestine and settled in Arab lands, eventually
forcing or "tricking" the Arabs out of their villages and farms, so that
almost every acre of the new state, which was formed by a United
Nations decision in 1947–1948, was "robbed" from the Palestinians by
these foreigners who came from Germany or Poland or Rumania or
Hungary or Czarist Russia. Seeing it this way, the Arabs could never
find any justice in the claim that these Europeans had a right to Arab
territory — any more, they said, than it would be rational for the Romans to claim England or the Algonquins to claim Manhattan. Europe's persecution of the Jews had nothing to do with the Arabs, they
said, because local Jews and Arabs in Middle Eastern countries had
always lived in reasonable harmony, and the Arabs had never persecuted the Jews. Most Egyptians therefore saw the new state of Israel

not as a new homeland for a persecuted people but as a continuation of European occupation. They further looked upon Zionist claims for the right to safeguard the new state by military force as an expansionist policy, and like most Arabs the Egyptians felt that the Jews of Europe had brought with them an alien European culture, so that they were not trying to be Semites among Semites but were determinedly remaining superior Europeans among inferior Arabs. Witness, they said, the treatment in Israel itself of Arab Jews, who were more or less second-class citizens to the European Jews.

Though this view was common to most Egyptians, there were many different ideas on what should be done about Israel. The extreme right talked of destruction, and the left wing favored a sort of live-and-let-live position. Gamal Abdel Nasser himself believed that Israel was created by the British as a long-range means of dividing and ruling the Middle East when they were eventually expelled themselves. But what seems to have been forgotten is that in his *Philosophy of the Revolution* Nasser admires the Jews for their resistance to the British, and he quotes favorably a Jewish officer in Palestine named Yerdan Cohen talking in 1948 about Nasser himself: "The subject that Gamal Abdel Nasser discussed with me was Israel's struggle against the English, how we organized our underground resistance in Palestine and how we succeeded in mobilizing world public opinion behind us against them." A few months before the 1956 attack on Egypt, Jean and Simonne Lacouture asked Nasser: "Don't you think that all Arabs are convinced that sooner or later Israel has to be suppressed and cease to exist as a state and be reduced to something like a Jewish Vatican City?" And Nasser replied: "No. As far as we in Egypt are concerned we merely ask that the state of Israel should respect Arab rights. It has to recognize them the same as other states do."

Nasser had just sat down to dinner with the Indonesian ambassador on the evening of October 31, 1956, when Cairo was shaken by the first British bombs on the city's military and civilian airfields. Cairenes, including Nasser, had a dark grandstand view of British jets coming in high and low and dropping high explosives and incendiaries and napalm on the neatly packed Egyptian jets, which were not expecting (as Nasser later admitted) British and French intervention. By morning Egypt had no real air force left, which freed the sky over the Sinai for the French and Israeli air forces. They proceeded with napalm to destroy most of the Egyptian armor, which was now exposed to the skies.

Reading many years later what is still the best account of the Suez war — *Secrets of Suez*, by Merry and Serge Bromberger, who were with the Israeli and French armies — it is quite clear that the battle of the Sinai was won by the French and Israeli air forces rather than by Moshe Dayan on the ground, however brilliantly he outmaneuvered and outfought the Egyptians. "The four decisive battles of the six-day campaign were won by aircraft which frequently used napalm bombs carried in Israeli Mustangs," the Brombergers wrote in their admiring account of the combined attack. As the British themselves had learned before Alamein, armies in the open desert exposed to air attack had no choice but to run as fast as they could. The panic of the British before Rommel was no different militarily than the panic of the Egyptians before the French and the Israelis in the Sinai in 1956. The war was officially ended on November 7, after the Russians (in a speech by Mr. Khrushchev) had more or less threatened to rocket Britain and the United States had denounced the attack. All four contestants agreed to the cease-fire demanded by the United Nations.

Almost nothing of the war ever reached Cairo except the bombing of the airfields. The city was blacked out at night, and the policemen guarding banks and bridges and post offices wore steel helmets and had sandbagged shelters hastily erected for them. But traffic, commerce, daily life and night life went on almost as before. There were noisy demonstrations in the streets, and sometimes at night armored columns moved heavily through the city, their metal tracks creaking and clanging grittily. Once or twice a lonely Egyptian Mig was seen in the sky. But there was no violent reaction by the population against anyone. There were no anti-Jewish demonstrations, the synagogues were not touched, and Jews went about their business, though a little more cautiously than before.

Yet something *had* happened to the city, and only when the war was over did the true effect on the Egyptians begin to show. The real exodus of foreigners from Cairo now began, but this time the Egyptians made it tougher and only allowed Europeans to take out forty Egyptian pounds cash and whatever valuables they could pack into a half dozen suitcases. What drove most Europeans out was not so much physical hostility towards them but the Egyptian realization, which the Suez war had inspired, that Egypt must more than ever be a nation of Egyptians, in which there was no place for a privileged European minority. Unfortunately, many Europeans who had been born and brought up in Cairo now found that they were going "home" to a country they did not know. Many Cairo Greeks with Greek passports had never seen Greece and didn't want to see it. Greeks made up the largest foreign population group in the city, and most of them were small merchants or shopkeepers or importers and exporters or cotton buyers or clerks, and Greece was full of small shopkeepers and importers and clerks. It was the better-off Greek or Cypriot who packed up first, the poorer Greeks stayed. Many of them had been given arms by the Egyptians during the Suez war, and they had fought side by side with Egyptians against the British in Port Said. There were thousands of Armenians who had fled to Egypt from the Turks after the First World War, and European Jews who had fled the Nazis. After the Suez war the European Jews were not forced to leave, but most of them wanted to because they felt the hostility now. Australia, France, Italy, Greece, South America, Soviet Armenia, the United States, and almost every country in Europe began to receive thousands of Europeans from Cairo. But for every one who packed up and left, another one wanted to stay, still under any circumstances preferring the city of his birth to anywhere else. Now, too, many of the local Europeans regretted that they had not become Egyptian nationals when they could easily have done so.

In human terms this exodus was a sad and preoccupying affair. From the day the Suez war ended the Europeans in the city thought and talked and gossiped about nothing but their uncertain future. The telephone would ring. Had you heard the news? Michel had just gotten a visa for Venezuela, or Giselle was going to her uncle in Naples, or a brother had sent from Australia for his sister. Day after day those remaining would ask each other: "When are you going? Where to?" Café talk, shop talk, family talk, business talk went on and on with the same problem, and day by day the Italian clerk or the Jewish typist or the Greek accountant disappeared.

After 1956 the shops employed mostly Egyptian girls behind the counters; European barbers became Egyptian barbers, European restaurants became Egyptian restaurants. The streets themselves began perceptibly to lose their European pedestrians, and already one noticed large numbers of poor Egyptian men in galabias and Egyptian peasant women in black meliyas (shapeless gowns) walking the streets of European Cairo, not trying to sell you something but simply being there as part and parcel of their own city. At first they were a sort of lower-middle-class overflow from their old territory across the Ezbekiya, but by 1960 they were established in the western part of the city for good.

Inevitably too, as these poorer and lower-middle-class Egyptians began to fill up the European places, the modern city deteriorated a little. The Europeans had insisted on European standards, but the poorer Egyptian had poorer standards. Pavements began to get bumpy, paint began to peel, trams began to rattle, porches went un-

Shoeshop in the
fashionable Kasr el Nil.

A study in
hand expressions.

Boats at Cairo.

swept, metros got dusty and the back streets filthy. The shops began to lose their chic and their European skin, and Cairo seemed to be steadily reverting to a sort of heavy-lidded Orientalism.

Yet imperceptibly every aspect of life in the city was undergoing a great change. Almost every author who has written about Egypt during this period comments on the national awareness which was the most important legacy of the Suez war. The courage of the citizen defenders of Port Said in 1956 and the powerful sense of injustice which the war left with most Egyptians began to weld them together far more effectively than any propaganda. This also affected the direction which the economy was taking. In his book *The Revolution in Egypt's Economic System 1952–1965*, published under the auspices of the Royal Institute of International Affairs in 1966, Patrick O'Brien has written: "After 1956 the Free Officers moved away from their previous policy for the development of the economy through the encouragement of private investment in favor of higher rates of public capital formation." In 1952–1953, he says, 72 percent of gross capital formation was carried out by the private sector, but by 1959–1960, 74 percent was undertaken by the state.

Nasser called this "controlled capitalism," but what it reflected was the desire and the willingness of Egyptians after 1956 to submit themselves to anything they considered necessary for their new national image of themselves. A new constitution in 1956 gave some political meaning to these hopeful ideas of "controlled capitalism," and once again Cairo became the headquarters of dozens of new organizations built up around the National Planning Committee, where two hundred economists and foreign experts from Norway, East Germany and Holland worked out long-term projects for the economy. What gave them some prospect of success was the Soviet agreement to finance and engineer the construction of the high dam at Aswan — the one project upon which all others depended. Cairo now began to grow again on its own hopes, and almost every day some new law was published in the press which made it clear to the citizens that their lives were being changed for them by economic necessity.

In 1959, for instance, a law was passed fixing the working week at forty-eight hours and the maximum working day at eight hours, an incredible step in a country like Egypt. In the same year a new law said that 25 percent of a company's profits should be set aside for its employees, of which 10 percent should go to them in cash, 5 percent for social services and housing, and the remaining 10 percent to government social services fund. The same law limited directors' salaries to five thousand Egyptian pounds a year, and every company had to

[261]

have on its board a representative of its employees and its workers. In 1957 the government decreed that all banking had to be organized in Egyptian joint-stock companies, with shares owned by Egyptians only. The same law applied to insurance companies. All export and import agencies and commercial representatives had to be Egyptian as of 1958, and once again a law was passed making Arabic compulsory in business and requiring that a majority of directors be Egyptian. Control of investment, dividends and volume of production, and participation in the production of petrol, minerals, transport and refining, brought the government directly into every aspect of Egyptian life, and there was hardly a man or woman in Cairo at this time who was not affected in some way by these new economic laws.

As early as 1957 Nasser had made a speech saying that Egypt would eventually become a "socialist, democratic and cooperative society," but no one, even in Egypt, took much notice of it. By 1960, however, socialism was the word all the planners in Cairo were using, but it did not become official policy until June 1961, when the government began what is now called in Egypt "the social revolution." In the short period of a few months all the banks and insurance and shipping companies of Egypt were nationalized, so were the forty-four principal industrial companies of Egypt which controlled timber, cement, motor transport, copper and electric power. All firms engaged in external trade were taken over, so were the cotton baling and pressing companies, and eighty-six firms which controlled light manufacture and commercial distribution had half their capital nationalized. One hundred and forty-seven other companies were simply appropriated, and later, in 1963, pharmaceutical manufacture, civil engineering, heavy road transport and water transport were taken over by the state. When all these nationalization decrees became law, Egypt had become in essentials a socialist society, although there were still many areas where private enterprise survived, such as small factories, internal trade, commercial concerns, housing, and the reformed land ownership, although new lands reclaimed by the Aswan dam scheme were scheduled to be state-owned and state-operated.

This economic revolution was given a political backbone when in May 1962 President Nasser presented to the Congress of Popular Powers a "charter" which gave Egypt a socialist ideology all its own. The charter was more or less an outline of accepted socialist doctrine: revolutionary ardor; heavy dependence on working class and peasantry (though it deplored class war); a foreign policy whose main theme was anti-imperialism, support for the United Nations and protection of national progress; and the high ideal of international cooperation against poverty. But in over one hundred pages of policy only a passing reference, in a few words, was made to the need to "liquidate the Israeli aggression on a part of Palestine." Egypt was much too preoccupied with its own affairs to bother much about Israel.

Officially, Cairo had now become the socialist capital of a socialist state. For a while Cairo had also been the capital of a United Arab Republic of Syria and Egypt, a union which had been conceived by Syrian politicians to prevent Syria's going Communist. It was eventually dissolved when Syrian soldiers found even Nasser's socialism a little too much for them, and all that was left for Egypt was its hopeful but lonesome identity as *the* United Arab Republic. Even when Syria eventually became socialist herself the union was not restored, although President Nasser's hope for it persisted. It hardly mattered, because Cairo felt itself thoroughly established as the capital of the Arab world and as the city to which all "unliberated" Arabs looked to for guidance and leadership. But not everybody in Cairo agreed that Arab socialism was the answer. Gamal Abdel Nasser's opponents had almost no public voice but they had a great deal of political power, and in September 1967 they would try to use it to bring the whole structure tumbling down. In the meantime, Cairo remained the master city of Arab socialism, and visually, at least, that is the city one sees now, even after the painful dramas of 1967.

19

The European Memory

THOUGH it *is* a socialist city, there is still a sort of neutrality in Cairo's atmosphere, as if it still straddles a halfway mark between one form of society and the other, as if it still wanted to hesitate a little before making up its mind. Cairenes are still deft and light-edged and mercurial. There are still rich and there are still poor. But the weight has shifted. The poor seem to be the moral masters of the city now, and the rich are more modest about themselves than they used to be, although they are by no means in disorderly retreat.

There is in fact almost no aspect of social and economic life in Cairo that is quite clear-cut. Cairo's largest stores, for instance, look like old-fashioned capitalist stores, whereas much of their business is controlled, though not owned, by the state. Most shops in Cairo are not so much polished aluminum and stark sheet glass as solid wood and creaking floors which smell of the kerosene used to clean them with. They looked much the same in 1967 as they did in 1947. Au Salon Vert, one of Cairo's best shops, has moved up to about 1960 by European standards. In the old days these stores in Cairo would have been as good as any in Europe, particularly big ones like Cicurel. But for anyone who remembers the old Cicurel the present one is a sad shadow of its former self, not because it is run down or neglected, but simply because its atmosphere is austere, and its business un-French and un-English and un-Italian.

One of the reasons why these stores remain old-fashioned is the government limitation on the purchase of foreign goods and the increased local production in cheaper versions of almost everything that a shop can sell. It is surprising now to see just how much of Cairo's consumer goods, from socks to electric light bulbs and bicycles, are manufactured in Egypt. Most of them are copies of European items, but on the whole they are not bad. Chemist shops have always been very important in Cairo because everybody in the city is permanently suffering stomach disorders, liver complaints, urinary upsets, ear infection or eye trouble, and every new drug or aperient is snapped up as a fashionable necessity. Europe's big drug makers used to consider Egypt a gold mine, but Egypt now makes most of its own drugs, and though pill takers and injection maniacs would probably prefer the European originals, nonetheless Egyptian drugs are just as good, and Cairo's chemist shops are always as busy as its cafés, bars and restaurants.

Local manufacture, the new labor laws, and government control of distribution have all had their effect on modern Cairo, because the man who owns a business is fighting hard to keep his profit up and his overhead down, because his level of investment, his rate of profit, the wages he pays his workers, and the hours they work are all under the government's omnipresent eye. What used to be a rather leisurely and pleasant and almost social affair of bargain and display in a Cairo shop, when time was cheap and taxes nil, is now a more streamlined and no-nonsense transaction — strictly business. You want a pair of shoes? They will still bring down the whole shop for you, but in half the time it used to take and with none of the gossiping humor that this sort of thing used to provoke. But the hard sell, a limitation on variety, an increasing competition from equally hard-pressed competitors, and a narrow margin on prices all keep the bazaar alive in Cairo's shops; you can still bargain even for a pair of shoes. But the old-fashioned Oriental sport has gone out of it forever.

Another influence on the appearance of Cairo now is its steady withdrawal westward, farther and farther away from the old medieval city. Commercial Cairo is now being built not only along the river but across it on the island of Gezira, and even on the Giza and Imbaba side. Big hotels are going up one after the other along the water's edge, and oil company offices and other big business concerns — Egyptian and foreign — are slowly cutting deep in the residential parts of Garden City. The opulent villas of Gezira which have not already been taken over by embassies are becoming government offices, and Imbaba across the river is now a new suburban city in itself. This push westward is naturally bringing the center of the city nearer to its original mother, the river, and though one is delighted

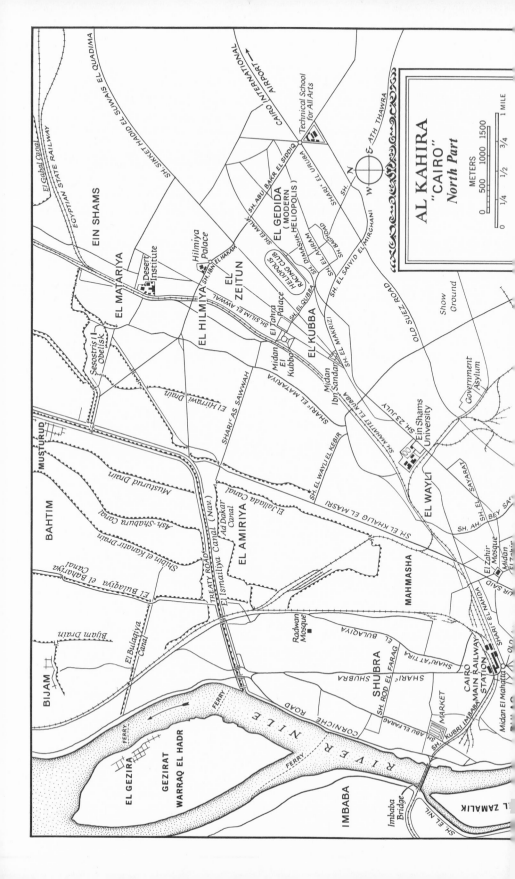

AL KAHIRA
"CAIRO"
North Part

METERS
0   500 1000 1500
0   1/4   1/2   3/4   1 MILE

EIN SHAMS

EL GABAL CANAL

EGYPTIAN STATE RAILWAY

SH. SIKKET EL HADID EL SUWAIS EL QUADIMA

CAIRO INTERNATIONAL AIRPORT

Technical School
for All Arts

SH. ATH THAWRA

N
W   E
S

EL MATARIYA

Desert
Institute

Sesostris II Obelisk

EL HILMIYA

SH. IBN EL HAKAM

Hilmiya
Palace

SH. ABU BAKR EL SIDDIQ

SH. DIMASHK

EL GEDIDA
(MODERN HELIOPOLIS)

SHARI' EL URUBA

SH. EL MALIK

EL ZEITUN

HELIOPOLIS
RACING CLUB

SH. AHRAM

BAGDAD

SHARI' EL MIRGHANI

SH. EL SAYID ELMIRGHANI

OLD SUEZ ROAD

Show
Ground

El Zahra
Palace

EL KUBBA

SH. EL QUBBA

SH. EL MAKRIZI

SH. EL SANDAR

Government
Asylum

EL HIRRAWI Drain

SH. AS SAWWAH

Midan
El Kubba

Midan
Ibn Sandar

SH. EL MATARIYA

SH. EL WAYLI EL KEBIR

SH. MAHATTET EL KUBBA

Ein Shams
University

SH. 23 JULY

SAYARAT

MUSTURUD

Mustrurud Drain

Ash-Shabura Canal

Shibin el Kanatir Drain

EL JALLADA Canal

Ad Dakar Canal

El Ismailiya Canal (Nav.)

TREATY ROAD

EL AMIRIYA

SH. EL KHALIG EL MASRI

EL WAYLI

SH. AH.

SH. EL

BEY SA

BAHTIM

El Bulaqiya el Bahariya Canal

El Bulaqiya Canal

Bijam Drain

BIJAM

EL NILE

RIVER NILE

FERRY

GEZIRAT
WARRAQ EL HADR

EL GEZIRA

CORNICHE ROAD

FERRY

MAHMASHA

Radwan
Mosque

EL BULAQIYA

SH. ROD EL FARAG

EL FARAG

SH. ABU EL FARAG

SHARI'AT TIRA

SHUBRA

SH. ROD EL FARAG

MARKET

SH. KUBRI IMBABA

CAIRO
MAIN RAILWAY
STATION

SHARI' EL NAHDA

UR SAID

El Zahir
Mosque

Midan

EL NAHDA

Midan El Mahatta

IMBABA

Imbaba
Bridge

SH. EL NIL

L. ZAMALIK

with the rediscovery of the Nile, it is possible that this modern commercial growth across it will eventually ruin some of the most delightful garden enclaves in that part of the city.

Maybe something has to be lost, but what an old friend of the city finds himself doing more and more now is not only looking for its medieval past but walking around the older European streets making sure that all the best European landmarks are still standing. An obvious one, Shepheard's Hotel, is simply a heap of red dust surrounded by a paling fence, but the British Embassy has survived as it was in Cromer's day, and so have the old royal stables in 21st of July Street and the cottage-like Scottish Church in Bulaq. Building by building one finds cosmopolitan, occupied Cairo still breathing, but more and more each fragment of it becomes a little island of memory in a rather troubled Egyptian sea. Even architecturally the city is losing its French look. It never had a British look. I cannot think of one beautiful "modern" building in Cairo which is distinctly British. The most attractive British buildings still left in Cairo are one or two unnoticed and unimportant Victorian and colonial edifices which only a few people find beautiful. The Victoria Hospital, for instance, is an almost perfect example of India Office–Ministry of Works colonial architecture. Set back a little from the street (Shari' Abdel Khalid Sarwat Pasha, not far from the Nile Hilton), its old wooden veranda suggests long cool evenings — not in Egypt, but in the faraway hill country of the Pathan gate or Katmandu. Another one of these evocative colonial houses has become the Tawfikiya secondary school in Shubra, and some of the original colonial barrack buildings in Abbasiya are still standing. The barracks at least are probably doomed, although the Egyptians show no inclination yet of wanting to tear them down. In fact as buildings they are all well kept, particularly the Tawfikiya school.

There is also another sort of colonial memory clinging to the city which has nothing to do with its architecture or its old buildings but simply with places. A few hundred yards upriver from the Nile Hilton is the place where Thomas Cook's steamer landing stage used to be. From here Gordon set out for the Sudan, and so did the relief expedition that went to rescue him. It is now a neat little river port for "casino" houseboats and restaurants which serve also as overflow accommodation for the big hotels. These romantic old riverboats move no more, and because the river no longer rises or falls very much since the High Dam was built at Aswan, the riverbank along the new roadway is planted with vegetables and flowers and fruit. The landing stage itself has long since gone, but as long as the boats are there one

Looking up the Nile from the Nile Hilton Hotel.

does not have to dig too deep into the mind to picture the 1884 Gordon relief expedition loading up twenty-seven steamers here with 11,000 British soldiers, 7,000 Egyptians, 130,000 tons of stores of all kind. It was Lord Wolseley, the conqueror of Egypt in 1882, who stepped onto one of those tacky little steamboats and made the long haul upriver only to arrive off Khartoum two days too late to save Gordon. Today there is neither plaque nor tree nor spot of blood to placard the site in memory of Gordon and Co., but the recollection is always there.

Looking about like this for the European past in Cairo, one is always confronted with the Egyptian present. It may seem odd, but the sort of life which the prosperous foreigners lived in occupied Cairo is not a bad measure to bring to the modern city, because the differences between then and now tell us what is happening to the city and to Egyptians themselves. Tourism, hotel life, night life and "Oriental" entertainment: the foreign *taste* for this sort of Cairo is the same, but what they actually get now is very different. The tourist who came to Cairo just before the Second World War was not much different from the tourist fifty years before, except that the gentlemen no longer wore pith helmets and the ladies no longer carried those pretty little white parasols which Thomas Cook once advised their lady tourists to carry as excellent weapons against the natives. Tourists used to ride donkeys, then bicycles, then horse-drawn gharries and later taxis. Now there are no more tourist donkeys or bicycles or gharries, only taxis and glass-sided buses. In this jet age the volume of tourists who come hurriedly to look and to eat and to sleep and then disappear forever is determined by a computerized system of accommodation and travel time which seems to infect the tourist himself. In the jargon of tourist statisticians, 10,400,731 "tourist" nights were spent in Egypt in 1965 (the best year ever) by 542,000 tourists. Most were Europeans and Arabs from neighboring countries, but the greatest number from any single country came from the United States: 52,118 of them. Next came Britain with 41,655, and then Germany — only 27,695, which will probably surprise those who complain that the Germans are everywhere these days. Greece sent almost as many: 24,661.

More than 90 percent of these tourists spent at least one glorious "tourist" night in Cairo. Previously, no tourist came to Cairo in the summer, or very few. In summer now you can see large tourist groups from the United States (up till 1967 anyway), Europe, and Arab countries walking around the hot city streets not at all deterred by the summer sun, and statistics show that Cairo hotels are fuller in July-

August than they are in December-January, a complete reversal in the kind of tourism that used to pack Cairo in the winter.

It is impossible to find out exactly how much money tourists spent in Egypt before the war, but in another good year after the war, 1964, foreign tourists spent £E 37.5 million in foreign currency in Egypt, most of it in Cairo. This is not as much as Egypt was getting then from the Suez Canal, but it was a large sum for a country like Egypt, and tourism has become one of Egypt's biggest sources of foreign exchange. It is, in fact, very big business, but whereas the bulk of the money from tourism used to end up in the pockets of the privately owned hotels, tourist companies, bus companies, restaurants, guides and shops, now a lot of it goes directly to the state, because the state owns the hotels, the airlines and the bus companies, and they have a stake now in many of the souvenir shops and guides because they are able to collect taxes from them.

The hotel industry itself is a big state business. There are four big hotel companies in Egypt owning thirty-six big hotels, and in every one of them the Egyptian government has a 60–40 percent interest as well as owning some hotels outright, such as the new Shepheard's on the river. Some of the business is shared with foreign companies. The Nile Hilton in Cairo is owned by the Misr Company, which is itself 60 percent state-owned; the Hilton Company, which shares it with Misr, runs the hotel and takes out 33 percent of the profits as its managers. What is intriguing about the financial structure of the Nile Hilton is the merger between Trans World Airlines and Hilton International, which means that the financial pyramid of the Nile Hilton in Cairo now is part U.S. airlines, part U.S. hotel company, part private Egyptian capital and part Egyptian government — a very peculiar partnership, but one that apparently works very well. The Sheraton company is doing the same thing with the new Sphinx Hotel on the Giza side of the river near the Gala' Bridge.

Who can afford to patronize all these luxury hotels in Cairo? The fourteen-day package tourist is Cairo's most frequent visitor, and the best hotels in Cairo are as full of this new kind of tourist as the more modest ones. Before the war the society visitor to Cairo simply moved into one of the best hotels for the "season," but that sort of thing has gone forever. There is still a kind of well-off international-diplomatic-U.N.-business-professional-managerial-academic-middle-class "society" which comes regularly to Cairo. They drift in season through places like the Nile Hilton, where the atmosphere is both tourist and well-off transient American or European. But their social stuffing is not up to the prewar *Almanach de Gotha* crowd, who were really a very cohesive international set — stuck-up, arrogant and self-perpetuating. The "society" hotels then were the British colonial hotels like Shepheard's and the Continental-Savoy. Old Shepheard's is a grave, but anyone who remembers the prewar Continental-Savoy might weep now to see its famous terraces built over with arcades of tourist shops. The dusty old courtyard behind it, and its pleasant garden, have been filled in with a cheap shopping center, and you can no longer enjoy tea in the wicker chairs of the wide salons because there aren't any salons. If you want tea in the Continental-Savoy now you have to sit somewhere behind the entrance hall and survive the non-stop TV. The tourists who come to the Continental now are Moroccans or Tunisians or Lebanese — people who are not much better off than the ordinary Egyptian effendi. South Africans or white Kenyans or, for a while, American students or Irish factory workers also put up there, and sometimes the mixture of all these groups at the same time makes it a far more interesting place than it used to be.

What has taken the bite out of Cairo for the tourist since 1952 is the city's new puritanism. What tourists have always expected to see in Cairo is vice and sex and succulent nightclubs. In Farouk's time there were several hundred high and low dives in the city that could offer the flushed visitor every kind of aberration, and one variety or another of the famous belly dance, which was either incredibly indecent or cleverly exotic. Tahia Carioca, who was at her best during the Second World War, was probably the most famous belly dancer Cairo has ever known. Nobody knows how many English generals and French diplomats and Egyptian pashas and Arab sheikhs and occasional kings longed to get their hands on her, but Carioca, who was a strikingly beautiful girl, was also intelligent, and after the 1952 revolution she became left-wing and attached herself to one of the young officers in the revolution who happened to be a Marxist. Now she is a talented film actress and is a plump, motherly figure wearing glasses who also has her own variety troupe.

Tahia Carioca closed an era on Cairo's Turkish harem entertainments. Since the revolution the belly dancers of Cairo, though still very beautiful and voluptuous girls, must dance with a curious Egyptian discipline which takes away most of the dance's orgasmic excitement. Instead of being a public conversation with sex it never quite gets that far now. It is still a waist-curling innuendo, but the moment it begins to suggest an eruptive ecstasy it suddenly switches to a jazz-like whirling which takes all the corruption out of it. It is almost too decent, and there are dozens of casinos and nightclubs all over Cairo (particularly in the big hotels) where this cleaned-up version of belly

elly dancer in one
Cairo nightclubs.

Restaurant along the Nile.

dancing is offered. Even respectable middle-class Egyptians take their wives along to enjoy it. The districts of the city where you could once indulge in some of the most corrupt entertainments ever conceived (like Clot Bey, where the Australians used to throw pianos out of the brothel windows) are now poor but respectable streets of small shops and cheap cafés.

Blatant prostitution has also disappeared from the streets of the city, at least visibly it has. But there is still plenty of evil hidden in the back streets of Cairo, and one is still invited to go and enjoy it by a well-dressed "effendi" who quietly takes your arm and whispers in your ear as you walk along a busy street. Some of the undercover brothels these days are just as likely to be in the quiet streets of the respectable Garden City, where I was accosted recently by a plump, respectable-looking middle-aged woman who approached me with a serious question which turned suddenly into an indecently put invitation. That other cousin of corruption and poverty — beggary — has also been suppressed. Someone once said that beggars were Cairo's oldest and purest citizens. But Cairo's beggars have always been the banner of its misery and its poverty. For many thousands of tourists in the last hundred years "Gimme a piaster, mister. C'mon, lady, half a piaster" were usually the first words they heard on their arrival in this glamorous city. If the tourist gave the boy, girl, baby, woman or man a piaster, he was then attacked by wave upon wave of reserve troops waiting in the rear.

At first the revolutionary government got rid of the beggars by simply rounding them all up and telling them forcefully to stay off the streets. Some of them were convinced by police "arguments," but plenty of them returned to the streets and begged again. But as Egypt has slowly begun to pull itself up by its bootstraps, beggars have more or less disappeared from Cairo, and though there were always a few left, just after the June war of 1967 they seemed to have disappeared completely. But Egyptians and Europeans still like to dispense charity to the attendant poor at mosques, hospitals and churches, or to car door openers who appear from nowhere. That isn't quite the same thing, and in any case dignity has now become the poor man's privilege.

The fact that there are still poor in Cairo evokes the question: Who are the rich, and how do they enjoy their wealth? After the socialist measures of 1961 the officers became less noticeably a privileged class, and President Nasser began to lean more heavily on civilians in government. Plenty of rich officer-businessmen remained, but their grip on the government machine (though not on the army) diminished every day. Nasser himself has always lived modestly, and so have most of his ministers, but between 1961 and 1967 there were still people who lived on their investments, on rents, on speculation (however limited), on buying cheap and selling dear. Wholesale distribution and building were still in private hands up to 1967. President Nasser, preparing to change this, said angrily in a speech in 1966 that the wholesale merchants and the builders were becoming a "new capitalist class." Wholesale merchants, he said, could make up to a thousand pounds in a day. What had happened was that investment in industry was impossible, so vigorous capitalist cash had found a place to thrive which was not yet forbidden, and it made fortunes for some men. Some landowners working their maximum two hundred acres were still rich, some shopkeepers or garage proprietors or nightclub owners were rich, and so were some film stars. Famous singers like Om Kalthoum and Abdel Wahab were very rich. These two artists were also rich in foreign currency, and were even allowed to live more than half the year in Switzerland. But both singers were so popular in Egypt and in the rest of the Arab world that almost nobody begrudged them their money and their privileges.

Because Cairo has become a socialist city, one is inclined to look suspiciously now for any display of this capitalist wealth. As recently as 1966 big villas were still being built in Heliopolis or along the Pyramid road, and there were plenty of American limousines on the streets and mink coats in the theatres and rich private entertainments in the hotels. Gezira Sporting Club was still the last stronghold of the privileged. There, the lawns and tennis courts and swimming pool and card tables still reflect its curious isolation from the rest of the city. Gezira has become a permitted indulgence for anyone who can afford it, as if by leaving it alone President Nasser has siphoned off some of the bitter discontent of the old upper classes. Here, at least, they could complain around the swimming pool to their heart's content.

There used to be other British clubs in Cairo for other levels of the well-off. Heliopolis Sporting Club was once a middle-class club for the middle-class Europeans, now it is a middle-class club for the middle-class Egyptians. All the advantages and privileges of the sporting clubs and the new flats and the rich houses of European Cairo are still being enjoyed by better-off Egyptians, who still have a taint of Europe on them. The old European city is still the privileged half of Cairo.

The other half, which is still poor and dirty and old, is crowded into the winding lanes and unclean alleyways of the medieval city. The old

city is still lived in by the same uneducated but highly alert population who are supposed to be on the way to inheriting the whole city.
But like the rich, the poor also seem to be hesitant and to be waiting
cautiously before abandoning their well-proven poverty for something
as yet undefined. They go on living in their medieval mess as if the
mess will last forever. What determines their future is not visible at all
in their famous old streets, and you have to be clever to see that even
in the thick of this awful poverty the past is actually dead, and that
something different is being born behind all the crumbling decay of its
antique façade.

20

The Medieval City Now

WHEN you cross Ezbekiya and walk straight up Shari' el Muski you come to a rather peculiar double road with tramlines on it. This is the Shari' el Khalig, Canal Street, and when you step over the shiny tramlines you have stepped into medieval Cairo. You have also stepped across the canal, now filled in, which was always the jugular vein of the old city. As you enter the older city the appearance, custom and character, and even the economy all seem to go backwards the deeper in you get. Buses run through the comparatively new thoroughfares and cars pile up noisily in the alleyways, there are neon-lit booths and big shops and boys on bicycles and women in European clothes, but all of this seems to be forgotten when you try to remember what you have seen that day. The lingering impression is still of a semi-medieval city and a semi-medieval population.

A large portion of this population always seems to be new, because so many country people are continuously arriving in Cairo looking for work. Though the agrarian reform of 1952 broke up the old feudal structure of land ownership, the economy is too deeply embedded in its need to go on producing for all of its feudal character to be wiped away with a magic reform wand. Egypt had about nine million people when the British came in 1882, now it has over twenty-six million, and as the death rate of children falls with better social conditions, by 1970 it will probably have thirty-five million or more. Cairo has had to absorb an unequal share of this increase. A sample survey made in 1961 revealed that only 53 percent of the city's population was born there. Its population in 1966–1967 was estimated at over four million.

Street scene in Shari' es Sukkariya.

Street scene in Shariʿ el Khiyamiya.

Coppersmiths' bazaar in Shari' el Nahhasin.

Twenty years previously it was just under one and a half million; and some quarters of the city are as densely populated as the most crowded cities of India. Day by day the poorer quarters fill up with more new arrivals from God and the countryside, and as you push your way through the overcrowded streets of the old city you can feel its raw fertility throbbing in the packed, narrow houses, overwhelming all European ideas of restraint with a reality that is sometimes frightening even to Egyptians.

But what you find here is still the natural Egyptian character as well as its massive presence; and there is always the hidden difference which European clothes and Mercedes taxis on the other side of Ezbekiya partly obscure and partly suppress. Even the noise in these streets is different, because it is made by people rather than by traffic. A woman selling an ounce of watermelon seeds or a man selling a few mouthfuls of hot rice are engaged not only in commerce but in a thoroughgoing exchange of themselves. Some sort of intimate social relationship is built into every act, word, curse, conflict and joke, because contact is life itself to an Egyptian. Over in the modern and more spacious half of the city the crude passions of involvement are slowly being lost, but in the old city they thrive on renewal and over-crowding.

This excess of relationship has persuaded many people that the medieval half of the city is just an overgrown, fecund village, surviving on its ignorance and poverty, and doomed to destruction once its people can be educated and rehoused elsewhere. But this is wrong, for although the old city looks like a ruin it has its own right to preservation, not only for its monuments but for its domestic traditions. The medieval Arab merchant, traveling great distances with his goods, wanted at the end of a long hot day to find a place to sleep, a safe warehouse for his goods, a lively bazaar to sell them in, and a cool, clean mosque to pray and talk business in. This is still the domestic character of the medieval city, even though merchants no longer arrive from afar, and caravanserais don't really function any more. Only the bazaars still function as if the world had not caught up with them, the only difference being that now they seem to sell the worst goods instead of the best. The barrow boys and shopkeepers of the Khan el Khalili cater to the poor, not the rich; the armorers' bazaar is now a secondhand ball-bearing bazaar; and even the Sagha (goldsmiths'), which is the only bazaar left that deals in real wealth, operates behind a façade of dusty poverty and sells fake gold as well as the real stuff.

The genuine artisan bazaars such as the tentmakers and the coppersmiths (Suq el Nahhassin) are still intact, even if skinned to the sad shadow of what they once were. You can still see small boys squatting outside a coppersmith's suq in the Bein al Kasrein noisily hammering sense into a huge copper pot with a ball peen hammer, and just outside the Bab Zuweila the tentmaker pours acres of canvas through his sewing machine, running up the huge decorated "tents" that still adorn every kind of festivity in Cairo. It is really the crafts and manufactures of this old city which give it away, because once you have seen, and seen again, the Sagha and the Khan el Khalili and the crowded Woolworth madness of the Shari' el Mu'iz, it is far more revealing to walk around the hidden back alleyways and count the actual manufactures going on under your feet. I once toted up a hundred different trades in less than a morning, including the manufacture of weights for weight lifters, and bath plugs out of old motor tires. It is nothing to see small boys making brass locks in sand molds on the footpath, or tinsmiths cutting dustpans out of kerosene tins, or other experts making mousetraps and furniture out of apple boxes, string out of paper, carpets out of rags. There is even the more serious manufacture of petrol lanterns, hubble-bubbles, motor car parts, torch batteries, spades, donkey carts, pots, books, wheels, shoes, suitcases, bottle caps, taps, and cooking pots. All you need do is wander in and out of the back streets, and a European's mechanical-engineering-carpentering-chemical eyes will boggle at what they see an ignorant man or boy can do, squatting in some filthy corner.

This is the sort of cottage industry working class of Cairo. The real factory proletariat who do all the organized work of a modern industrial state may live here, but they work elsewhere in proper factories which are usually on the outskirts of the city. Medieval Cairo is not therefore the industrial quarter of Cairo. It is simply an exciting place of unorganized manufacture and of hand-to-mouth subsistence, where poverty is an ocean, and the remnants of past glories are the romantic archipelagoes of its neglected beauty. But nothing can hide the fact that it is really a large festering slum, however romantically enclosed it is. You have to occasionally tear your eyes away from its exciting streets and look up at the awful old houses. Sometimes five people live in one tiny room in these tipsy tenements, and some people sleep and eat under stairways or in kerosene-tin shacks on the roofs, or they bed down on balconies among the chickens and goats. Every house in these streets is a contaminated hive. Hygiene cannot exist in them, and almost every man, woman and child living here suffers from some sort of unpleasant disease, which they pass on to each other by hand, by touch, by refuse, by filth. There is no real starvation, and there never has been in modern times, but not many people here get enough

Fruit merchant
in Cairo.

Fortuneteller in
the streets of Cairo.

to eat, few have more than one change of clothing, if that, and not many adults can read or write.

Yet you can also find tucked away in the strangest corners of these streets dozens of primary and elementary schools. Before the war there were seventy-nine elementary schools in Cairo which were traditionally attached to "fountains," like Abdel Rahman's in the Bein el Kasrein. Most of these fountain schools are still functioning, as well as the new ones which the Ministry of Education is opening as fast as they can get trained teachers for them. Every one of these schools is a discovery in this old city, because one is inclined to forget in the anarchy of all this poverty and street commerce that children here go to school, and that after all, medieval Cairo has in it one of the oldest seminaries in the world — the Azhar.

The Azhar is now a mosque, a religious school and a fully fledged university. When General Gawhar finished building the first version of it in 972 it was simply a place of worship. A few years later, when the Caliph Mu'iz arrived in his new city, he went straight to the Azhar to offer prayer after he had inspected the rest of Kahira. It was the Caliph Mu'iz who turned the mosque into a theological academy in 996, and since then it has remained the most important university in Islam for the study of the religion and religious law. The Azhar has been rebuilt so many times since 971 that no part of the original Fatimid building is left except the middle of its sanctuary and the cupolas over it. Before the British came to Egypt in 1882, it had 7,600 students and 230 teachers, but by 1912 it had 14,599 students and 587 teachers, and in 1969 it had 13,420 students and 428 teachers.

In Taha Hussein's day (the early 1900s), when this blind literary genius was studying at the Azhar, almost every column in the great liwan had a teacher and a class around it. The method then was to squat on the floor around a teacher (mudarris) and repeat and repeat again the text of the Koran, and then to learn the official interpretations of the words and the arguments in support of whatever attitude the teacher himself took on each sura (verse). The principal subjects taught at the foot of these columns were Islamic law, monotheistic divinity, the science of traditions of the Prophet, Koranic exegesis, grammar, morphology, rhetoric and logic; and students could also learn arithmetic, algebra, poetry and other subjects as part of their course, but not around the columns of the seminary. In 1930 and 1936 the Azhar was reformed by royal decree into a proper university, but it hardly changed its methods of teaching. It only did that after the revolution. By 1969 there were only two or three classes left under the columns of the madrasah and about a third of these pupils were blind.

Mosque of al Azhar,
west liwan of the
courtyard.

Teaching around the columns in al Azhar.

These open classes are no longer a serious academy, even for religion, and they are mostly attended now by simple men who will leave here after five or six years, word-perfect in the Koran, and go into the villages as literate but uneducated village sheikhs — the very thing that Taha Husain hated about the Azhar's methods in his day.

The real university is just behind the mosque, where a sophisticated education is offered on a modern campus. In fact the principal faculties of the Azhar now are medicine, agriculture, engineering and industry, as well as religion and Islamic studies. But it seems a pity that the classical method of gathering students around a master to learn by listening and then by discussion has gone from here. Even so, the Azhar remains a stubborn, religious fortress in this old city, and it is still used as a temple by poor men in long robes who take off their dusty sandals and wash their feet and bend over their prayers in the dirt courtyard; and on feast days, when they put up the big decorated canopies to keep the sun out, the city outside its walls dies away and the desert itself creeps up around the high stone barrier. Like the Moslem religion, the Azhar still has its roots in the faraway deserts of Arabia.

This everlasting attachment to the desert keeps cropping up in the medieval city. So many of its buildings are really Bedouin tents made of mud, and the poor Egyptian still dresses for the desert rather than the city. Yet when you see all these "Arabs" en masse in the streets, you find yourself wondering how "Arab" the Egyptians really are. They all speak Arabic, and culturally they are Arabs because they can hardly be anything else after more than a thousand years of Arab indoctrination. But there are no pure Arabs in Egypt, any more than there are pure Britons in Great Britain. Looking back on Cairo's complicated tangle of foreign occupation, one is tempted to imagine that all the people you see in the city's streets are so mixed, racially, that they are racially nothing at all. But this is not so.

It is true that Cairo has always had a very mixed population and that it has always been full of Arabs, Turco-Persians, Turco-Mongols, Syrians, Sudanese, Armenians, Georgians, Tartars, Africans, Abyssinians, Turks, Greeks, Jews, and every kind of European. There were also, of course, the last of the original Egyptians themselves, the Copts, who never intermarried much with anyone else. This extraordinary mixture of races was mostly concentrated in the city, while the peasants in the countryside remained comparatively undiluted by all these foreigners. When the first Arabs came to Egypt the sitting peasants were the indigenous and original Egyptians. The early Arab migrations undoubtedly seeped Arab blood into the Egyptians, because the Arabs

Moslem mother
and her son.

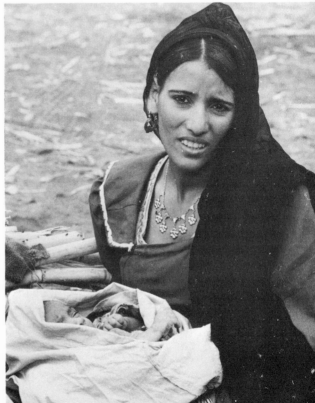

Fellaha mother and child
waiting for the bus.

did mix with the peasants and did marry them. But none of the other conquerors took their own population with them into the countryside the way the Arabs did. Most conquerors simply occupied Cairo, and the towns and took over the large estates, but always as the ruling class or the administrators or the army. The old Egyptian ruling class, therefore, has in it the greatest mixtures of races — Greek, Arab, Circassian, Turk, Syrian, Persian and European.

This is not true, however, of the poorer Egyptians from the village. The peasantry have remained predominantly Egypto-Arab, and because the streets of Cairo are continuously replenished and overrun by the country population, the mass population of Cairo is mainly this Egypto-Arab mixture. To most people, therefore, being an Arab doesn't exactly mean race. Being an Arab in Egypt is rather like being an American in the United States. It is national, cultural, social and religious, not racial. And since the culture is "Arab," the other question one asks oneself as one bumps along with this turbulent, gregarious, joking, argumentative city peasantry is just how much "Arab" culture they are aware of.

There is no real answer to this question yet. Arab art is all around them, but what do they know about it, and what right has the foreigner to point it out to them? One thing seems clear. The foreigner did a great deal to rescue the fragments of Arab art left in this old city, but now he is no longer needed because Arab art is finally in the hands of the Arabs themselves, and whatever is done with it now is their own affair. Take, for example, the Museum of Islamic Art which is about halfway up towards the Citadel in the Bab el Khalq Square. The history of the museum itself, and of the Committee for the Preservation of Arab Monuments which helped sponsor it, tells us something about this problem of popular Egyptian participation in their own culture.

In 1880 the Egyptian government of the Khedive Tawfik began to assemble the loose bits and pieces of Cairo's mosques and monuments and to store them in a corner of the Mosque of el Hakim so that ravaging European "antiquarians" could not get their hands on any more of them. So much Islamic art had been stolen, and went on being stolen, that the loss to Egypt is still incalculable. Not only was the loss of movable objects disturbing, but the condition of almost every important historical mosque or wall or gate was appalling. In the latter part of the last century a few foreign enthusiasts like Franz Pasha, Max Herz, Stanley Poole and Rogers Bey formed a Committee for the Preservation of Arab Monuments, and the khedive recognized it as an official body in a decree of 1882. The committee's official duties were to make an inventory of the Arab monuments and to preserve them, repair them accurately, and decide what loose objects were valuable and worth storing. In 1890 the great Max Herz was appointed architect in charge of the work of the committee, and the two European names you still hear mentioned most often in Cairo when talking of Islamic art are Herz and Creswell, who was still on the committee in 1969.

This committee has rescued or looked after almost every great monument of Islamic art now standing in Cairo, including the madrasahs and the mosques and gates and the walls, and the present Museum of Islamic Art owes its existence to this committee. Herz wrote its first catalogue in 1895, and in 1903 it was shifted out of Hakim's mosque into its present building on Bab el Khalq Square. Though the khedival government was the main fund provider and kept up its cautious interest, it was mostly Europeans who were involved at first. Egyptians became the directors and keepers of the museum only in comparatively recent times. After the revolution, the museum changed its name to the Museum of Islamic Art rather than of Arab Art because many of its most beautiful objects were not ethnically Arab at all.

What a westerner sees in this museum now often disappoints him, because Islamic art can appear very repetitious if you don't study it a little. There is almost no representation of the human form in it, since Moslem dogma forbids all iconography and self-worship, but the substitute for it — an exuberance of geometric and abstract designs — has left us one of the most passionate decorative arts ever conceived. "Illegal" animal figures are, in fact, represented right up to the fourteenth century, and in this little museum some of the carved hunting and domestic scenes look almost Greek. But what one mainly finds here are the arabesqued pulpits, ceilings and doors, and the finely worked lamps and fountains, from houses and palaces and mosques. Fustat is also here. You can even trace the continuity of Greek influence and Coptic influence on the Arabs if you study the material closely, and maybe the best things in the place are the fragments of that fragile specialty of medieval Cairo — stucco. Somehow or other, by what extraordinary excess it is still hard to determine, the Egyptian craftsman made something exhilarating out of this art of carved plaster. But many of the museum's most beautiful artifacts, which were found in the cosmopolitan debris of the old city, originated elsewhere, finding their way to Cairo because, after all, it was the richest city in the world. Hispano-Mooresque luster-painted dishes, ceramics from Transoceania and Persian bowls: the exquisite beauty one sees instantly in this art is what the ordinary Egyptians still have to discover.

[289]

So what, one finally asks, are the Egyptians themselves doing to get all this to their people? How are they going to continue the work begun by the Committee for the Preservation of Arab Monuments? — which with all its dedication barely touched the surface beauty of the medieval city. The last time I saw Professor Creswell in Cairo he said that the committee had to be prodded to do anything at all. But in talking to Egyptians it seems clear that they are now thinking differently about the way they are going to preserve their monuments. Undoubtedly they respect the committee and will use it, but they are trying to find some other approach. The museum itself is a comparatively simple affair of accumulation, restoration and display. But in deciding the fate of their most famous buildings the Egyptians dislike this remnant of foreign patronage telling them what to do, even though almost all its members are Egyptian. In the past the committee worked as a rather esoteric group who had no burning desire to encourage popular interest in their activities. What the new culture of Egypt wants now is not only popular interest but public participation.

Yet something seems to be missing in the official Egyptian approach to Islamic art. It isn't a lack of profundity or respect. On the contrary, respect at least is excessive now. It is hard to say what is wrong. Maybe it is only a matter of money. Egypt still can't afford to spend much on the very expensive restoration of the medieval city's beautiful buildings. There is also a religious problem. Scholarship and modernity have always had a difficult job going to work on the Islamic past because many of the Egyptian scholars themselves are fenced in by their cautious attitude to religious taboos, and after all most of Cairo's monumental buildings are religious. What seems odd is that Islam itself has never really helped much in the preservation or protection of its ancient buildings, not over a long period of time anyway. The Ministry of Wakfs, the vast endowed institution of inalienable properties administered by the government, has often helped restore some of the mosques, but not enough to matter.

Ironically, the only great monument of the medieval city which has been well looked after for almost eight hundred years, and continuously in use in that period, is the very fortress which kept the city in subjugation — the Citadel. It sits up on the little spur of the Mukattam Hills as if it were always something apart, a permanent foreigner in the city. That is what it was supposed to be in the first place. It was the military castle of a conqueror, Saladin, and it became the fortified castle of every other conqueror after him, including Napoleon, Mohammed Ali, and the British. Not much of its original construction is left; in fact Professor Creswell's detailed detective work on its many

Looking towards the Citadel from the mosque of Qigmas al Ishaqi.

additions is really a study of architectural cannibalism. Functionally the fortress ceased to have any military significance early in the nineteenth century when Mohammed Ali put a battery of artillery on the Gebel Giyushi (Giyushi Hill) above it and forced the Turkish garrison in it to surrender. Nonetheless, it went on being the main barracks for anyone who wanted to rule the city, and it is still a "gendarmes" fortress for government presence in Cairo.

Most of it, the biggest and best part of it, is now closed to the public. The only parts of it that you can see freely today are the outside walls, the Mohammed Ali mosque, the old harem palace where the trapped Mamelukes hammered on the doors begging the women for sanctuary (it is now a military museum), and Saladin's Well of Joseph, which is 280 feet deep. (This famous old well looks rather like the big hole that Conan Doyle's Professor Challenger dug in the Surrey Downs to penetrate the earth's crust and touch its underskin, which made the earth scream in pain.) But even though it has been generally looked after, inside the Citadel some of the mosques and the palaces have been thoroughly neglected. In fact it has always been the walls and the barracks that have been fairly well cared for and rebuilt and added to, because they were always needed. The Citadel is probably Cairo's greatest monument, because more than any other building it is simply *there*. But like the Matterhorn it is a desolate place, and the only way you can really see it properly now is from the Gebel Giyushi above it. From up there it looks rather like a child's complicated sand castle — all castellated walls and towers.

Because the Citadel is not really part of the ordinary life of the city, Cairenes have always been more or less detached from it, sometimes fearfully so, whereas foreigners and occupiers have always been fascinated and attracted by it. Perhaps the real point of departure between Egyptian and foreigner here is an aesthetic one. Foreigners see beauty in medieval Cairo as foreigners. But for Egyptians the old city is still lived-in up to the hilt, and what hides the beauty and buries the history and spoils the art for them is the condition of their own lives. For Cairenes the real loveliness of their old streets is covered over by an ancient crust of oppression which has been left behind by too much history, and the only thing that is going to initiate their own rediscovery of medieval Cairo is the recovery first of themselves. People live here on a historical treasure island, which is becoming smaller and smaller but more and more precious as the new city spreads out all around it into the fields and farms and deserts, and even up into the Mukattam Hills. But it is this new city which will recover the old one, and it won't be done building by building as much as man by man.

21

The New City

In 1967 Greater Cairo looked rather like Chicago the way Dreiser portrayed it. All around the outskirts of the city tall hard blocks of pale dry buildings, built with abundant Tura cement, were opening up their flat glass petals to the glaring sun. New communities emerged from sand heaps, and the streetcars followed. The metro railways crossed and recrossed each other in Heliopolis as if it were a rail siding, and along the back wall of Abbasiya barracks on the desert side, under the gum trees, a new metro track was being laid from Cairo to the new suburb of al Nasr, which has been built between Abbasiya and Heliopolis. Eventually al Nasr will occupy the entire area of Abbasiya barracks, and will spread into the desert far to the east.

What used to be open desert around Heliopolis and Almaza a few years ago is all built up now, and houses are already touching the perimeter of Cairo airport. Dokki and Imbaba and Giza and even the Mukattam are all being built on so rapidly that what used to be the empty horizon of Cairo is now becoming its most important new living quarters, and because there is unlimited space around the city there is little doubt that in ten or twenty years Cairo will cover about twice the area it did ten years ago, if it hasn't done so already.

This seems to suggest that Cairo is abandoning its old center, but there is hardly a district in the modern middle of Cairo which is not rebuilding, although most of it is still in the European half. At least four new hotels have gone up near the river, and the old Shepheard's Hotel site at Ezbekiya was about to be developed, but the 1967 war interrupted the plan. Around Abdin and in Saiyida Zeinab and even under the ears of the Citadel the cement tiers of cold stone floors are going up and up, and when you walk around the old medieval city you suddenly find a dirty little alleyway running into a new cement apartment block. Even the slums of Babylon (Old Cairo) are being cleaned up, and the government is building two new hospitals just outside the old fortress. A large community development has been built in the very middle of the Fustat-Askar spaces.

About the only large area of Cairo which has been left untouched is the Arafa, the City of the Dead, south of the Citadel; but even this untouchable old cemetery is being gently clipped around the edges. New ring roads have also been built around the city and through it. You can now drive from the pyramids to Heliopolis via Roda Island, Old Cairo (Babylon), Ain el Sira, alongside the aqueduct to the Citadel, east of the old walls of Kahira, and up into Abbasiya. Another new road runs south along the river to Ma'adi. There are underpasses in Giza and there's a river taxi running from Roda to Kasr el Nil which chugs up the wide yellow river like an old man walking painfully uphill.

The most important part of this vast rebuilding scheme is the Medinat al Nasr, the city within a city which is being built over the skeleton of Abbasiya barracks. Al Nasr is really being built to house the greater part of the ministries and departments of the government, as well as the people who work in them. In 1969 it was still a naked group of tall apartment blocks and glassy offices, which looked far too exposed to desert winds and hot sun. But already the whole area, extending into Heliopolis, is a place for Egypt's new politics. The tax collector's office is already there, so are the census office, the headquarters of Egypt's Transport Ministry and the head office of the National Oil Company. As a relief, perhaps, there is also a new Olympic-size stadium, and a dusty parade ground (a desert Red Square) with a ghostly reviewing stand waiting patiently for some fine military victory to justify its existence. The new headquarters of the Council of Ministers is just across the road in Heliopolis, and the Heliopolis Palace Hotel has been turned over to the Arab League.

Heliopolis itself is going through a change of life. The old racecourse is now a public garden, with a rather antiseptic but attractive nightclub in it. A new racecourse has been built on the southern tip of Cairo's airport. There are at least three new quarters to Heliopolis, one even extending as far as Ein Chams, and the sandy and unfinished avenues of small houses, blocks of flats and villas still have the desert in their backyard. There are probably more new churches being built in Cairo than in any European city, and many of them are in Heliopolis. President Nasser himself has become the patron of a new mosque near his house is Manshiet el Bakri, which borders Heliopolis. Another two or three mosques are going up in Heliopolis, and one of them at least is original and interesting to look at. The new churches in Heliopolis are not all Coptic; there are Chaldean, Maronite, Orthodox and Catholic churches. None of them looks beautiful, but none of them is empty on Sundays either.

Imbaba, on the west bank of the river, is also unfolding like a tattered butterfly. Ten years ago it was a native village, now it has a new complex of little houses and schools and shops. This community is in fact a special cooperative for architects and teachers, and it is steadily pushing its nose out towards the toy airfield. This cooperative idea is playing a more and more important part in Cairo's rebuilding. Up till 1967, most of Cairo was being built by private enterprise, though with government help. If you wanted to build an office block, apartments, or a house in Cairo (and the government encouraged it) the state provided cement at cost, provided you had a license to put your building up. But the license system gave the government the right to control the rents you asked as well as to specify what sort of building you built. Before 1965 controls were not so tight and you could also build without a license, although the government still had to sanction the site. But if you did it that way, you could get cement only at open market prices, which came to about twice the cost. The government has a monopoly on cement, but until 1967 allowed about a third of the total production to find its way to the open market. That means that up until 1967–1968 a little more than a third of all new buildings in Cairo were privately built without a license and with only minimum government control of the process.

Most of the unlicensed blocks of flats were built in the best positions, because the companies who built them had more capital to pay high prices for land, which was bought and sold on the open market. Before the new outlook of July 1967 there were areas where building speculators could persuade government officials to "cooperate" with them in getting the good sites. On the other hand, the licensed flats were a good idea because Cairo needed new homes at low rentals. However, the companies who owned and built these licensed blocks often charged an exorbitant sum for key money, usually five hundred to two thousand Egyptian pounds, so in 1966 the city government passed more stringent measures against the key money system, and by 1967 almost all rents in Cairo were under some sort of government restraint and were kept low.

Most of the professions, the army, the civil services and even the unions have built their own blocks of flats in Cairo, so that rents are also being forced down as more houses become available through social organizations. Some unions have even invested in ordinary commercial building. The new el Borg Hotel on Gezira was built by the Teachers' Union. They keep the top two floors for themselves as a headquarters and a club, and rent the rest to the government as a hotel.

This rather delicate mixture of private enterprise and state control and cooperative investment brought a building boom to Cairo in the 1960s.

In 1965–1966 the government finally decided that Cairo needed a planning authority, because the simple permit system gave them too little control over the appearance of the city. In 1966 the city set up a new committee to safeguard the historical and traditional and aesthetic appearance of Cairo and to veto any demolition or any new construction which did not conform to certain standards. Knowing how much damage and how much good has been done to London since the war by a similar planning authority, I wondered how it would affect the old medieval city, where the slum and the monument and the eyesore and the beauty are so mixed up together. In 1966 I asked Dr. Saleh Abdel Wahab, a member of Cairo's city council, what plans they had under the new law for the old city. He said that nothing would be done to interfere with either the atmosphere or the architecture of Kahira. The committee intends to preserve it as a medieval city, to keep its narrow winding streets and alleys intact, to close a great deal of it to motor traffic, and to restore the houses, gardens, walls, shops and marketplaces to their "original" condition, and perhaps even improve them. What about cleaning up the filth? I asked. Dr. Abdel Wahab insisted that this would be the first requirement, not only cleaning up the back streets and removing piles of decay and dirt (which the archaeologists euphemistically call "rubbish") but painting the houses, paving the alleyways, and taking away all suggestion of its slum character.

It seemed admirable; in fact for anyone who admired the old city it sounded like a miraculous solution. But how were they planning to deal with the chronic overcrowding? Either the dense concentration of population would have to be thinned out by removing large numbers of people or the old city would have to be considerably rebuilt. The emphasis seems to be on thinning out, shifting people into new housing estates to give those who remain a chance to develop a hygienic and modern community, even in a city which will always remain a medieval modular pile. This is, of course, a project, not a reality; but one influence which may help to clean it up is its future attraction to the tourist. At the moment a tourist sees little of the old city because the back lanes are so disgusting, but when the western tourist begins to discover the untainted glories of Islamic art in the now neglected streets, no doubt restoration will be speeded up considerably.

Almost every aspect of Cairo's development depends on the ability of the present government to solve the social problems first. Overpopulation is so much a factor that the government is vigorously encouraging birth control. A big family may be a virtue in the Moslem religion, but there is apparently no serious religious taboo against contraception. Every district in the poorer parts of the city now has a women's committee which advises and helps women to get and use contraceptives, usually the pill or some sort of uterine device. There is also a weekly birth control program on television.

The overcrowding of living space is not the only problem in conceiving a new Cairo. Getting people in and out of the city is a big problem. Already, at noon every day, Cairo's buses are jammed with people going home to lunch and to their siestas, hanging on to the open doors like bees swarming on a hive. I have even seen men riding a bus having no physical contact with it at all — simply hanging on to the shoulders of others and wrapping their legs around their fellow bees. A young woman typist hoping to get on one of these chariots simply takes a look at the impenetrable mess and gives up. An older woman doesn't even look at it. Gestures towards solution have been made — collective taxis now cover set routes at a flat rate, and fast express buses, the 500s, to most outer suburbs siphon off some of the clustering madness. On the whole, the permanent public crush of Cairo at noon is probably not much worse than it is in most cities at peak hours these days, but there is much more drama to it, more noise, more sport, more contest, more laughter, and a lot more death.

Most of Cairo's other problems are simply exacerbated copies of those facing most world capitals. Sometimes, standing in the middle of the big midans and looking at the sunburned skyscrapers, one longs for a sign that will make it clear to all that this is Cairo, not Rome or Paris or Dallas. There is, in fact, one special feature which does make Cairo unique, only you can't see it from ground level.

On the roofs of Cairo there is a third city which is not European or medieval, but a suspended township of modern roof dwellers. Tens of thousands of people live on Cairo's rooftops, and in the days when you could fly a small plane over Cairo you could clearly see its two levels of life: one on the ground and one in the air. The medieval city's roofs are a warren of poor habitations, but even in the European part

[297]

Looking across Cairo's rooftop slums to the Citadel, from the mosque of Qalaun.
To the right, the minarets of the university mosque of al Azhar, and to their right,
in the background, the twin minarets of the mosque of al Mu'aiyad.

there are many of these poor little "villages" which are, in fact, the rooftop rooms of the servants and porters who attend the people in the building. But I have seen on a roof opposite the Continental Hotel a fairly large chicken run, someone cooking on a primus under a bamboo shelter, village women washing clothes, naked children, a goat or two, and a mangy dog.

Obviously these rooftop slums are mostly servants' quarters, but in the old city at least they are the byproduct of overcrowding. Remembering the picture one has of Fustat's wonderful rooftop gardens, with the likelihood that you could have walked clean across that city on its roof as well as on its floor, there seems to be a chance here to use this unique condition to better advantage. A modern rooftop Cairo could at least have the courtyards and terraces and tangled passageways, gardens, fountains, balconies and shady corners that Fustat once had. Maybe the rooftop gardens of fruits and flowers in Fustat, which were irrigated by a water buffalo turning a sakia, can hardly be copied on top of the Bank Misr, but the weather and the nature of Egyptian domestic life would permit the style to be repeated. Why not? It is simply a matter of developing and beautifying and redesigning what is already there.

Unfortunately, it is not a likely proposition at the moment because it would obviously be an indulgence. Cairo is going to emerge first along conventional lines. For a long time yet it will have to go on facing its problems of housing, transport, work hours and hygiene in the usual way, so that after all the new city will be little different from any other city. Already, in fact, the sort of detachment which dehumanizes all great cities is getting the better of it. Twenty years ago Cairo used to be a very personal city. Everyone living in it seemed to have a special connection with it. But now its size alone is undermining the feeling of local attachment. Curiously enough it is still a children's city, not only because one sees so many of them on the streets but because they are among its busiest and most responsible working citizens. Very few of them beg any more, and now they must all go to school (although many do not). There are also strict laws now about exploiting children. But they do work, and you can see them in the hole-and-corner laundries of the old city practically sitting on the huge hot irons they are pressing shirts with, or you might see a boy of about ten solemnly carrying a tin tray of coffees from a sidewalk café to a nearby shop, or even more fascinatingly you can still find a twelve-year-old mechanical genius lying along the fender of a car and probing at its innards with a handful of tools. But all these child occupations are visibly dying out as the labor laws are more strictly enforced.

Children at work in Cairo; in charge of horse and cart (ABOVE), and punching brass tray pattern (BELOW).

So much is changing in new Cairo that many of the everyday things that one hardly noticed before now have a special flavor all their own: the kites, for instance, flying lazily on the hot air above the city and soaring endlessly on their wing tips waiting to dive on some succulent morsel of refuse, or the English Church bells ringing loudly on a dry Egyptian Sunday, or the steel shutters closing up the city tight at noon every day. But it is probably a mistake to go on looking for the personality of this changing city in the peculiarities of its activities or in the transformation of its appearance. After all, it is the people in it and what they think and feel that really give it shape and character, and one must try to understand the citizens if one is ever going to understand the place.

22

The Morals and the Manners

In 1836, when Edward Lane published *An Account of the Manners and Customs of the Modern Egyptians,* Europeans considered it a revelation. And so it was, because Lane's was the most truthful and detailed account in English of how Egyptians lived and behaved. It was one of the books that inspired several subsequent generations of Europeans to dress up in Arab clothes (as Lane did) and play the role of the Arab (as Lane did) and even embrace Islam (as Lane pretended to do.) There was a scientific purpose in Lane's apostasy, but those who followed him, including Lawrence of Arabia, usually became "Arabs" for flimsier and more dangerous reasons.

When the tribal Arab first came to Egypt with Islam he brought the special morality of the desert with him, but it didn't take long for the older prejudices and deeper superstitions of the Pharaonic people to be woven into local Islam, and the combination made the Egyptian what he is now. He is still partly a feudal man, even though he hates feudalism and wants to get rid of it. The campaign against feudalism has gone so far in modern Egypt that even the religion is trying to switch itself from medievalism to Arab socialism. Gamal Abdel Nasser himself said in a speech in 1962 that Islam and socialism were not incompatible, and that it was actually under Islam that the first great experiment of socialism was tried out in the Middle Ages. Nonetheless, the ordinary superstitious Cairene still believes in the djins, who are all great pilferers, hate salt, were created two thousand years before Adam, and love to hide in cellars, behind doors, at crossroads, in market squares, and in buckets, wells and old clothes. Anyone using a lavatory in Cairo or taking a bath should, if he has any sense, first say "Permission?" to the resident djin. A modern professor of physics may not believe in djins any more, but he may very well decorate his baby daughter with a blue bead against the evil eye. Superstition has always helped the poor man of Cairo get on with his daily life in the face of lavish misfortunes, so that any philosophy that wants to offer an alternative to religion and superstition in Egypt has to persuade the Egyptian that he at least has a chance without them. Egypt today seems to be searching desperately for a new moral system which will not go too fast nor be too slow; which will not antagonize existing hard-held beliefs but will never surrender to the old restraints of ignorance and custom. But it can only do this if it takes the existing character of the Egyptian into account.

For instance, the intensity of the disarray in ordinary life in Cairo seems to typify the Arab way of doing things. But it is never as bad as it seems. Two well-dressed men shouting at each other in the middle of Cairo and looking as if they are dismantling a long friendship are probably trying to decide which one will visit the other for lunch. If someone in Cairo asks you to come in at that moment and have a cup of tea, you have to politely decline twenty times before you finally accept. The basis of ordinary Egyptian intercourse is protestation, and though it makes a wonderful game, full of wit and good fun and sting, it is debilitating if you want to get something done. Modern Egyptians are now becoming fed up with all this elaboration; they long to have a simple yes-and-no relationship with their friends, as well as a much simpler way of getting on with their daily work.

It isn't all false, of course, and Egyptians can't be classified as hypocrites. Very few foreigners who have lived in Cairo for any length of time have thought of them as being anything but as honest as their lives permit them to be, as well as kindly, unwarlike, and very forgiving. On the other hand, their sensitivity to moral and mental suffering can become comical. In 1956 Mother's Day was introduced officially to Egypt, but ten years later it had to be changed to Family Day because Mother's Day was considered too terrible a reminder for all the orphans. Yet Egyptians can be very cruel to animals, often needlessly so. Anyone who has seen a donkey in Cairo pulling an overloaded cart of heavy bricks, and being beaten mercilessly to keep it working, will weep for the animal. The British always did. One of the first social organizations the British set up in the 1890s was a society against cruelty to animals. But even today, given the choice of man or beast, the man is comparatively so much the worse off that worrying over a suffering ass can seem immoral. Even the skinny cats and dogs of Cairo seem to be social victims rather than personal ones, as in fact most animals are in all poor peasant countries. But the nearest child with fly-encrusted eyes is always the more real sufferer.

For that matter, even the dirt of the city is a condition rather than a nature. Egypt has not always been dirty. Ancient Egyptians were fanatically clean, they dressed in the purest white, and they wouldn't even kiss a Greek because all Greeks (the classical and the beautiful) were considered filthy. The ancient Egyptian washed his fingers after each course he ate, the Greek used bread to wipe his mouth and fingers and then threw the bread to the dogs, a habit which the Egyptians found repulsive. All the big mosques in Cairo have taps or a fountain in the courtyard, and every Moslem is supposed to clean himself thoroughly before praying. Middle-class Egyptian women in Cairo always considered the Englishwomen who came out to rule them very unclean because their personal hygiene was not up to the mark of the educated Egyptian woman.

But the more you tangle like this with the manners and customs of Cairo the more you long for a new volume like Edward Lane's, only without Lane's nostalgia for the medieval merchant. What is needed now is a report on the morals of transition, because Egyptians need a new explanation of themselves, in the light not of their browbeaten past but of whatever new outlook they are trying to shape their future with.

Unfortunately most Egyptians are inclined to undermine their own character before it has been tested. They often seem to disbelieve in themselves to the point of cowardice. Taha Husain, the literary guardian of all that is best in the ordinary Egyptian, understood this fatal self-denigration in his people, particularly when they compared themselves with the west. He countered it by emphasizing Egypt's Mediterranean connection, her long attachment through Arab civilization to classical Greek and Roman culture. Maybe Egyptian culture is "European" enough for Taha Husain to make such a point of it, but that hardly seems to be the answer now.

The things of Europe which will rescue Egypt now from her pathetic self-effacement are the physical sciences and the conveyor belt, not classicism. It is technology which must impress the morality and uproot the slavishness. Women, for instance, can hardly go on being chattels and semi-beasts of burden in an industrialized Egypt. In ten short years after 1952 Egyptian working women were given more freedom than in the previous ten thousand years. Today, when you see a neatly dressed "peasant" girl in the streets of Cairo, with perhaps a colorful sweater and wearing shoes and stockings, it means more than simple abandonment of the veil. In 1934 only 235,000 girls were in school in Egypt, by 1966 the figure was 1,252,000 or 37 to 40 percent of the school population. The revolution gave Egyptian women the vote, which Swiss women still don't have. Someday that will count, though not yet, because the morality for their new outlook has not been settled. Many women now hold important positions in Egypt. There are women members of parliament, women professors, doctors, writers, lawyers, painters, pilots, and administrators. This is mostly new, but not entirely so. In the past women usually made up for their lack of public position by wielding enormous power in the home, but even before the revolution women were fighting their way into public life. Suffragettes like Doria Shafik and Hoda Shaarawi and Seza el Nabarawi have been known to most Egyptian women for almost forty years. Egyptian women have always been good airplane pilots, for instance, and since the revolution the government's primary training school for airline pilots at Embaba near Cairo has been run by a woman pilot — Captain Aziza. All these women belong to an older generation, but all of them are models for the rest, except perhaps Doria Shafik, who, after years of struggle to free women from the harem, anticipated Egypt's defeat in the Suez war and called for an end to all "dictators," meaning Gamal Abdel Nasser. Since then she has been politely but officially ignored.

But the strong woman doesn't really solve the problem of women in Egypt, nor of a new morality for them, because even middle-class girls from liberal Arab families still live in a very restricted atmosphere of moral and physical chaperonage which prevents any rapid liberation. Among the peasantry the moral taboos are just as strict, but there is a freer give-and-take between the sexes, which the educated classes don't have. In Cairo University, which has a very large number of women in the student body, the relationships between young men and women seem to be fairly free, but in fact the sexes are isolated into separate puritanical compartments by the old morality.

The only way for a boy and a girl to get around the restrictions would be to abandon the rules altogether and take their chances, which is a far more serious step in Moslem Cairo than it would be in New York or London. There are no bed-sitters in Cairo. A liberal Moslem friend of mine, the mother of a young girl at the university who was just unfolding her butterfly wings, said to me despairingly one day: "If you forbid too much, the girl will find a way of going to where *he* lives, and who knows what happens there?" But nonetheless she had to forbid. She explained to me that male understanding was changing far more slowly than the role of women, and though she was willing to trust her daughter, there was a good chance that the young

Somberly dressed mother and her more up-to-date daughters stop
for ice cream.

Mineral baths near Fustat.

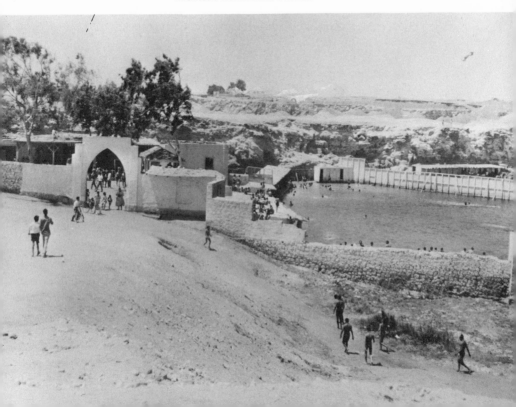

man, who had been brought up in this sexually repressed atmosphere, would "take advantage" of her if he could. The only thing that saved my friend from losing her mind with worry was the girl herself, who admitted she had visited a young man in his rooms but said to her mother: "I did not do anything, and will not do anything that would be untrue to myself or hurt others." In Arabic this is even more high-sounding than it is in English, but the situation of the girl was far, far worse than it would have been in a western country, so her reply was the best the mother could hope for.

But many young men in Cairo cling to the special sexual sport of the country. A vulgar core of these young men have bold eyes for all women, and plenty of salacious comment as well. The young women too have a curious way of inspecting a man, as if he were someone they are fascinated with and suspicious of and attracted to and contemptuous of. It can be a far more electrifying experience to be looked at by a beautiful woman in Cairo than encouraged by one in Paris. This is probably because the veil is always invisibly present on a Cairo woman's face. The veil used to allow a woman's eyes all kinds of sensuous abandon, as if, with the nose, mouth and chin hidden, the eyes could go mad and do whatever they liked. The veil is gone now, but the eyes of most Egyptian women still operate as if they had a right to annihilate you. On the whole, though, the men are free and the women are not.

One of the unfortunate side effects that this liberty for men and strict morality for women has in a city like Cairo is the petty brutalization of a certain number of its footloose adolescent young men, who have another furtive street sport of their own. Many a girl in Cairo suffers at some time or other from subtle nudges and pinches on hips, breasts and arms by ill-mannered young men who can do astonishing things to a girl with forefinger and thumb. As a rule, about all the girl can do is to shout "Mougrim" (blackguard) after him and hit him with her handbag. In October 1966 a new law gave the police the right to shave a man's head if he molested women in the streets. This has had some success, but the problem remains the social relationship itself. Even the average Egyptian marriage is still so formal that for a woman it suggests bondage. The bride and bridegroom still don't go to a mosque together to get married. The marriage ceremony is really the signing of the marital contract by the husband and the wife's family, at which she is not present. A week later, rather than a ceremony there is a celebration called "the entry," when the husband comes to the bride to begin his conjugal life. Perhaps it doesn't really matter when or how the marriage ceremony takes place, but as long as it takes place without the woman, there is an element of male purchase in it.

The question that most westerners ask about a Moslem marriage is whether it is as sacred as a Christian one. For years Europeans looked with delicious horror on the polygamy of the Moslems, although it was by no means a purely Moslem privilege. The Jewish religion not only allows a man two wives under special circumstances but two concubines as well. No doubt some Egyptian Jews enjoyed these pleasures equally with the Moslems, though I only know two who have had two wives. But like most Jews, most Moslems had only one wife and no concubines. Today the harem no longer exists in Cairo. In the poor countryside it never really existed. But easy divorce still gives the man an unfair advantage. All a man has to do in the Moslem religion to divorce his wife is to say "I divorce thee" and it is done. His wife can come back to him twice, but the third time he says that he divorces her the divorce is absolute. Or if he says "I divorce thee" three times at one go, the divorce is absolute and instantaneous and irrevocable. It is the man who pays the dowry in a Moslem marriage, not the woman, and if he divorces his wife, she keeps a portion of the dowry money and takes all her other worldly goods with her. Most people imagine that a Moslem woman can't divorce her husband at all, but she can go to a court and force him to divorce her if he is cruel or neglectful. If she does this she loses all the dowry.

There are plenty of loopholes in the Moslem law which a woman can use to her advantage, and now the civil law begins to back her up. Now, too, the religion is frowning on polygamy as contrary to what Mohammed really meant. But there are other inequalities of marriage which haven't yet become a problem, but probably will, some day soon. A Moslem man can marry a Christian or a Jew or a woman of any religion, provided the children are brought up Moslems. But a Moslem woman can't marry anyone but a Moslem, because if she did her children would be fathered by an unbeliever, which is untenable. Cairo's courts are always full of cases arising out of marital disputes, and because witnesses are such an important factor in any proceeding in Egyptian law, the scandalous stories you can hear are often very high drama. When the British introduced the system of native courts into Egypt in the last century the book of instructions they eventually produced for the parquets, written by J. F. Kershaw, said that the only way to get the truth out of an Egyptian witness was to let him ramble on in his own way, and in these marital cases the witnesses can hold you spellbound with their lengthy and intimate description of what really happened between a quarreling couple: no detail is clouded and no joy unrevealed.

In 1939 the census figures showed that 43 percent of all marriages in Cairo ended in divorce, and by 1959 the figures were about the same. Unlike the western world, where divorce is being made easier, both state and religion in Egypt are now trying to make it more difficult, and by 1969 the divorce rate was beginning to decrease. The religion in particular is preaching discipline and discretion and offering "try again" counsel. This is obviously an important step towards improving the status of women, but the real point of this new religious attitude is not so much the influence it has on women but what it reveals about the religion itself.

Like all religions Islam has suffered serious distortions over the centuries, and as with all Middle Eastern religions, what was a good moral system for half a dozen desert tribes one or two thousand years ago is hardly a sound one now for an industrial nondesert society. On Fridays the mosques of Cairo are always crowded, and mats extend even out on the roadway among the traffic. (In Cairo a mat distinguishes the praying area of a mosque, even when put down temporarily in the street outside.) Loudspeakers on the minarets take the religion even farther: they are so loud on Fridays that you can lock yourself up in a thick-walled apartment and still hear the fluid exhortations of the imam or the sheikh, standing halfway up the pulpit steps, telling Moslems they must obey the will of God or else face terrible results. Young men in nylon socks and rich men with Mercedes, generals who arrive in staff cars and poor men still wearing the galabiya — all worship in the same line in the same mosque in the same way. The one virtue before God in Islam is this égalité.

Nobody knows how religious the leaders of the revolution in Egypt really are. President Nasser is very strict about the form. There is little doubt that he believes in God, but there is every doubt that he accepts the kind of dogma which has ruled Egypt for so long. In fact the way he has interpreted the Moslem religion in his speeches and writings is in total contradiction to the traditional shape of it. But he obviously wants to reform the religious attitude rather than directly oppose it — he wouldn't have a chance of opposing it anyway. But somehow the new Egypt still has to undermine that awful fatalism of the Islamic code if it hopes to do anything with its people. Fatalism once gave tremendous courage to Islam's all-conquering soldiers, but it eventually turned courage into its opposite to persuade the peasant to remain helpless and submissive.

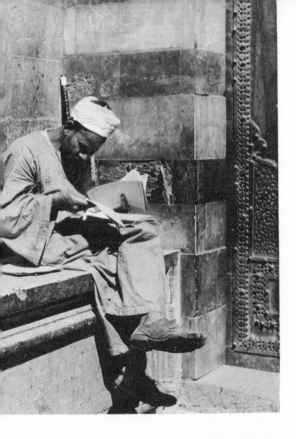

Student priest.

Moslem worshippers
praying in the street
in a "sajud" position.

The present attack on this situation is roundabout. It is part of the new doctrine, for instance, that Mohammed said you should do good and serve your people. Another new encouragement says that if work and prayer conflict, you should work. God will understand. There is even a blanket escape clause which now allows you to think for yourself, suggesting that if you use your judgment and act primarily as a thinking man you are quite safe, because God has determined what you are anyway, so you have nothing to fear from him. This helps the morality of the simple man come to grips with his new opportunities without overthrowing his firmly held conviction of the rightness of God and the prophecy of Mohammed.

But the problems of dogma are not a purely Moslem affair in Egypt. Coptic peasants are just as fatalistic as their Moslem brothers, and most Coptic peasant women have worn the veil like Moslem women and lived under the same sort of moral regulations. On the whole the indigenous Egyptian Jews in Cairo have also lived close to the Mohammedan code. Until recently the indigenes of all these three religions in Cairo were very little different in *moral* outlook and behavior. Although some Copts and local Jews identified themselves partly with their European co-religionists and took on European characteristics, the poor Copt and the poor Jew of Cairo went on living exactly like the poor Moslem.

The situation of the Jewish population in Cairo is a special one. After the British came there were two kinds of Jews in Egypt: indigenous Jews, who were mainly poor, and foreign Jews, who came as Europeans and refused to consider themselves Egyptians. The effect this produced is revealed in a survey of Middle East Jews prepared by Siegried Landshut for the American-Jewish and Anglo-Jewish Association and published by the *Jewish Chronicle* in London in 1950. The Landshut report says that "the increasingly western orientation of the majority of Egyptian Jews, aggravated by the acquisition of foreign nationality by so many of them, has led to their alienation from the rest of the indigenous population." In religious matters, however, there was never much of a problem for the Jews in Cairo. The Moslem and the Jewish religions are similar, and they often allied themselves against the Christians. On the whole the Jews suffered far more prejudice in Cairo from the European Christian community than they ever did from the Moslems.

After the revolution, laws were passed in Egypt forbidding anti-Semitism. After the Suez war of 1956 Nasser did not specifically expel Jews, but he did expel the British and the French. What drove many European Jews out of Cairo, even before 1952, was the great restriction put on non-Egyptians in business (the Landshut report also makes this clear). Most Jews who left after 1956, with all the other Europeans, were treated no differently from them. In fact there was far more anti-Semitism in Egypt before 1952 than after 1956, and there is probably more real anti-Semitism (as distinct from anti-Israelism) in European cities today than there is in Cairo.

Before the June war of 1967 there were still about twenty-six hundred Jews left in Egypt (mostly in Cairo), and a day before the war started the London *Times* correspondent in Egypt, Peter Hopkirk, went to see the chief rabbi, Ben Haim Douek, in Cairo. His report, published in *The Times* of June 5, 1967, said that there were almost certainly Jewish soldiers serving in the Egyptian army, and that "it may come as a surprise to many people, although it emphasizes a point the Egyptians never tire of making — that it is Israel they aim to destroy, not the Jews." Hopkirk reported that Jews had "full Egyptian citizenship with equal rights and responsibilities," and he found twenty-six Cohens in the Cairo telephone book. When he asked the chief rabbi if there was any anti-Semitism or hostility in Cairo, the chief rabbi replied that there were occasional incidents of the sort you get even in England. "But the government does all it can to prevent them," the chief rabbi said. "Anyone found guilty of causing an incident of this kind is punished." There were twenty-six functioning synagogue in Egypt, principally in Cairo, in June 1967.

The status of Jews in Egypt has never been a serious racial or religious problem; it is mostly an external political one. It would not even have a place in this book at all if the indigenous Jews of Cairo had not been such a valuable part of Cairo's life. The Landshut report says, "There has been a Jewish community in Egypt for the past 1,900 years." But there were "noncommunity" Jews in Egypt before that; the earliest reference to them in Egyptian monuments in 1220 B.C. Curiously enough, as Alfred Lucas points out in his sympathetic book *The Route of the Exodus of the Israelites from Egypt,* there is "not a single mention in the ancient Egyptian records of the entry of the Israelites into Egypt, of their sojourn in Egypt, or of their exodus from Egypt." This seems worth noting, since ancient Egyptians were inclined to put down on tablets every mortal thing that happened, and the other events of the period are very well recorded.

In any case during the "1,900 years" the Jews have been in Egypt there has always been a community of them in what is now Cairo, and there still is. In 1966 I walked into the big synagogue in Shari' Adly Pasha behind some cheerful old Jewish ladies and stood in the big Pharaonic doorway and watched men and women coming and going into the synagogue. Nobody in the street took any notice of them, and the worshipers themselves did not behave as if they had to be furtive about their religion. This was still true in 1969. Many of Cairo's most important shops, though owned now by Egyptians and even by the state, have kept their old Jewish names. But for obvious reasons the Jews of Cairo have no role in the city's affairs any more.

Coptic Christianity, on the other hand, still has a big role because there are about three million or more Copts in Egypt. The Coptic peasant living under a Coptic landlord was often worse off than the Moslem, but the middle-class Copts have always been more liberated in their ordinary relationships than the Moslems. The religion itself is just as narrow and as bigoted as the Moslem, and being Christian it hasn't the egalitarian virtues that make Islam a refuge for the poor man. But it too is now facing a revolt among its youth. Educated Copts may still look down on Moslems as new arrivals in Egypt, but as the morality of the new society has less and less to do with religion, it seems as if religious differences between Copt and Moslem will be slowly forgotten in the creation of something else.

In any case, what counts more in the everyday life of a Cairene (be he Moslem, Copt or Jew) is not so much loyalty to the politics of religion but attachment to all the ancient rituals. Cairo life is full of them: what you do when someone gets born, comes of age, is married or dies. A Moslem corpse, for instance, has to leave the house over blood, so something is slaughtered, anything, even a pigeon. When the corpse has gone the slaughtered flesh is given to the poor, and the richer you are the bigger the slaughter. Some Jews sit on the floor and eat boiled eggs after they have come back from a funeral, and the Oriental ones go on sitting on the floor for seven days. The Moslems still employ professional mourners (though it has never been a favored custom), and the wail of the women, the waloul, is a wild screech that has to be heard to be believed. Professional mourners tear their hair and beat their faces and work everybody up into a frenzy, and then collect their pay and pack up and go home, having turned a wake into an agonizing display of theatrical tragedy.

On a dusty vacant lot near the Omar Makram mosque in Cairo, not far from the Nile Hilton, one sometimes sees a large colored tent lit by white petrol lamps or electric lights. It is a beautifully decorated Arabian tent, the kind that is used in Egypt for official receptions. The dirt floor is carpeted and there are usually about a hundred little golden chairs and some inlaid tables set up inside it. This particular tent is used when some great personage dies. The male mourners walk in casually (the dead man's house is left to the women), greet each other with the elaborate handshakes that Egyptians love, stop awhile, sit in one of the rows of golden chairs talking to their friends, lay their fingers elaborately on their heart for a moment — amber beads dangling from a plump hand — and then sigh and get up and go away. This tent seems to be up almost all the time, and there are plenty of other places in the city where there are similar tents, which can also be used for wedding receptions. Mourning goes on and on in Cairo. Every religion — Catholic, Protestant, Maronite, Chaldean, Jewish, Greek, Copt — has official ceremonies that drag out death for seven days or fourteen or even forty days after the funeral.

The Copts in particular hold a service forty days after death which is called the arbe'en, and the last one I attended was almost too much for my European nerves. There seems to be something cruel in this organized mourning. The widow was led into the church almost unable to stand. She threw herself on the black-ribboned portrait of her husband which was propped up against the little pulpit surrounded by flowers, letting out a shocking scream of agony which I would prefer never to have heard. The church was ugly and hung around with bad holy pictures, and all its decorations of tragedy seemed to be in such bad taste that death became a mere suburban visitor. A poor man's funeral is much better because his friends always seem to be in a hurry to carry the corpse to the grave, to bury it, to weep a little in regret, and then get home for supper.

In a city where there is so much ritual of death it is understandable that one of its largest quarters is actually called the City of the Dead just south of the Citadel; it has streets and avenues of mausoleums and tombs, and some are the size of a small house. There are other large cemeteries quite near the middle of Cairo, and the famous Tombs of the Caliphs (also called the City of the Dead) and the Tombs of the Mamelukes are inseparable from the old city. On certain public feast days Mohammedan cemeteries in Cairo come to life like revitalized ghost cities, because relatives visit their dead and picnic around the tombs, eating special dishes and making something festive of the whole affair. Though the big cemeteries are important places, every domed building in Cairo is a tomb, sometimes a collective one for a famous family. In 1966 quite by accident I discovered the grave of ex-King Farouk under one of these family domes.

I was really visiting the Imam Shafi'i mosque, and I noticed a bijou building behind it which I had always intended to take a look at. This was the Hosh el Basha, where most of the Mohammed Ali family are buried. The inside walls of this large family mausoleum are of polished marble, and the gold leaf and green decorations running up the walls are romantically French and have nothing to do with Islam. About twenty or thirty tombs lie close together on the floor, all high above ground as Moslem tombs are, and looking like the attractive bakers' ovens you see in some Egyptian villages. These tombs are richly cut and decorated, excepting one belonging to the Princess Fatima Daoud, a granddaughter of Mohammed Ali. The princess was so pious or so rebellious that she asked to be buried in a plain wooden box; her family obliged, and it stands out among these marble sarcophagi like a beggar in a Turkish palace.

The most important tomb belongs to Ibrahim, who was Mohammed Ali's soldier son. The tomb he occupies was originally prepared for his father, but because Ibrahim died first he was buried there instead. When I was looking at it I noticed that the flagstones in front of the tomb had been dug up recently and replaced unevenly. That could only mean that someone had been into Ibrahim's grave. What for? I pressed the question on the old guardian, who eventually bubbled over with the explanation. "About a year ago," he said, "some officials came here at two-thirty in the morning with torches and dug up the pavement of Ibrahim Pasha's tomb. They found the steps leading to the chamber underneath. Then they went outside and came back in here with King Farouk's body. They laid him down side by side with Ibrahim, who was his great-great-uncle. That man Ibrahim," the old man said with his gravedigger's inspirational admiration for the dead, "had a very big head. His skull was enormous." And he swelled his hands around his own wizened skull. "But Farouk," he added sadly, "was not so blessed." Most Egyptians know that Farouk is buried somewhere in Cairo, but outside a few officials very few people know where.

All the other ceremonial acts of Cairo life — birth, coming of age, marriage and parenthood — are also heavily celebrated in the same Oriental way. In the western world, Jewish families are probably the only ones to celebrate the coming-to-be of one thing or another with the same verve and conviction which Moslems and Copts make of these ceremonies in Cairo. Even the word "feast" has lost its meaning for us, so that Christmas is about the only real feast we have left. But there are half a dozen feasts still celebrated to the full in Cairo. The most important one is the Mulid el Nabi — the birth of the Prophet. A hundred years ago in Cairo this mulid was specially celebrated around the lake of Ezbekiya, but now that the lake has gone the festivities are spread out through the main streets of the old city, which is decorated and hung with lamps and lanterns. Until fifty years ago the dervishes used to perform their flagellating zikrs as the main entertainment of the mulid, but their self-inflicted tortures and live snake swallowing have long been banned. A. J. Butler, the British scholar, described one of these public zikrs near the English Church in the 1890s, when a very stout pasha mounted on an "Arab" galloped his steel-shod horse along a line of prostrate dervishes who were lying along the ground like sardines. Many were killed, almost all were cut and severely wounded. Butler was instrumental in having the ceremony (called dossah) stopped. Nasser has thoroughly dispersed the dervishes, who were too fanatical and ignorant to be safe companions in a city like Cairo.

Apart from the banned zikr, most of the ordinary popular Egyptian mulid festivities in the old city are still the same as they have always been: conjurers, reciters, performing baboons, children's games, Punch and Judy shows. Now you can see children's swings and rather battered-looking tricycles for hire as well. The Mulid el Nabi feast lasts nine days, and during it Egyptians go mad for anything sweet. Children get sugar dolls and adults eat their way through mountains of cakes and pastries, which you can buy from hundreds of booths or street sellers or shops or street ovens.

All these pastries are really sweetmeats, a word which in Cairo means what it says. The basis of most of them is layer upon layer of flaky pastry, which you can see being made in little shops almost everywhere in Cairo. The pastry is rolled out until it is paper-thin and then it is whirled in the air by a twist of the wrist. The baker folds it and then cooks it stuffed with nuts or meat, and you can buy this pastry prepared in brittle threads that make a sweet called kunafa. Another one is called "palace bread" and is made of flat native bread fried in butter, soaked in honey, and then coated thickly with ishta, which is a rich white buffalo-milk cream. If you prefer European pastries you can buy them in places like Groppi's or Lappa's or A l'Américaine, and for a sweet lover Cairo is still a paradise of self-indulgence. During a mulid I have eaten my way clean across the city from one kiosk to another on a river of sugar. The aftereffect of such excesses is usually a badly frightened stomach, but in Cairo you learn to live with fears of that sort because you have to go on surviving the feast tables laden with chicken, macaronis, pigeon, vegetables of all kinds, breads, kebabs, meatballs, syrups, fruits, cakes, nuts, and so on.

But the most demanding Moslem celebration is not a feast, it is a fast which celebrates Ramadan — the month in which God handed down the Koran to Mohammed. It begins after sunset on the last day of the previous month, when a cannon on the Citadel is fired like a starting gun for a hungry race. Thereafter for thirty days you have to abstain during daylight hours from food, drink, sex, perfume and alcohol. As long as you can distinguish a white thread from a dark one you cannot eat, but another cannon shot at dusk officially ends the day's fast, and you can then rush home and indulge to your heart's content.

Some people are exempted from fasting all day during Ramadan — pregnant women, the sick and the aged. But most of Cairo's working population touch nothing from dawn till dusk during these thirty days, and because this is such an important and well-kept festival for Egyptians the government has not yet worked a way around it. Something will have to be done about it sooner or later because a Cairo bus driver, for instance, gets through his day's driving during Ramadan in a state of semi-collapse; and what happens to a steel puddler in Helwan, or a bulldozer operator in Aswan? The religion has just begun to stretch a point in favor of the working population, but so far most workers still go on fasting. Maybe they insist on fasting to justify the small pleasure of the night, when Cairo's streets are crowded with noisy celebrating people buying and eating the usual piles of sweetmeats and food and drinks. Towards the end of the thirty days, however, the white petrol lamps and the gaiety of the night wear a bit thin, and most people are finally glad when it is all over.

Moslems and Copts share at least one festival between them, but they both tolerate each other's activities. The common one to both is Sham el Nessim, the first sniff of the breeze, the first day of spring. It is also officially the first day of the khamsin, the period of the hot, southerly winds which bring thick dust into Cairo. Khamsin means fifty, and the dusty winds last on and off for about fifty days. When the khamsin blows, Cairo lives under an oppressive yellow, gritty blanket, and when you stand on Kasr el Nil bridge during a khamsin and look at the city, at the river, at the gardens, the skyscrapers, the trams and the buses and the horizon, that simple little line which the Beatles sing so feelingly, "Nothing is real," is what the city seems like.

The celebration of Sham el Nessim is supposed to be especially gay. If you're a miraculously average happy family in Cairo you probably take a picnic out to the Barrage Gardens and join all the other happy families along the riverbank. Cairo is bombed mercilessly on Sham el Nessim by youths who carry around in their pockets little grenades made of a small stone and gunpowder, wrapped up in paper and tied with cotton. They hurl these things to the footpath, and the blast cracks open the night and the day. The same happy Egyptian family that went to the barrage almost certainly went the day before to a special shop in Cairo where you can buy a putrefied fish called fesseekh which is prepared on Lake Menzalah near Port Said. Egyptians can eat this rotten delicacy all the year round, but Sham el Nessim is the time to make a point of it, and the smell of it is so high a dwarf cedar I once saw which had been planted in an old fesseekh barrel did not smell pleasantly of cedar but exuded the stinking smell of the rotten fesseekh.

Almost every feast or fast in Cairo is an excuse for family-tribal get-togethers. Like those other tribal and allied people, the Jews, Egyptians are inclined to be clannish, and the way that brothers and sisters and cousins and second cousins and cousins-in-law and friends visit each other in Cairo often suggests the grand arrival of a desert tribe rather than a mere family call to say hello. The way guests are received, too, is the way of the desert, not the concrete city; and the exchange of these Oriental courtesies in a modern Cairo flat always seems incongruous, because everybody should be sitting cross-legged on a tent floor instead of upright in stiff-backed European chairs.

Of all the morals and manners of Cairo, this old intimacy of family relationships is one of the best things that remain from a very complicated past. Nobody in Egypt quite escapes these close family ties, not even that skilled craftsman of isolation, the intellectual. Often, in fact, Egyptian intellectuals are profoundly influenced by this social remnant of a noncapitalist past, although it is obviously beginning to change.

Where any of these traditional morals and manners will lead in Egypt's new society is hard to guess. The intellectuals usually reflect what the rest of society will be thinking and feeling and arguing about tomorrow, so it is possible to approach some of the future through them. In many ways they have benefited most by the tangled mess which ordinary social intercourse in Egypt seems to be. It has provided them with a limitless source of wonderful human material, and now that they are finally liberated from intellectual bondage to Europe and are beginning to discover their own sources of culture in these rich fields, Cairo is once more becoming an intellectual city which might very well develop an influence far beyond Egypt and the Arab world.

23

The Intellectual City

Before the revolution of 1952 Egypt's best writers and artists and painters were not exactly underground, but as far as any serious artistic activity was concerned they were living in an oppressive society. On the day that Cairo was set on fire, in January 1952, political divisions among the intellectuals had prevented their playing any effective role in developing events. They did not lead the revolution. That was left to the young officers, who were mostly nonintellectuals, but who were determined, disciplined and dedicated, even if some of them were narrow and ignorant. Not all Cairo's intellectuals welcomed the army as their new master, and not all the young officers had any sympathy for the intellectuals.

After the revolution and up till 1956 there was nothing much in the young officers' social ideology to attract the artists. Most of Cairo's smart young men continued to look admiringly at the west. Just before the revolution Albert Cossary, who was one of Egypt's brightest young writers, was still writing beautiful Durrell-like novels (in French, not Arabic) about the tired and lackadaisical Egyptian peasantry and workers who couldn't quite get up enough energy or willpower to rescue themselves. That was still the young intellectual's position even after the revolution.

This attitude was killed stone-dead by the Suez war of 1956, which revealed Egyptians to themselves. Poets, writers, painters and playwrights suddenly came into their own, and they began to take part in this Egyptian kind of revolution. But the contempt and dislike of the right-wing officers, who didn't want longhairs telling them what to do, made the intellectuals a little nervous of what they said and did, though Nasser himself had encouraged them.

This situation changed radically in 1962 when Nasser pushed through the socialist charter. He needed the help of the intellectuals to persuade the entire society that the only hope for Egypt lay in this new militant, popular, scientific, anti-imperialist, industrialized, slogan-heavy socialism. On the whole the intellectuals not only agreed but gladly involved themselves. In 1962–1963 Nasser also let the Communists out of jail. Most of the imprisoned Communists were intellectuals — important ones. Many had been in jail since the revolution, but in the peculiar catalepsy of Egyptian politics they had often supported Nasser from their prison cells, even when they were being beaten up and tortured by the political police for refusing to renounce their Communism. What Nasser asked them to do now was to accept the policy of the Arab Socialist Union without necessarily renouncing Communism, and since the Communists found the charter to their liking, they agreed to do so. When they were released some of them were immediately given important intellectual positions.

Politically, therefore, the intellectuals found themselves more and more attached to the revolution. External events also forced them to make up their minds on issues which intellectuals usually like to keep safely open at both ends. In the press, theatre, TV, cinema and literature they now began to tell their own people that Egyptians were not fools or knaves, and that the nation must have dignity, courage and social purpose. This new emphasis on social awareness even put inflammatory words like "socialism" and "revolution" into the mouths of the respectable middle classes. Only a few years before, you had to whisper a word like "socialism" behind your hand, but the intellectuals now began to change all that.

Perhaps no nation has ever been able to fix the proper balance between responsibility and freedom for its intellectuals, and Egypt is no exception. But if an outsider looks at all the Oriental alleyways which are now leading Egyptians towards their future, there is a certain logic to the direction they are taking. Not every intellectual may like the idea of his new responsibility, but like it or not, they all have to live with it. And the forces involved are very powerful. One of the best examples of just what is involved is Cairo's press.

What in the west is usually called a "free" (privately owned) press no longer exists in Egypt. In 1960 the entire press was handed over to the Arab Socialist Union. When Cairo's newspapers lost their private owners they lost some of their backbiting scurrility (which was often delightful) and became instead organs of social pressure. It suited some, but not all. Even so, famous weeklies, like *Rosa el Youssef* (which is the name of its founder, a woman) and *Akhbar el Yom* and *Akher Sa'a*, are probably much better papers since they became less scandalously lightheaded, even if they have become duller.

The one newspaper which took this social transformation more seriously than the rest is *al Ahram*, which is the New York *Times* or London *Times* or *Pravda* of Egypt. Few papers in the world can be read to such advantage by "experts" who want to discover exactly what the leaders of the nation are actually thinking. *Al Ahram's* editor, Hassanein Haikal, writes not only what President Nasser officially wants, but what he himself is troubled about, what he finds difficult, disappointing, encouraging or discouraging in Egyptian society, and sometimes the results of this critical soul-searching by *al Ahram* are extraordinary. Haikal himself will often go along to a public meeting of a local Arab Socialist Union branch and deliberately provoke sharp and critical discussions of policies and ideas. Like Nasser's, his attempts in *al Ahram* to stimulate public participation have become almost an obsession. Egypt's press was always inclined to be provocative, but now the provocation has a specific social aim.

What is always astonishing to anyone looking at the newsstands of Cairo is the amount of stuff still published. The official yearbook of 1965 listed nine Arabic dailies in Cairo, as well as 44 Arab weeklies, 22 fortnightlies, 146 monthlies and 51 occasional journals. Today there is still at least one daily paper in English, as well as about ten English weeklies and five monthlies, some of them propaganda journals. There are also a French daily and about ten weeklies or monthlies, and a Greek and an Armenian daily, as well as weeklies and monthlies in those languages. The list also mentions dailies in Persian, German and Italian. Until recently Cairo's most important literary journals were monthlies, but after 1962 the government decided that it was important for the big dailies to carry a serious cultural section once a week, to take Egyptian culture into every household that can read a newspaper. On the whole, most serious writers have welcomed this back door into Egyptian minds, and the social responsibility of the press, in providing it, finds an easy equivalent in the social realism of the writers and artists who use it. There is no strong desire in modern Egypt for intellectuals to remove themselves from unintellectual society. It might look to an outsider as if it is all being done to order, but nobody who understands modern Egypt thinks of it that way. The Lacoutures reported that Egypt's new social realism "corresponds pretty well to the present state of Egyptian culture and the country's immediate problems, and it allows some synthesis to be made between the struggle for national independence, social reforms, and the needs of art itself."

This brings literature into the arena with Hassanein Haikal, the editor of *al Ahram,* and social realism in literature fits in very well with the socialist charter of 1962. In 1956 the Lacoutures in their book mentioned about ten writers as Egypt's best, among them Abdel Rahman Sharqahi, Naguib Mahfuz, Rushdi Salih, Taha Husain and Tawfik el Hakim. All but one (Tawfik el Hakim) could be called social realists. Not only are they Egypt's best, but the struggle of Egyptian literature to exist at all in the last fifty years is embedded in their work. Writers like Taha Husain and Tawfik el Hakim in particular are just as important in Egyptian literature as Mauriac is in France or Hemingway in America or Sean O'Casey in Britain, and their work can be compared favorably with any of these great Western writers. Most of these Egyptian writers were established even before the revolution. They were household names among Egypt's intelligentsia. But only since the revolution have they become widely known among the ordinary nonintellectual Egyptians.

One of the reasons why Egypt's best writers never had a proper audience before the revolution was the large amount of bowdlerized trash published in Egypt which absorbed a large portion of the reading public's time and interest. I would guess that about a third of all titles used to be crudely translated and "adapted" European and American novels. Along the sidewalk of the Ezbekiya Gardens, near the Opera House, is one of Cairo's many clusters of street bookstalls, and it is worth taking a look at them. Once you've overcome your fascination for the sort of English books you can find there — Victorian and pre-1914 popular fiction, and every conceivable kind of medical book sold by returning students — you get involved in the hundreds of Arabic paperbacks. All you need to know about them is in the cover design, and if you open some of them at random you can almost follow, without understanding a word of Arabic, the terse language of the French *policiers* or the American detective story. I once found a paperback *Moby Dick* written almost entirely in Hemingwayesque dialogue.

But this sort of thing is disappearing now. In Cairo's real bookshops (there are more bookshops in the center of Cairo than seems reasonable) you can now find serious translations of almost every important European and American author, as well as a fairly up-to-date selection of modern French, Italian, English, American and Russian books. Many of these bookshops in the center of Cairo were originally European. Sometimes they did not stock any Arabic books at all, but there are very few now that haven't a few Arabic books on their shelves.

The old city is full of Arabic bookshops, because even in its darkest, trashiest days Cairo published a lot. These older Arabic bookshops have a special smell and feeling about them which is not like a European bookshop. They are dry and a little dusty and have a smell of the desert in them. Most books in Arabic have paper covers, and if you take one down that has been undisturbed on the shelves for some time the paper is so dry that if you flick over the pages they may snap in half with a crack.

What is so revealing about an Arabic bookshop now is the kind of titles it has on its shelves. Almost every book written now, and the number is becoming quite formidable, is worrying about Egypt's future. This is where social realism is seen in the flesh, but what remains unseen by most foreigners is not the difficulties of the content but the complicated problems of the form, because the Arabic language becomes hellish if you try to write realistically in it. There are really three Arabic languages in use in Egypt — classical, modern and colloquial. In general, classical Arabic is the language of literature, modern Arabic is the language of newspapers, cinema and TV, and colloquial Arabic is the language of the uneducated. The uneducated or half-educated Egyptian cannot understand classical Arabic, even when it is spoken.

Nothing has divided people from their own culture as much as this awful gap in language. Modern Arabic is trying to bridge it, and though writers like Taha Husain and Tawfik el Hakim write, fundamentally, in classical Arabic, they have also tried over the years to find a meeting point with the colloquial tongue. And it has to be done. It would be ridiculous, for instance, for Naguib Mahfuz, who writes wonderfully about the lively, vulgar population of the old city, to have his truck drivers talk in pure literary Arabic. On the other hand, what holds the structure of any book together is the profound strength of good literary Arabic. Good style is absolutely essential in Arabic.

The people who are having the most trouble are the poets, because the complicated but inescapable relationship between grammar, meter, rhyme and style gives Arabic an inborn sort of poetry which very few other languages have. But it is formal. You cannot abuse Arabic the way you can English and get a certain kind of native poetry out of it. The problem for modern poets therefore is to overcome the conventions. I think it was in the thirteenth century that poets at the court of one of the sultan's were forbidden to build their rhymes on any but a codified set of permitted comparisons. Eyes, ears, lips, cheeks, love, sex could be compared only with specific things like pearls, pomegranates, gazelles, a rose or a she-camel. The list was long, but the rules were strict, and though this sort of thing was only a brief episode in the life of the language, nonetheless Arab poetry has remained in the grip of similar conventions.

What makes the modern poet rebel against this elaborate form is the need to say something about what is happening now, and to communicate quite informally the fact that a rose is a rose is a rose. Some young poets have tried a kind of colloquialized classicism. Others, like Kamel Abdel Halim, whom some Egyptians have called their Mayakovski, have tried to use the startling simplicity of everyday language. In the 1960s many of the young poets went back to a more primitive pre-Islamic style: pre-Koran, so to speak. (The Koran is the real creator of the enriched Arabic language.) The man some of these new young poets and many older ones have chosen as their master is Ahmad Shawki, a late nineteenth-century poet and playwright who broke many of the strict conventions of rhyme and meter and used a very free form of rhymed prose to convey the feeling of character and action. Those who dislike his influence accuse his young disciples of simply copying a copier.

In any case this search for new ways of expression is leading to a renaissance in the Arabic language. For an educated Egyptian this is a very exciting prospect. Poetry is now booming. In 1966 Malak Abdel Aziz, one of Egypt's leading women poets, who had just published a second edition (three thousand copies) of her collected poems, said to me: "What surprises me about the French is the small size of their editions of poetry. A thousand is very good in Paris. But I suppose that's because they don't believe in anything, so why should anyone look for poetry that leaves them no better off?" This sounds tendentious, but Malak's own poetry is quite feminine and solicitous, and her particular search in Arabic for the informality of a field of prairie flowers sounds like this in English:

I leaned toward them.
My heart inclined:
"Darling,
How lovely you are.
How lovely is the glow of colors on your cheeks.
How lovely is the excitement,
How sweet is the giddiness from your intoxicating, odorant
  scents."
I look in their eyes,

[325]

I drank dew of their eyes,
I caressed tenderly their delicate stem.
I asked about their names,
And with the tremble of anxiety
I heard their deep whisper.
I found in their depths tales wanting to be confessed
Mixed with honey, scents and melodies.

The informal lyricism is obvious even in English, but it gives no idea of the problems of the language itself. Egyptian poets are going to go on suffering and arguing a great deal before they find a language and style fit for their changing world.

What has probably emerged more successfully than poetry is the theatre, which also enjoyed a remarkable renaissance in the 1960s. Egyptian theatre is only about a hundred years old, because theatre in the European sense is not part of Arab culture. Professor H. A. R. Gibb of Harvard University in his preface to an excellent book on twentieth-century Arab art by Dr. Jacob M. Landau (*Studies in the Arab Theatre and Cinema*, 1958) says that European theatre derives from Greece, but somehow this missed the Arabs. The result was that serious theatre did not develop among them, although there was a lively popular tradition in Egypt of mimicry, shadow plays, puppetry and buffoonery. But one must add that Arabic poetry had its own kind of theatricality, even though it was not acted out. The religion made any serious use of acting difficult, but Arab preoccupations with epic poetry, with play upon language, and with that remarkable dialectical exercise — the public poetry contests — each created a sort of serious theatre of its own. It was not European in style, but it had drama enough for the European-style theatre to find a natural home in Egypt when it came.

European theatre was introduced in the nineteenth century, and many French and Italian troupes were imported into Cairo. By the time the British came, Cairo's ruling classes probably knew European drama and opera better than the average British officer. The British never brought any serious English drama to Cairo. The first English theatre performance in Egypt between 1882 and 1900 that I could trace was a performance of a farce written by an army subaltern. It was quite a social event. What the English didn't know then and never knew was that in the back streets of Cairo at this time they could have seen Arabic adaptations of Racine, Molière, Corneille, Voltaire, and even of Shakespeare himself.

Once it had arrived, the theatre never again left Cairo, and in a hundred years, as Dr. Landau shows, it has developed its own traditions and its own style and its own remarkable playwrights, among them Ahmad Shawki, Hassan el Mar'i and Mahmoud Taimour. Today Egypt undoubtedly has one of the world's greatest playwrights, Tawfik el Hakim. His dramas are almost unknown in the west, yet he has been writing his clever, intellectual, probing plays for almost thirty years, and they mean a great deal now in Egypt's present mood of self-analysis. Like Shaw, Tawfik el Hakim often deals in the exaggerated moral choice. He has always reflected what was happening in the minds of his thoughtful countrymen, although he is often so intellectual that he antagonizes the social realists. Nonetheless, it is only since 1952 that Tawfik el Hakim has been given adequate recognition in Egypt.

Despite his artistic nonrealism, Tawfik el Hakim is very much part and parcel of the political realism which now dominates the Egyptian theatre. After 1962 almost every theatre in Cairo began to put on plays about ordinary Egyptian life, not simply domestic comedies and dramas, but plays with a social message. Most of them contrasted conditions before and after the revolution, and the hero was usually the revolutionary. Just after 1956 Yussef Wahby put on a series of plays about British occupation and how Egyptians fought it; and Nouman Akhour wrote some of the first plays in modern Egypt to make a genuine point of the social conflict between the old and the new. It was Akhour who began to suggest the socialist alternative. A dozen other playwrights were saying the same things in the 1960s. In 1966–1967 a play by Yussef Idriss called *Al Ghafeer* (The Overseer) was an intellectual sensation because it attacked the old Egyptian (?) habit of telling someone else what to do, then taking the credit if it turned out well, but blaming the other chap if it turned out badly. As this kind of committed theatre began to emerge in Cairo, so did new troupes for folk dancing and folk singing, which up till the revolution had hardly existed as an art form at all.

All this awakened interest in drama and music had to be organized and have a place to live in, and by 1967 Cairo had eight theatres, two folklore ensembles, two revue troupes, a symphony orchestra, a choral group, a new National (classical) Ballet, a circus, and a song and dance ensemble. In the first three years after the social revolution of 1962 theatre performances tripled in Cairo, and the audience increased by 600 percent. All Cairo theatres are either owned or sponsored by the government, and almost every production is subsidized. In 1967 Cairo was probably one of the few cities in the world where the government took over several large cinemas and turned them into theatres, although new cinemas were also being built. A new theatre for the new National Ballet was planned for 1967 or later, but the June war of 1967 interfered with the scheme. The ballet has been trained by the Russians, and their first ballet, *Bakhtchissarai Fountain*, which I saw performed in the little wooden Opera House in 1966, was about as good as Western ballet five or six years before. A new puppet theatre has been built in the Ezbekiya Gardens for a very clever puppet troupe which turns the traditional Egyptian village art of shadow play and puppetry into professional entertainment.

The influence of the European theatre on the Egyptian is obvious, but the form, as a rule, is uniquely Egyptian; in fact much that is still experimental in European theatrical invention is normal to Arab audiences. Avant-garde techniques now being rediscovered so forcefully in Europe and America are similar to those used primitively for hundreds of years in ordinary Arab entertainment, particularly the use of song and dance to comment on or carry a moment of the drama. What is often considered nonrealistic theatre in the west, therefore, is perfectly acceptable to Egyptians, even within the bounds of their own conventions. But modern European dramatists are now fairly popular in Egypt anyway. Since 1956 Egyptians have performed in their Arabic theatre, or on the TV or radio, plays by Tennessee Williams, Beckett, Osborne, Pinter, Wesker, N. F. Simpson, Rattigan, Chekhov, Gorki, Arthur Miller, Ionesco, Dürrenmatt, Brecht, O'Neill, O'Casey, and many others not so well known, as well as Greek classical dramas, which are always an experience in good translation, because classical Arabic sounds so classically Greek.

In December 1966 in Cairo I attended a rehearsal in Arabic of Brecht's *The Good Woman of Sezuan*. Brecht never meant *The Good Woman . . .* to be taken literally, but in Egypt this play about poverty and corruption became something quite real for Egyptians, even though performed in the Brechtian way. The Egyptians have had trouble with Brecht, because it was only recently that Brecht's wife, Helene Weigel, agreed to let them use Arabic music for the songs in his works. The Egyptians had tried the European music with *The Caucasian Chalk Circle*, but the songs were so ridiculous to Arab ears that they stopped the production. The modern symbolistic Greek play by Theodakis about fear and individual responsibility, *The Bridge of Arta*, also had a meaning for Egyptians which it probably never quite had for Europeans, even though it too is primarily an intellectual exercise. This play was performed in Arabic by Egypt's International Theatre Troupe, and written on the drop curtain of the theatre in Arabic was their heaven-kissing credo: "For the sake that the roses in our garden will ripen, so that all the hands of love and peace and human brotherhood would meet for deep culture, and the high policy of Arab international art."

The reason this new role for the intellectual has been easier in the theatre than in any other art is that the familiar conflict between content and form was already partly solved. But like the poets, the painters have had a much more difficult time. There is no genuine tradition of Arab "painting," not the sort of painting that can be fitted into the modern context anyway. All modern Egyptian painting is influenced, at one gulp, by almost every European development over the last sixty years, so it is hard to call it uniquely Egyptian. So far the influence of Islamic art on modern Egyptian art has been negligible. Like the historians, painters are still rather afraid of the religious taboos attached to Islamic art, and maybe they dislike it for its long history of suppression and restraint. But what is attractive about new young painters is their attempt to find what is their own, even though there is no evidence yet that they have found it.

It is quite impossible for Egyptian artists today to avoid the social problem, and the painters' approach is still fairly naïve. Eventually they will either come up with a new and vigorous art of their own, or they will produce the same sorts of things you can find in Paris or Rome or London or New York, which will really be failure for them. At the moment it is too early to tell what will happen. It seems fitting, though, that the artists use the old Sinnari house, where Napoleon put his artists, as their headquarters and their atelier. Every now and then a group of Cairo artists will set out from the Sinnari house and go looking for something in Cairo they seem to have lost, something that is still hidden in the city itself, although they don't quite know what it is. One Sunday I joined some friends on one of these outings and we went down to the medieval city, to the Bein el Kasrein, and when we were all looking up at the minaret of Qalaun mosque someone said in an awed voice: "It's emotional!"

The man who said it was then the high, official priest of Egyptian aesthetics in art — al Arabli: a small lean man who had stubborn, highly intellectual tastes which Cairo's artists did not always agree with, even though he was an enthusiast for almost everything they were doing. If Egypt had an art censor it would have been al Arabli, but there was no sign of censorship, although it was clear that artists were expected to produce something that could be measured by what Egypt was trying to do socially and intellectually. So far this has not excluded abstract art; in fact it has excluded nothing at all. A painter like Rateb Sadek, who makes fleshy ironical comments on *"la paix,"* is hardly a conformist; nor is the famous Bulaq painter Rifaat Ahmad, nor is Ramses Yunan, who is a very shy and gentle Copt with a Polish wife. He paints quite unrealistically. It is possible that Egypt's best artist at the moment is a woman, Gazbia Sirry. At any rate she deserves the reputation she has won abroad. The Egyptians are very pleased with her because she is a woman painting like a woman, which is an obvious encouragement to the social revolution, but her studies of Nubia, before it was drowned by the Aswan High Dam, hardly appear feminine.

What some critics say is lacking in Egyptian art is a true folk motif. There is a degree of folk art everywhere in Egypt, but its usefulness to the sophisticated artist is not visible yet. There is, for instance, a primitive village weaving art, and there is also a very popular "mural" art — a sort of cartoon painted on the walls of many village houses showing how the occupant got to Mecca and back on his holy pilgrimage there. You don't see such paintings much in Cairo. The last one I saw there was over a sugar-cane shop in Bulaq, and it was old and peeling. None of these folk arts has helped the modern artist discover what his own people think and feel. His problem is still to bridge that gap between the seventh and twentieth centuries when Islam forbade any kind of representational art. Islam's iconoclastic hatred of holy faces cut Egypt off during all those centuries from evolving the sort of art they could do with now. Unfortunately, when Egyptian painters try to bridge the gap, they tend to go all the way back to the beginning. They see themselves in Pharaonic colors wearing an antique cloak. The rich culture of Islam might never have existed for them.

Painting, anyway, is not yet considered one of the big implements of social change, so it can go on groping around wherever it likes. Trouble begins with more applicable arts like cinema and TV. In 1934 Cairo was already the Hollywood of the Arab cinema world, and though it developed unevenly, the Egyptian film industry was always an important one and an interesting one too. By 1946 it was producing seventy films a year. It was eleventh in world cinema production in 1960, and most of its films were produced in the Misr Studios, which you can see along the irrigation canals out near the pyramids. There are about eighty cinema houses in Cairo, and an Egyptian film shown in a Cairo cinema often has to survive an extraordinary amount of noisy comment. In some of the poorer cinemas, catcalls, whistles, interruptions, vulgarities and tears involve the audience in everything that is happening on the screen, even when the films are silly melodramas.

Before 1956 most films were cheaply made and their subject matter

Main street in Cairo.

was usually puerile. Domestic dramas or village comedies bore no relationship to anybody's life at all, and like the paperbacks many of the scripts were plagiarized versions of western dramas or Hollywood films. No serious writer would write for the films, and though there were excellent directors and first-class actors like the great Naguib al Rihani or the singer and actress Om Kalsoum, both of whom had an enormous following, the main idea was to pander to a mass market.

After 1960 the government set up a committee for the consolidation of the cinema to help finance films, and the government began to produce its own documentaries. A Higher Institute for Cinema was set up in Cairo, and the government began to insist on "better" films — usually something social and realistic. But it was only when serious writers like Naguib Mahfuz began to write for the screen that the real transformation started. The results were immediately visible in the response this new kind of film got from Cairo's critical and noisy audiences. The most popular films in Cairo in the 1960s became well-written realistic dramas about the ordinary inhabitants of the Khan Khalili rather than the old peasant–upper-class tearjerkers and comedies. That wonderful prewar American film *The Grapes of Wrath* would have found itself in good company in Cairo thirty years later.

There was something inevitable and even necessary in the way Egypt's cinema cut a path through all the trash to create a genuine style of its own. As a result it is far superior to Egypt's TV, which was born ready-made in the middle of the social revolution. But like the cinema before it, TV is not yet taken seriously by the talented men. It started in 1960 with two channels, and by 1967 there were three. The first channel is popular, the second is intellectual and educational, and the third is for French and English programs. By 1967 Cairo had 174,-588 TV sets, almost all of them made in Egypt, and every year since then the numbers have increased considerably. Since TV audiences are semicaptives, one might imagine that Cairo's programs would be heavily political, but like TV in western countries the popular channel concentrates on sport, light entertainment, serials, domestic comedies, documentaries, and a fairly good news service, which has been much better since it began to treat the news more objectively. American, French, English, Italian, Russian and Czech films still form a big part of the programs, just as they do in many European countries, because most of the state investment in its TV has so far been in equipment rather than artistic talent. But it manges somehow to look very professional. The women announcers are sophisticated and are famous. In 1968 everybody in Cairo knew that one of them wore an expensive wig she brought back from London, and that another one (who was also head of Cairo TV's cultural department) was the beautiful wife of a released "Communist" who was himself in charge of state publishing.

Despite its modern beginnings, TV is obviously going to become more important than radio in the Middle East because it is such a powerful propaganda weapon. It won't be long before a desert Arab will have a battery set perched on his camel, instead of the transistor radio he lives with now and which plays such a big part in shaping his opinions. In the meantime, ordinary radio is still the most powerful political voice that Cairo has, not only in the Arab world but in Africa. From time to time one reads angry complaints in the letters column of the London *Times* suggesting that Cairo Radio ought to be forcefully closed down, or at least be taken over by the United Nations. Charles Issawi (*Egypt in Revolution*) said of it in 1962 that "for sheer venom, vulgarity and indifference to truth it has few equals in the world." This depended on which way you looked at it, but objectively speaking Issawi was probably right — until 1962 anyway.

The one unhealthy aspect of it from anyone's point of view was its exaggeration. Before 1962 Cairo Radio was very much in the hands of the right wing of the regime, who used Arab hyperbole and machiavellian invention to present the Arab case to the world. The stupidity of this policy was that the Arabs could have made a very good case with no deception or exaggeration. Its venom and its provocation were possibly forgivable, but boasts and threats and idiotic claims eventually undermined anyone's belief in what Cairo Radio said, even among the Arabs themselves.

The social revolution changed the methods somewhat. The Voice of the Arab went on attacking western interests, but it began to use facts and rational argument rather than exaggeration. It even began to use western material against the west, and to disseminate straight news in much the same way the BBC and the Voice of America use it to make propaganda with. On the whole, however, Cairo's Voice of the Arab remained the voice of the right-wing up to 1967. In the 1960s Cairo Radio was broadcasting in twenty-one languages besides Arabic. This went on right around the clock, including broadcasts in the middle of the Egyptian night beamed to the United States (about sixty hours a month), and many of these programs were edited and broadcast by American Negroes living in Cairo.

The most important broadcasts were to Africa: 324 hours a month in 1964–1965, over a hundred hours more than to Middle East countries. In 1969 the figure was slightly reduced, though not by much. This fits in quite well with Cairo's considering itself the most important city not only in the Arab world but in Africa as well. Almost every African revolutionary or unification movement has an office or a representative in Cairo. The top half of Africa is mostly Moslem, and this is very important to Cairo. In his *History of Nigeria*, Sir Alan Burns says that in the evangelical rivalry for the African soul at least ten heathens become Moslem for every one who becomes Christian, and Cairo Radio counts on this religious advantage. The main burden of these broadcasts to Africa is their attack on imperialism and neo-colonialism. Almost every week, it seems, Cairo holds some sort of conference for those Africans who enjoy this subject, and Cairo Radio speeds the word of these long, hot summer discussions as far south as Capetown. Cairo is full of African students studying the one language which is common to much of Africa — English. Many of them broadcast Egyptian ideas in English to Kenya or Zambia or Ghana, and now that social revolution as well as political liberation is the song Cairo sings, the poor African listens.

One is talking here of Cairo Radio's broadcasts to other countries, but the one voice which seemed to be far more embittered than all the others from Cairo was the Palestinian Program. This functioned up till 1967 as the voice of the million Palestinian refugees who had once lived where Israel is now. It was a more or less autonomous station, run by the Palestine Liberation Organization, and it insisted that Israel was a nonstate which had no right to exist because it had stolen all its territory from the Arabs by tricks and ruthless expulsions. The Palestinian Program went much farther than Cairo Radio's own Voice of the Arab broadcasts, and it continuously called on all Arabs to launch themselves at Israel. It predicted the day, soon, when every Israeli would be thrown into the sea, and the land restored to its rightful inhabitants. It was these broadcasts by the Palestinians which were widely disseminated as Egyptian policy towards Israel, although in fact there were serious differences.

It would be a mistake to imagine that these broadcasts caused the war of June 1967. They did not. After 1967 they changed their tactics and no longer threatened Israel with annihilation, but before 1967 they certainly helped to popularize the idea in Israel and abroad that it was either attack first for Israel or be thrown into the sea. The Egyptians, as distinct from the Palestinian refugees, believed that pushing Israel into the sea was not going to be easy. But by 1967 they felt that they were as good as the Israelis and that they were finally ready to face them on equal terms.

The June war shattered this unreal conviction. Even more, the June war put in jeopardy the very existence of Cairo, since the Israelis made it clear that if they were attacked on the positions they held after June 1967, they would retaliate with all their resources. Knowing this, every Cairene realized that his city could very well become a target in a new war, and as a result Cairo once more became a city waiting for another big event to decide its future for it.

24

The Destiny of Necessity

IT would be hard to convince anyone in Cairo that Israel was not the aggressor in the June war, just as it would be hard to convince any Israeli that as a nation they had no choice but to attack first. Since Israel's Prime Minister Levi Eshkol and Moshe Dayan have more or less admitted that Israel struck first, the two issues of the June war are what they always were: the right of Israel to exist at all, and the totally different points of view represented by Israel and Egypt on the future of the whole area.

The immediate sequence of events leading up to June 1967 can be interpreted according to which side you favor, but the Egyptian position is that Israel began, in April 1967, to prepare to attack Syria, which had recently taken a sharp political turn to the left. On April 7, 1967, Israel launched a full-scale attack on Syria with air force, tanks and artillery, in retaliation, Israel said, for several incidents on the borders. The Israeli foreign minister, Abba Eban, called for further large-scale punitive actions against Syria and suggested that Israel would have to strike "a decisive blow" against Syria. On May 9 the Israeli Knesset gave the government powers to conduct full military operations against Syria; Israeli troops on the Syrian border were alerted; and finally Israel was mobilized. The entire Arab world believed that an Israeli attack was imminent. Egypt had a mutual defense agreement with Syria, so she asked the United Nations troops stationed in Egypt along the Sinai border with Israel to get out of the way. Replying to western criticism of this move, Nasser said that the United Nations had been stationed exclusively on the Egyptian side of the border for eleven years, and he proposed that they cross over and stay on the Israeli side. But Israel refused to have them.

The Egyptians looked on this sequence of events as proof that Israel had aggressive intentions against the Arab states from the start. The Israelis, however, looked upon the same events as proof that the Arabs were proposing to attack Israel. They could point to continuous raids by groups of Arab al Fatah guerrillas from Syria and Jordan, and to statements by President Nasser that it was the Arabs' intention to "destroy" the state of Israel. In an interview on the eve of war, Nasser implied that he meant the word militarily rather than politically — that he was talking about the armed forces, not the people. But it was too late for this kind of explanation; that one phrase as much as anything else in the bitter war of words between Israel and the Arabs brought western sympathy heavily on the side of Israel, particularly among intellectuals. When Israel did launch her attack on June 5, she had the sympathy of almost the entire population of Europe and the United States of America, who felt that Israel was always under offensive threat and that the Arabs (in particular President Nasser) had been "asking for it," and now they were going to get it.

The war was brilliantly conceived and executed by Israel. The Israeli strategic premise was very simple — destroy the Arab air forces on the ground before they ever get off it. The Israelis had learned the old lessons of desert warfare very well. They knew that whoever won the air won the desert, no matter how good the army on the ground was. When the Israeli air force took off before dawn on June 5 and pounded every important Arab airfield as far apart as Luxor in Egypt and Habbaniya in Iraq, the decision of the whole war depended on their success. There is no doubt that, flying as they did without rest or respite in order to destroy every vestige of the Arab air forces, the Israelis succeeded beyond their wildest dreams, and within six hours rather than six days the Arabs were defeated. In June 1969 the Israelis released a propaganda film of this air attack and said that the war was won in the first three hours.

In the four days it took the Israeli army to win the battle on the ground, the Israeli air force continued undisturbed to do to the Arab armies what it had done to the air forces — destroy them before they got going. Napalm was again their principal weapon, and their pounding of Egyptian armor, transport and soldiers in the open deserts enabled the Israeli army to clean up what was left very quickly and then shift itself safely from one front to the other, to attack on land what was left of the other Arab armies after the air force had finished with them also.

Perhaps the most decisive factor, aside from the victory of the Israeli air force, was the skill of Israel's intelligence service. It seems clear that Israel chose June 5 for the attack because of a message they had intercepted on June 3 or 4 from GHQ Cairo to Egypt's Sinai command saying that the general staff would be arriving early at dawn on the morning of the 5th. In fact they were all trapped in the air by the Israeli attack, with nowhere to land, and for about six hours Egypt's army was without proper orders. The Egyptians believe now that all their military communications to the Sinai were picked up by the U.S. intelligence ship *Liberty* (which was anchored off the coast of Egypt with British personnel on board) and handed over to the Israelis. The Israelis also knew all the Egyptian army codes, and they sent (with the *Liberty*'s help, the Egyptians believe) false orders on Egyptian wavelengths to almost every divisional unit in the Sinai. This not only caused more confusion, but many units obeyed the false orders, which took them into exposed positions. From the outset, therefore, Egypt had made all the mistakes and the Israelis had made none at all.

Though there were bombings all around Cairo during the six days of the war, and every night the city was a noisy, black hole, with people crowding into air raid shelters listening to the din of the antiaircraft batteries, Cairo was not damaged. During the six days of the war Cairo also returned to its old habit of pouring out onto the streets to demonstrate and denounce, and since the people did not know at first that they had lost their entire air force, Cairenes were confident that any reversal their troops suffered in the Sinai would soon be put right, and that the result of the war would be heavily in their favor. Only those who listened to the BBC or the Voice of America began to doubt. On the second day of the war a rumor went through the city that the Egyptian armies had suffered complete disaster in the Sinai, but other rumors suggested that the Russians would intervene politically any minute, as they had in 1956. The city itself went on functioning as if the war was on, but very far away.

The streets looked military simply because there was plenty of military presence in them. Bridges, post offices, ministries, and most of the important buildings were given a façade of sandbags and brick barricades. The Nile Hilton looked like a man with sandbag earmuffs on. Police were given shelters they could jump into in case of air raids, and the steel shutters which have always given Cairo its hours of summer sleep at midday, as well as its flavor of tomorrow's troubles, were kept permanently down in many of its shops and businesses. You could still get a suit made at your tailor's, or sit in Groppi's garden sipping a lamoon on those balmy June evenings, but day by day between June 5 and June 11 the tensions and the daily fear of air raids, and a steadily oppressive sense of disaster, suggested calamity to every thinking person.

For Cairo the war came to an end not so much with the cease-fire agreement in the United Nations but with the resignation of President Nasser on June 9. Expectancy of some dramatic twist to their lives is so inbred in Cairenes that they knew something politically dramatic was about to happen, and President Nasser's speech that day was probably heard by almost all Cairo's adult population. Nasser began by telling the Egyptians they had suffered a severe setback, and he analyzed events leading up to the week before the outbreak of war. He said that on May 26, 1967, President Johnson had warned him that if Egypt struck first in any conflict, the results for Egypt, as far as the United States was concerned, would be serious. After this warning by America, he said, the Soviet ambassador called on him at 3:30 the next morning to say that the Soviet government requested that Egypt should not open fire. (It was revealed later that President Johnson had been on the hot line to Moscow urging them to restrain Egypt just as he would restrain Israel.) But on June 5, Nasser said, Israel had attacked, and he went on to accuse Britain and America of direct intervention with planes and aircraft carriers. After analyzing the reasons for Egypt's defeat, he said that he took full responsibility for what had happened, and added in a broken voice: "I have decided to give up completely and finally every official post and every political role, and to return to the ranks of the public to do my duty with them like every other citizen." He handed over the Presidency to Zakaria Mohieddin, and concluded by saying that the working class in Egypt must now be the source for new leadership of the Arab revolution.

What happened in Cairo then has never been properly understood, but almost from the moment this speech was delivered, people began to collect in the streets of the city, and though there was an air raid alert that night and the whole sky at one moment seemed to be cracking open, many thousands of people walked about simply shouting, "Nasser! Nasser!" At the same time an emergency meeting of the National Assembly was held, and President Nasser's resignation was rejected. By dawn next morning large numbers of people began to pour into Cairo from the villages and towns near Cairo, and also from Alexandria and the Canal Zone. They carried crude banners telling Nasser to change his mind and they converged on the National Assembly. By noon all the streets and squares for some distance around the National Assembly were packed. For a full day Cairo was an extraordinary sight, as thousands of people kept on arriving in the city on trucks and buses and in cars and taxis and on foot, so that overnight what had looked like the end of President Nasser became in fact a new beginning for him.

It is widely believed in the west that Nasser resigned deliberately so that carefully prepared demonstrations in his favor could be organized and his authority publicly restored. Serious students of the man and his methods deny this absolutely. This theory also ignores two factors in recent events. The first is that Nasser's increasing appeal and dependency on the ordinary people as the major factor in Egyptian life gave him genuine support from these sections of the population, and the second factor is his way of telling the Egyptians the worst of their predicament, so that most Egyptians believed what he said when they were inclined to disbelieve everybody else. There was genuine weeping in the streets of Cairo that day, as well as long-lasting organized rhythmical chanting of Nasser's name. When he tried to get to the National Assembly to be reinstated, his car was held up by crowds and he could not get through.

Much of this passionate activity in Cairo lay on the surface of the city like a covering of rime on a deep dark pond. What was really happening beneath the surface was that right-wing elements in the army and the police were telling people not to demonstrate but to go home, insisting that it was "dangerous" for large crowds to collect in the city — and so it was. But the real danger was political rather than military. The steadily increasing conflict between right and left wings in Egypt was coming to the surface again. There was clearly a group of right-wing army, air force and intelligence officers who wanted to get rid of Nasser, abandon the Arab revolution, and reverse Egypt's international attitudes, in order to come to an agreement with the United States. Since Nasser now knew he had vast popular support for his own policies, he not only used the demonstrations in his favor as a means of restoring his own authority, but immediately purged the armed forces of the senior officers most to blame for Egypt's being caught so easily on June 5. The commander in chief of the air forces was dismissed, and his three most senior staff officers. So was the director of the army's intelligence service, and the governor of Cairo's military prison. All these men were subsequently arrested and put on trial.

But the political conflict was by no means over. Day by day throughout July and August, Cairo was a city in a daze, far more concerned with what was happening to itself and to its leadership than it was about the pressure of Israel just across the Suez Canal. Everybody waited for something new to happen. Most people realized that a struggle was still going on for political leadership, and that groups of offices, including many senior staff officers, were plotting against Nasser. At the end of August, Nasser was to go to Khartoum for an Arab summit conference on the Middle East situation, and Cairo knew that something dramatic was likely to happen before he left. They were right. On August 26 fifty officers were arrested, and Field Marshal Abdel Hakim Amer was put under house arrest.

Field Marshal Amer had been President Nasser's closest friend and collaborator since their days together as young army officers. More than any other two men they were the architects of the original Free Officers corps; they had together organized the 1952 coup and thereafter been close allies in Egypt's new future. When Nasser had resigned as president in June, Hakim Amer had also given up his posts as vice-president and deputy commander in chief of the army. But unlike Nasser, nobody had asked that Amer be reinstated, and he had not been reinstated because he as much as any man was blamed for what had happened. Nominally, of course, Nasser was the commander in chief of the armed forces, but the real role belonged to Hakim Amer. He had always considered his authority over the armed forces to be his share in the authority of the revolution. When army and air force officers were insulted in the streets of Cairo after the June debacle (they were told to appear when possible in civilian clothes) Hakim Amer felt the sting of this popular reaction.

He had never been popular himself, and many people now accused him of using his position to amass wealth. This seems doubtful, but what is true is that the nonsocialist senior officers and even the old landowner class looked on Amer as their man. Many of the senior officers dismissed by President Nasser were Hakim Amer's closest friends, and not only had they turned to him for help, but some of those the military police were still looking for had been given asylum in Hakim Amer's house in Cairo, which had become a little fortress, guarded by dissident officers and armed retainers brought in from a farm belonging to Hakim Amer's brothers.

Towards the end of August, Nasser appealed to Amer to cooperate, particularly in army matters, in the totally new approach needed in Egypt's serious situation. Amer refused. His own plot to regain control of the army and eventually of Egypt itself was almost ready. It was Amer's plan that he and some of the dismissed senior officers would take over the eastern command of the army (on the Suez Canal facing the Israelis), using a forged presidential decree. Amer would then telephone to President Nasser an ultimatum demanding that he be given back command of the army and that all accusations against the dismissed senior officers be withdrawn. If Nasser refused, the army would dismiss him, and the group then planned to blame the Russians for their own strategic mistakes and for not intervening on Egypt's side. This implied that Russian advisers had been responsible for Egypt's overall strategy, a rather thin excuse, since Amer had always made a point of rejecting any Russian advice or help.

There was a nursery garden near Hakim Amer's villa in Dukki (west Cairo) and a helicopter was standing by at the nearby airfield of Imbaba to land among the flower beds and take Amer off to the Canal Zone on the night of August 27. Nasser knew the details of the plot, and on the eve, August 26, he sent for Amer, presumably using the persuasion of a strong escort. Once more these two men argued bitterly as they sat together in the president's office. Another old friend of both, Zakaria Mohieddin, now the vice-president, was also present. But again Nasser failed to convince Amer that he must accept a totally new approach. Amer refused to compromise, so "with sadness and regret" (according to *al Ahram*) Nasser told Amer that he was now under house arrest, and that all the officers collected in his villa had been arrested and his peasant bodyguard disarmed and locked up. All together more than fifty people were arrested that night.

Cairo only heard officially of these events a week later on September 4, and when *al Ahram* published the details of this plot there was no popular reaction in favor of the field marshal. Amer meant "the army" to most people, and the army was in disgrace — though somewhat unjustly, since it was not the army's fault that it had been so exposed to annihilation from the air. But it seemed fair to most people that Amer himself, as the man responsible above all others for Egypt's armed forces, should suffer some sort of severe punishment.

The last act of the tragedy was yet to be performed. On September 12, Amer took poison while he was being questioned in his house about his part in the plot. But the doctors managed to save him. He was then shifted to another house in Giza, where he was under permanent surveillance by two army doctors. Sometime on September 14 he went into the bathroom and pulled a strip of plaster off what was supposed to be a cut in his flesh, but which was in fact a hidden capsule of poison. He gulped it down, and when the doctors realized what he had done they rushed him to a hospital, where he died three hours later.

There is something almost traditional to Cairo in this drama of two men, close friends all their lives, emerging together with a new and powerful force in Egypt only to part bitterly when calamity threatened, so that a violent end to one or the other became inevitable. But the makeup of this tragedy was far from traditional. It reflected more than anything else Nasser's attempts to break with what had been the Free Officers Committee which had implemented the revolution. For many years, as Nasser had leaned more and more heavily on socialist and working class sympathies in Egypt, Hakim Amer's political ideas did not really change from what they were in 1952. He had gone along with Nasser's new political and socialist ideas only as long as the army and the air force were not greatly affected by them. Socialism was all right for the masses, but not for the soldiers, and until June 1967 the armed forces of Egypt remained curiously outside the social changes which were shaking Egypt.

Nobody has been able to report how Nasser took Hakim Amer's death, but obviously there was a Hamlet in both these men. Politically, Amer's suicide did not interfere or interrupt the course of Nasser's new policy, which was not only to change the very social basis of the army's role, but also to bring the population of Egypt more and more into the everyday affairs of the government by telling them everything, good and bad, that seemed important. The way Nasser set about doing this was through Mohammed Hassanein Haikal, editor of *al Ahram*, who began on August 20, 1967, to write an article every Friday in his paper (and broadcast on the radio) dealing ruthlessly with the military and political predicament of Egypt.

Haikal's first articles analyzed in critical detail the reasons for Egypt's defeat, with no attempt to excuse it. The analyses of Israel's armed forces and methods of training and warfare were objective. The point he made was that Egypt must learn from Israel just how to do it. Israel's superior intelligence service was admitted — in fact Haikal called it the best intelligence service in the world — and Israel's use of scientific methods and clear-cut thinking were analyzed and admired. No excuses were made for Egypt's own forces — lined up and fully equipped with excellent material, but without the strategy of inevitability which gave Israel its inner strength. The way Egyptian planes were kept exposed, the criminal lack of anticipation, and the poverty of tactical thinking were laid bare. "We are facing a modern, educated enemy," Haikal wrote, "and we have no alternative but to be as modern and as educated." Week by week this sort of analysis exposed the weaknesses and deceptions and failures not only of Egypt's military might but of her ordinary social life.

Finally, on November 17, 1967, Haikal made it quite clear that the old concept of the army as an outside growth was no good, that if the army did not grow healthily out of the society it was useless. "The army," he wrote, obviously thinking aloud for Gamal Abdel Nasser,

[343]

"any army, is the hard bark formed by the society to protect itself, but the bark has no value unless it is sustained through the living cells of the body." And the body, in this sense, was the body politic.

The June war affected every Egyptian with a reaction against himself, but in their highly self-critical mood the first signs of a political awareness of ordinary citizens was visible in Cairo soon after it. By November 27, 1967, the London *Times* was reporting that "a new element of efficiency has come to Egypt since the war. So humiliated have the Egyptians been that whenever business or social obligations are not honored these days, the common retort is: 'That's just the reason why we lost the war.' " This kind of response in a society which had always been politically nervous and quite unused to acceptance of popular responsibility was quite new in Egypt. On December 10, 1967, the London *Sunday Times* correspondent Rawle Knox reported from Cairo that the Arab Socialist Union had been organizing public meetings to discuss and debate Egypt's situation, and that after a week of seminars all over the city and the country, in which the discussions were heated and frank, the Arab Socialist Union was told to go ahead and "stimulate criticisms and find out how much a people who have become totally unused to public comment can take." Knox reported that a concentrated drive had begun to inform the country people about what goes on in the government ("Nasser believes this is good insurance against those in authority who might intrigue against him") and Knox concluded that "Egyptian democracy is the right to know the wrong." Even the idea of letting the people know was a new one in Egypt. But all this public involvement simply underlined the unresolved tensions that continued to pull Egypt this way and that.

Economically Egypt was not left broken-backed by the June war, even though the Suez Canal was closed and her entire economy upset. But the war did have a disastrous effect on the economic rate of growth which is so dear to modern economic planners. Egypt's balance of payments problems were partly solved by the Arab oil-producing countries agreeing at the Khartoum conference in August 1967 to contribute enough hard currency to make up for Egypt's loss in canal dues. The really serious problem for Egypt continued to be what it had been for twenty years — how to find enough land and jobs for her rapidly increasing population. In this respect the Aswan High Dam remained the key to Egypt's salvation.

But after the June war, everything that Egypt was trying to do internally had to be measured by what happened to her externally. The problem of how to recover the Sinai was probably less important even two years after the war to most Egyptians walking the streets of Cairo

On 26th July Street (the date King Farouk was deposed in 1952), businessmen gossip in a coffee shop (above), and people stroll along or drink coffee at tables on the pavement.

than how to cope with Israel as a reality: how to accept her or not accept her, how to live with her or once more think of defeating her. Israel has always thought it necessary for her own survival that the Arabs should acknowledge her in their midst as "a fact." When Ahmad al Shukairy was dismissed as head of the Palestine Liberation Organization in January 1968 his successor, Yahia Hamuda, said of Israel: "We must face facts and not demand the impossible." In general most political observers of Middle Eastern affairs in 1968 and 1969 believed that President Nasser wanted some kind of political solution with Israel, but only through the United Nations. Israel has always been adamant that the only way to settle the dispute is by direct talks between the two countries. This sounds sensible to anybody but an Arab, who feels that direct talks at any time with Israel would be a pre-admission of Israel as she is, which Arabs find impossible to accept, particularly after June 5. They point out that the United Nations created Israel, so that is where the problem must be settled. They also point to America's nonrecognition of Communist China and the NATO nations' refusal to recognize East Germany as the west's own version of whom to recognize and whom not to recognize. But it seems clear that any solution in the Middle East is not simply a matter of the Arabs recognizing Israel. Most Arab countries continue to see Israel as a sort of prehensile limb of imperialism, and anyone hoping to bring peace to the Middle East will have to prove to the Egyptians at least that this is not so.

What Egypt has agreed to accept is the British resolution passed by the Security Council after the June war. It provides for a withdrawal of Israeli armed forces from territories occupied in June, and at the same time it insists on acceptance of the sovereignty and territorial integrity and political independence of every state in the area, including Israel. It defines the right of Israel and the Arabs to live in peace within secure and recognized frontiers, and it provides for freedom of navigation through international waterways for Israel. A just settlement of the Arab refugee problem is included, but the most important clause is obviously the one guaranteeing the territorial inviolability of all the states in the area.

Egypt has accepted this resolution in full, without any strings, although it is clearly a reluctant admission. Israel has continued to reject it, feeling that any withdrawal to her pre-June frontier without better guarantees than the U.N. can give would be foolish, if not suicidal. Israel is also smarting under the attacks on her airliners in Zurich and Athens, and though her avowed policy of retaliation of ten to one has immediately followed these attacks, there is little hope that any Arab country will restrain the guerrillas who make them.

Up till the end of 1968 Egypt was still hoping for a political settlement based on the U.N. resolution. But when it seemed clear that there was no hope of this, and no hope of four-power insistence on it, the Egyptian attitude began to harden. She not only began preemptive artillery strikes across the canal to prevent Israel's building up her armor and rocketry and artillery in the occupied Sinai, but also began to give more and more moral and physical support to the various Arab guerrilla movements. In 1969 a four-power conference (United States, Soviet Union, Britian and France) tried to find a formula for settlement, but Israel rejected the authority of the conference from the outset.

New military factors had already begun to appear in Egypt's thinking just after the June war, when the Soviet Union began to re-equip the Egyptian army and air force. Soviet officers came to Egypt to help train the army in this new equipment, with a particular emphasis on artillery, which the Russians have always believed to be the "god of war." There have been many estimates of how many Russians there are in Egypt training this new army. American reports say thousands, but the London *Times* in September 1968 limited the figure to "hundreds." In any case there is no noticeable Russian presence in Cairo, and most Cairenes would probably be surprised to read a report in *Life* (November 1968) that "Zamalek . . . once the favorite residential area of wealthy westerners, is now a Russian ghetto."

What is acknowledged in Cairo is that the Russian military experts insisted on a much harder training schedule than Egyptian officers were used to. It is known that they had President Nasser's blessing in this. And what you see of all this in Cairo is the new kind of face the Egyptian officers wear, the different look about the Egyptian army, which doesn't seem to be a body of heavy-footed soldiers any more but a force of far more acute men with something on their minds.

The thing that is permanently on their minds, of course, is when does the next round begin, and when and where and how? Though the Israelis have been twice successful in their initial air strikes against Egypt, it seems unlikely that Israel can repeat it so successfully a third time. What Egypt is particularly worried about is not only the obvious escalation of techniques to sophisticated rocketry for the next attack, but a possible Israeli attack on the Aswan High Dam, which would effectively cripple Egypt's hopes of emergence for years to come. In the speculations you hear in the drawing rooms and kitchens and cafés and trams and streets and peasants' huts of Egypt, this factor is one that makes people almost drop their voices when they suggest the possibility.

Egypt is also convinced that Israel is making a nuclear bomb, and that she will undoubtedly use it if she ever feels she is finally meeting her match militarily. What convinces Egypt of this is that she herself has agreed to let the United Nations inspect all her atomic installations, but Israel has refused. In January 1969, American reports claimed that Israel already had the bomb. In February, President Nasser told an American correspondent that he did not think Israel had the bomb. It is inconceivable to anyone outside Egypt and the Arab world that Israel would use an atom bomb — nobody in the west can believe it possible — but it is nonetheless one of the strategic factors which will shape the future of this bitter conflict if it continues for long without a solution.

Cairo's future as a city and as a place and as a capital and as a monument to a great deal of Egyptian history is therefore held delicately in the two shatterable hands of the Arab revolution and the Arab-Israeli dispute. It took only a few months after the June war for Cairo to look like a normal city again. The lights were lit, the coffee bars were full, the cinemas and theatres were packed, the tourists (not Americans at first) had returned and the shops were busy, but today when you walk down a Cairo street and suddenly see a young Egyptian girl in military uniform, the rickety peace of the city is drowned by the thunder of tomorrows' guns.

Despite its problems Cairo continues to be a thriving and curiously untouched city. When there is a momentary crisis the city is once again sandbagged and blacked out and gotten ready for trouble. The idea that you must be prepared for trouble is now so deep in the city's nervous system that it is almost over-ready for any emergency. But visibly it still does not wear a military cloak. The girls are also wearing minis, and the well-off young men can still go every spring to the local tailor and have their new trousers cut from locally made cloth, which is not as good as imported material but is good enough to justify the extraordinary passion Egyptian youths still have for wearing perfectly pressed pants and whiter-than-white shirts.

It all looks very normal, very much the same city it was before June 1967. But in fact it is more than ever a revolutionary city, and it is more than ever the ideological fountainhead for the troublesome ideas that are breaking up the old political structures of the Arab countries. To the Arabs there are only two ways of looking at Cairo's influence on the Arab world. Either the Arab revolution is not necessary, or the revolution is desirable and inevitable, in which case Cairo justifies itself. The fact that not all Arabs think the way Cairo thinks is almost the point of the revolution. If all Arabs were like-minded there would be no problem. As it is, the patchwork of Arab unity which the June war inspired in half a dozen quite inimical Arab societies only emphasizes that the revolution is in progress. Any serious analysis of what is said by Cairo's intellectuals and politicians and ordinary people might reveal that nobody believes there is going to be any solution to the problem of the Middle East until the Arab revolution has genuinely united all Arabs and begun the economic and social restoration of an impoverished and hard-pressed people.

What is really in the balance now is not only Cairo's survival as a city but its extraordinary legacies of the past and its great hope for the future. More people will die if there is a war and if Cairo is destroyed, and maybe that is all one should worry about. But one cannot quite forget those acres of rubble which used to be Fustat. Utter destruction has happened here before and presumably it could happen again, so one is inclined to get emotionally involved, if only because the fabulous old city of the tent, Fustat, once had a soul of its own. That is what one longs to add for consideration in all the violent situations that now threaten Cairo.

Nobody can breathe in this city and not feel its nervous whispers and its carefree ecstasies for simple things. You don't need to give yourself to this city because it gives itself to you, and there is hardly a man, woman or child in it who, in the space of an hour or two, wouldn't lay his entire life bare for you to judge or admire or condemn. Men still walk innocently hand-in-hand in Cairo, and one of its most passionate principles is that you must never be unequal to a jest. A casual greeting can become a dialectical argument, and an argument can become an elemental tragedy. Emotion always runs high and thin and unbearably close, but possibly no city in the world laughs so much, not only at its ridiculous jokes but at its ridiculous self.

There is no measure, really, which does it justice, because its only fair measurements are its own. And though one can sit up all night on the Mukattam and watch the night fall suddenly flat on the rooftops and the day rise like a diaphanous bubble behind the crumbling minarets, there is still no sight or sound in this city, no matter how romantic, that is better than the gay little donkey bells which still tinkle musically in the streets the way Saint-Saëns heard them. The donkeys are dying out and the modern city beats like a hot bat against the outside walls of its dusty sky and its clean, dry deserts. It grows like a

Schoolchildren with their teacher having their picture taken inside
the Egyptian Museum.

cactus, becomes noisier, harsher, less credulous, more efficient, and it fills itself hungrily with the four winds of fate. Day by day it lives a little more and dies a little less, and like the Egyptian himself it offers to a visitor more heart than sense. But it still guards for itself the prospects of the future it has only just defined.

Bibliography

THE bibliography is a shortened list of the vast amount of material consulted for this story of Cairo. I have arranged the list chapter by chapter because it was agreed between editor and author at the outset that there would be no footnotes and only the very minimum text references to sources. But I can't leave the final result without some sort of support, and by making this bibliography consecutive to the text I hope to ensure that anyone interested will be able to find the appropriate source he may want to consult.

GENERAL

Kuran (*Koran*) (tr. Al Haj Hafiz Ghulam Sarwar, 1929).
Encyclopaedia Britannica (Chicago 1968).
Encyclopaedia of Islam (London 1960–68).
Arab Review
The Middle East and North Africa, 1968–1969 (A Survey and Directory . . . London 1968).
Basic Statistics of the U.A.R. (Cairo 1963–68).
Karl Baedeker. *Egypt* (Leipzig 1929).
Carl Brockelmann. *History of the Islamic Peoples* (London 1952).
Mrs. R. L. Devonshire. *Rambles in Cairo* (Cairo 1917).
Phillip K. Hitti. *History of the Arabs* (London 1956).
T. P. Hughes. *A Dictionary of Islam* (Lahore 1964).
William Yale. *The Near East: A Modern History* (Ann Arbor, Mich. 1958; new ed. 1968).

1. FOUNDATIONS

Jane Harrison. *Ancient Art and Ritual* (London 1914). *Prologomena to the Study of Greek Religion* (Cambridge 1903). *Themis* (Cambridge 1912).
Sir W. M. Flinders Petrie. *Corpus of Proto-Dynastic Pottery* (Cairo 1953). *Gizeh and Rifeh* (Cairo 1898). *Prehistoric Egypt* (Cairo 1920).
W. J. Arkell and K. S. Sandford. *Paleolithic Man and the Nile Faiyum Divide* . . . (Chicago, 1929). *Paleolithic Man and the Nile Valley in Lower Egypt* (Chicago 1939).
J. H. Breasted. *Ancient Times* (Boston 1916). *Development of Religion and Thought in Ancient Egypt* (New York 1959).
W. B. Emery. *Archaic Egypt* (London 1961).
W. C. Hayes. *Most Ancient Egypt* (Chicago 1965).
O. Menghin and Mustafa Amer. *The Excavations of the Egyptian University in the Neolithic Site at Maadi* (Cairo 1932).

[353]

2. DYNASTIC CAIRO

Sir W. M. Flinders Petrie. *A History of Egypt* (London 1894–1905; vols. I–III, from 1st to 30th dynasty).
Herodotus. *History* (tr. George Rawlinson, ed. E. H. Blakeney, London 1910).
J. H. Breasted. *Ancient Records of Egypt* (Chicago 1906). *A History of Egypt* (New York 1950).
Selim Hassan. *The Great Sphinx and Its Secrets* (Cairo 1953).
Ahmed Fakhry. *The Pyramids* (Chicago 1961).
Adolf Erman. *Egyptian Grammar* (tr. J. H. Breasted, 1894). *A Handbook of the Egyptian Religion* (London 1907). *The Literature of the Ancient Egyptians* (London 1927).
Sir J. G. Wilkinson. *Manners and Customs of the Ancient Egyptians* (3 vols. London 1878). *Materia Hieroglyphica* (London 1828). *The Egyptians at the Time of the Pharaohs* (London 1857).
Sir Alan Gardiner. *Egypt of the Pharaohs* (Oxford 1961).
I. R. S. Edwards. *The Pyramids of Egypt* (London 1961).
Manetho. *Manetho* (tr. F. E. Robbins, London 1940).
Karl Richard Lepsius. *Denkmäler aus Ägypten . . .* (1849).
Sir William Dampier. *A History of Science* (Cambridge 1942).
J. F. Champollion. *L'Egypte sous les pharaons* (*Description géographique*, 2 vols. 1814).

3. HELIOPOLIS

Sir W. M. Flinders Petrie. *Heliopolis, Kafr Ammar, and Shurafa* (Egyptian Research Account, 1915). *Religion and Conscience in Ancient Egypt* (London 1920). *Social Life in Ancient Egypt* (London 1923).
J. H. Breasted. *Development of Religion and Thought in Ancient Egypt* (New York 1959).
Diodorus. The Bibliotheca Historica of Diodorus Siculus (Oxford 1956–57).
Sir Alan Gardiner. *The Attitude of the Ancient Egyptians to Death and the Dead* (Cambridge 1935). *Egyptian Grammar* (Oxford 1927).
Strabo. *The Geography of Strabo* (8 vols. London 1917–32).
G. Posener. *La première Domination perse en Egypte* (Institut Français d'Archéologie, Bib. d'Etudes, vol. II, 1936).
Pierre Jouguet. *L'Impérialisme macedonien et l'hellenisation de l'orient* (Paris 1926).
Henri Frankfort. *Ancient Egyptian Religion* (New York 1949).

4. BABYLON

Sir Harold Idris Bell. *Cults and Creeds in Graeco-Roman Egypt* (Liverpool 1953). *Egypt from Alexander the Great to the Arab Conquest* (Oxford 1948). *Evidences of Christianity in Egypt During the Roman Period* (Cambridge, Mass. 1944). *Jews and Christians in Egypt* (London 1924).
J. G. Milne. *Egypt Under Roman Rule* (London 1894).
E. R. Bevan. *Egypt Under the Ptolemaic Dynasty* (London 1927).
Pierre Jouguet. *La Vie municipale dans l'Egypte romaine* (Bib. des Ecoles Françaises d'Athènes et de Rome, #104, 1911).
C. H. Oldfather. *Literary Texts from Graeco-Roman Egypt* (Univ. of Wisconsin Social Science Studies #9, Madison, Wis. 1923).
E. Amelineau. *La Géographie de l'Egypte à l'époque copte* (Paris 1893). *Histoire du patriarche copte Isaac* (L'Ecole Supérieure des Lettres d'Alger, #2, 1890).
A. J. Butler. *The Arab Conquest of Egypt* (Oxford 1902). *Babylon of Egypt* (Oxford 1914). *The Ancient Coptic Churches of Egypt* (Oxford 1884).

Bibliography

Ahmad Ibn Ali al Makrizi. *Mémoires géographiques et historiques sur l'Egypte*
. . . (tr. E. M. Quatremère, 2 vols. Paris 1811). *A Short History of the
Copts* . . . (Original Documents of the Coptic Church #3, 1873).
John, Bishop of Nikiou. *The Chronicles of John* (London 1916).
Flavius Josephus. *Complete Works* (London 1963).

5–8. FUSTAT AND AL KAHIRA

A. R. Guest. *Offprints on Egyptian History* (1902–26). *The Governors and
Judges of Egypt* (*El Kindi* 1912). "The Foundation of Fustat and the
Khittahs of That Town" (*Royal Asiatic Society Journal*, 1907).
Aly Bahgat and Albert Gabriel. *Fouilles d'al Foustat* (Musée National de l'Art
Arabe, 1921).
Eustace K. Corbett. "The History of the Mosque of Amr at Old Cairo" (*Royal
Asiatic Society Journal*, July 1890).
Muhammad Ibn Ahmad (Ibn Ayas). *An Account of the Arab Conquest of
Egypt* (tr. W. H. Salmon, London 1921).
Sir William Dampier. *A History of Science* (Cambridge 1942).
Ahmad Ibn Ali al Makrizi. (Edgard Blochet) *Histoire d'Egypte de Makrizi*
(Paris 1908). (Urbain Bouriant) *Description topographique et historique
de l'Egypte* (*al Makrizi*) (Mémoires du Mission Archéologique Française
au Caire, vol. XVII, 1895). (Paul Casanova) *Kitab al Mawa'idh wa'li'tibar*
(*Livre des admonitions*) (Mémoires de l'Institut Français d'Archéologie
Orientale au Caire, vol. III–V, XVII, 1906). *Essai de reconstruction
topographique de la ville d'al Foustat ou Mist* (Mémoires de l'Institut
Français d'Archéologie Orientale au Caire, vol. XXXV, 1919). (E. M.
Quatremère) *Mémoires géographiques et historiques sur l'Egypte* . . .
(2 vols. Paris 1811). (Paul Ravaisse) *Essai sur l'histoire et sur la topo-
graphie du Caire d'après Makrizi* (Mémoires Mission Archéologique Fran-
çaise au Caire, vol. 1886–89). (Gaston Wiet) "Le Traité des famines
— al Makrizi" (*Journal of Economic and Social History of the Orient*,
Leiden 1962).
Ibrahim Ibn Muhammad (Ibn Duqmuq). *Description de l'Egypte* (ed. C.
Vollers, 2 vols. in Arabic, Cairo).
Muhammad Ibn Haukal. *The Oriental Geography of Abu Ishak al Farisi al
Istakhri* (in Arabic, Cairo 1882).
Abd al Rahman Ibn Muhammad (Ibn Khaldun). *Prolégomènes historiques
d'Ibn Khaldoun* (tr. Baron MacGuckin de Slane, 1862–1868). Académie
des Inscriptions et Belles Lettres, *Notices* . . . (vol. XIX pt. 1, XX pt. 1,
1787).
Ali Ibn Husain al Mas'udi. *An Account of the Establishment of the Fatimite
Dynasty in Africa* (1840). *Les Prairies d'or* (*Meadows of Gold*) (tr.
Barbier de Meynard and Pavet de Courteille, 9 vols. Paris 1861–77). *Al
Mas'udi's Historical Encyclopaedia* (tr. A. Sprenger, vol. I, London 1841).
Nasir Ibn Khusrau. *Sefer Nameh* (tr. and annotated by Charles Schefer; Ecole
des Langues Orientales Vivantes, ser. 2, vol. I, Paris 1881). "Nasir Ibn
Khusrau" (tr. E. G. Browne, *Royal Asiatic Society Journal*, 1905).
Ahmad Ibn Muhammad (Ibn Khallikan). *Ibn Khallikan's Biographical Dic-
tionary* (tr. Baron MacGuckin de Slane, London 1842–71).
A. I. Silvestre de Sacy. *Exposé de la réligion des Druzes* (Paris 1838).
K. A. C. Creswell. *The Muslim Architecture of Egypt A.D. 939–1326* (Oxford
1952–59). *A Bibliography of Painting in Islam* (Cairo 1953).
Paul Casanova. *Mohammed et la fin du monde — l'Islam Primitif* (Paris 1911).
Stanley Lane Poole. *The Story of Cairo* (London 1902).
Concise Encyclopaedia of Arabic Civilization (ed. Stephen and Nandy Ronart,
Amsterdam 1959).

Guglielmus (William), Archbishop of Tyre. *A History of Deeds Beyond the Sea* (tr. Emily A. Babcock and A. C. Krey, New York 1943).

Gaston Wiet. *L'Égypte arabe de la conquête arabe à la conquête ottomane, 642–1517* (*Histoire de la nation égyptienne*, vol. IV, Paris 1937). *Catalogue générale du Musée Arabe au Caire* (8 vols. Musée Nationale de l'Art Arabe, Cairo 1929).

Ali Ibn Ridwan. *Climate and Health of Old Cairo According to Ali Ibn Ridwan* (Comptes Rendus de Congrès International de Médecine Tropicale et de Hygiène, Cairo, December 1928, vol. II, Cairo 1929). On the Prevention of the Harm of Bodily Ills in Egypt (biography of Ibn Ridwan by Ibn Abu Usaibi'a, MS. Cairo).

Raymond C. Smail. *Crusading Warfare, 1097–1193* (Cambridge 1956).

Rev. T. P. Hughes. *Notes on Muhammadanism* (London 1894).

9. SALADIN'S CAIRO

Paul Casanova. *Histoire et description de la citadelle du Caire* (Mission Archéologique, Cairo 1894).

Ahmad Ibn Ali al Makrizi. *Histoire des sultans mamlouks de l'Egypte . . .* (tr. E. M. Quatremère, Oriental Translation Fund, London 1837).

Stanley Lane Poole. *Saladin and the Fall of the Kingdom of Jerusalem* (London 1926). *A History of Egypt in the Middle Ages* (London 1894). *The Art of the Saracens in Egypt* (London 1886).

Edward Lane. *Arabian Society in the Middle Ages* (ed. S. Lane Poole, London 1883). *Arabian Nights* (tr. Edward Lane, London 1877).

Muhammad Ibn Ahmad (Ibn Gubayr). *The Travels of Ibn Jubayr* (Gubayr) (tr. R. J. C. Broadhurst, London 1952).

Muhammad Ibn Abd Allah Ibn Batuta. *The Travels of Ibn Batuta A.D. 1325–1354* (tr. H. A. R. Gibb, Cambridge 1958). *Voyages d'Ibn Batoutah* (Société Asiatique, 1853).

Abd al Rahman Ibn Muhammad (Ibn Khaldun). *An Arab Philosophy of History* (tr. Charles Issawi, London 1950).

Lodovico di Varthema. *The Travels of L. di Varthema* (tr. John W. Jones, London 1863).

Abdel Latif Ibn Yusuf al Baghdadi. *Extrait de l'autobiographie d'abd el Latif* (tr. Baron MacGuckin de Slane, Académie des Inscriptions et Belles Lettres, *Historiens orientaux*, vol. III, Paris 1884). *Relation de l'Egypte* (tr. A. C. Silvestre de Sacy, Paris 1810).

Muhammad Ibn Ali Talib al Dimashki (Dimishqi). *Manuel de la cosmographie du moyen age* (tr. A. F. Mehren, Copenhagen 1874).

Muhammad Ibn Ahmad (Ibn Ayas). *L'Odeur des fleurs dans les merveilles de l'univers: Cosmographie* (tr. L. M. Langlès, Académie des Inscriptions et Belles Lettres, vol. VIII, pt. 1, 1787, Paris 1810). *Journal d'un bourgeois du Caire* (tr. Gaston Wiet, Paris 1955).

D. A. Cameron. *Egypt in the Nineteenth Century* (London 1898).

Gaston Wiet. *Les Mosques du Caire* (Paris 1932).

Albert Champdor. *Saladin, le plus pur héros de l'Islam* (Paris 1956).

Kenneth Meyer Setton, ed. *A History of the Crusades* (Philadelphia 1955).

Henri Gambier. *Histoire de la république de Venise* (Venice 1955).

Freddy Thiriet. *La Romanie vénitienne au moyen age* (*XIIe-XVe siècles*) (Bib. des Ecoles Françaises d'Athènes et de Rome, #193, Paris 1959).

Ali Ibn Musa Ibn Said. *Kitab al mugrib fi, hula al magrib* (Book I, tr. K. L. Tallqvist, Leiden 1899).

Les Enfants enlevés par les Tcherkesses: le sort des enfants dans les pays païens (Paris 1870).

Bibliography

10. OTTOMAN CAIRO

D. A. Cameron. *Egypt in the Nineteenth Century* (London 1898).
Abd al Rahman Ibn Hasan al Jabarti (Gabarti). *Merveilles biographiques et historiques* (tr. Chefik Mansour Bey, Abdulaziz Kali Bey, Gabriel Nicolas Kalil Bey, and Iskander Ammoun Effendi, 9 vols. Cairo 1888–96).
Sir G. C. M. Birdwood, ed. *Register of Letters of the East India Company, 1600–1619* (London 1893).
Richard Pococke. *A Description of the East and Some Other Countries* (2 vols. London 1743–45).
Carsten Niebuhr. *Voyage en Egypte* (Nouvelle Bibliothèque des Voyages, vol. II, 1841). *Traveles Through Arabia and Other Countries in the East* (tr. R. Heron et al., Edinburgh 1792).
Constantin François de Volney. *Voyage en Syrie et en Egypte* (*Les Ruines* . . .) (3 vols. Paris 1792).
W. G. Browne. *Travels in Africa, Egypt, and Syria, from the Year 1792 to 1798* (London 1799).

11. NAPOLEON'S CAIRO

Description de l'Egypte: un recueil des observations et des recherches qui ont été faites en Égypte pendant l'expedition de l'armée française (20 vols. Paris 1809–28; 24 vols. Paris 1821–29).
D. A. Cameron. *Egypt in the Nineteenth Century* (London 1898).
Napoleon I. *Memoirs* (tr. Somerset De Chair, London 1948).
Napoleon I and Louis Alexandre Berthier. *An Account of the French Expedition in Egypt* (with Sir William Sidney Smith's letters; Leeds 1800).
L. Luis de Boisey. *Bonaparte au Caire* (Paris 1799).
F. Charles-Roux. *Bonaparte, gouverneur d'Egypte* (Paris 1936).
Christian Cherfils. *Bonaparte et l'Islam* (Paris 1914).
P. G. Elgood. *Bonaparte's Adventures in Egypt* (London 1931).
Al Gabarti. *Merveilles* (see under chapter 10 above).
Courier de l'Egypte (Cairo 1798–1801).
Dominique Vivant Denon. *Travels in Upper and Lower Egypt* (2 vols. London 1802).
M. F. Rousseau. *Kléber et Menou en Egypte* . . . (Paris 1900).
Sir Robert T. Wilson. *History of the British Expedition to Egypt* (London 1802).
"Carlos Bey." *A Non-Military Journal* (London 1863).
A Faithful Journal of the Late Expedition to Egypt, by a private on board the *Dictator* (London 1805).

12. MOHAMMED ALI'S CAIRO

D. A. Cameron. *Egypt in the Nineteenth Century* (London 1898).
R. and G. Cattan. *Mohamed Aly et l'Europe* . . . (Paris 1950).
F. Charles-Roux. *L'Egypte de 1801 à 1882* (Paris 1936).
Shafik Ghurbal. *The Beginnings of the Egyptian Question and the Rise of Mehemet Ali* . . . (London 1928).
Felix Mengin. *Histoire de l'Egypte sous le gouvernement de Mohammed Aly* . . . (2 vols. Paris 1823).
Stanley Mayes. *The Great Belzoni* (London 1959).
Maurice W. Disher. *Pharaoh's Fool* (London 1957).
John Lewis Burckhardt. *Travels in Arabia* (London 1829). *Travels in Egypt and Nubia* (2 vols. London 1829).
Sir Richard Howard-Vyse. *Operations Carried on at the Pyramids of Gizeh in 1837* (3 vols. London 1840–42).

[357]

E. Deseille. *Les Débuts de Mariette-Pacha* (Paris 1881).
A. L. Champollion-Figeac. *Les Deux Champollions* (Paris 1887).
Joseph Moyle Sherer. *The Imagery of Foreign Travel* (London 1838).
Edward Lane. *An Account of the Manners and Customs of the Modern Egyptians* (2 vols. London 1836). *Cairo Fifty Years Ago* (London 1896).
John L. Stephens. *Incidents of Travel in Egypt, Arabia Petraea and the Holy Land* (Edinburgh 1839).
George R. Gliddon. No. 1 *A Memoir on the Cotton of Egypt*. No. 2 *An Appeal to the Antiquaries of Europe* . . . (London 1841). *Otia Aegyptiaca* (London 1849).
James E. Cooley. *The American in Egypt* (New York 1842; refutation by Gliddon, Philadelphia 1842).
Hon. Mary G. E. Dawson Damer. *Diary of a Tour in Greece, Turkey, Egypt and the Holy Land* (2 vols. London 1841).
Sarah Haight. *Letters from the Old World* (New York 1840).
Rose Macaulay. *Pleasure of Ruins* (London 1953).
Sophia Poole. *The Englishwoman in Egypt* (London 1844–46).
Gerard Labrunie de Nerval. *Scènes de la vie orientale* (2 vols. Paris 1850).
Harriet Martineau. *Eastern Life* (3 vols. London 1848).
Pehr Forskal. *Flora Aegyptiaco-Arabica* (ed. Carsten Niebuhr, 1775).
Adolphe L. Joanne. *Voyage en Egypte et en Grèce* (Brussels 1850).
Sir John Bowring. Blue Book for British Government on Egyptian finances (1840). *Autobiographical Recollections* (London 1877).
Frederic Bonola Bey. *L'Egypte et la géographie* . . . (Paris 1889).
A. J. Butler. *Court Life in Egypt* (Oxford 1914).
Gaston Wiet. *Les Mosques du Caire* (Paris 1932).
Charles Didier. *Les Nuits du Caire* (Paris 1860).

13. EUROPEANIZED CAIRO

Charles Didier. *500 Ligues sur le Nil* (Paris 1860). *Les Nuits du Caire* (Paris 1860).
D. A. Cameron. *Egypt in the Nineteenth Century* (London 1898).
Thomas Cook. *The Business of Travel* (London 1891). *Programmes of Personally Conducted and Independent Tours Palestine* . . . (London 1874–1899). *Up the Nile by Steam* (London 1874–82).
James MacCoan. *Consular Jurisdiction in Turkey and Egypt* (London 1873). *Egypt As It Is* . . . (London 1877). *Egypt Under Ismail* (London 1889).
Ismail I, Khedive of Egypt. *Itinéraire des invités aux fêtes de l'inauguration du canal de Suez* . . . (Paris 1869).
Sir Samuel Baker. *Ismailia* (expedition organized by Ismail, Khedive of Egypt; 2 vols. London 1874).
M. F. Shukry. Equatoria Under Egyptian Rule (unpublished correspondence of Gordon with Ismail; Cairo 1953).
Pierre Crabites. *Ismail the Maligned Khedive* (London 1933). *Americans in the Egyptian Army* (London 1938). *Ibrahim of Egypt* (London 1935).
Charles Chaille-Long. *Central Africa* (London 1876). *My Life in Four Continents* (2 vols. London 1912).
Sir Auckland Colvin. *The Making of Modern Egypt* (London 1906).
Olympe Audouard. *Les Mystères de l'Egypte dévoilés* (Paris 1865).
Lady Lucie Duff Gordon. *Letters from Egypt, 1863–1865* (London 1865). *Last Letters from Egypt* (London 1875).
Wilfred Scawen Blunt. *Secret History of the English Occupation of Egypt* (pts. I and II, London 1907).
Thomas Archer. *The War in Egypt and the Sudan* (4 vols. London 1885–87).
E. W. Polson Newman. *Great Britain in Egypt* (London 1928).

14. CROMER'S CAIRO

Parliamentary Papers: Reports on the financial situation of Egypt, prepared by the Earl of Cromer.

British Foreign Office: Draft Instructions to her Majesty's Agent in Cairo, London, 1879.

Sir Evelyn Baring, Earl of Cromer. *Modern Egypt* (London 1908). *The Situation in Egypt* (address; London 1908).

Sydney A. Moseley. *With Kitchener in Cairo* (London 1917).

Sir Ronald Storrs. *Orientations* (London 1937).

Thomas Cook & Son. *Guide to Egypt* (London 1876–1921).

Karl Baedeker. *Egypt* (handbook; Leipzig 1877–1914).

Paul Joanne. *Guide to Egypt* (Paris 1900).

Douglas Sladen. *Egypt and the English* (London 1908). *Oriental Cairo . . .* (London 1911).

Alfred W. Sansom. *I Spied Spies* (London 1965).

Pierre Cachia. *Taha Husayn* (London 1936).

Taha Husain. *The Stream of Days* (London 1948).

Sir Valentine Chirol. *The Egyptian Problem* (London 1920).

Eustace A. R. Ball. *Cairo of Today* (London 1898–1914). *The City of the Caliphs* (Boston 1897).

Garrison Directory (army lists, Egypt, 1906).

15. REVOLUTIONARY CAIRO

Egyptian Government Agricultural Statistics: *Report on the Cost of Living* (Cairo 1920).

Aubrey Herbert. *Mons, Anzac and Kut* (London 1930).

Joseph Maxwell. *Hell's Bells and Mademoiselles* (Sydney 1932).

Sir Ronald Storrs. *Orientations* (London 1937).

E. J. Rule. *Jacka's Mobs* (Sydney 1933).

Archibald (Lord) Wavell. *Allenby* (London 1940). *Allenby in Egypt* (London 1943). *The Palestine Campaigns* (London 1928).

Foulad Yeghin. *Saad Zaghloul, le "père du peuple" égyptien* (Paris 1927).

E. M. Forster. *Egypt* (Labour Research Department, London 1921).

Emil Ludwig. *The Nile in Egypt* (London 1937).

George A. (Lord) Lloyd. *Egypt Since Cromer* (2 vols. London 1933).

Sir Thomas W. Russell. *Egyptian Service, 1902–1946* (London 1949).

Sir George Young. *Egypt* (London 1927).

P. G. Elgood. *The Transit of Egypt* (London 1928).

Ahmad Shafik. *L'Egypte moderne et les influences étrangères* (Cairo 1931).

The English School Magazine (Cairo 1938).

Jockey Club of Egypt: *Racing Calendar* (1915–16).

Egyptian Ministry of Justice: Native Penal Code.

Charles Issawi. *Egypt: An Economic and Social Analysis* (London 1947).

Anthony M. Galatoli. *Egypt in Mid-Passage* (Cairo 1950).

16. THE END OF OCCUPATION

Alan Moorehead. *African Trilogy* (London 1944).

Alfred M. Sansom. *I Spied Spies* (London 1965).

Gamal Abdel Nasser. *Egypt's Liberation: The Philosophy of the Revolution* (Washington 1955).

G. Vaucher. *Gamal Abdel Nasser et son équipe* (2 vols. Paris 1959).

Rustom K. Karanjia. *The Arab Dawn* (London 1958).

Mohammed Neguib. *Egypt's Destiny* (London 1955).

Anwar el Sadat. *Revolt on the Nile* (London 1957).

Jean and Simonne Lacouture. *L'Egypte en mouvement* (Paris 1956; English version *Egypt in Transition,* London 1958).
Anthony M. Galatoli. *Egypt in Mid-Passage* (Cairo 1950).

17–24. EGYPTIAN CAIRO

Serge and Merry Bromberger. *Les Secrets de l'expedition d'Egypte* (Paris 1957; English version *Secrets of Suez,* London 1957).
Jean and Simonne Lacouture. *L'Egypte en mouvement* (see under chapter 16 above).
Anthony Nutting. *I Saw for Myself* (London 1958). *No End of a Lesson: The Story of Suez* (London 1967).
Max Herz. *Catalogue sommaire des monuments exposés dans le Musée National de l'Art Arabe* (Cairo 1895).
Keith Wheelock. *Nasser's New Egypt* (London 1960).
Walter Z. Laqueur. *Nasser's Egypt* (London 1956).
Simonne Lacouture. *Egypt* (London 1963).
J. F. Kershaw. *Hints on the Conduct of Criminal Investigation* (Cairo 1907).
Siegried Landshut. *Jewish Communities in the Muslim Countries of the Middle East* (American-Jewish and Anglo-Jewish Association, London and New York 1950).
Alfred Lucas. *The Route of the Exodus of the Israelites from Egypt* (London 1938).
A. J. Butler. *Court Life in Egypt* (Oxford 1914).
Jacob M. Landau. *Studies in the Arab Theatre and Cinema* (Philadelphia, Pa. 1958).
Sir Alan Burns. *History of Nigeria* (London 1958).
Charles Issawi. *Egypt in Revolution* (Oxford 1963). *Egypt: An Economic and Social Analysis* (London 1947).
Patrick O'Brien. *The Revolution in Egypt's Economic System, 1952–1965* (Royal Institute of International Affairs, Oxford 1966).
Randolph and Winston S. Churchill. *The Six Day War* (London 1967).
Doreen Warriner. *Land and Poverty in the Middle East* (New York 1948). *Land Reform and Development in the Middle East* (London 1962).
Taha Husain. *The Stream of Days* (London 1948).

Index

Index

Index

Index

Index

Khedive Club, 199
Khedivial Sporting Club, 215
Khrushchev, Nikita, 257
Khufu, pyramid of, 7, 8, 9, 12, 13, 179
Khumaraweh, 55–57
Kishkadam quarter, 141
Kitchener, Lord, 212, 213, 220, 221, 224
Kléber, General Jean Baptiste, 158, 165–167, 168, 170
Knox, Rawle, 344
Koran, influence on Arabic literature, 325
Koutouz, 105
Kubba, 216
Kulzum (Suez), 27
kuttab, 133

Lacouture, Jean and Simonne, 249, 250, 256, 322, 323
Lagim, 113
lake of mercury, Khumaraweh, 57
lakes, 177, 214. *See also* names of lakes
Lampson, Sir Miles, 221
Land reform law (1952), 249
Landau, Dr. Jacob, 326, 327
Landshut report, 312–313
Lane, Edward William, 110, 179, 183, 187, 303, 305
Lappa's, 317
Lavicy, Baron, 160
Lawrence, T. E., 99, 213, 222, 223, 303
Lazarist Fathers, 217
Lebanon, 83
Leibnitz, Baron Gottfried Wilhelm von, 157
Lepsius, Karl Richard, 180
Lesseps, Ferdinand de, 187, 197, 202, 209
Liberty (ship), 338
lion house of Khumaraweh, 56
literature and the arts, 320–335
Little West Palace, 78, 80
Livingstone, David, 205
Loring, General W., 204
Louis IX, 106
Louis XIV, 157
Louis Philippe, 189
Louvre, 180
Lucas, Alfred, 313
Ludwig, Emil, 224
Luli Pavilion, 78, 80
Luxor, 237, 337
Lycée Français, 228

Ma'adi, 294
McClellan, Major Edwin N., 209
MacCoan, James, 203, 206, 207
Machiavelli, Niccolò, 123
Macmillan's Magazine, 205
Madrasahs, 98, 101; Barkuq, 118, 126; Beibars (Zahiriya), 108; al Ghury, 135–136; Hasan, 56, 117, 118, 120, 131; Kamilya, 103; al Nasir, 117–118; Qait Bey, 133; Qalaun, 109–110; el Shafi'i, 101
Mahdi, the, 76, 83
Maher, Ali, 242
Mahfuz, Naguib, 323, 324
Maho cotton, 185
Mahroussa (yacht), 246
Makaukus, the, 30
al Makrizi, Ahmad Ibn Ali, 49, 123–124; quoted *passim*, chapters 7–9

al Maks, 73, 78; mentioned, 75, 81, 99, 107, 126, 127
al Maleki, Mohammed Chanan, 141
Malik Kaher, 107
Malik Rudwan, 94
Malik Salih, 109
Maliki, 62
Mamelukes, 100, 103–136; Bahri, 100, 103–120; Circassian (Burji), 100, 120–136; system and culture, 103–105, 113–114, 123–124, 137–138, 204; monuments, 108–109, 117–120, 124–126, 131–134, 135–136; trade, 109, 113–114, 116, 128–131, 134; horses, 116, 123, 127; under Ottomans, 137–140, 151, 158–159, 166–168, 170; destruction by Mohammed Ali, 173–176
Mamelukes, Tombs of the (cemetery), 315
Mamun, 50, 51
al Mansuriya (al Kahira), 75
maps of Cairo, mentioned, 73, 77–78, 160
el Mar'i, Hassan, 327
Mari Girgis, Convent of, 32
Mariette, Auguste, 179
markets, 129–130, 188, 281–282
Martineau, Harriet, 184, 188
Mashhads. *See* mausoleums
Masjids. *See* mosques
Masr el Atika. *See* Babylon
Mastabat Far'un, 14
al Mas'udi, Ali Ibn Husain, 62, 63
Matariya, 17, 32, 218
Mausoleums: Barkuq, 124–126; al Ghury, 135–136; Hosh el Basha, 315; al Nasir, 117–118; Qait Bey, 133; Qalaun, 109–110, 112; Saiyida Rukaya, 96, 104; Sayida Atika, 96; el Shafi'i, 101; Shaggar ad Durr, 104
Meadows of Gold (al Mas'udi), 62
Mecca, 41, 46
Medina, 41, 174
Medinat el Nasr, 293, 294
Mehanna, Rashed, 242
Melchites, 29, 30, 42
Memnon, 179
Memphis, 8, 21, 60
Mendrici, Doctor, 176
Mengin, Félix, 176, 177, 188
Menkure, pyramid of, 14
Menou, General Jacques, 168, 170–171, 172
Menou, Said Soliman Mourad Jacques, 168
Menzalah, Lake, 319
Metro Cinema, 241
Midan Ismailiya, 238–239
Midan el Katai, 52
Midan el Tahrir, 243
Milne, J. G., 28
Milner, Alfred (Lord), 207, 226
Misr, 60, 61. *See also* Fustat-Misr
Misr Company, 271
Misr Studios, 330
Missions, Christian, 148, 216–218
al Mitwalli, 93
Modern Egypt (Cromer), 212
Mohammed, 50, 75, 76, 99, 134
Mohammed (son of Safiya), 152
Mohammed Ali, 172; Mameluke wars, 173–176; confiscates land, 174; massacre of Mamelukes, 175–176; daily life under, 177–178, 187–188; introduces cotton, 185;

Index

financial involvement with Europe, 178, 186, 194; and Suez Canal, 187; death, 194; mentioned, 105, 144, 170, 182, 189, 194, 217, 246, 290, 315. *See also under* mosques

Mohammed Amin Pasha, 142

Mohammedanism. *See* Islam

Mohieddin, Zakaria, 248, 332, 342

Monge, Gaspard, 158

Mongol Wars, 105, 114, 116

Mons, Anzac and Kut (Herbert), 222

Montgomery of Alamein, Bernard (Lord), 233, 237–238

Montreux Conference, 207

Moore, Sir John, 168

Moorehead, Alan, 232

Morgan, Major, 204–205

Moslem Brotherhood, 96, 240–241

mosques (*see also* madrasahs; mausoleums); Akmar, 93, 94; Amr Ibn el 'As, 38, 39, 42, 44–45, 46–47, 55, 61–62, 65, 69; al Azhar. *See* Azhar; Barkuq, 124–126; Beibars, 108, 115, 162; el Fakahani, 93; el Garhi, Abu el Su'ud, 70; al Ghury, 135–136; al Giyushi (Badr), 88, 89, 96; Hakim, 56, 80, 93, 94–95, 289; Hasan, 56, 117, 118–120, 131; el Hasanein (Saiyidna'l Husein), 95; Ibn Ruzzik, 95, 96; Ibn Tulun, 51, 53–55, 69, 113, 127, 142; Mohammed Ali, 117, 152, 188–192, 292; al Mu'aiyad, 131–133, 299; al Nasir, 117; Qait Bey, 132, 133, 188; Qalaun, 109–111, 329; Qigmas al Ishaqi, 134; Safiya Malika, 152; al Salih Ayyub, 103; el Shafi'i, 101, 315

Mott, Captain Thadeus P., 204

al Mou'men, fountain, 139

al Mu'aiyad, mosque, 131–133, 299

al Mu'allaka (Hanging Church), 31, 32–36

mudirs, under Mohammed Ali, 174

Mu'iz, 74, 75, 76, 77, 78–79, 80, 284

Mukattam Hills, 4; mentioned, 5, 24, 51, 52, 57, 68, 75, 83, 88, 99, 141, 162, 196, 290, 292, 293, 349

Mulid el Nabi, 316–317

Murad Bey, 46, 151, 153, 155, 163, 166

Murat, Marshal Joachim, 158

Muristans: of Qalaun, 109–110, 117, 118; of Saladin, 100–101. *See also* hospitals

Museum of Islamic Art, 71, 120, 288, 289

musharabiya (carved window screen), 142, 143

music, 327. *See also* Opera House

Musk, Iz ed Din, 178

Muski Bridge, 178

Muski quarter, 178, 187

Mussolini, Benito, 233, 234

Mustafa Kamel, 220, 230

Mustafa Pasha, 220

al Mustansir, 85–88, 90

My Life in Four Continents (Chaillé-Long), 205

Mystères de l'Égypte Dévoilés, Les (Audouard), 207

el Nabarawi, Seza, 306

Naguib, Mohammed, 244, 245, 248

Nahas Pasha, 240, 241

Napoleon I, 149–164 *passim;* mentioned, 7, 46, 108, 127, 146, 168, 290

al Nasir, 113–118; mosque, 117; college and mausoleum, 117–118; aqueduct and canal, 117–118, 127

Nasr (suburb), 293, 294

Nasriya quarter, 163

Nasser, Gamal Abdel: 1952 Revolution, 238, 240, 244–246; 248–254; attitude to Israel, 255–256; Suez War, 256; and United Arab Republic, 263; and intellectuals, 321–322; and June War, 337, 339–340; Hakim Amer plot 341–343

Nassouh, 167

National Ballet, 327–328

National Oil Company, 294

National Planning Committee, 261

Nationalist Party, 225

Nazli, Princess, 220

Nelson, Horatio (Lord), 157, 158

Nerval, Gerard de, 184

New Hotel. *See* Continental-Savoy

newspapers. *See* press

Niebuhr, Carsten, 146–149, 150, 151

Nile, the, 5, 18, 61, 126, 196, 202; steamers, 181; mentioned, 27, 52, 63, 66, 69, 212

Nile, battle of the, 158, 163

Nile in Egypt, The (Ludwig), 224

Nile Hilton Hotel, 127, 267, 271, 314, 338

Nile–Red Sea Canal. *See* Red Sea Canal

Nilometer, 61

Nokrashy Pasha, 239–240

Non-Military Journal ("Carlos Bey"), 171

Nubar Bey, 181

Nubia, 330

Nur ed Din, 67, 91

Oakes, Sir Reginald, 218

Obelisks (Heliopolis), 21

O'Brien, Patrick, 261

Old Cairo. *See* Babylon

al Oleimi, 139

Omar (Caliph), 41, 42, 43

Omar Khayyam Hotel, 199, 216

omdehs, under Mohammed Ali, 174

Opera House, 198, 205, 328

Oppenheims (banking house), 203

L'Orient (ship), 158

Orientations (Storrs), 213

Osman Bey, 167

Osman Bey Zulficar, 142

Ottoman Turks, 100, 123; conquest of Egypt, 134–135; Ottoman Cairo, 137–156; system of government, 137–138, 142, 145–146; houses, 141–143; trade, 148; taxes and wages, 151; revolt against (1796–97), 153; defeat by Napoleon, 155. *See also* names of rulers

painting and painters, 329–330

Palestine Liberation Organization, 334, 346

Palestine War (1948), 239

Palestinian Program, Cairo Radio, 334

Peninsular and Oriental Steamship Navigation Company (P & O), 182

le Père (architect), 179

Persian conquest, 17, 18

Petrie, Sir W. M. Flinders, 20

Pharaonic Museum, Egyptian, 127, 180

Index

Shawar, 68, 72, 91, 96
Shawki, Ahmad, 325, 327
Shepheard's Hotel, 159, 200–201, 232, 293; burned, 159, 242, 267; English social center, 188, 198–199, 272
Shepheard's hotel (new), 271
Shepseskaf, 14, 15
Sheraton Hotel Company, 271
Sherer, Captain Moyle, 180
Sherman, General William T., 206
Shi'a and Shi'ites, 48, 49, 64, 75–76, 81, 90, 92; mentioned, 67, 83, 96, 97, 100
Shirkuh, 68, 91, 92
Shubra, 162, 178, 183, 198, 216, 267
Shukairy, Ahmad M., 346
sibil of Abd er Rahman Kikhya, 152
Sinai, 254, 257, 336, 338, 344, 347
al Sinnari, Ibrahim (house), 163, 164, 329
Sirry, Gazbia, 330
Sisters of the Good Shepherd, 217
Sitt el Mulk, 83
Six-Day War. See June War
Sladen, Douglas, 215
slave market, 160
slave rulers and soldiers, 48, 50–51, 80. See also Mamelukes
Smith, Sir Sidney, 165
Soames, Christopher, 234
Socialist Cairo, 264–341; "controlled capitalism," 261–262; socialist charter, 262–263; economic classes, 274–276, 282–284; government offices, 294; city planning and building, 293–297; social problems, 296–302; socialism and Islam, 303–312, 316–319; socialist press, 321–323; after June 1967 War, 344–351. See also literature and the arts; television; theatre; etc.
Solitary Ruins (Volney), 183
Sphinx, 10, 12, 13, 15, 179
Sphinx, The (weekly), 214
Sphinx Hotel, 271
Stack, Sir Lee, 226
Stanley, Henry, 205
Stephens, John L., 181
Stephenson, Robert, 196
Stereo Club, 9
Stone, General Charles P., 208
Storrs, Sir Ronald, 213, 222, 223, 232
Strabo, 13, 22, 23
Street of Lamps, 65
Stuart, Colonel, 169, 172
stucco carving, art of, 131
Studies in the Arab Theatre and Cinema (Landau), 326
Sudan, 76, 177, 212, 237, 297
Suez Canal, 187, 189, 195, 196, 197; opening, 198, 199, 202; Ismail sells his shares to British, 203; British bases demilitarized, 248, 249; nationalized, 250; closed, 344; mentioned, 157, 165, 170, 206, 209, 239, 240, 341
Suez War (1956), 253, 255–260, 306, 320
Sunday Times, London, 344
sundial, invention of, 23
Sunna, 75
Sunni and Sunnites, 48, 62, 75–76, 92; mentioned, 84, 90, 100, 118
Suq el Nahhassin, 280, 281
Sutherland, Duke of, 199

Syria, 67, 83, 99, 165, 263, 336–337
al Syuti, 129

Taimour, Mahmoud, 327
Talisman, The (Scott), 102
Talleyrand-Périgord, Charles Maurice de, 158
Tawab, Dr. Abdel Rahman Abdel, 69, 70, 110, 120
Tawfik, 194, 207–209, 211, 216, 217
Tawfikiya Secondary School, 267
Teachers' Union, 296
Tel el Kebir, 240; battle of (1882), 209–210, 220
television, 330, 332–333
Tennyson, Alfred (Lord), 157
theatre, 326–329
Théâtre Français, 205
Thomson, James, 175
Thutmose III, 21
Times, The, London, 21, 313, 333, 347; Sunday Times, 344
Tombs of the Caliphs, 133, 315
Tombs of the Mamelukes, 315
Torah, 36–37
Tourism, 13, 14, 197, 270–272. See also travelers' accounts of Cairo
Trade and trade routes, 3–4, 67, 128–129, 134
Trajan, Emperor, 25, 27
Transit of Egypt, The (Elgood), 224
transportation, 296–297; Transport Ministry, 294
travelers' accounts of Cairo, 144–151, 180–185. See also tourism
Tribunaux Mixtés, 207, 227
Tulun (father of Ibn Tulun), 51
Tulunids, 51–58
Tura, 9, 27, 214
Turf Club, 213, 215, 232, 241
Turks, 48 50–51, 80, 87–88. See also Ottoman Turks and Seljuk Turks
Tushtu ("Green Chickpeas"), 115
Tusun, 175, 177

Ubadah ibn al Samit, 30
Uganda, 205–206
United Arab Republic, 263
United Nations, 257, 336, 346, 348
United States, 204–206, 338–339

Valid fountain, 154
Van Buren, Martin, 182
Varthena, Lodovico di, 145
Venice, 116, 128–129, 134
Verdi, Giuseppe, 68
Victoria and Albert Museum, 65, 120
Victoria Hospital, 214, 267
Virgin's Tree, 32
Voice of America, 338
Voice of the Arab (Cairo Radio), 333
Volney, Constantin François, 149–151, 157, 171, 183
Voyage en Egypte et en Grèce (Joanne), 187

Wafd party, 225, 238
Waghorn, Lt. Thomas, 185, 187
Wahby, Yussef, 327
Wahhabis, 177
Wakf, 174; Ministry of Wakfs, 290

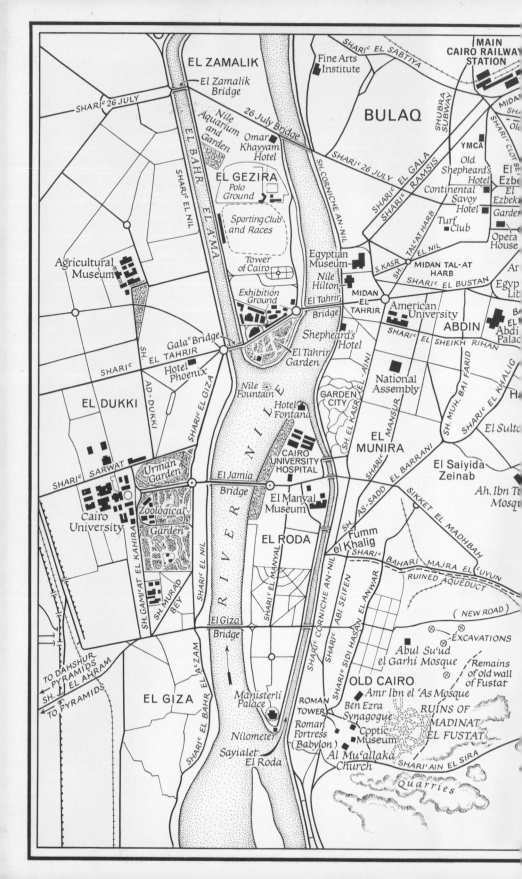